ASCENT
CENTER FOR TECHNICAL KNOWLEDGE

Autodesk® Revit® 2019
BIM Management: Template and Family Creation

Learning Guide
Imperial Units - 1st Edition

AUTODESK.
Authorized Publisher

ASCENT - Center for Technical Knowledge®
Autodesk® Revit® 2019
BIM Management: Template and Family Creation
Imperial Units - 1st Edition

Prepared and produced by:

ASCENT Center for Technical Knowledge
630 Peter Jefferson Parkway, Suite 175
Charlottesville, VA 22911

866-527-2368
www.ASCENTed.com

Lead Contributor: Martha Hollowell

ASCENT - Center for Technical Knowledge is a division of Rand Worldwide, Inc., providing custom developed knowledge products and services for leading engineering software applications. ASCENT is focused on specializing in the creation of education programs that incorporate the best of classroom learning and technology-based training offerings.

We welcome any comments you may have regarding this guide, or any of our products. To contact us please email: feedback@ASCENTed.com.

Contents

Preface

Building Information Modeling (BIM) is an approach to the entire building life cycle. Autodesk® Revit® for Architecture, MEP, and Structure is a powerful BIM program that supports the ability to coordinate, update, and share design data with team members throughout the design construction and management phases of a building's life. A key component in managing the BIM process is to establish a company foundation for different types of projects by creating standard templates and custom family elements. Having this in place makes the process of any new project flow smoothly and efficiently.

The objective of the *Autodesk® Revit® 2019 BIM Management: Template and Family Creation* learning guide is to enable users who have worked with the software to expand their knowledge in setting up office standards with templates that include annotation styles, preset views, sheets, and schedules, as well as creating custom system, in-place, and component families.

This learning guide contains practices that are specific to each discipline.

Topics Covered

- Create custom templates with annotation styles, title blocks, and custom element types.
- Create schedules, including material takeoff schedules with formulas.
- Create custom wall, roof, and floor types as well as MEP system families.
- Set up a component family file with a parametric framework.
- Create family geometry.
- Create family types.
- Modify the visibility of components and incorporate additional family items such as controls, MEP connectors, and nested components.
- Create specific families, including in-place families, profiles, annotations, and parameters.

This learning guide also contains discipline-specific practices for families, including: doors, windows, railings, pipe fittings, light fixtures, gusset plates, and built-up columns.

Prerequisites

- Access to the 2019 version of the software. The practices and files included with this guide might not be compatible with prior versions.

- Students should be comfortable with the fundamentals of the Autodesk Revit software, as found in the *Autodesk Revit 2019 Architecture Fundamentals*, *Autodesk Revit 2019 Structure Fundamentals*, or *Autodesk Revit 2019 MEP Fundamentals* learning guides. Knowledge of basic techniques is assumed, such as creating standard element, copying and moving elements, and creating and working with views, etc. Information on Collaboration Tools, Conceptual Design, and Site and Structural Design are covered in additional learning guides.

Note on Software Setup

This guide assumes a standard installation of the software using the default preferences during installation. Lectures and practices use the standard software templates and default options for the Content Libraries.

Students and Educators can Access Free Autodesk Software and Resources

Autodesk challenges you to get started with free educational licenses for professional software and creativity apps used by millions of architects, engineers, designers, and hobbyists today. Bring Autodesk software into your classroom, studio, or workshop to learn, teach, and explore real-world design challenges the way professionals do.

Get started today - register at the Autodesk Education Community and download one of the many Autodesk software applications available.

Visit www.autodesk.com/education/home/

Note: Free products are subject to the terms and conditions of the end-user license and services agreement that accompanies the software. The software is for personal use for education purposes and is not intended for classroom or lab use.

Lead Contributor: Martha Hollowell

Martha incorporates her passion for building design and education into all her projects, including the learning guides she creates on Autodesk Revit for Architecture, MEP, Structure, Landscape, as well as Advance Steel. She started working with AutoCAD in the early 1990's, adding AutoCAD Architecture and Autodesk Revit as they came along.

After receiving a B.Sc. in Architecture from the University of Virginia, she worked in the architectural department of the Colonial Williamsburg Foundation and later in private practice, consulting with firms setting up AutoCAD in their offices.

Martha has over 20 years' experience as a trainer and instructional designer. She is skilled in leading individuals and small groups to understand and build on their potential. Martha is trained in Instructional Design and has achieved the Autodesk Certified Instructor (ACI) and Autodesk Certified Professional designations for Revit Architecture.

Martha Hollowell has been the Lead Contributor for *Autodesk Revit BIM Management: Template and Family Creation* since its initial release in 2008.

In this Guide

The following images highlight some of the features that can be found in this guide.

Practice Files

To download the practice files for this student guide, use the following steps.

1. Type the URL shown below into the address bar of your Internet browser. The URL must be typed exactly as shown. If you are using an ASCENT ebook, you can click on the link to download the file.

Address bar

http://www.ASCENTed.com/getfile?id=xxxxxxxx

File Edit View Favorites Tools Help

2. Press <Enter> to download the .ZIP file that contains the Practice Files

3. Once the download is complete, unzip the file to a local folder. The unzipped file contains an .EXE file

4. Double-click on the .EXE file and follow the instructions to automatically install the Practice Files on the C:\ drive of your computer.

Do not change the location in which the Practice Files folder is installed. Doing so can cause errors when completing the practices in this student guide.

http://www.ASCENTed.com/getfile?id=xxxxxxxx

Stay Informed!
Interested in receiving information about upcoming promotional offers, educational events, invitations to complimentary webcasts, and discounts? If so, please visit: www.ASCENTed.com/updates/

Help us improve our product by completing the following survey:
www.ASCENTed.com/feedback
You can also contact us at: feedback@ASCENTed.com

Link to the practice files

Practice Files

The Practice Files page tells you how to download and install the practice files that are provided with this guide.

Chapter

1

Getting Started

In this chapter you learn how to start the AutoCAD® software, become familiar with the basic layout of the AutoCAD screen, how to access commands, use your pointing device, and understand the AutoCAD Cartesian workspace. You also learn how to open an existing drawing, view a drawing by zooming and panning and save your work in the AutoCAD software.

Learning Objectives in this Chapter

- Launch the AutoCAD software and complete a basic initial setup of the drawing environment.
- Identify the basic layout and features of AutoCAD interface including the Ribbon, Drawing Window, and Application Menu.
- Locate commands and launch them using the Ribbon, shortcut menus, Application Menu, and Quick Access Toolbar.
- Locate points in the AutoCAD Cartesian workspace.
- Open and close existing drawings and navigate to file locations.
- Move around a drawing using the mouse, the **Zoom** and **Pan** commands, and the Navigation Bar.
- Save drawings in various formats and set the automatic save options using the **Save** commands.

Learning Objectives for the chapter

Chapters

Each chapter begins with a brief introduction and a list of the chapter's Learning Objectives.

1.3 Working with Commands

Starting Commands

The main way to access commands in the AutoCAD software is to use the Ribbon. Several of the file commands are available in the Quick Access Toolbar or in the Application Menu. Some commands are available in the Status Bar or through shortcut menus. There are additional access methods, such as Tool Palettes. The names of all of the commands can also be typed in the Command Line. A table is included to help you to identify the various methods of accessing the commands.

When typing the name of a command in either the Command Line or Dynamic Input, the **AutoComplete** option automatically completes the entry when you pause as you type. It also supports mid-string search by displaying all of the commands that contain the word that you typed, as shown in Figure 1–12. You can then scroll through the list and select a command.

Figure 1–12

You can also click (Customize) to display the Input Settings for the AutoComplete feature

To set specific options for the **AutoComplete** feature, right-click on the Command Line, expand Input Settings, and select from the various options, such as the ability to search for system variables or to set the delay response time, as shown in Figure 1–13.

Figure 1–13

If you need to stop a command, press <Esc> to cancel. You might need to press <Esc> more than once.

As you work in the AutoCAD software, the software prompts you for the information that is required to complete each command. These prompts are displayed in the drawing window near the cursor and in the Command Line. It is crucial that you read the command prompts as you work, as shown in Figure 1–14.

© 2015 ASCENT - Center for Technical Knowledge®   1–9

Instructional Content

Each chapter is split into a series of sections of instructional content on specific topics. These lectures include the descriptions, step-by-step procedures, figures, hints, and information you need to achieve the chapter's Learning Objectives.

Side notes

Side notes are hints or additional information for the current topic.

Practice 1c   **Saving a Drawing File**

Practice Objectives
- Open and save a drawing.
- Modify the **Automatic Saves** option.

Estimated time for completion: under 5 minutes

In this practice you will open a drawing, save it, and modify the **Automatic saves** option, as shown in Figure 1–51.

Figure 1–51

1. Open **Building Valley-M.dwg** from your class files folder.
2. In the Quick Access Toolbar, click (Save). In the Command Line, _QSAVE displays indicating that the AutoCAD software has performed a quick save.
3. In the Application Menu, click Options to open the Options dialog box.
4. In the *Open and Save* tab, change the time for *Automatic save* to 15 minutes.

Practice Objectives

Practices

Practices enable you to use the software to perform a hands-on review of a topic.

Some practices require you to use prepared practice files, which can be downloaded from the link found on the Practice Files page.

Chapter Review Questions

1. How do you switch from the drawing window to the text window?
   a. Use the icons in the Status Bar.
   b. Press <Tab>.
   c. Press <F2>.
   d. Press the <Spacebar>.
2. How can you cancel a command using the keyboard?
   a. Press <F2>.
   b. Press <Esc>.
   c. Press <Ctrl>.
   d. Press <Delete>.
3. What is the quickest way to repeat a command?
   a. Press <Esc>.
   b. Press <F2>.
   c. Press <Enter>.
   d. Press <Ctrl>.
4. To display a specific Ribbon panel, you can right-click on the Ribbon and select the required panel in the shortcut menu.
   a. True
   b. False
5. How are points specified in the AutoCAD Cartesian workspace?
   a. X value x Y value

Chapter Review Questions

Chapter review questions, located at the end of each chapter, enable you to review the key concepts and learning objectives of the chapter.

Command Summary

The Command Summary is located at the end of each chapter. It contains a list of the software commands that are used throughout the chapter, and provides information on where the command is found in the software.

Autodesk Certification Exam Appendix

This appendix includes a list of the topics and objectives for the Autodesk Certification exams, and the chapter and section in which the relevant content can be found.

Practice Files

To download the practice files for this guide, use the following steps:

1. Type the URL shown below into the address bar of your Internet browser. The URL must be typed **exactly as shown**. If you are using an ASCENT ebook, you can click on the link to download the file.

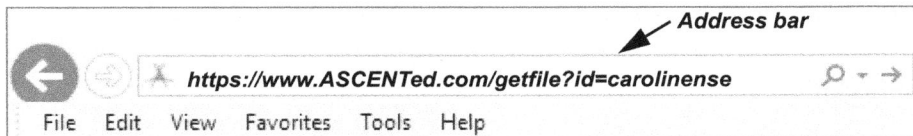

Address bar

https://www.ASCENTed.com/getfile?id=carolinense

File   Edit   View   Favorites   Tools   Help

2. Press <Enter> to download the .ZIP file that contains the Practice Files.

3. Once the download is complete, unzip the file to a local folder. The unzipped file contains an .EXE file.

4. Double-click on the .EXE file and follow the instructions to automatically install the Practice Files on the C:\ drive of your computer.

   Do not change the location in which the Practice Files folder is installed. Doing so can cause errors when completing the practices.

https://www.ASCENTed.com/getfile?id=carolinense

Creating Custom Templates

Custom templates can save you time and provide consistency in applying office standards when creating similar projects. Templates can include items such as levels, views, sheets, schedules, and annotation types for text, dimensions, and tags. A typical family that is added to templates is a custom title block, which helps you to ensure that sheets are created with the appropriate information. You may also want to add rule-based view filters and view templates to project template files.

Learning Objectives in this Chapter

- Create project templates.
- Use resource projects to store additional system families, details, schedules, and other data.
- Create standard text and dimension types for use in your projects.
- Modify callout, elevation, and section tags and specify which tags are loaded in a template.
- Create title blocks including detail lines, text, labels, symbols, regions, and revision schedules.
- Set up Visibility/Graphic override filters for various categories of elements.
- Create and apply view templates.

1.1 Preparing Project Templates

A project template is a file that contains information that can be used over and over to create new projects. The goal is to save time by using company standards, enabling you to concentrate on the design. For example, predefined levels (as shown in Figure 1–1 for a residential project) and the associated plan views and elevations provides a starting point for a model.

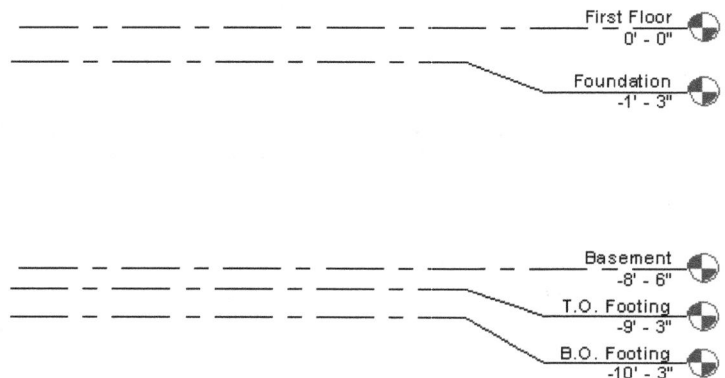

Figure 1–1

- Some items in a project template include:
  - Levels
  - Project-based settings (e.g., Project Units, Object Styles and discipline-specific settings, etc.)
  - System Families
  - Component Families
  - Annotation Types
  - Sheets with associated title blocks
  - Views
  - View Templates
  - Schedules and Legends

- You can have several project templates for different types of projects or building types, such as residential, commercial, and industrial.

- If you provide constant work to a specific client (e.g., a school system), you can create a template specific to their projects with associated title blocks and other information.

- You can also store items such as sheets, schedules, families, and drafting views (details) in a separate resource file and add the elements to the current project, as required.

How To: Create a Project Template File

1. In the *File* tab, expand ⬜ (New) and click 🗔 (Project).
2. In the New Project dialog box, in the *Template File* area, select a template file to build from or select **None** to use a blank project file.
3. In the *Create new* area, select **Project template**, as shown in Figure 1–2.

Project template files have the extension .RTE.

New Project   ✕

Template file

| Construction Template | ⌄ | Browse... |

Create new

○ Project   ◉ Project template

OK   Cancel   Help

Figure 1–2

4. Click **OK**.
5. Add settings, families, views, etc., as required to the new file.
6. Save the project template file.

- To save time, use an existing project or template that includes some of the basics you need rather than starting from scratch.

- If you select <None> in the Template file list, you are prompted to specify the initial unit system for the project: **Imperial** or **Metric**, as shown in Figure 1–3.

Undefined System of Measurement

Which system of measurement do you want to use in your project?

→ Imperial

→ Metric

Figure 1–3

Managing Settings

Most of the settings stored in a template file are found in the *Manage* tab>Settings panel, as shown in Figure 1–4. These settings include Units, Snaps, Temporary Dimensions, Object Styles (Lineweights, Line color, and Line patterns), Line Styles, Materials, Fill Patterns, etc.

- Specific Structural Settings, MEP Settings, and Panel Schedule Templates are also included in this panel.

Figure 1–4

For more information on managing settings see:

- A.1 General Settings
- A.2 Creating Object Styles
- A.3 Creating Fill Patterns
- A.4 Creating Materials
- A.5 Settings for Mechanical Projects
- A.6 Settings for Electrical Projects
- A.7 Settings for Structural Projects

Families in Templates

There are two types of families that can be setup in template files: system families, such as the Duct shown in Figure 1–5, and component families, such as the Air Terminal shown in Figure 1–5.

Figure 1–5

System Families are created by duplicating an existing type and modifying the Type Properties, as shown in Figure 1–6. This must be done within a project and it helps to have the company standard for these families setup in a template file. System families include Walls, Wall Foundations, Floors, Slabs, Ceilings, and Roofs. They also include Duct, Pipe, Cable Tray and Conduit types and annotation elements such as text and dimensions.

For more information on setting up system families see Chapter 3 Custom System Families.

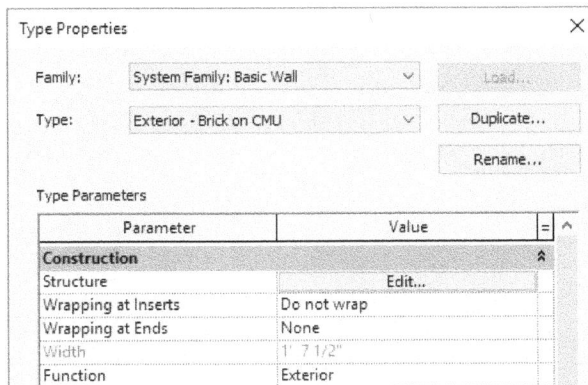

Figure 1–6

Component Families are created outside of a project and can be loaded directly in a template file if there are types and sizes that are used frequently. Component families include elements such as furniture, trees, beams, columns, mechanical equipment, and electrical fixtures, as shown in the Type Selector in Figure 1–7.

For more information on creating component families see Chapter 4 Component Family Concepts.

Figure 1–7

Using Resource Projects

Although you can use a template file to start a project, you might also want to have resource projects that include additional system and component families, pre-drawn details (as shown in Figure 1–8), schedules, and sheets. You can then copy these elements into a new template or the current project, as required.

Figure 1–8

- To copy drafting views (details), sheets, schedules, or reports into the current project, use **Insert Views from File**.

- To copy system families (e.g., wall, floor, duct, pipe, wire types, etc) or annotations (e.g., text and dimension styles, materials, etc.), use **Transfer Project Standards**.

- To copy component families from a resource project, use **Copy to the Clipboard** and either **Paste Aligned to Selected Levels** or **Paste Aligned to Selected Views**.

How To: Insert Views from an Existing Project

1. In the *Insert* tab>Import panel, expand ⬚ (Insert from File) and click ⬚ (Insert Views from File).
2. In the Open dialog box, select the project file you want to copy from.
3. In the Insert Views dialog box, select the views you want to insert into the current project, as shown in Figure 1–9.

Figure 1–9

4. Click **OK**. The views are added to the file.

- Schedules are completed with the information in the current project. Sheets are added, but do not include any views.

How To: Transfer Project Standards

1. Open the project from which you want to transfer information.
2. Switch to the current project you are copying to.
3. In the *Manage* tab>Settings panel, click (Transfer Project Standards).
4. In the Select Items To Copy dialog box, expand the Copy from drop-down list and select the file to copy from.
5. Select the items you want to copy into the current project, as shown in Figure 1–10. Then, click **OK**.

*Click **Check None** or **Check All**, as required.*

Figure 1–10

- If the Duplicate Types dialog box displays (shown in Figure 1–11), choose **Overwrite** or **New Only** to update the existing project.

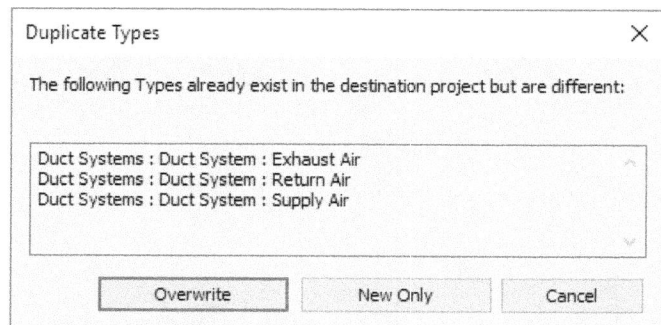

Figure 1–11

Setting Default Template Files

If your company uses several different templates, you can create a list that displays in the New Project dialog box, as shown in Figure 1–12. The top five templates also display on the Recent Files page.

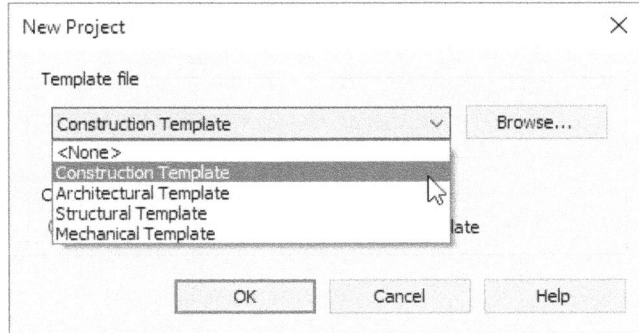

Figure 1–12

How To: Set the Default Template Files List

1. In the *File* tab, click **Options**.
2. In the Options dialog box, in the left pane, select **File Locations**, as shown in Figure 1–13.

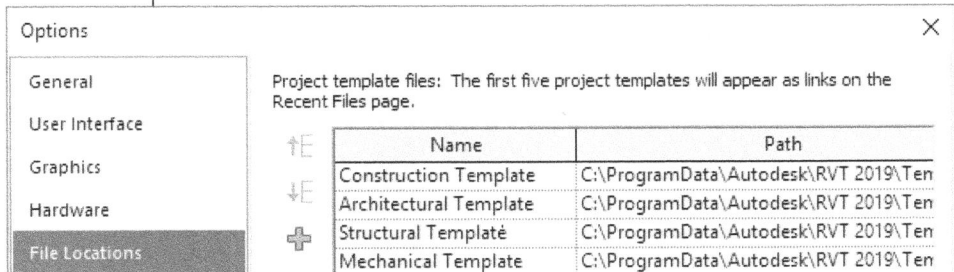

Figure 1–13

- Use ✛ (Add Value) to list additional templates.

- Use ⬆E (Move Rows Up) and ⬇E (Move Rows Down) to order the templates. Move the templates that are used most often to the top

- Use ▬ (Remove Value) if you do not require a template anymore.

3. Type in a *Name*.
4. Click on the *Path* column and select the browse button. In the Browse for Template File dialog box, navigate to the correct folder, select the template file, and click **Open**.

Practice 1a | Prepare Project Templates

Practice Objectives

- Create a new project template file.
- Add levels with plan views.
- Review existing system and component families
- Load a component family
- Insert views and transfer project standards from a resource project.

In this practice, you will create a new template file based on an existing template and add several levels to the project. You will review the existing system and component families and load a component family. You will then insert views and transfer project standards from a resource project, as shown for Text Types before in Figure 1–14 and after in Figure 1–15.

Before

Figure 1–14

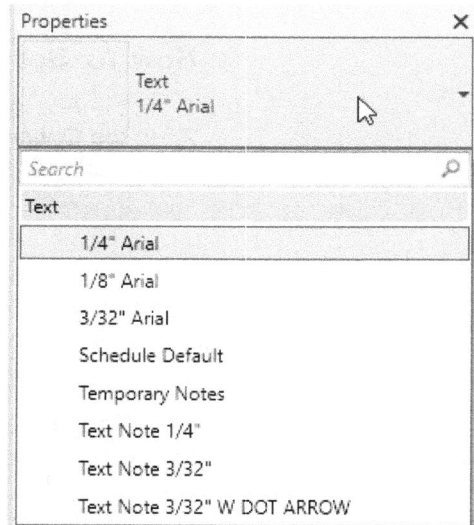

After

Figure 1–15

Task 1 - Establish a project template file.

1. In the *File* tab, expand ☐ (New) and click ☝ (Project).

2. In the New Project dialog box, select an existing template file similar to your primary discipline. Do not select the Construction Template.

   • For electrical, click **Browse...** and select **Systems-Default.rte or Electrical Default.rte**

3. In the *Create New* area, select **Project template** and click **OK**.

4. In the Quick Access Toolbar, click 🖫 (Save) and save the template in the practice files folder as **Midrise-Template.rte**.

Task 2 - Add Default Levels (Architectural and Structural only).

• MEP templates typically do not have additional levels. They are created using **Copy/Monitor** with a linked file. Skip to the next task.

1. Open an elevation view.

2. Click on the level head and rename *Level 1* to **Floor 1** and *Level 2* to **Floor 2**. Click **Yes** to rename the corresponding views.

3. Change the **Floor 2** height as shown in Figure 1–16.

Figure 1–16

4. In the *Architecture* or *Structure* tab>Datum panel, click ↴ (Level).

5. In the Options Bar, verify that the **Make Plan View** option is selected and click **Plan View Types...**.

6. In the Plan View Types dialog box, select the view types that you want to create:

   • Architectural template: Select **Ceiling Plan** and **Floor Plan**, as shown in Figure 1–17.
   • Structural template: Select only **Structural Plan**, as shown in Figure 1–18.

Figure 1–17

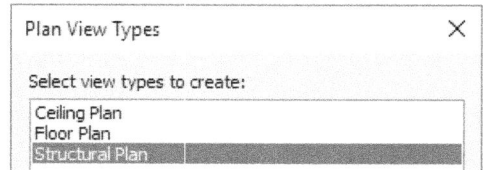

Figure 1–18

7. Add three more levels above the current levels and two levels below **Floor 1**. Rename them as shown in Figure 1–19. Click **Yes** to rename the corresponding views as needed.

Scale change and dimensions are added for clarity.

Figure 1–19

8. Return to the plan view.

9. Save the template.

Task 3 - Review Existing Family Elements in the Template.

1. In the Annotate tab> Text panel click **A** (Text).

2. Expand the list in the Type Selector. Only a few text types are available, as shown in Figure 1–20.

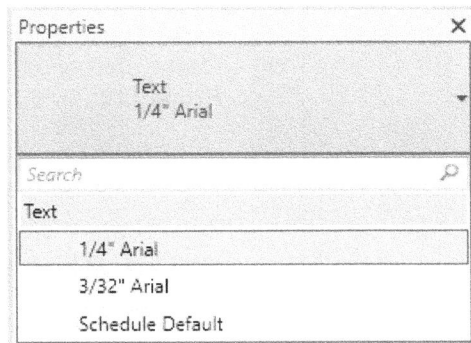

Figure 1–20

3. Select a command that uses a system family such as **Wall, Duct, Pipe**, or **Conduit** and review the list in the Type Selector.

4. Select a command that uses a component family such as **Component, Structural Column, Mechanical Equipment**, or **Electrical Equipment** and review the list in the Type Selector.

5. In the ribbon in the Select panel, click **Modify**.

6. In the *Insert* tab>Load from Library panel, click 🗇 (Load Family).

   • By using the **Load Family** command you can load any type of component. If you use a specific command such as **Column** or **Mechanical Equipment** you can only load that type of family.

7. In the Load Family dialog box, navigate to an appropriate folder and select a family to load and click **Open**.

8. Review the list in the Type Selector again to see the new component added.

9. Click **Modify**.

10. Save the template.

Task 4 - Copy Information from a Resource Project.

---

1. Close any open projects other than the template file.

2. In the *Insert* tab> Import panel, expand (Insert from File) and click (Insert Views from File).

3. In the Open dialog box, navigate to the practice files>*Reference* folder, select **Construction Resource Project.rvt**, and click **Open**.

4. In the Insert Views dialog box, scroll through the list of options.

5. Select one or two drafting views and one or two schedules from the list as shown in Figure 1–21.

Figure 1–21

6. Click **OK**.

7. If the Duplicate Types warning displays, click **OK**.

8. In the Project Browser of your template file, review the new Drafting Views and Schedules that are added.

9. Return to the original plan view.

10. In the *Manage* tab> Settings panel, click 📑 (Transfer Project Standards.

11. In the Select Items to Copy dialog box, note that *Copy from:* is set to **Construction Resource Project.rvt**, the one that was just used for inserting a view from a file.

12. Click **Check None**, select **Text Types** (as shown in Figure 1–22), and click **OK**.

Figure 1–22

13. In the Duplicate Types dialog box, select **New Only**, if required.

14. Start the **Text** command and look at the expanded list of text types that are now available, as shown in Figure 1–23.

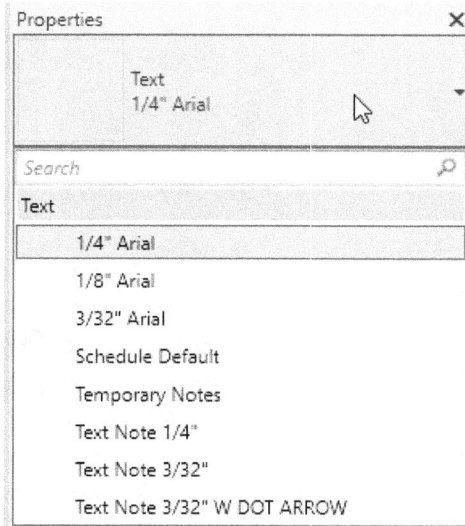

Figure 1–23

15. Click **Modify**.

16. Save the template file.

1.2 Customizing Annotation Types

You can customize Annotation types in your project template file including dimensions, text types, and tags, as shown in Figure 1–24.

Figure 1–24

Text, Dimensions, and Arrowheads are all system families. This means they have a standard set of parameters, which you can modify and save as a type. Callout, Section, and Elevation tags can be modified in the Autodesk Revit software. Most other tags are created using component families.

Creating Text Types

Text types are used to standardize text formatting (such as the font, text height, etc.), as shown in Figure 1–25. They can be created for both annotative text and Model Text.

A FANCY FONT AT 1/4"

A HAND LETTERING FONT AT 1/8"

A HAND LETTERING FONT AT 5/32"

Figure 1–25

- The **Text** command places text at the height you need for the final plot. The view scale controls the height of the standard text in the views.

- The **Text Size** parameter represents the height of a capital letter. (Verify that the text in projects created in earlier versions of the software displays as expected.)

- The **Model Text** command places text that is typically used on the building, such as the signage shown in Figure 1–26. Text types for Model Text should be the full height of the final element and are not affected by the view scale.

Figure 1–26

How To: Create a Text Type

1. Start the **Text** command. In Properties, click 🔲 (Edit Type) or in the *Annotate* tab>Text panel title, click ⌄ (Text Types).
   - For **Model Text** you first have to place an instance, select it, and modify the type properties.
2. In the Type Properties dialog box, click **Duplicate...**.
3. Type a new name and click **OK**.The new type is activated.
4. Modify the parameters as required for the new type, as shown for annotation text in Figure 1–27.

Type Parameters	
Parameter	**Value**
Graphics	⌃
Color	■ Black
Line Weight	1
Background	Opaque
Show Border	☐
Leader/Border Offset	5/64"
Leader Arrowhead	Arrow 30 Degree
Text	⌃
Text Font	Arial
Text Size	1/4"
Tab Size	1/2"
Bold	☐
Italic	☐
Underline	☐
Width Factor	1.000000

Figure 1–27

5. Click **OK** to finish.

Creating Dimension Types

Dimensions are one of the more complex system families in terms of the number of parameters you can modify. They include options for the Dimension Text, Dimension Line, Tick Marks, and Witness Lines. You can specify information such as the units, color, and all of the gap sizes between elements, as shown in Figure 1–28.

Dimension Text

Dimension Line

Tick Mark

Witness Line

Set gap between witness line and reference

Figure 1–28

How To: Create Dimension Types

1. In the *Annotate* tab>Dimension panel, expand the Dimension panel title (as shown in Figure 1–29), and click ✐ next to the dimension type you want to create.

You create separate types for each dimension method.

Figure 1–29

2. In the Type Properties dialog box, click **Duplicate...**.

Values for parameters (such as text size, witness line extension, etc.) are the actual plot size for these elements. The view scale controls how large they are in the specific view.

3. Type a new name and click **OK**. The new type is activated.
4. Modify the parameters as required for the new type, as shown in Figure 1–30.

Figure 1–30

5. Click **OK** when you are finished.

- For Linear dimensions, you can specify a *Leader Type, Shoulder Length, Leader Tick Mark, and Show Leader When Text Moves* that is used when the text is pulled away from the dimension string. You can also specify the text inserted for **Equality Text** (the default is EQ).

- You can specify a *Text Background* option. If you set the value to **opaque**, it automatically masks any elements behind the text. If it is set to **transparent**, anything the text overlaps is still visible.

- If you are dimensioning doors and windows by their widths rather than their centers, you can also have the opening height displayed with the dimension. Select **Show Opening Height**.

Loading Tags and Symbols

Tags and symbols are 2D component families that must be loaded into a project. Not all types of tags need to be in each project, so you can choose which ones you want to include in your templates. For example, if you are working in an architectural project, you can load tags such as the door, window, and wall shown in Figure 1–31.

Figure 1–31

How To: Specify Loaded Tags and Symbols

1. In the *Annotate* tab>Tag panel, expand the panel title and

   click ⚲ (Loaded Tags and Symbols).
2. In the Loaded Tags and Symbols dialog box, use the *Filter* field to limit the types of tags you are looking for by discipline, as shown in Figure 1–32.

Some elements, such as Floors and Structural Fabric Reinforcement, have both tags and symbols. They can both be specified in this dialog box.

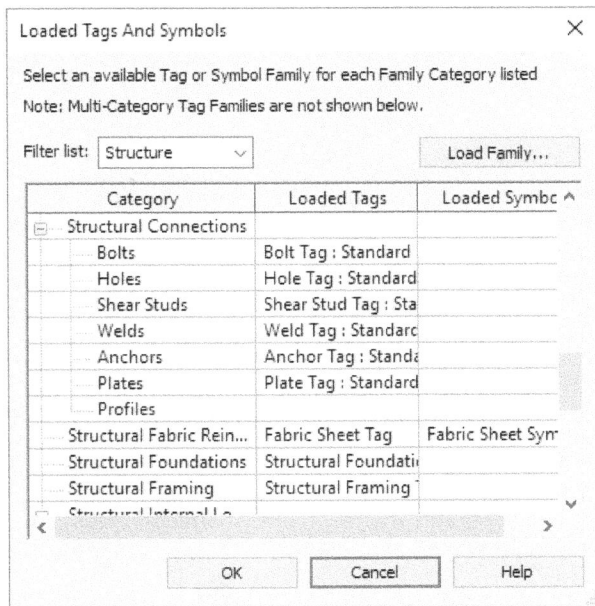

Figure 1–32

3. Click **Load Family...**.
4. In the Load Family dialog box, navigate to the appropriate library and folder.
5. Select the required tags and click **Open**. Hold <Ctrl> or <Shift> to select multiple tags.
6. When you have loaded all of the tags that you typically need for a project, click **OK**.

Specifying View Tags

Callout, Elevation, and Section tags can be modified to suit an office standard. The tag is actually part of a view type. For example, you can create a new Elevation view type containing a tag that displays the view name, as shown in Figure 1–33.

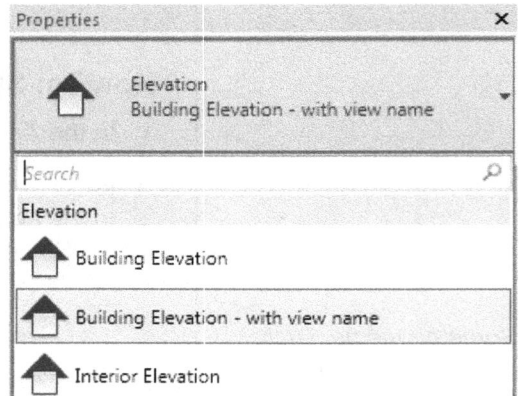

Figure 1–33

How To: Create Tags for View Types: Callout, Elevation, and Section

1. Click ⬚ (Callout), ⬆ (Elevation), or ⬙ (Section), as required, and in Properties, click ⬚ (Edit Type). Or, in the *Manage* tab>Settings panel, expand ⬚ (Additional Settings) and click ⬚ (Callout Tags), ⬆ (Elevation Tags), or ⬙ (Section Tags).

2. In the Type Properties dialog box, select an existing type, then duplicate and name the new view type, as shown for an elevation view in Figure 1–34.

Each view type has different parameters.

Figure 1–34

3. Beside the **Tag** parameter, click in the *Value* column and then click ⌶ (Browse).

4. In the Type Properties dialog box for the tag, select from an existing type or duplicate a type, and specify a new mark element from a list of families that have been inserted into the project, as shown in Figure 1–35.

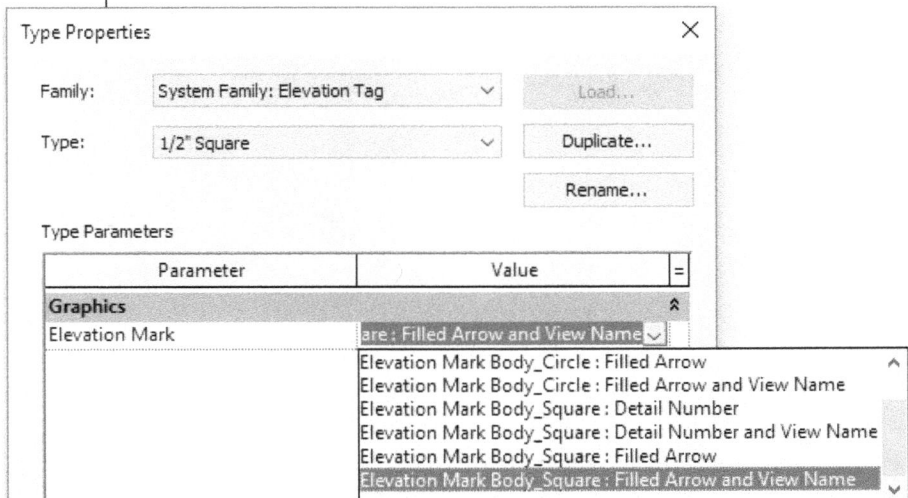

Figure 1–35

5. Click **OK** to apply the tag type.
6. Modify the other parameters as required and click **OK** to close the Type Properties dialog box.

• Levels (shown in Figure 1–36) and Grids (shown in Figure 1–37) are also system families that are setup in Type Properties and include component families such as the *Symbol* **Level Head-Circle** and **Grid Head-Circle**.

Figure 1–36

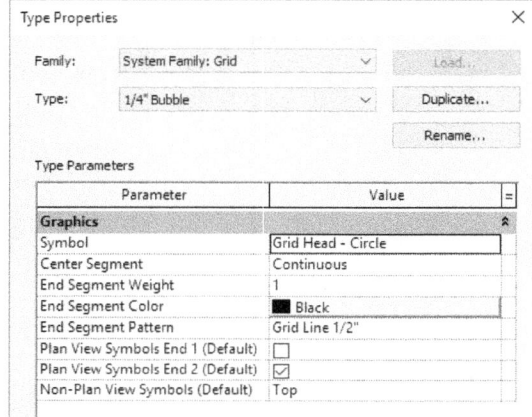

Figure 1–37

Practice 1b

Customize Annotation Types

Practice Objectives

- Set up text and dimension types.
- Load tags.
- Create a new view tag.

In this practice, you will create text types, duplicate and modify dimension styles (as shown in Figure 1–38), and load typical tags into the project template file. You will also create a new elevation tag that includes the view name information.

Title Small

Title Large

Figure 1–38

Task 1 - Create Text Types.

1. Open the project template **Midrise-Template.rte** that you created in the previous practice. If you did not complete the previous practice, open the template found in the practice files folder:
   - *Architectural>***Midrise-Template-Architectural-1.rte**
   - *MEP>***Midrise-Template-MEP-1.rte**
   - *Structural>***Midrise-Template-Structural-1.rte**

2. Start the **Text** command.

3. In Properties, click ⬚ (Edit Type)

4. In the Type Properties dialog box, click **Duplicate....**

5. Type the *Name* **Title Small** and click **OK**.The new type is activated.

6. In the *Text* area, select a font and other options, as required. Set the *Text Size* to **1/4"**, as shown in Figure 1–39.

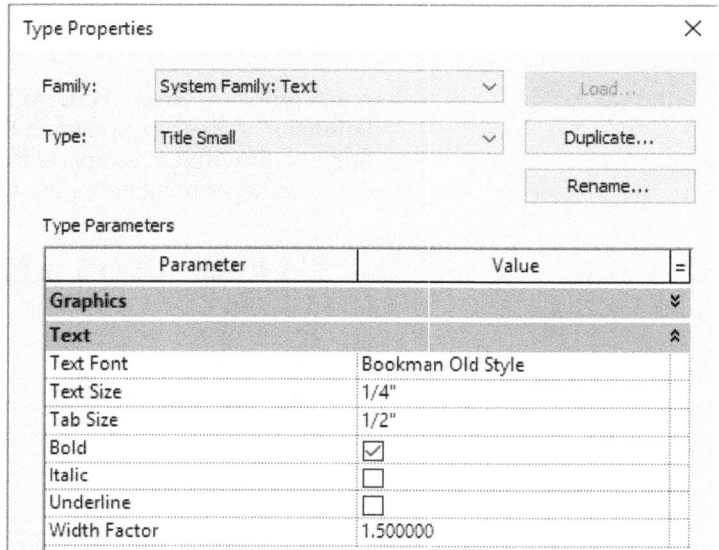

Type Properties ✕

Family:	System Family: Text	⌄	Load…
Type:	Title Small	⌄	Duplicate…
			Rename…

Type Parameters

Parameter	Value	=
Graphics		⩔
Text		⩕
Text Font	Bookman Old Style	
Text Size	1/4"	
Tab Size	1/2"	
Bold	☑	
Italic	☐	
Underline	☐	
Width Factor	1.500000	

Figure 1–39

7. Click **OK** and type in some text using the new text type.

8. Create a duplicate of the new text type named **Title Large**. Change the *Text Size* to **1/2"** and add some text using the new type, as shown in Figure 1–40.

Title Small

Title Large

Figure 1–40

9. Save the template file.

Task 2 - Create Dimension Styles

1. Model a few linear elements (such as walls, beams, or duct) and add two linear and two angular dimensions shown in Figure 1–41.

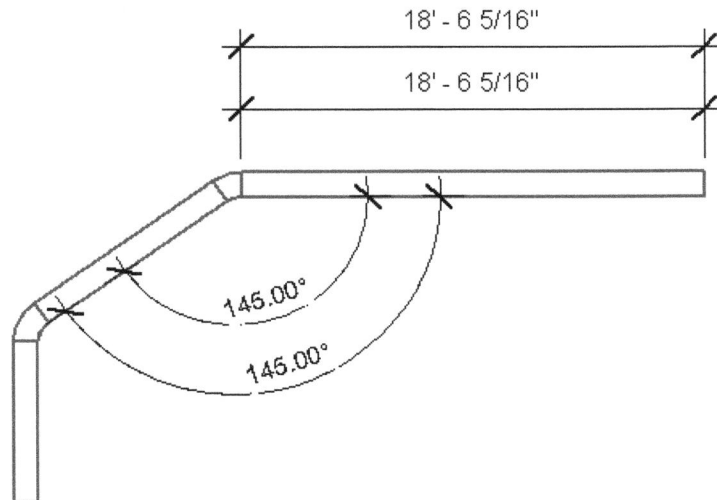

18' - 6 5/16"

18' - 6 5/16"

145.00°

145.00°

Figure 1–41

2. Click **Modify**.

3. Select the outer most linear dimension.

4. In the Properties, click **Edit Type**.

5. In the Type Properties dialog box, duplicate the type and name it **Linear - Standard**.

6. In the *Text* area, change the *Text Size* to **1/8"**.

7. Click on *Units Format.* In the Format dialog box, clear the checkmark for **Use project settings** and change the *Rounding* to the **nearest 1/8"**, as shown in Figure 1–42.

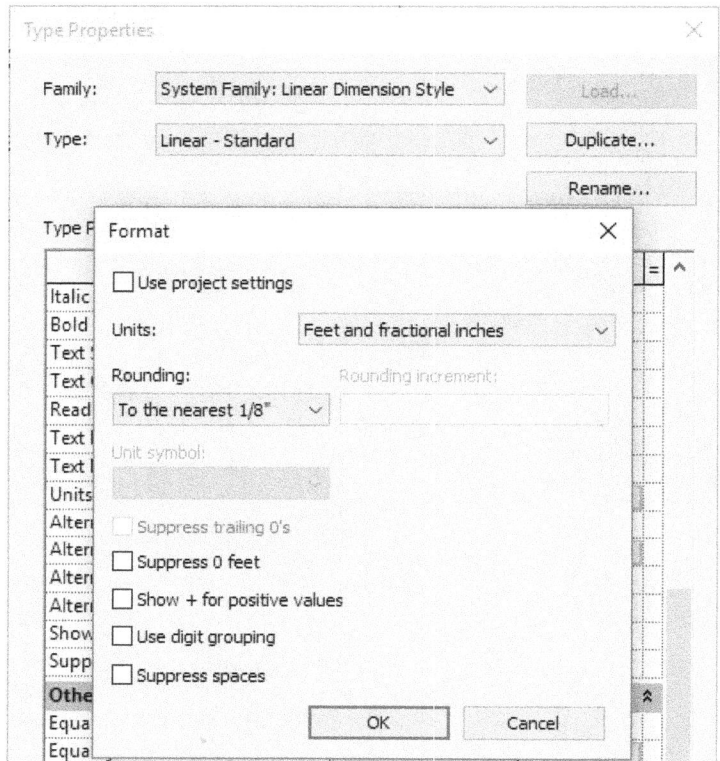

Figure 1–42

8. Click **OK** twice to finish. The linear dimension updates to the new style.

9. Select the outermost angular dimension. Duplicate the type and name it **Angular - Standard**.

10. In the Type Properties dialog box, in the *Graphics* area, change the *Tick Mark* to **Arrow Filled 30 Degree**.

11. In the *Text* area, change the *Text Size* to **1/8"** and the *Units Format* to **0 decimal places**.

12. Click **OK** twice to finish. The angular dimension updates as shown in Figure 1–43.

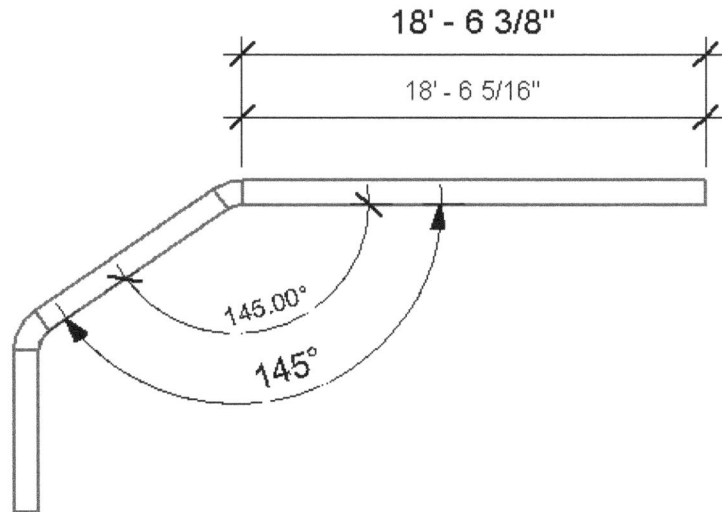

Figure 1–43

13. Select and delete the sample text, elements, and dimensions.

14. Save the template.

Task 3 - Load Tags

---

1. In the *Annotate* tab, expand the Tag panel title, and click

   (Loaded Tags and Symbols).

2. In the Loaded Tags and Symbols dialog box, set the *Filter List* to match your discipline(s).

3. Click **Load Family...** and load the following tags from the Revit Library>*Annotations* folder subfolders into the discipline-specific project template:

Architecture:

Folder	Tag Name
Architectural	Casework Tag.rfa, Furniture Tag.rfa, and Furniture System Tag.rfa

MEP:

Folder	Tag Name
Mechanical> Duct	Duct Fitting Tag.rfa
Electrical	Lighting Fixture Tag.rfa
Piping	Pipe Fitting Size Tag.rfa

Structure:

Folder	Tag Name
Architectural	Wall and Floor
Structural	Select any different Structural tags you might want to use in place of those already loaded.

4. The tags are automatically assigned to the correct *Category*, as shown for the Architectural tags in Figure 1–44.

Figure 1–44

5. Click **OK**.

6. Save the template file.

Task 4 - Modify a Elevation Tag

1. In the plan view, zoom to where you can see one of the existing building elevation view markers.

2. Select the pointed end of the marker.

3. In the Type Selector, verify that **Elevation> Building Elevation** is selected.

4. In Properties, click **Edit Type**.

5. In the Type Parameters, select the Value beside *Elevation Tag* and then click the **...** (Browse) button.

6. A second Type Properties dialog box displays for the Elevation Mark. Duplicate this type and add **...with Name** to the end.

7. In the *Elevation Mark* drop-down list, select **Elevation Mark Body_Square: Detail Number and View Name**, as shown in Figure 1–45.

Figure 1–45

8. Click **OK** twice. The Elevation Tag updates as shown in Figure 1–46.

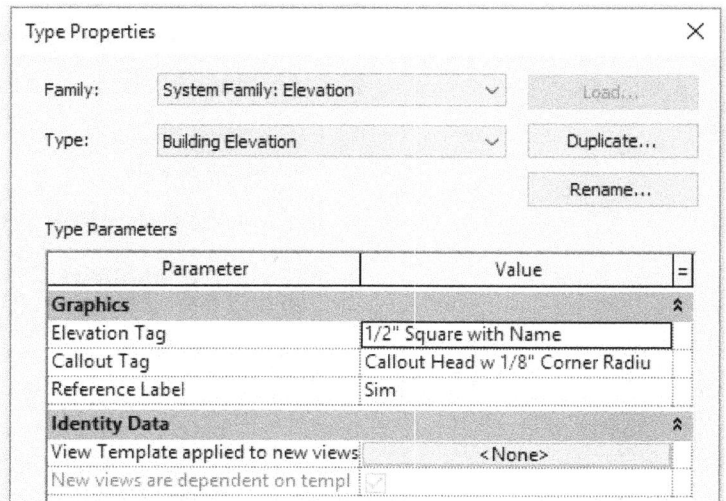

South - Mech

Type Properties   ✕

Family: System Family: Elevation   ⌄   Load...

Type: Building Elevation   ⌄   Duplicate...

                                                           Rename...

Type Parameters

Parameter	Value	=
Graphics		⌃
Elevation Tag	1/2" Square with Name	
Callout Tag	Callout Head w 1/8" Corner Radiu	
Reference Label	Sim	
Identity Data		⌃
View Template applied to new views	\<None\>	
New views are dependent on templ	☑	

Figure 1–46

9. Zoom to fit the view.

10. Save the template.

1.3 Creating Title Blocks

Title blocks (as shown in Figure 1–47) contain information about the company and consultants designing the project, project information (such as project name and number), and sheet-specific information (such as sheet numbers and drawn by). They are created by sketching detail lines and adding text, symbols, and regions, as well as image files for company logos. The variable information is stored in labels.

Some of these parameters never change, some are project-specific, and some are sheet-specific.

Figure 1–47

• Once you have title blocks customized you can add them to templates and setup views and sheets in the template.

How To: Create a Title Block

1. In the *File* tab, expand ▢ (New) and click ▣ (Title Block).
2. In the New Title Block - Select Template File dialog box, select a template file size from the list and click **Open**. A new family file opens and the Family tools display in the ribbon, as shown in part in Figure 1–48.

You can select from several preset sizes or create a custom size.

Figure 1–48

3. Add lines, filled regions, symbols, text, labels, etc., as required.
4. Save and close the file.

- If you select a template with a standard size, a rectangle of that size displays in the view.

- If you select **New Size**, a rectangle with dimensions displays. Edit the dimensions to modify the size.

- You can use reference lines and dimensions to help place the elements in the title block family, they are not displayed when the title block is inserted.

Adding Labels

Labels are not just text but elements that are assigned to specific parameters and can be added to title blocks or tags. They can change without modifying the rest of the elements. For example, you would use annotation text for the words **Drawn By:** and a label for the initials of the person who did the work (by default displaying DRW in Figure 1–49), because that varies from sheet to sheet.

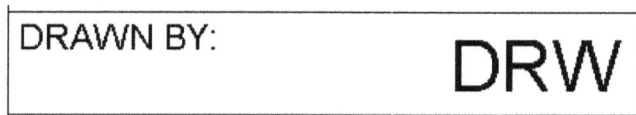

DRAWN BY:	DRW

Figure 1–49

- The title block template comes with one text type and one label type already defined. You can create additional types in Properties by duplicating types. The **Text** and **Label** parameters are similar, but you must create separate types for each of them.

- Labels use Rich Text Format so that they match text notes.

How To: Create a Label

1. In the Family Editor, in the *Create* tab>Text panel, click
   𝗔 (Label).

2. In the *Modify | Place Label* tab>Format panel, specify the alignments: **Left**, **Center**, **Right**, **Top**, **Center Middle**, or **Bottom**, as shown in Figure 1–50.

Figure 1–50

3. Click in the view window to place the label, as shown in Figure 1–51.

Figure 1–51

4. In the Edit Label dialog box (shown in Figure 1–52), select a label in the *Category Parameters* list and double-click or click

(Add parameter(s) to label). You can select more than one by holding <Ctrl> or <Shift>.

Figure 1–52

5. Enter the *Sample Value* and specify any other options, as required.

    -   If you are using several parameters in one label, select **Wrap between parameters only** and **Break** (in column) options to separate them while still permitting a word wrap, as shown in Figure 1–53.

Project Name Project Address

Two labels without break

Project Name
Project Address

Two labels with break

Figure 1–53

-   Click ↑E (Move parameter up) and ↓E (Move parameter down) to reorder multiple parameters.

-   If you select a numerical parameter, click (Edit parameter's units format) to change, if required.

-   Click f_x (Add calculated parameter to label) to use a formula based on other parameters.

-   Click (Add Parameter) to create a new parameter for the project.

6. Click **OK** when you have finished editing the label.

-   While placing the label, you can rotate or stretch it (as shown in Figure 1–54), or select a point for an additional label.

•DRW

Figure 1–54

-   You can also rotate or stretch a label once it has been placed in the title block.

For more information on creating parameters and calculated parameters, see 2.6 Working with Project Parameters.

Adding Revision Schedules

A table of revisions included in a project and/or sheet is typically added to a company title block, as shown in Figure 1–55. In the Autodesk Revit software, you can create a Revision Schedule that is then linked to the Revision Table in the project.

No.	Description	Date

Figure 1–55

How To: Add Revision Schedules to Title Blocks

1. In the Family Editor, in the *View* tab>Create panel, click (Revision Schedule).
2. In the Revision Properties dialog box, select the fields you want to use. Several are already selected for you, as shown in Figure 1–56.

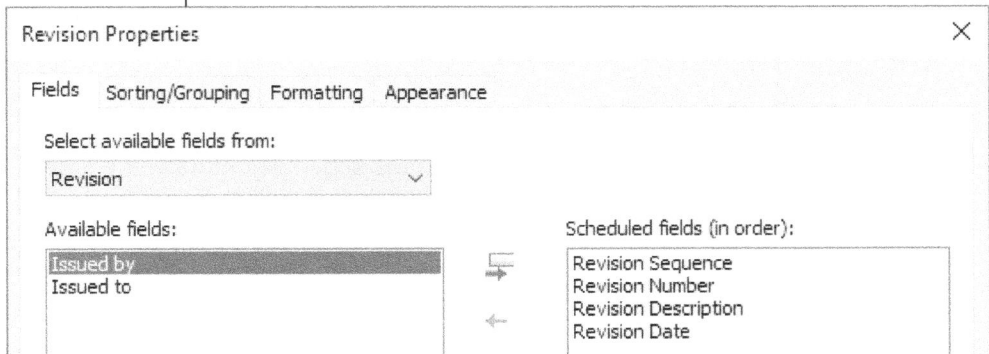

Revision Properties ✕

Fields   Sorting/Grouping   Formatting   Appearance

Select available fields from:

Revision ∨

Available fields:

Issued by
Issued to

Scheduled fields (in order):

Revision Sequence
Revision Number
Revision Description
Revision Date

Figure 1–56

3. Modify the options in the *Sorting/Grouping* and *Formatting* tabs, as required.

4. In the *Appearance* tab, select how you want to build the schedule: from the **Top-down** or **Bottom-up**. You can also set the *Height* to **Variable** or **User-Defined**, as shown in Figure 1–57.

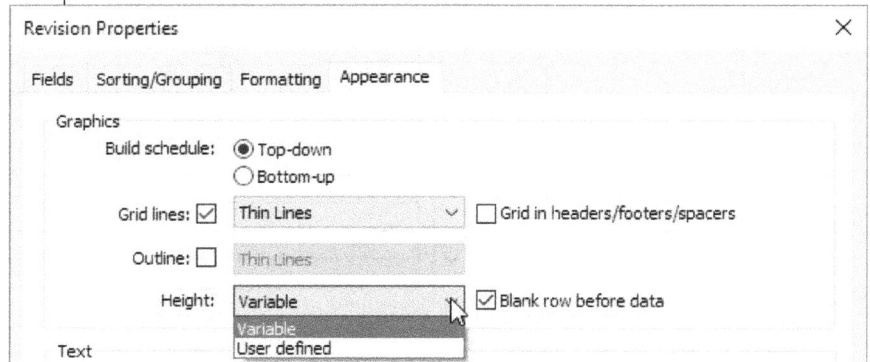

Figure 1–57

5. Click **OK**. The schedule view displays, as shown in Figure 1–58.
6. Click on the sheet view tab (it has no name) to reopen it as shown in Figure 1–59.

Figure 1–58

Figure 1–59

7. Drag and drop the schedule onto the sheet and modify the controls, as shown in Figure 1–60.

If the height is set to ***User-Defined****, an additional control displays at the bottom of the schedule. Use it to set the height of the schedule.*

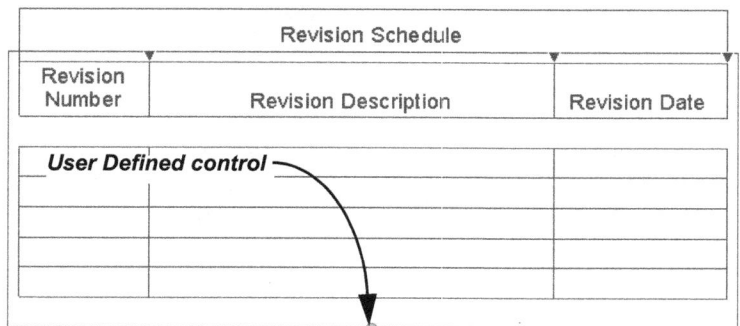

Figure 1–60

- In the Options Bar, you can change the *Rotation on the Sheet* to **None**, **90° Clockwise**, or **90° Counterclockwise**.

Adding Sheets to Project Templates

You can create sheets that are typically used in projects in the template and even place views on them, as shown in Figure 1–61. Note that the view is empty in the template, but as you draw elements in the project they automatically display in the view and on the sheet.

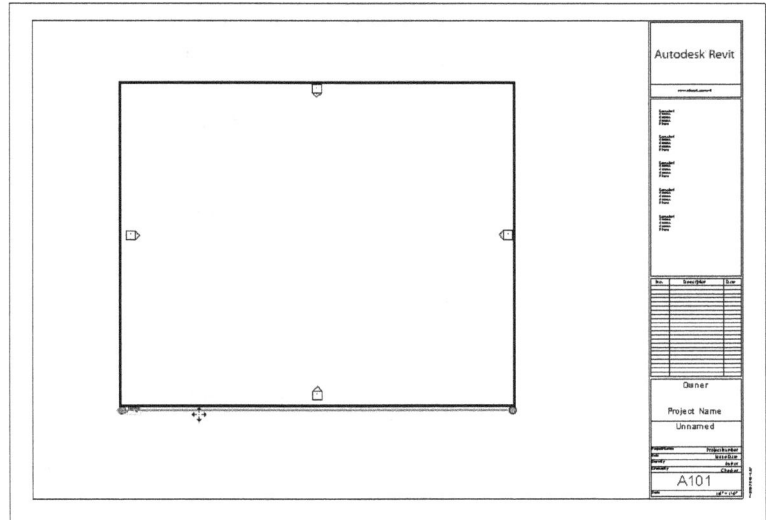

Figure 1–61

- You can create as many sheets as are typically used in a project or you can create a Sheet List and populate it with sheet names that can be used as placeholder sheets.

- You can also copy sheets from a resource project.

- For more information on creating Sheet Lists, see *A.8 Additional Schedule Types.*

Presetting a Starting View

When you create a project template or project, it can help to specify a starting view. This can be any of the standard views, such as plan, elevation, 3D view, or one that is specifically created. This is often a Drafting View (as shown in Figure 1–62), or a Legend View with information about the project or the cover sheet for the project.

Figure 1–62

How To: Set a Starting View

1. Set up the view or sheet that you want to use as the starting view.

2. In the *Manage* tab>Manage Project panel, click (Starting View).

3. In the Starting View dialog box, select the view or sheet that you want to use as shown in Figure 1–63.

The Default starting view is <Last Viewed>.

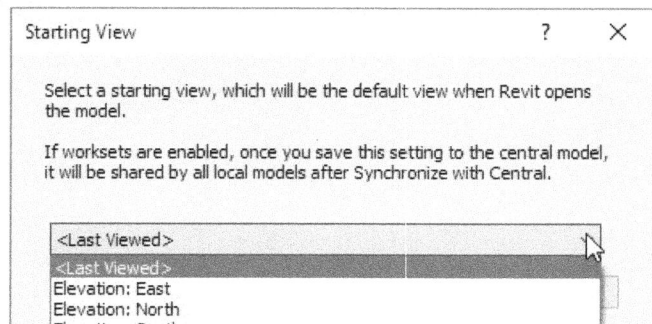

Figure 1–63

4. Click **OK**.

Practice 1c | Create Title Blocks

Practice Objectives

- Draw a custom title block including detail lines, text, labels, and a revision table.
- Set up sheets in the template using the new title block.

In this practice, you will create a new title block by adding lines, text, labels, logo, and a Revision Schedule similar to Figure 1–64. You will then load it into a project template file and create several standard sheets.

Figure 1–64

Task 1 - Create a title block.

1. In the *File* tab, expand ⬜ (New) and click ⬚ (Title Block).

2. In the New Title Block - Select Template File dialog box, select **D - 36 x24.rft** and click **Open**.

3. In the *Create* tab>Detail panel, click ⌐ (Line) and create lines on the inside of the existing rectangle **1/4"** away from the top, bottom, and right sides. Draw a line **1"** away on the left margin. Trim the lines as required.

4. Draw lines in the lower right corner of the title block, as shown in Figure 1–65.

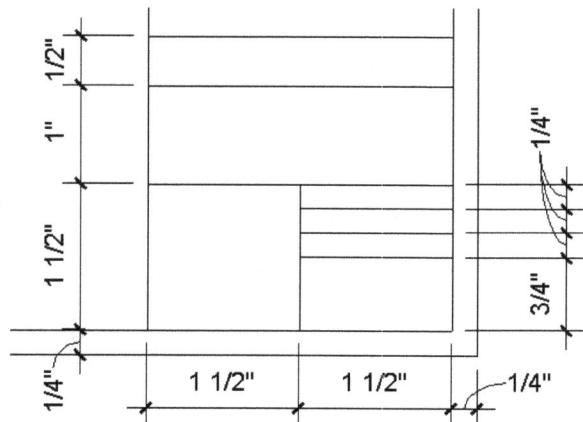

Figure 1–65

5. In the *Create* tab>Detail panel, click ⬕ (Symbol).

6. In the *Modify | Place Symbol* tab>Mode panel, click ⬓ (Load Family).

7. Navigate to the practice files>*Reference* folder, select **Company Logo.rfa**, and click **Open**.

8. Add the symbol to the lower left corner of the new title block. It is designed to fit within the square.

9. In the *Create* tab>Text panel, click **A** (Text).

10. In Properties, click ⊞ (Edit Type) and create the following Text type:

Type Name	Font	Size	Bold	Background
Arial 1/16"	Arial	1/16"	No	Transparent

11. In the *Create* tab>Text panel, click 🅰 (Label).

12. In Properties, click ⊞ (Edit Type) and create the following Label types:

Type Name	Font	Size	Bold	Background
Arial 1/8"	Arial	1/8"	No	Transparent
Arial 1/4"	Arial	1/4"	No	Transparent

13. Using the following steps, add text and labels to the title block, as shown in Figure 1–66.

Sheet Name

Project Name
Project Address

Company Logo

Date
Project Issue Date

Project Number
Project Number

Drawn By
DRW

Sheet Number
A101

Figure 1–66

You can use Reference Lines to place the text and labels exactly.

- Use **A** (Text) with the *text type* **Arial 1/16"** to add text in the lower right spaces for the *Date*, *Project Number*, *Drawn By*, and *Sheet Number*.

- Use **A** (Label) with the *label type* **Arial 1/4"** and

  ≡ (Align Center) justification to add the *Sheet Name*, *Project Name*, and *Sheet Number*. Move and stretch the labels to fit in the title block.

- Using the *label type* **Arial 1/8"** and ≡ (Align Center) justification, add the *Project Address* below the *Project Name*.

- Using the *label type* **Arial 1/8"** and ≡ (Align Right) justification, add the *Project Issue Date*, *Project Number*, and *Drawn By*. Save the title block in the practice files folder as **Company TBLK.rfa**.

Task 2 - Add a Revision Schedule to the title block.

1. In the title block Family Editor, in the *View* tab>Create panel,

   click ⬚ (Revision Schedule).

2. In the Revision Properties dialog box, *Fields* tab, set up the fields as shown in Figure 1–67.

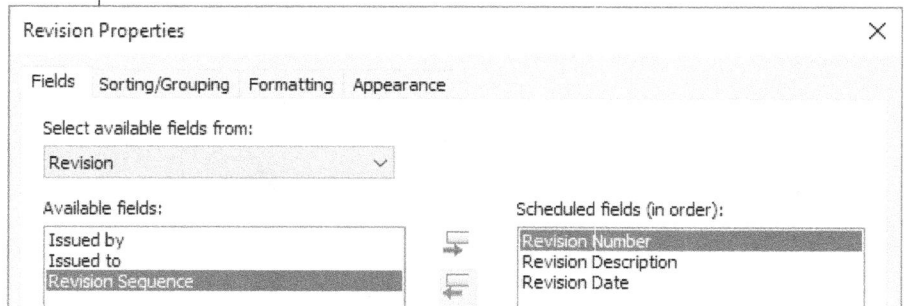

Figure 1–67

3. Accept the defaults for the *Sorting/Grouping* and *Formatting* tabs.

4. Select the *Appearance* tab and change the *Height* to **User defined**.

5. Click **OK**.

6. Return to the Sheet view.

7. In the Project Browser, expand *Views (all)* to display the *Schedules* and *Sheets (all)* areas, as shown in Figure 1–68.

Figure 1–68

8. Drag and drop the Revision Schedule onto the sheet.

9. Move it above the sheet name and resize it to display several lines, as shown in Figure 1–69. Align it to the edge of the title block.

Figure 1–69

10. Save and close the title block.

Task 3 - Set up sheets in a project template using the new title block.

---

1. Open the template found in the practice files folder that relates to your discipline:

   - *Architectural*>**Midrise-Template-Architectural-2.rte**
   - *MEP*>**Midrise-Template-MEP-2.rte**
   - *Structural*>**Midrise-Template-Structural-2.rte**

2. In the *View* tab>Sheet Composition panel, click 🗋 (Sheet).

3. In the New Sheet dialog box, click **Load...**.

4. In the Load Family dialog box, navigate to the practice files folder, select **Company TBLK.rfa** (that you just created), and click **Open**.

   - If you did not complete the previous tasks, open **Sample TBLK.rfa** from the practice files>*Reference* folder.

5. Select the title block that you just loaded and click **OK**.

6. In the Project Browser, select the sheet and rename it as **CS000 – Cover Sheet**.

7. Using the **Title Large** text type, add placeholder text for the project name and address, as shown in Figure 1–70.

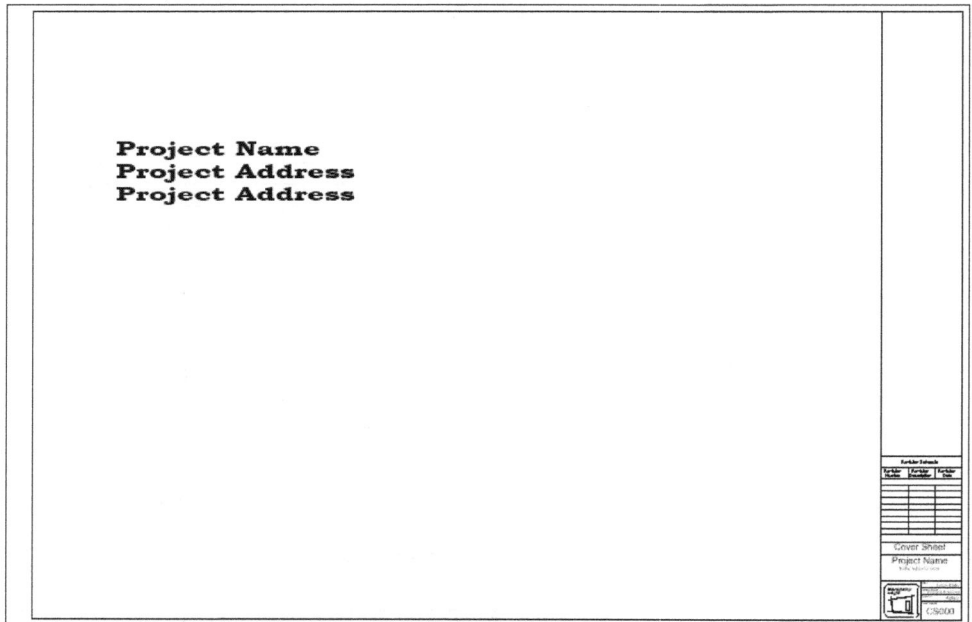

Figure 1–70

8. In the *Manage* tab>Manage Project panel, click 🗗 (Starting View).

9. In the Starting View dialog box, select **Sheet: CS000 - Cover Sheet** as shown in Figure 1–71.

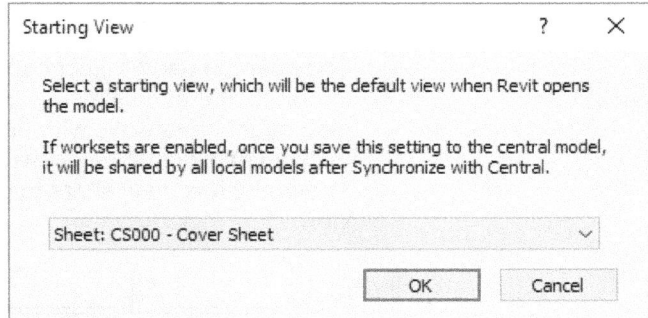

Figure 1–71

10. Create another sheet with the new title block and name it according to your discipline:

- **A201 – First Floor Plan**
- **M201 - First Floor Plan Mechanical**
- **E201 - First Floor Plan Electrical**
- **P201 - First Floor Plan Plumbing**
- **S201 - First Floor Plan Structural**

11. Open this sheet view. Drag the associated **Level 1** floor plan view onto the sheet, as shown in Figure 1–72.

No elements are on the view, but it acts as a placeholder on the sheet. Elements display as they are drawn.

Figure 1–72

12. Save and close the template file.

1.4 Setting Up View Filters

Rule-based view filters used in conjunction with Visibility/Graphic Overrides are a powerful tool that can be saved in template files. They can be used to test conditions in a project or modify the information that display in a view. For example, a fire evacuation plan might have walls with different fire ratings that display with thicker lineweights, as shown in Figure 1–73. MEP projects frequently use view filters to control which systems display in a view.

Figure 1–73

*   Rule-based Filters are used in Visibility/Graphic Overrides and Selection Filters are used by Selection Sets.

How To: Create Filters

1. In the *View* tab>Graphics panel, click (Filters). The Filters dialog box opens as shown in Figure 1–74.

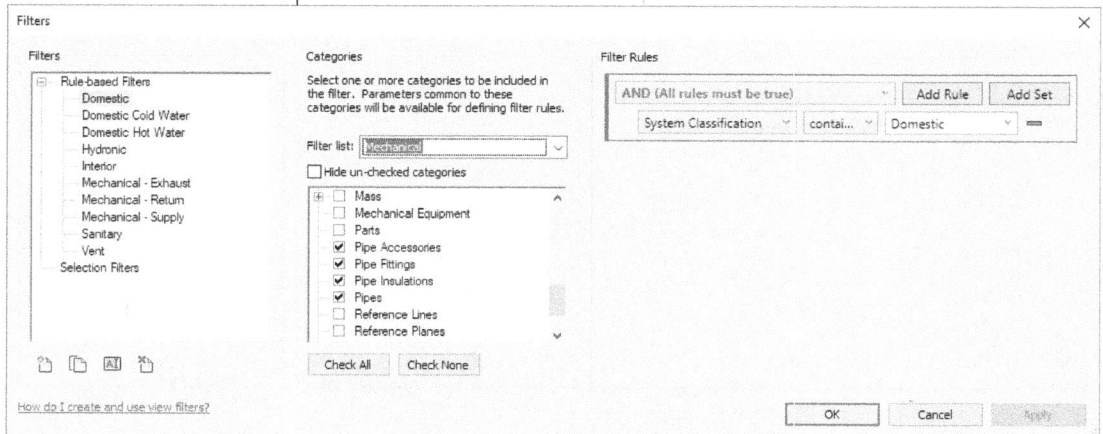

Figure 1–74

2. In the *Filters* area, select the **Rule-based Filters** node or an existing filter and click ⬚ (New) or ⬚ (Duplicate), as shown in Figure 1–75. Name the new filter and click **OK**.

3. In the *Categories* area, filter the list by discipline and then select the categories to include in the filter, as shown in Figure 1–75. Use **Check All** and **Check None** to help select the categories.

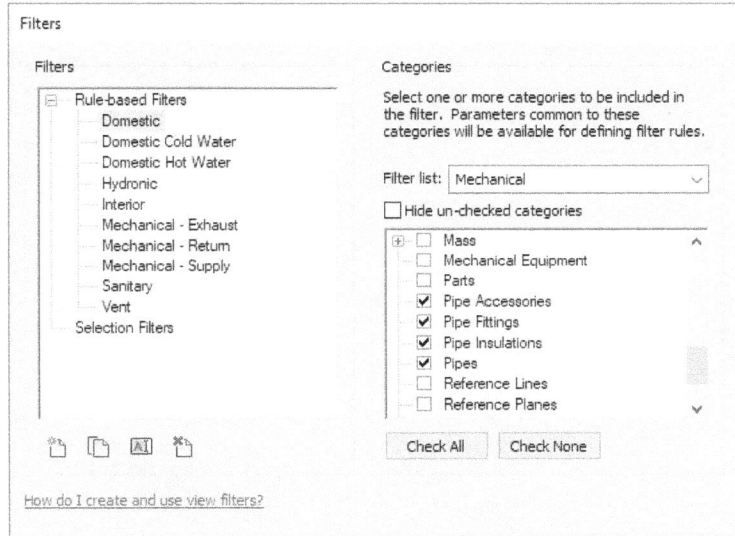

Figure 1–75

- Although you can select multiple categories, you can only filter by the parameters the categories have in common.

4. In the *Filter Rules* area, select the *Condition* (type of filter) you want to create (**AND** or **OR**) as shown in Figure 1–76.

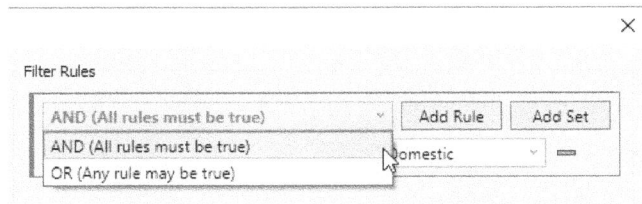

Figure 1–76

5. Then, for each filter, specify the *Parameter*, *Operator*, and *Value*, as shown in Figure 1–77.

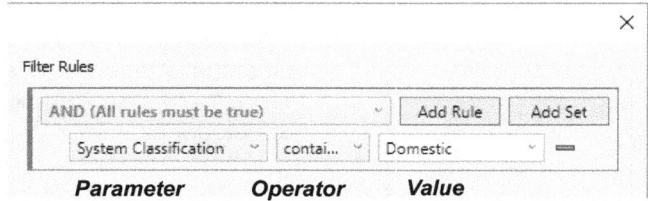

Figure 1–77

- Click **Add Rule** to add a rule to the existing Condition.
- Click **Add Set** to add a nested Condition and filters.

6. Click **Apply** to save the changes and remain in the dialog box, or click **OK** to finish.

- If you create more than one filter rule, they are applied in order.

- Building nested filters is complex. It is recommended to start with an **AND** condition and then add **OR** conditions to further identify the elements.

- Test your filters thoroughly before applying them in a template.

How To: Apply Visibility/Graphic Overrides Filters

1. Type **VG** or **VV** or in the *View* tab>Graphics panel, click

   (Visibility/Graphics) to open the Visibility/Graphic Overrides dialog box. Select the *Filters* tab, as shown in Figure 1–78.

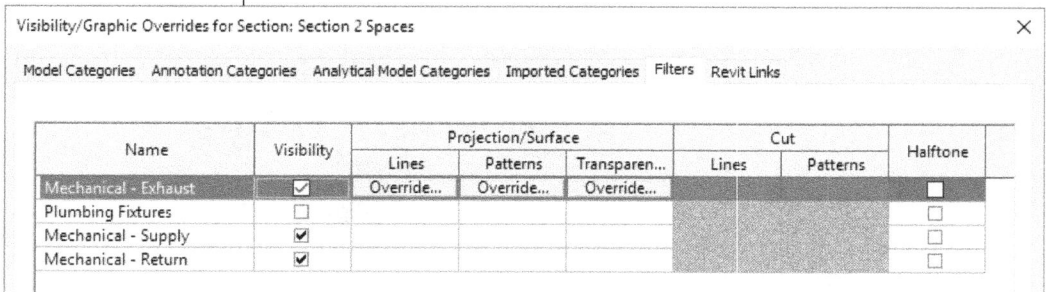

Figure 1–78

2. Click **Add** to add a filter to the list.
3. In the Add Filters dialog box, select the filter(s) you want to add, as shown in Figure 1–79. Then, click **OK**.

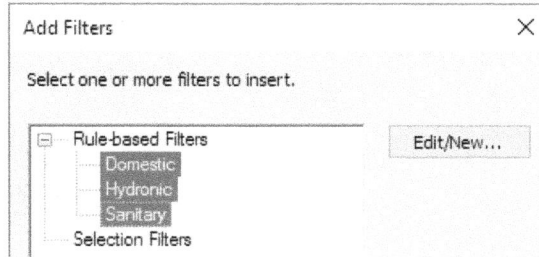

Add Filters ×

Select one or more filters to insert.

⊟ Rule-based Filters   Edit/New...
    Domestic
    Hydronic
    Sanitary
  Selection Filters

Figure 1–79

- If the filter you want is not defined, click **Edit/New...** to open the Filters dialog box, where you can define a new filter or edit an existing one.

4. In the Visibility/Graphic Overrides dialog box, assign the overrides you want for the filter, as shown in Figure 1–80.

| Name | Visibility | Projection/Surface | | | Cut | | Halftone |
		Lines	Patterns	Transparen...	Lines	Patterns	
Mechanical - Exhaust	☑	Override...	Override...	Override...			☐
Domestic	☐						☐
Hydronic	☐						☐
Sanitary	☐						☐
Plumbing Fixtures	☐						☐
Mechanical - Supply	☑						☐
Mechanical - Return	☑						☐

Figure 1–80

5. Click **OK**.

Practice 1d | Set up View Filters - Architecture

Practice Objectives

- Create rule-based filters.
- Add view filters to a view and setup overrides.

In this practice, you will create rule-based filters. You will duplicate a view and add the filters with overrides setup in Visibility/Graphic Overrides. The original view and modified view are shown in Figure 1–81.

Original View   *Duplicated View with Filters and Overrides*

Figure 1–81

Note: This practice uses view filters in an existing project so you can see the impact of what they do. They should be setup originally in a template.

Task 1 - Create filters.

1. In the practice files *Architectural* folder, open **Office-Fire Ratings.rvt**.

2. In the *View* tab>Graphics panel, click 🗹 (Filters).

3. In the Filters dialog box, click 🗋 (New), name the new filter **Fire Rating - 1 Hour**, and click **OK**.

4. In the *Categories* area, set the *Filter list* to **Architecture**. Select **Walls**.

5. In the *Filter Rules* area, set the **AND** condition to **Fire Rating - equals - 1 Hour**, as shown in Figure 1–82.

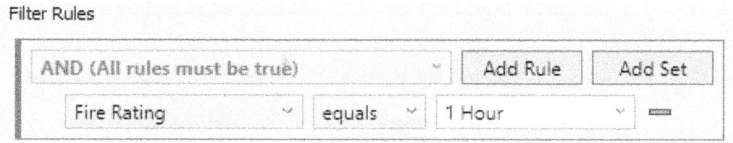

Filter Rules

| AND (All rules must be true) | ⌄ | Add Rule | Add Set |

| Fire Rating | ⌄ | equals | ⌄ | 1 Hour | ⌄ | ▬ |

Figure 1–82

6. Click **Apply** and remain in the Filters dialog box.

7. Select the new **Fire Rating - 1 Hour** filter and click (Duplicate).

8. Right-click on the duplicated filter and click (Rename). In the Rename dialog box, type **Fire Rating - 2 Hours** and click **OK**.

9. Modify the *Filter Rule* to **Fire Rating - equals - 2 Hours**, as shown in Figure 1–83.

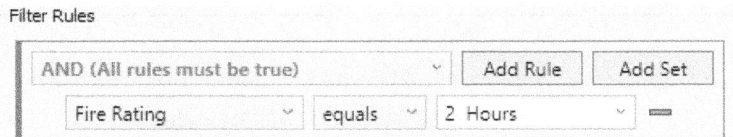

Filter Rules

| AND (All rules must be true) | ⌄ | Add Rule | Add Set |

| Fire Rating | ⌄ | equals | ⌄ | 2 Hours | ⌄ | ▬ |

Figure 1–83

- Note: You will need to type in **2 Hours** because this fire rating does not yet display in the project.

10. Click **OK** to close the Filters dialog box.

Task 2 - Test the View Filters

1. Duplicate the Floor Plans>**Level 1** view and name it **Level 1 - Fire Ratings**.

2. Open only the **Level 1** and **Level 1 - Fire Ratings** views and type **WT** to tile them side by side.

3. Zoom in on the core of the building in both views.

4. In the **Level 1 - Fire Ratings** view, open the Visibility/Graphic Overrides dialog box.

5. In the *Filters* tab, click **Add**.

6. In the Add Filters dialog box, select the fire rating filters, as shown in Figure 1–84. Then, click **OK**.

Figure 1–84

7. For the **Fire Rating - 1 Hour** filter, in the *Cut>Patterns* column, select **Override**.

8. In the Fill Pattern Graphics dialog box, change the *Foreground Pattern* to **Solid Fill** and *Color* to an orange, as shown in Figure 1–85. Click **OK**.

Figure 1–85

9. Repeat the process for the 2-hour fire wall using a different color, as shown in Figure 1–86.

Figure 1–86

10. Click **OK**. The Filter overrides display in the Fire Ratings view but not in the original view.

11. Select one of the exterior walls (**Basic Wall (WT-04)**) and in Properties, click **Edit Type**.

This is an example. Typically, exterior walls are not setup with this type of fire rating unless they are part of a fire wall.

12. Scroll down to the *Identity Data* section and beside *Fire Rating*, type in **2 Hours**, as shown in Figure 1–87. Then, click **OK**.

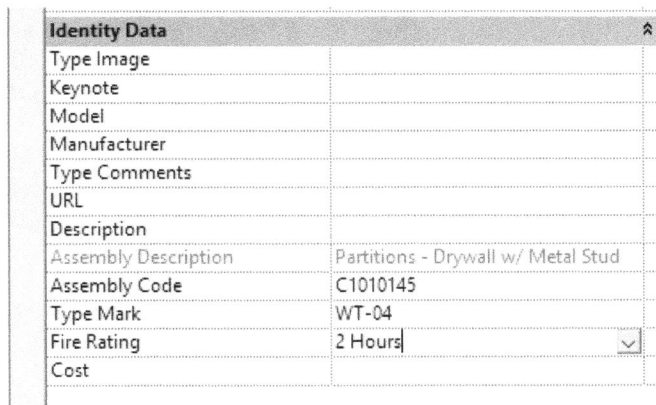

Figure 1–87

• The value of the Fire Rating parameter must match the name of the filter exactly. Edit the filter if the walls do not change color.

13. Save and close the project.

Practice 1e | Set up View Filters - Structure

Practice Objectives

- Create rule-based filters.
- Add view filters to a view and setup overrides.

In this practice, you will create rule-based filters. You will duplicate a view and apply the filters with overrides setup in Visibility/Graphic Overrides. The modified view is shown in Figure 1–88.

Figure 1–88

Note: This practice uses view filters in an existing project so you can see the impact of what they do. They should be setup originally in a template.

Task 1 - Create filters.

1. In the practice files *Structural* folder, open **Office-Materials.rvt**.

2. In the *View* tab>Graphics panel, click ⬚ (Filters).

3. In the Filters dialog box, click 🗋 (New), name the new filter **Concrete** and click **OK**.

4. In the *Categories* area, set the *Filter list* to **Structure**. Select **Structural Columns**, **Structural Foundations**, **Structural Framing** and **Walls**.

An alternate way to make these filters is to do one for each material.

5. In the *Filter Rules* area, set the **OR** condition to **Structural Material - equals - Concrete - Cast-in-place Concrete**, as shown in Figure 1–89.

Filter Rules

| OR (Any rule may be true) | | Add Rule | Add Set |

Structural Material   equals

<By Category>
Concrete - Cast-in-Place Concrete
Masonry - Concrete Masonry Units
Metal - Steel - ASTM A500 - Grade B -
Metal - Steel - ASTM A992
Metal - Stud Layer

Figure 1–89

6. Click **Add Rule** and add another rule: **Structural Material - equals - Concrete Mason Units.**

7. Click **Apply** and remain in the Filters dialog box.

8. Select the new **Concrete** filter and click 🗋 (Duplicate).

9. Right-click on the duplicated filter and click 🔤 (Rename). In the Rename dialog box, type **Steel** and click **OK**.

10. Modify the *Filter Rules* to **Structural Material - equals - Metal - Steel - ASTM A500 - Grade B - Rectangular and Square** and **Metal - Steel - ASTM A992**, as shown in Figure 1–90.

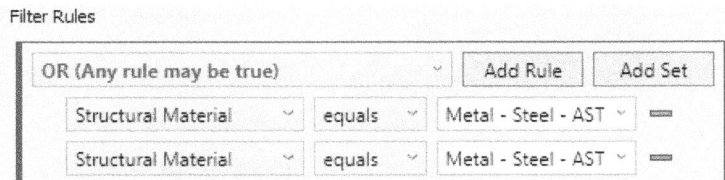

Filter Rules

| OR (Any rule may be true) | | Add Rule | Add Set |

Structural Material   equals   Metal - Steel - AST

Structural Material   equals   Metal - Steel - AST

Figure 1–90

11. Click **OK** to close the Filters dialog box.

Task 2 - Test the View Filters

1. In the Project Browser, duplicate 3D Views>**{3D}** view and rename it to **Structural Materials - 3D**.

2. Open the Visibility/Graphic Overrides dialog box.

3. In the *Filters* tab, click **Add**.

4. In the Add Filters dialog box, select both of the filters, as shown in Figure 1–91. Then, click **OK**.

Figure 1–91

5. For the Concrete Filter in the *Projection/Surface>Patterns* column, select **Override**.

6. In the Fill Pattern Graphics dialog box, change the *Foreground Pattern* to **Solid Fill** and *Color* to an orange, as shown in Figure 1–92. Click **OK**.

Figure 1–92

7. Repeat the process for the Steel using a different color, as shown in Figure 1–93.

| Visibility/Graphic Overrides for 3D View: Structural Materials - 3D | | | | | | | × |

Model Categories   Annotation Categories   Analytical Model Categories   Imported Categories   Filters

Name	Visibility	Projection/Surface			Cut		Halftone
		Lines	Patterns	Transparen	Lines	Patterns	
Concrete	✔						☐
Steel	✔	Override...		Override...	Override...	Override...	☐

Figure 1–93

8. Click **OK**. The Filter overrides display in the view.

9. Save and close the project.

Practice 1f

Set up View Filters - MEP

Practice Objectives

- Create rule-based filters.
- Add view filters to a view and setup overrides.

In this practice, you will create rule-based filters. You will duplicate a view and add the filters with overrides setup in Visibility/Graphic Overrides. The original view and modified view are shown in Figure 1–94.

Original View   *Duplicated View with Filters and Overrides*

Figure 1–94

Note: This practice uses view filters in an existing project so you can see the impact of what they do. They should be setup originally in a project template.

Task 1 - Create filters.

1. In the practice files *MEP* folder, open **Office-Velocity.rvt**.

2. In the *View* tab>Graphics panel, click ⬚ (Filters).

3. In the Filters dialog box, click ⬚ (New), name the new filter **Mechanical - Low Velocity**, and click **OK**.

4. In the *Categories* area, set the *Filter list* to **Mechanical**. Select **Ducts** and **Flex Ducts**.

5. In the *Filter Rules* area, set the **AND** condition to **Velocity - is less than or equal to - 900 FPM**, as shown in Figure 1–95.

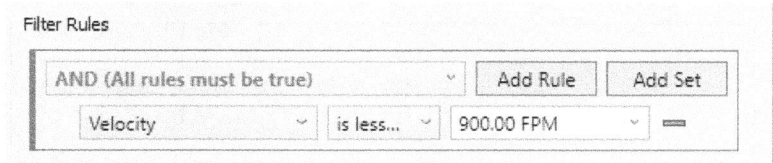

Figure 1–95

6. Click **Apply** and remain in the Filters dialog box.

7. Select the new **Mechanical - Low Velocity** filter and click ⬚ (Duplicate).

8. Right-click on the duplicated filter and click ⬚ (Rename). In the Rename dialog box, type **Mechanical - Medium Velocity** and click **OK**.

9. Click **Add Rule** to create a second rule and set the rules up as shown in Figure 1–96.

Figure 1–96

10. Create an additional filter named **Mechanical-High Velocity** set up as shown in Figure 1–97.

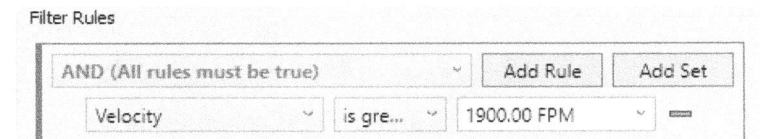

Figure 1–97

11. Click **OK** to close the Filters dialog box.

Task 2 - Test the View Filters

1. Duplicate the Mechanical>Floor Plans>**1 - Mech** view and name it **1 - Mech - Velocity**

2. Open only the **1 - Mech** and **1 - Mech - Velocity** views and type **WT** to tile them side by side.

3. Zoom in on the central core of the building in both views. Both views display the duct colors setup in the Duct System properties for Supply, Return, and Exhaust.

4. In the **1 - Mech - Velocity** view, open the Visibility/Graphic Overrides dialog box and open the *Filters* tab. Three existing filters are available for the Mechanical duct systems.

5. In the *Filters* tab, click **Add**.

6. In the Add Filters dialog box, select the new filters as shown in Figure 1–98. Click **OK**.

Figure 1–98

7. If required, move the Velocity based filters to the top of the list using the **Up** and **Down** buttons.

8. For the **Mechanical-Low Velocity** filter, in the *Projection/Surface>Patterns* column, select **Override**.

9. In the Fill Pattern Graphics dialog box, change the *Pattern* to **Solid Fill** and the *Color* to an orange, as shown in Figure 1–99. Click **OK**.

Figure 1–99

10. For the other velocity filters, create a similar overrides using other colors.

11. For the Supply and Return filters, set the *Lines* override *Color* to **Black** with no additional *Weight*. Then, clear the *Visibility* check on the Exhaust filter, as shown in Figure 1–100.

Figure 1–100

12. Click **OK**. The Filter overrides display in the velocity view, but not in the original view.

13. Save and close the project.

1.5 Adding View Templates

View templates, consisting of specific view properties and visibility options, ensure that company standards are applied to views. For example, you can create a view template that displays spaces, but hides the MEP systems in a view (as shown in Figure 1–101), while another view template displays duct systems but not plumbing fixtures (as shown in Figure 1–102).

Figure 1–101

Figure 1–102

- Many companies lock in view templates for their views to be placed on sheets. This prevents anyone from making changes, as shown for the detail level in Figure 1–103.

Figure 1–103

How To: Create a View Template from an Existing View

1. Set up a view the way you want it with *Scale*, *Detail Level*, *Visibility Graphic Overrides*, and other *View Settings*. For example, you can create a view template for furniture plans, such as that shown in Figure 1–104.

Figure 1–104

2. In the Project Browser, right-click on the view and select **Create View Template from View** or, on the *View* tab> Graphics panel, expand ⬛ (View Template), and click ⬛ (Create Template from Current View).
3. In the New View Template dialog box, type a name for the view template.
4. Click **OK**.
5. In the View Template dialog box, make adjustments as required and then click **OK**.

How To: Set up a View Template

1. In the *View* tab>Graphics panel, expand ⬛ (View Template) and then click 🔧 (Manage View Templates).
2. In the Apply View Template dialog box, in the *Names* list, select a view similar to the one you want to create and click ⬛ (Duplicate).
3. In the New View Template dialog box, type a new name for the view template and click **OK**.

4. Select the new view template (as shown in Figure 1–105), and modify the parameter values in the *View Properties* area, as required.

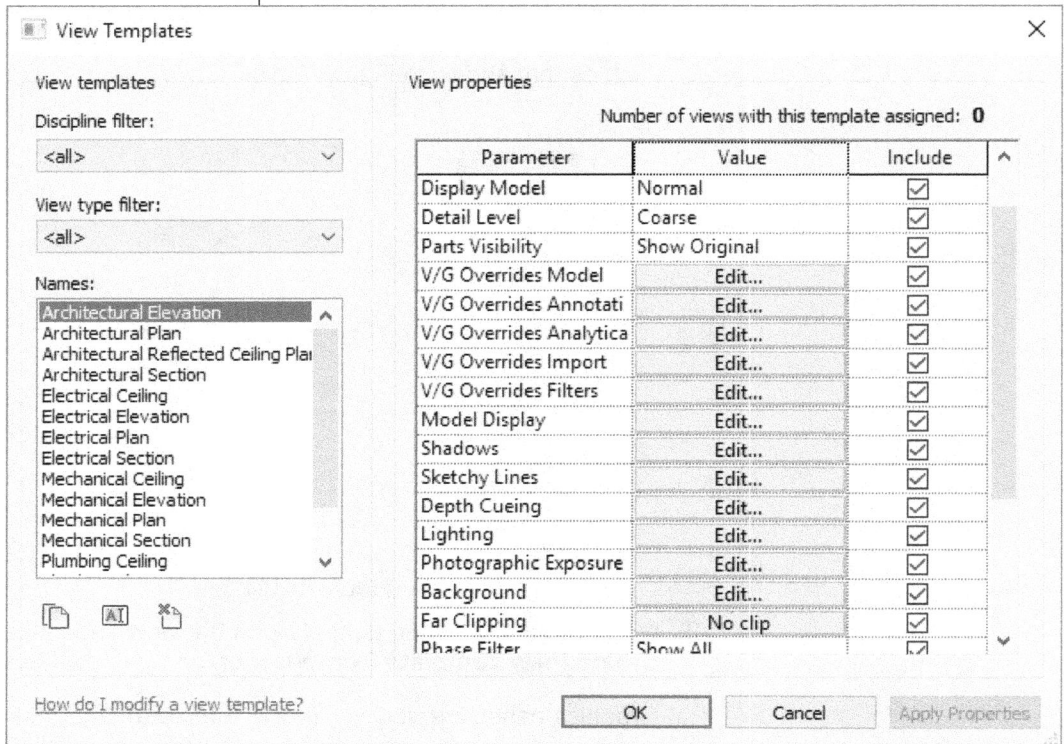

Figure 1–105

5. Click **OK** to finish.

• To limit the number of view templates that display, filter the list by selecting an option in the *Discipline filter* and *View type filter* drop-down lists, as shown in Figure 1–106.

Figure 1–106

- If you do not want specific view properties to be part of the view template that is applied to views, clear the checkmark in the *Include* column for the parameters you do not want to include. You can also create overrides to the view template by changing parameter values.

- Note that the different view types have different view parameters. For example, 3D views have options for Rendering and Perspectives that plan views do not have.

Hint: Setting the View Scale-to-Detail Level Correspondence

One view parameter is the *Detail Level*. There are three options: **Coarse**, **Medium**, and **Fine**. You can modify the table of scales that are related to the levels. In the *Manage* tab>

Settings panel, expand 🔧 (Additional Settings) and select

▦ (Detail Level). The View scale-to-detail level correspondence dialog box displays, as shown in Figure 1–107.

Figure 1–107

How To: Create a New View Type with a View Template

1. Open a view of the type you want to create. For example, if you want to create a new plan view type, select an existing Floor Plan view, or if you want to create a new elevation view type, select an existing Elevation view.
2. In Properties, click **Edit Type**.
3. Duplicate the existing type and give it a new name.

4. Specify the *Callout Tag* and *Reference Label*, set the *View Template is applied to new view* option, and select **New views dependent on template**, if required, as shown in Figure 1–108.

Figure 1–108

5. Click **OK**.

- When you create a new view, you can select the view type from the drop-down list, as shown for a new floor plan in Figure 1–109. The view is also placed in its own group in the Project Browser, as shown in Figure 1–110.

Figure 1–109

Figure 1–110

How To: Set the Default View Template for a View

1. In the Project Browser, select one or more views.
2. In Properties, in the *Identity Data* section, click the button next to *View Template*, as shown in Figure 1–111. The name on the button varies according to the template that has already been assigned.

Identity Data		☆ ∧
View Template	Space Plan	
View Name	Level 1	
Dependency	Independent	

Figure 1–111

3. In the Apply View Template dialog box, select the appropriate template and click **OK**.

•   You can apply view templates to any view as many times as required, unless it is set as the default template in the view properties.

•   If you want to start a new view template based on an existing view, select **Show Views**. The *Names* list expands to include all of the related views in the project.

Hint: Temporary View Properties

As you are working, it can be helpful to temporarily override the view. You can do this by selecting a view template from the View Control Bar, as shown in Figure 1–112.

Enable Temporary View Properties
Temporarily Apply Template Properties...
Recent Templates
✓ Mechanical Section
Electrical Section
Restore View Properties

Figure 1–112

1. In the View Control Panel, expand 🖾 (Temporary View Properties) and select **Enable Temporary View Properties**.

2. Expand 🖾 (Temporary View Properties) again and select **Temporarily Apply Template Properties**. Alternatively, if you have already used the process, you can select from a list of view templates, as shown in Figure 1–112.

3. In the dialog box, select the view template you want to apply and click **OK**.

4. When you are finished, expand 🖾 (Temporary View Properties) and select **Restore View Properties**.

•   Some companies create a "working view" template to be used as a temporary override, rather than having separate working views.

Practice 1g | Add View Templates - Architecture

Practice Objectives

- Create a view template from an existing view.
- Create a view template from within Manage View Templates.
- Duplicate views and apply the view templates.

In this practice, you will create view templates from an existing view and modify the view template using **Manage View Templates**. You will then duplicate views and apply the view templates to other views, as shown in Figure 1–113.

Figure 1–113

Note: This practice uses view templates in an existing project so you can see the impact of what they do. They should be setup originally in a project template.

Task 1 - Create a View Template from an existing view.

1. In the practice files *Architectural* folder, open **Office-Rooms.rvt**.

2. In the **Level 1 - Fire Ratings** view hide the grids, elevations, sections, furniture, plumbing fixtures, and similar elements. (Hint: Select one element of each category and type **VH**).

3. In the Project Browser, in the *Floor Plans* area, right-click on the **Level 1 - Fire Ratings** view and select **Create View Template From View**.

4. Name the new view template **Fire Ratings** and click **OK**.

5. In the View Templates dialog box, next to **V/G Override Filters**, click **Edit...**.

6. In the Visibility/Graphic Overrides dialog box, *Filters* tab, review the Filters and overrides.

7. In the *View properties* area, in the *Include* column, clear the checkmarks from all of the options except *Detail Level, V/G Overrides Model, V/G Overrides Annotation, V/G Overrides Filters,* and *Model Display,* as shown in Figure 1–114.

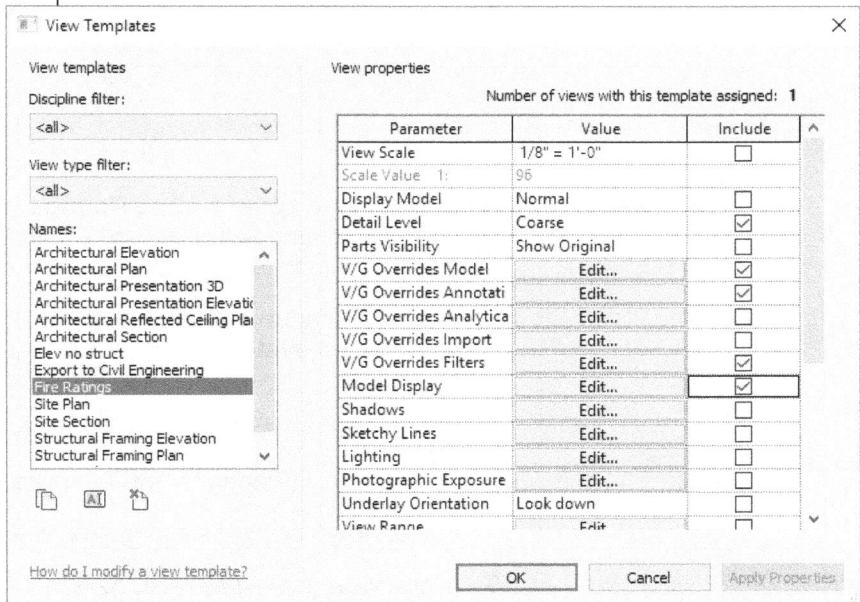

Figure 1–114

8. Click **OK**.

Task 2 - Apply View Templates to views.

---

1. Duplicate the **Level 2** view and rename it as **Level 2 - Fire Ratings**.

2. In Properties, in the *Identity Data* group, select the button beside *View Template*.

3. In the Assign View Template dialog box, select **Fire Rating** and click **OK**.

4. Review the View Control Bar options. Note that you can't make any changes to the view controls of this view, as shown in Figure 1–115.

Figure 1–115

5. Switch to the **Level 1 - Fire Ratings** view. Note that you can still make changes to the View Controls of this view because the view template is not linked to the view.

6. Return to the **Level 2 - Fire Ratings** view. The floor is showing in **Level 2** but you do not want this to display.

7. In the *View* tab>Graphics panel, expand (View Template) and click (Manage View Templates)

8. In the View Templates dialog box, select **Fire Ratings**.

9. In the *View properties* area, next to *V/G Overrides Model*, click **Edit**.

10. In the Visibility/Graphics Overrides dialog box, toggle off **Floors**.

11. Click **OK** to close each of the dialog boxes. The floor in the **Level 2 - Fire Ratings** view automatically toggles off.

12. Save the project.

Task 3 - Create a View Template through Manage View Templates.

1. In the *View* tab>Graphics panel, expand ⬚ (View Template) and click ✎ (Manage View Templates).

2. In the Apply View Template dialog box, set the *View type filter* to **Floor, Structural, Area Plans**.

3. in the *Names* list, select **Architectural Plan** and click ⬚ (Duplicate).

4. Name the new view **Room Plan**.

5. Next to *V/G Overrides Model*, click **Edit...**.

6. In the Visibility/Graphic Overrides dialog box, set the *Filter List* to **Architecture**.

7. Select **All** and clear the checkamrks from all of the model elements.

8. Select **None**.

9. Toggle on **Doors, Stairs, Walls,** and **Windows**.

10. Select and expand *Rooms* and select **Interior Fill**, as shown in Figure 1–116.

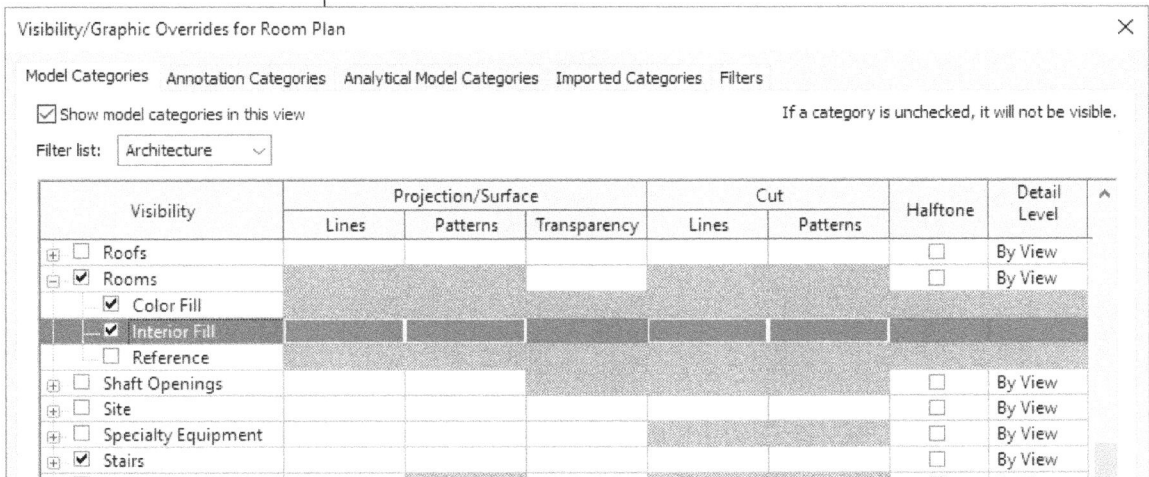

Visibility/Graphic Overrides for Room Plan							×

Model Categories Annotation Categories Analytical Model Categories Imported Categories Filters

☑ Show model categories in this view   If a category is unchecked, it will not be visible.

Filter list: Architecture ⌄

Visibility	Projection/Surface			Cut		Halftone	Detail Level
	Lines	Patterns	Transparency	Lines	Patterns		
⊞ ☐ Roofs						☐	By View
⊟ ☑ Rooms						☐	By View
☑ Color Fill							
☑ Interior Fill							
☐ Reference							
⊞ ☐ Shaft Openings						☐	By View
⊞ ☐ Site						☐	By View
⊞ ☐ Specialty Equipment						☐	By View
⊞ ☑ Stairs						☐	By View

Figure 1–116

11. Click **OK**.

12. In the View Templates dialog box, clear the checkmarks in the *Include* column beside *View Scale* and *View Range*.

13. Click **OK**.

14. Use the **Duplicate with Detailing** command on the **Level 1** and **Level 2** views and rename them as **Level 1 - Rooms** and **Level 2 Rooms.**

15. In the Project Browser, select both rooms views.

16. In Properties, in the *Identity Data* group, select the button beside *View Template*. and apply the **Room Plan** view template to the views.

17. Open **Level 1**, **Level 1 - Fire Ratings**, and **Level 1 - Rooms** views and compare them.

18. Save and close the project.

Practice 1h

Add View Templates - Structure

Practice Objectives

- Create a view template from an existing view.
- Create a view template from within Manage View Templates.
- Duplicate views and apply the view templates.

In this practice, you will create a view template from an existing view and modify the view template using **Manage View Templates**. You will then duplicate views and apply the view template to other views, as shown in Figure 1–117.

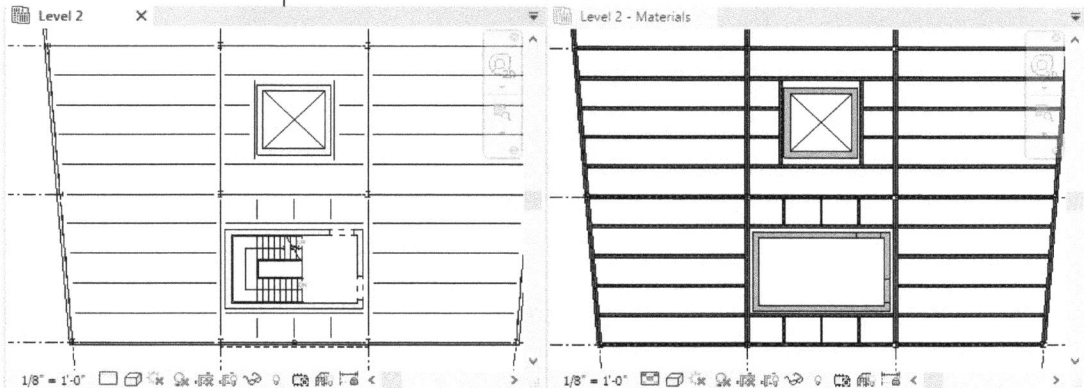

Figure 1–117

Note: This practice uses view templates in an existing project so you can see the impact of what they do. They should be setup originally in a project template.

Task 1 - Create a View Template from an existing view.

1. In the practice files *Structural* folder, open **Office-View Template.rvt**.

2. In the Project Browser, in the *3D Views* area, right-click on the **Structural Materials - 3D** view and select **Create View Template From View**.

3. Name the new view template **Structural Materials** and click **OK**.

4. Next to **V/G Override Filters**, click **Edit...**. The Visibility/Graphic Overrides dialog box opens with the *Filter* tab selected. You can see that the Filters and overrides setup in the view are included in the view template.

5. Click **OK**.

6. In the *Include* column, clear the checkmarks from everything except the *Detail Level, V/G Overrides Filters*, *V/G Overrides Model,* and *Model Display* categories.

7. Click **OK**.

8. Save the project.

Task 2 - Apply the View Template to Views.

1. Duplicate the Structural Plans>**Level 1** view and rename it **Level 1 - Materials**.

2. Right-click on the new view and select **Apply Template Properties**.

3. In the Apply View Template dialog box, set the *View type filter* to **<all>** and select **Structural Materials**, as shown in Figure 1–118. Click **OK**.

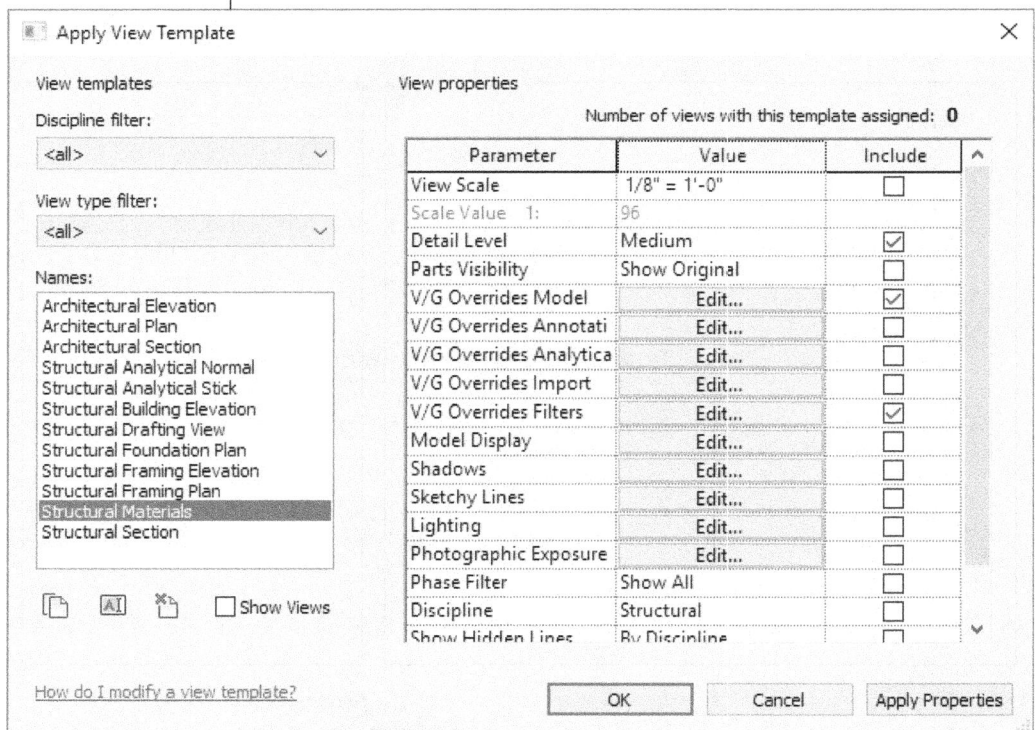

Figure 1–118

4. The plan displays with the most of the design in the concrete color. Compare the new floor plan view with the existing **Level 1** view, as shown in Figure 1–119.

Figure 1–119

5. Duplicate the **Level 2** view and rename it as **Level 2 - Materials.**

6. In Properties, in the *Identity Data* group, select the button beside *View Template*.

7. In the Assign View Template dialog box, set the *View type filter* to **<all>** and select **Structural Materials**. Click **OK**.

8. Review the View Control Bar options. Note that you cannot make any changes to the view controls of this view, as shown in Figure 1–120 and that the colors are not displaying as expected.

Figure 1–120

9. Switch to the **Level 1 - Materials** view. Note that you can still make changes to the View Controls of this view.

Task 3 - Modify a View Template through Manage View Templates

1. Switch to the **Level 2 - Materials** view.

2. In the *View* tab>Graphics panel, expand ⬚ (View Template) and click 🔧 (Manage View Templates).

3. in the *Names* list, select **Structural Materials**.

4. Next to *V/G Overrides Model*, click **Edit...**.

5. In the Visibility/Graphic Overrides dialog box, toggle off **Floors**.

6. Click **OK** twice to close the dialog boxes. The Steel color now displays because the floor has been removed, but the concrete walls do not display as expected, as shown in Figure 1–121.

Figure 1–121

7. Open the Manage View Templates dialog box again and select **Structural Materials**.

8. Edit the *V/G Overrides Filters*.

9. In the Visibility/ Graphic Overrides dialog box, add overrides to the *Cut Patterns* to match the *Projection/Surface Pattern* overrides, as shown in Figure 1–122.

Visibility/Graphic Overrides for Structural Materials								✕

Model Categories   Annotation Categories   Analytical Model Categories   Imported Categories   Filters

Name	Visibility	Projection/Surface			Cut		Halftone
		Lines	Patterns	Transparen	Lines	Patterns	
Concrete	☑						☐
Steel	☑	Override...		Override...	Override...		☐

Figure 1–122

10. Click **OK** to close the dialog boxes and the information is updated in the view as shown in Figure 1–123.

Color Added

Figure 1–123

11. Save and close the project.

Practice 1i

Add View Templates - MEP

Practice Objectives

- Create a view template from an existing view.
- Create a view template from within Manage View Templates.
- Duplicate views and apply the view templates.

In this practice, you will create view templates from an existing view modify the view template using **Manage View Templates**. You will then duplicated views and apply the view templates to other views, as shown in Figure 1–124.

Figure 1–124

Note: This practice uses view templates in an existing project so you can see the impact of what they do. They should be setup originally in a project template.

Task 1 - Create a View Template from an existing view and Apply View Template to views.

1. In the practice files *MEP* folder, open **Office-Spaces.rvt**.

2. In the Project Browser, in the *Mechanical>Floor Plans* area, right-click on the **1 - Mech - Velocity** view and select **Create View Template From View**.

3. Name the new view template **Velocity Duct Plan** and click **OK**.

4. In the View Templates dialog box, next to **V/G Override Filters**, click **Edit...** The Visibility/Graphic Overrides dialog box opens with the *Filter* tab selected. You can see that the Filters and overrides setup in the view are included in the view template.

5. Click **OK** twice to close the dialog boxes.

6. Duplicate the **2 - Mech** view and rename it as **2 - Mech - Velocity**.

7. In Properties, in the *Identity Data* group, select the button beside *View Template*.

8. In the Assign View Template dialog box, select **Velocity Duct Plan** and click **OK**.

9. Review the View Control Bar options. Note that you cannot make any changes to the view controls of this view, as shown in Figure 1–125.

Figure 1–125

10. Switch to the **1 - Mech - Velocity** view. Note that you can still make changes to the View Controls of this view.

Task 2 - Create a View Template through Manage View Templates

---

1. In the *View* tab>Graphics panel, expand ⬜ (View Template) and click ✏ (Manage View Templates).

2. In the View Templates dialog box, set the *View type filter* to **Floor, Structural, Area Plans**.

3. in the *Names* list, select **Architectural Plan** and click
   ⬀ (Duplicate).

4. Name the new view **Space Plan.**

5. Next to *V/G Overrides Model*, click **Edit...**.

6. In the Visibility/Graphic Overrides dialog box, set the *Filter List* to **Mechanical**, **Electrical**, and **Piping**.

7. Select **All** and clear the checkmark from all of the model elements.

8. Select **None**.

9. Scroll down, select and expand *Spaces,* and select **Interior**, as shown in Figure 1–126.

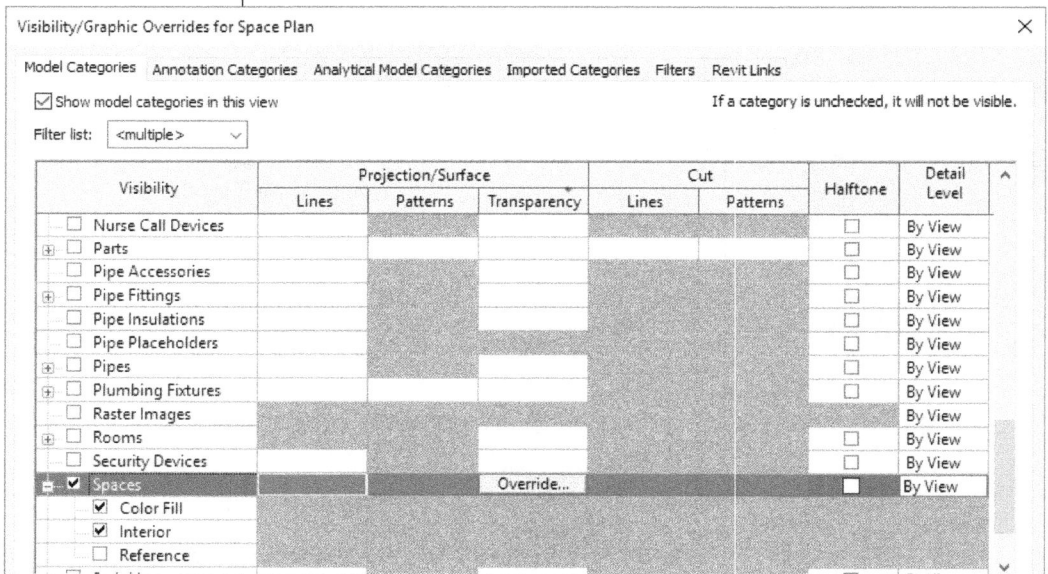

Figure 1–126

10. Click **OK.**

11. In the View Templates dialog box, clear the checkmarks in the *Include* column beside *View Scale* and *View Range.*

12. Change the *Discipline* to **Coordination** and click **OK.**

13. Save the project.

Task 3 - Apply View Template to Views

1. Use the **Duplicate with Detailing** command to duplicate the **1 - Mech** and **2 - Mech** views and rename them as **1 - Spaces** and **2 - Spaces.**

   • You can to include the space tags in the views so you must duplicate with detailing.

2. In the Project Browser, select both spaces views.

3. In Properties, in the *Identity Data* group, select the button beside *View Template*. and apply the **Space Plan** view template to the views.

4. In the Project Browser, the views are automatically moved to the **Coordination** node and the spaces display in the view but none of the MEP elements display, as shown in Figure 1–127.

Figure 1–127

   • If the spaces are not showing as expected, reload the linked file.

5. Save and close the project.

Chapter Review Questions

1. Which of the following items are NOT set in a template file?

   a. Units

   b. Annotation Types

   c. Title blocks

   d. Keyboard Shortcuts

2. What is a label?

   a. A text type used in title blocks.

   b. A dimension with text instead of numbers.

   c. A type of text with variable information.

3. When you want to create new Text Types, such as those shown in Figure 1–128, you need to copy an existing one.

   ## A FANCY FONT AT 1/4"

   A HAND LETTERING FONT AT 1/8"

   A HAND LETTERING FONT AT 3/32"

   Figure 1–128

   a. True

   b. False

4. Which of the following enables you to assign a view template consistently to a view so that no changes can be made to the view parameters?

   a. In the View Status Bar, lock the view.

   b. In Properties, select a View Template.

   c. In the Project Browser, right-click on the view and select **Lock**.

   d. In the Apply View Template dialog box, select a template.

5. Which of the following parameters are included in a View Template (as shown in Figure 1–129)? (Select all that apply.)

Figure 1–129

a. View Scale

b. V/G Overrides

c. Project Units

d. Detail Level

Command Summary

Button	Command	Location
Templates		
	Callout Tags	• **Ribbon:** *Manage* tab>Settings panel> expand Additional Settings
	Elevation Tags	• **Ribbon:** *Manage* tab>Settings panel> expand Additional Settings
	Floor Plan	• **Ribbon:** *View* tab>Create panel> expand Plan Views
	Loaded Tags and Symbols	• **Ribbon:** *Annotate* tab>Tag panel> expand the panel title
	Section Tags	• **Ribbon:** *Manage* tab>Settings panel> expand Additional Settings
Annotation		
	Dimension Types	• **Ribbon:** *Annotate* tab>Dimensions panel>expand the panel title
	Text	• **Family Editor** • **Ribbon:** *Create* tab>Text panel
Title Blocks		
	Label	• **Family Editor** • **Ribbon:** *Create* tab>Text panel
	New Title Block	• **Ribbon:** *File* tab> New
	Revision Schedule	• **Family Editor** • **Ribbon:** *View* tab>Create panel
View Templates and Filters		
	ApplyTemplate Properties to Current View	• **Ribbon:** *View* tab>Graphics panel> expand View Templates • **Project Browser:** (*right-click on a view*) **Apply Template Properties...**
	Create View Template From View	• **Ribbon:** *View* tab>Graphics panel> expand View Templates • **Project Browser:** (*right-click on a view*)
	Filters	• **Ribbon:** *View* tab>Graphics panel
	Manage View Templates	• **Ribbon:** *View* tab>Graphics panel> expand View Templates
	Temporary View Properties	• View Control Bar

Creating Schedules

Schedules are a critical component of BIM projects. They gather information about the model that is used in construction documents, and can also be used to test your model (for example, to verify the amount of air flow in a space). Several types of schedules can be created, including: building component schedules, key schedules, and material takeoff schedules. These schedules are all created using the same basic methods. Custom parameters can be added to schedules that include additional information about elements as well as formulas and other calculations.

Learning Objectives in this Chapter

- Schedule building components.
- Customize schedule tables using filters, sorting/grouping, formatting, and appearance.
- Modify the appearance and content of individual schedule cells.
- Create Key Style schedules by defining keys for elements with similar characteristics.
- Create material takeoff schedules.
- Apply conditional formatting to fields in a schedule.
- Embed a schedule into an existing room or space schedule.
- Create additional parameters including Calculated Value Fields and Percentage Fields.

2.1 Introduction to Schedules

Schedules can be created at any point in a project or included in template files. Each schedule is a separate view and can be inserted on a sheet, as shown in Figure 2–1.

Figure 2–1

You can create the following types of schedules:

(Schedule/ Quantities)	Generates schedules using parameters available at category level. There are two types of Schedule/ Quantities schedules: **Building Component** and **Key**.
(Material Takeoff)	Generates schedules from information about materials in a project and can be used to do quantity takeoffs.
(Sheet List)	Generates schedule from sheet information including who has designed and checked the sheet.
(Note Block)	Generates schedules that keep count of all of the symbols used in the project.
(View List)	Generates schedules that keep count of all of the views in the project, including their scale, phase, and use on sheets.
(Graphical Column Schedule)	(Structural only) Generates graphical schedules displaying heights of all columns in a project compared to levels. For more information on Graphical Column Schedules see *Figure A–72* .

- For more information on Sheet List, Note Block, and View List schedules see *A.8 Additional Schedule Types*.

Importing and Exporting Schedules

Schedules are views and can be copied into your project from other projects. Only the formatting information is copied; the information about individually scheduled items is not included. That information is automatically gathered from the elements in the current project. You can also export the schedule information to be used in spreadsheets.

How To: Import Schedules

1. In the *Insert* tab>Import panel, expand 🗋 (Insert From File) and click 🗋 (Insert Views From File).
2. In the Open dialog box, locate the project file containing the schedule that you want to use.
3. Select the schedules that you want to import, as shown in Figure 2–2.

*If the referenced project contains many types of views, change Views: to **Show schedules and reports only**.*

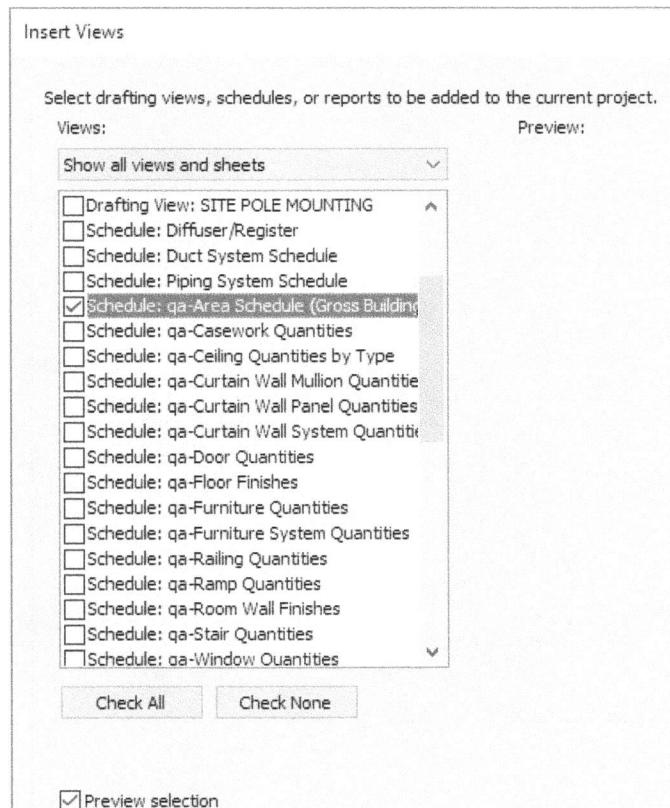

Insert Views

Select drafting views, schedules, or reports to be added to the current project.

Views: Preview:

Show all views and sheets ⌄

- [ ] Drafting View: SITE POLE MOUNTING
- [ ] Schedule: Diffuser/Register
- [ ] Schedule: Duct System Schedule
- [ ] Schedule: Piping System Schedule
- [x] Schedule: qa-Area Schedule (Gross Building
- [ ] Schedule: qa-Casework Quantities
- [ ] Schedule: qa-Ceiling Quantities by Type
- [ ] Schedule: qa-Curtain Wall Mullion Quantitie
- [ ] Schedule: qa-Curtain Wall Panel Quantities
- [ ] Schedule: qa-Curtain Wall System Quantitie
- [ ] Schedule: qa-Door Quantities
- [ ] Schedule: qa-Floor Finishes
- [ ] Schedule: qa-Furniture Quantities
- [ ] Schedule: qa-Furniture System Quantities
- [ ] Schedule: qa-Railing Quantities
- [ ] Schedule: qa-Ramp Quantities
- [ ] Schedule: qa-Room Wall Finishes
- [ ] Schedule: qa-Stair Quantities
- [ ] Schedule: qa-Window Quantities

Check All   Check None

[x] Preview selection

Figure 2–2

4. Click **OK**.

How To: Export Schedule Information

1. Switch to the schedule view that you want to export.

2. In the *File* tab, expand ⬚ (Export), expand ⬚ (Reports), and click ⬚ (Schedule).

3. In the Export Schedule dialog box, select a location and name for the text file and click **Save**.

4. In the Export Schedule dialog box, set the options in the *Schedule appearance* and *Output options* areas that best suit your spreadsheet software, as shown in Figure 2–3.

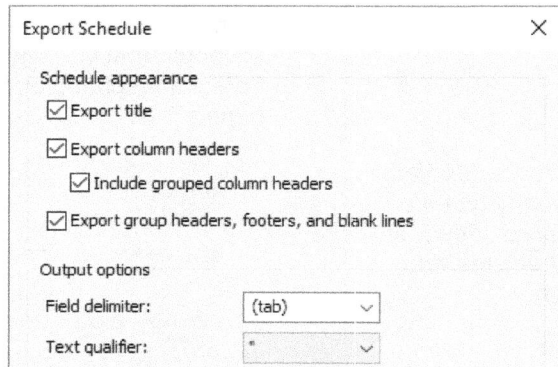

Figure 2–3

5. Click **OK**. A new text file is created that you can open in a spreadsheet, as shown in Figure 2–4.

Figure 2–4

2.2 Creating Building Component Schedules

A Building Component schedule is a table view of selected parameters of an element such as air terminals, structural foundations or doors, as shown in Figure 2–5. Some parameters are automatically filled in while others need to be added. Schedules can include both instance parameters and type parameters.

A	B	C	D	E	F	G	H
Mark	Height	Width	Fire Rating	Frame Type	Frame Material	Finish	Function
2	7' - 0"	10' - 0"	A	A	Steel	Brushed	Exterior
3	6' - 8"	3' - 0"	B	B	Wood	Paint	Interior
4	6' - 8"	3' - 0"	B	B	Wood	Paint	Interior
5	6' - 8"	3' - 0"	B	B	Wood	Paint	Interior
6	6' - 8"	3' - 0"	B	B	Wood	Paint	Interior

<Door Schedule>

Figure 2–5

How To: Create a Building Component Schedule

1. In the *View* tab>Create panel, expand (Schedules) and click (Schedule/Quantities) or in the Project Browser, right-click on the Schedule/Quantities node and select **New Schedule/Quantities**.
2. In the New Schedule dialog box, select the type of schedule you want to create (e.g., Doors) from the *Category* list, as shown in Figure 2–6.

In the Filter list drop-down list, you can specify the discipline(s) to show only the categories that you want to display.

Figure 2–6

3. Type a new *Name*, if the default does not suit.
4. Select **Schedule building components.**
5. Specify the *Phase* as required.
6. Click **OK**.
7. Fill out the information in the Schedule Properties dialog box. This includes the information in the *Fields*, *Filter*, *Sorting/Grouping*, *Formatting*, and *Appearance* tabs.
8. Once you have entered the schedule properties, click **OK**. A schedule report is created in its own view.

• Other elements that can be scheduled include model groups and Revit links.

Fields Tab

In the *Fields* tab, you can select from a list of available fields and organize them in the order in which you want them to display in the schedule, as shown in Figure 2–7.

Figure 2–7

You can also double-click on a field to move it from the Available fields to the Scheduled fields list.

How To: Fill out the Fields Tab

1. In the *Available fields* area, select one or more fields you want to add to the schedule and click ⬛ (Add parameter(s)). The field(s) are placed in the *Scheduled fields (in order)* area.
2. Continue adding fields, as required.

   - Click ⬛ (Remove parameter(s)) to move a field from the *Scheduled fields* area back to the *Available fields* area.

   - Use ⬛ (Move parameter up) and ⬛ (Move parameter down) to change the order of the scheduled fields.

Other Fields Tab Options

Select available fields from	Enables you to select additional category fields for the specified schedule. The available list of fields depends on the original category of the schedule. Typically, they include room information.
Include elements in links	Includes elements that are in files linked to the current project, so that their elements can be included in the schedule.
⬛ **(New parameter)**	Adds a new field according to your specification. New fields can be placed by instance or by type.
f_x **(Add Calculated parameter)**	Enables you to create a field that uses a formula based on other fields.
⬛ **(Combine parameters)**	Enables you to combine two or more parameters in one column. You can put any fields together even if they are used in another column.
⬛ **(Edit parameter)**	Enables you to edit custom fields. This is grayed out if you select a standard field.
⬛ **(Delete parameter)**	Deletes selected custom fields. This is grayed out if you select a standard field.

Filter Tab

In the *Filter* tab, you can set up filters so that only elements meeting specific criteria are included in the schedule. For example, you might only want to show information for one level, as shown in Figure 2–8. You can create filters for up to eight values. All values must be satisfied for the elements to display.

Schedule Properties			✕
Fields Filter Sorting/Grouping Formatting Appearance			
Filter by:	Level ⌄	equals ⌄	Level 1 ⌄
And:	(none) ⌄		

Figure 2–8

- The parameter you want to use as a filter must be included in the schedule. You can hide the parameter once you have completed the schedule, if required.

Filter by	Specifies the field to filter. Not all fields are available to be filtered.
Condition	Specifies the condition that must be met. This includes options such as **equal**, **not equal**, **greater than**, and **less than**.
Value	Specifies the value of the element to be filtered. You can select from a drop-down list of appropriate values. For example, if you set *Filter By* to **Level**, it displays the list of levels in the project.

Sorting/ Grouping Tab

In the *Sorting/Grouping* tab, you can set how you want the information to be sorted, as shown in Figure 2–9. For example, you can sort by **Mark** (number) and then **Type**.

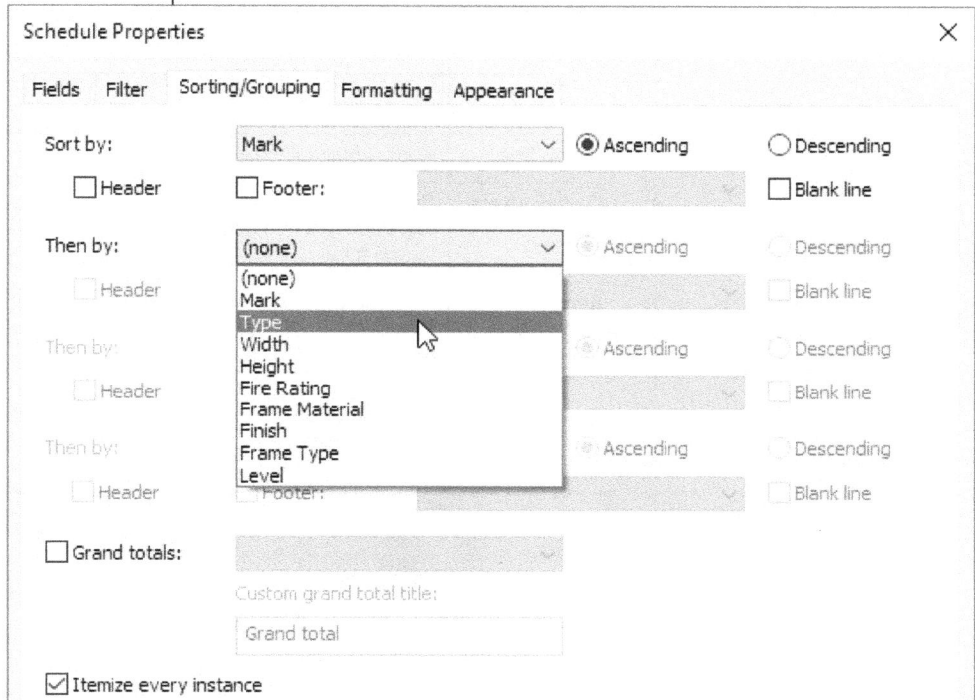

Figure 2–9

Sort by	Enables you to select the field(s) you want to sort by. You can select up to four levels of sorting.
Ascending/ Descending	Sorts fields in **Ascending** or **Descending** order.
Header/ Footer	Enables you to group similar information and separate it by a **Header** with a title and/or a **Footer** with quantity information.
Blank line	Adds a blank line between groups.
Grand totals	Selects which totals to display for the entire schedule. You can specify a name to display in the schedule for the Grand total.
Itemize every instance	If selected, displays each instance of the element in the schedule. If not selected, displays only one instance of each type, as shown in Figure 2–10.

Figure 2–10

Formatting Tab

In the *Formatting* tab, you can control how the headers of each field display, as shown in Figure 2–11.

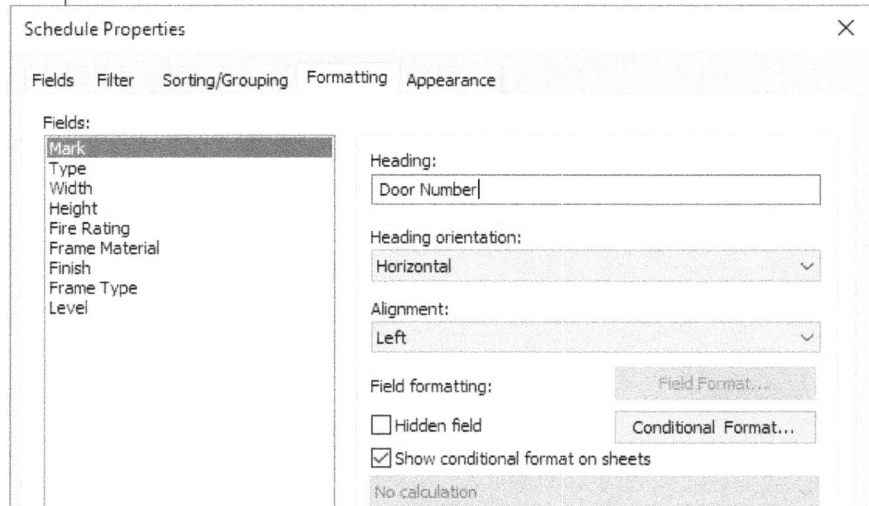

Figure 2–11

Fields	Enables you to select the field for which you want to modify the formatting.
Heading	Enables you to change the heading of the field if you want it to be different from the field name. For example, you might want to replace **Mark** (a generic name) with the more specific **Door Number** in a door schedule.
Heading orientation	Enables you to set the heading on sheets to **Horizontal** or **Vertical**. This does not impact the schedule view.
Alignment	Aligns the text in rows under the heading to be **Left**, **Right**, or **Center**.
Field Format...	Sets the units format for the length, area, volume, angle, or number field. By default, this is set to use the project settings.
Conditional Format...	Sets up the schedule to display visual feedback based on the conditions listed.
Hidden field	Enables you to hide a field. For example, you might want to use a field for sorting purposes, but not have it display in the schedule. You can also modify this option in the schedule view later.
Show conditional format on sheets	Select if you want the color code set up in the Conditional Format dialog box to display on sheets.
Calculation options	Select the type of calculation you want to use. All values in a field are: • **Standard** - Calculated separately. • **Calculate totals** - Added together. • **Calculate minimum** - Reviewed and only the smallest amount displays. • **Calculate maximum** - Reviewed and only the largest amount displays. • **Calculate minimum and maximum** - Reviewed and both the smallest and largest amounts display. • This is often used with rebar sets.

Hint: Hiding Columns

If you want to use the field to filter or sort, but do not want it to display in the schedule, select **Hidden field**. Alternatively, once the schedule is completed, select the column header, right-click on it, and select **Hide Columns**.

Appearance Tab

In the *Appearance* tab, you can set the text style and grid options for a schedule, as shown in Figure 2–12.

Figure 2–12

Grid lines	Displays lines between each instance listed and around the outside of the schedule. Select the style of lines from the drop-down list; this controls all lines for the schedule, unless modified.
Grid in headers/ footers/spacers	Extends the vertical grid lines between the columns.
Outline	Specify a different line type for the outline of the schedule.
Blank row before data	Select this option if you want a blank row to be displayed before the data begins in the schedule.
Show Title/Show Headers	Select these options to include the text in the schedule.
Title text/Header text/Body Text	Select the text style for the title, header, and body text.

Schedule Properties

Schedule views have properties including the *View Template, View Name, Phases* and methods of returning to the Schedule Properties dialog box as shown in Figure 2–13. In the *Other* area, select the button next to the tab that you want to open in the Schedule Properties dialog box. In the dialog box, you can switch from tab to tab and make any required changes to the overall schedule.

Figure 2–13

Figure 2–14

Just like other views, schedules can have View Templates applied. When you specify a view template directly in the view, as shown in Figure 2–14, none of the schedule properties can be modified.

- Schedule view templates are type-specific. If you apply one to a different type of element, only the *Appearance* information is applied.

- If you apply a schedule view template to a schedule of the same type, it overrides everything in the existing schedule including the fields.

- If you have a complicated schedule, you might want to create a view template for it to avoid losing that organization.

- To create schedule view templates, you need to create at least one from an existing view. Then, you can modify it and duplicate it in the View Templates dialog box.

Filtering Elements from Schedules

When you create schedules based on a category you might need to filter out some of the element types in that category. For example, in the Autodesk Revit software, doors (and windows) in curtain walls are automatically added to a door schedule, as shown at the top in Figure 2–15, but are typically estimated as part of the curtain wall rather than as a separate door. To remove them from the schedule, as shown at the bottom in Figure 2–15, assign a parameter that identifies them and then use that parameter to filter them out of the schedule.

	Door Size			Frame		Door Schedule- 1st
Door Type	Width	Height	Thickness	Frame Type	Frame Material	Head Detail
	8' - 3 1/2"	9' - 4 1/4"				
	3' - 0"	7' - 0"	0' - 2"	A	Aluminum	
	3' - 0"	7' - 0"	0' - 2"	B	Aluminum	
	3' - 0"	6' - 8"	0' - 2"	C	Aluminum	

Curtain Wall Doors Displayed

	Door Size			Frame		Door Schedule- 1st
Door Type	Width	Height	Thickness	Frame Type	Frame Material	Head Detail
	3' - 0"	7' - 0"	0' - 2"	A	Aluminum	
	3' - 0"	7' - 0"	0' - 2"	B	Aluminum	
	3' - 0"	6' - 8"	0' - 2"	C	Aluminum	
	3' - 0"	6' - 8"	0' - 2"	C	Aluminum	

Curtain Wall Doors Filtered Out

Figure 2–15

- This type of filtering can be used for any schedule in any discipline.

How To: Filter Elements in a Schedule

Create a type specifically for this if you are using one that is also used elsewhere.

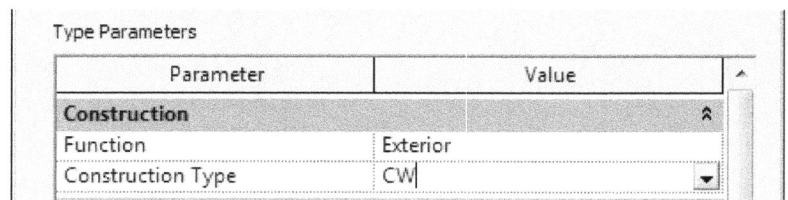

1. Select an element (such as a door used in curtain walls) and modify the Type Parameters. Add a value to one of the parameters that you are not otherwise using in your schedule. For example, set *Construction Type* to **CW**, as shown Figure 2–16.

Type Parameters	
Parameter	**Value**
Construction	
Function	Exterior
Construction Type	CW

Figure 2–16

2. Create a schedule and include the field, such as *Construction Type.*
3. Modify the *Filter* of the schedule so the parameter does not equal the specified value. In the example shown in Figure 2–17, *Construction Type* **does not equal CW**. Any types that match this filter are excluded from the schedule.

Schedule Properties				✕

Fields   Filter   Sorting/Grouping   Formatting   Appearance

Filter by:	Level ∨	equals ∨	Level 1 ∨
And:	Construction Type ∨	does not equal ∨	CW ∨

Figure 2–17

4. In the final schedule, the elements display with the specified value. Right-click on the column header and select **Hide Column(s)**, as shown in Figure 2–18. It is just used as a filter and not part of the final schedule.

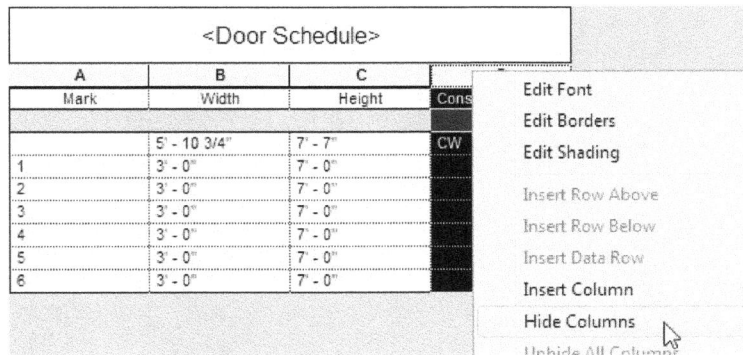

Figure 2–18

Practice 2a

Create Schedules for Architectural Projects

Practice Objectives

- Create building component schedules.
- Apply filters.
- Enter information.
- Place schedules on a sheet.

In this practice, you will create Door and Window schedules, filter out curtain wall doors, and add information to cells in the door schedule. You will also place the schedules on a sheet, as shown in Figure 2–19.

Figure 2–19

Task 1 - Create a Door schedule.

1. In the practice files *Architectural* folder, open **Clark-Hall-Schedules-Create.rvt**.

2. In the *View* tab>Create panel, expand (Schedules) and click (Schedule/Quantities).

3. In the New Schedule dialog box, set the *Filter List* to **Architecture** only to limit the number of categories and then set the *Category* to **Doors**.

4. Name the schedule **Door Schedule-Level 1**. Click **OK**.

5. In the Schedule Properties dialog box, in the *Fields* tab, add the following fields, as shown in Figure 2–20:

- *Level*
- *Mark*
- *Height*
- *Width*
- *Fire Rating*

- *Frame Type*
- *Frame Material*
- *Finish*
- *Comments*
- *Construction Type*

Figure 2–20

6. Click **OK** to create the schedule. Note that Level 1, Level 2, and Level 3 doors are included.

7. In Properties, in the *Other* category, next to **Filter**, click **Edit...**. The Schedule Properties dialog box opens with the *Filter* tab selected. Set *Filter by* to **Level - equals - Level 1**.

8. In the dialog box, in the *Sorting/Grouping* tab, sort the doors by **Mark**, and click **OK** to update the schedule.

9. Save the project.

Task 2 - Remove the Curtain Wall Doors from the schedule.

1. Continue working in the new **Door Schedule-Level 1** view, The doors in the curtain walls do not display with a **Mark**, as shown in Figure 2–21. Additionally, they are not included in door schedules and need to be removed.

A	B	C	D
Level	Mark	Height	Width
Level 1		6' - 11"	5' - 11"
Level 1		6' - 11"	5' - 11"
Level 1	1	7' - 0"	3' - 0"
Level 1	2	7' - 0"	6' - 0"
Level 1	3	7' - 0"	6' - 0"
Level 1	4	6' - 8"	3' - 0"
Level 1	5	6' - 8"	3' - 0"

Figure 2–21

2. In Properties, in the *Other* category, next to **Filter**, click **Edit...**.

3. In the Schedule Properties dialog box, in the *Filter* tab, add the additional Filter: **Construction Type - does not equal - CW**, as shown in Figure 2–22. Then, click **OK**.

*You need to type **CW** because the option does not yet exist in the project.*

Figure 2–22

4. In the Schedule, next to one of the curtain wall doors, in the *Construction Type* column, type **CW** and press <Enter>. An alert displays prompting you that this is a type property. Click **OK** and the curtain wall doors are no longer included in the schedule, as shown in Figure 2–23.

A	B	C	D
Level	Mark	Height	Width
Level 1	1	7' - 0"	3' - 0"
Level 1	2	7' - 0"	6' - 0"
Level 1	3	7' - 0"	6' - 0"
Level 1	4	6' - 8"	3' - 0"

Figure 2–23

5. Right-click on the *Level* column header and select **Hide Columns**. Repeat the procedure with the *Construction Type column* header. This removes the columns from the schedule (as shown in Figure 2–24), while still enabling you to use the fields as filters.

			<Door Schedule - Level 1>				
A	B	C	D	E	F	G	H
Mark	Height	Width	Fire Rating	Frame Type	Frame Material	Finish	Comments
1	7' - 0"	3' - 0"					
2	7' - 0"	6' - 0"					
3	7' - 0"	6' - 0"					
4	6' - 8"	3' - 0"					
5	6' - 8"	3' - 0"					
6	6' - 8"	3' - 0"					
7	6' - 8"	3' - 0"					
8	6' - 8"	3' - 0"					

Figure 2–24

6. Save the project

Task 3 - Fill in additional information in the Door Schedule

1. Continue working in the **Door Schedule-Level 1** view,

2. In the *Fire Rating* column, type a letter for one of the door types and press <Enter>. Because the door type controls the **Fire Rating** parameter, an alert box opens, as shown in Figure 2–25. Click **OK**.

Revit	✕
This change will be applied to all elements of type	
Single-Flush-Interior: 36" x 80".	
	OK Cancel

Figure 2–25

3. Repeat with the other doors until they all have a fire rating.

4. Open the **Floor Plans: Level 1** view and select one of the interior single doors.

5. Right-click and select **Select All Instances>In Entire Project**. In Properties, set the following parameters:

- *Frame Type:* **22**
- *Frame Material:* **Wood**
- *Finish:* **Stained**

6. Switch back to the schedule to verify that it has updated with the new information, as shown in Figure 2–26.

	A	B	C	D	E	F	G	H
	\<Door Schedule - Level 1\>							
	Mark	Height	Width	Fire Rating	Frame Type	Frame Material	Finish	Comments
1	7' - 0"	3' - 0"	B					
2	7' - 0"	6' - 0"	B					
3	7' - 0"	6' - 0"	B					
4	6' - 8"	3' - 0"	A	22	Wood	Stained		
5	6' - 8"	3' - 0"	A	22	Wood	Stained		
6	6' - 8"	3' - 0"	A	22	Wood	Stained		
7	6' - 8"	3' - 0"	A	22	Wood	Stained		
8	6' - 8"	3' - 0"	A	22	Wood	Stained		
9	6' - 8"	3' - 0"	A	22	Wood	Stained		

Figure 2–26

7. In the schedule view, set the rest of the doors to the following parameters:

- *Frame Type:* **21**
- *Frame Material:* **Aluminum**
- *Finish:* **Brushed**

8. Save the project.

Task 4 - Create a Window schedule.

1. Create a new window schedule with the following fields: **Count**, **Type**, **Manufacturer**, and **Comments**.

2. In the *Sorting/Grouping* tab, sort the windows by **Type**. Toggle on **Grand totals** and toggle off **Itemize every instance**.

3. Click **OK** to create the schedule. It lists the total count for a single type (only one type is used in the project), as shown in Figure 2–27.

<Window Schedule>			
A	B	C	D
Count	Type	Manufacturer	Comments
39	48" x 48"		
Grand total: 39			

Figure 2–27

4. In the **Floor Plans: Level 1** view, select the three windows in the Conference Room in the office wing. In Properties change the type to **Fixed with Trim: 36" x 72"**.

5. Switch back to the schedule view. A change should display in the schedule that reflects the new window type, as shown in Figure 2–28.

<Window Schedule>			
A	B	C	D
Count	Type	Manufacturer	Comments
3	36" x 72"		
36	48" x 48"		
Grand total: 39			

Figure 2–28

6. Open the **A601- Schedules** sheet. Drag and drop the schedules to this sheet. Modify the width of each field as required.

7. Save and close the project.

Practice 2b

Create Schedules for MEP Projects

Practice Objectives

- Create building component schedules.
- Place the schedules on a sheet.

In this practice, you will create schedules for two types of typical MEP schedules: a system schedule and a fixture schedule. In this case, they will be for duct systems and plumbing fixtures. If time permits, you will also create schedules for electrical circuits and lighting fixtures. You will then place the schedules on a sheet, as shown in Figure 2–29.

Duct Systems		
System Name	Comments	Flow
Exhaust Air		
Mechanical Exhaust Air 1		2000 CFM
Mechanical Exhaust Air 7		420 CFM
Mechanical Exhaust Air 9		200 CFM
Return Air		
Mechanical Return Air 1		0 CFM
Mechanical Return Air 2		0 CFM
Mechanical Return Air 3		205 CFM
Mechanical Return Air 4		500 CFM
Mechanical Return Air 5		500 CFM
Mechanical Return Air 6		500 CFM
Mechanical Return Air 10		0 CFM
Mechanical Return Air 14		205 CFM
Supply Air		
Mechanical Supply Air 1		4000 CFM
Mechanical Supply Air 2		2400 CFM
Mechanical Supply Air 3		2900 CFM
Mechanical Supply Air 4		3500 CFM
Mechanical Supply Air 8		0 CFM
Mechanical Supply Air 9		2900 CFM
Mechanical Supply Air 10		3900 CFM
Mechanical Supply Air 15		3090 CFM
Mechanical Supply Air 19		2400 CFM

Figure 2–29

Task 1 - Create a Duct System schedule.

1. In the practice files *MEP* folder, open
   Freel-Office-Create.rvt.

2. In the *View* tab>Create panel, expand 🔲 (Schedules) and

   click 🔲 (Schedule/Quantities).

3. In the New Schedule dialog box, set the *Filter list* to
   Mechanical and the *Category* to **Duct Systems** and name it
   Duct Systems, as shown in Figure 2–30.

Figure 2–30

4. Click **OK**.

5. In the Schedule Properties dialog box, in the *Fields* tab, add
   the following fields:
   - *System Classification*
   - *System Name*
   - *Comments*
   - *Flow*

6. In the *Sorting/Grouping* tab, sort by **System Classification**.
   Select **Ascending** and **Header**.

7. Click **OK** to create the schedule. Stretch the columns so that you can read all of the information, as shown in Figure 2–31.

<Duct System Schedule>			
A	B	C	D
System Classification	System Name	Comments	Flow
Exhaust Air			
Exhaust Air	Mechanical Exhaust Air 1		2000 CFM
Exhaust Air	Mechanical Exhaust Air 7		420 CFM
Exhaust Air	Mechanical Exhaust Air 9		200 CFM
Return Air			
Return Air	Mechanical Return Air 1		0 CFM
Return Air	Mechanical Return Air 2		0 CFM
Return Air	Mechanical Return Air 3		205 CFM
Return Air	Mechanical Return Air 4		500 CFM
Return Air	Mechanical Return Air 5		500 CFM
Return Air	Mechanical Return Air 6		500 CFM
Return Air	Mechanical Return Air 10		0 CFM
Return Air	Mechanical Return Air 14		205 CFM
Supply Air			
Supply Air	Mechanical Supply Air 1		4000 CFM
Supply Air	Mechanical Supply Air 2		2400 CFM
Supply Air	Mechanical Supply Air 3		2900 CFM
Supply Air	Mechanical Supply Air 4		3500 CFM
Supply Air	Mechanical Supply Air 8		0 CFM
Supply Air	Mechanical Supply Air 9		2900 CFM
Supply Air	Mechanical Supply Air 10		3900 CFM
Supply Air	Mechanical Supply Air 15		3090 CFM
Supply Air	Mechanical Supply Air 19		2400 CFM

Figure 2–31

8. Right-click on the *System Classification* column and select **Hide Columns**. (The System Classification is specified by the Header).

9. Open the **M601- Mechanical Schedules** sheet. Drag and drop the duct system schedule to this sheet. Modify the width of each field as required.

10. Save the project.

Task 2 - Create a Plumbing Fixture schedule.

1. In the *View* tab>Create panel, expand ⊞ (Schedules) and click ⊞ (Schedule/Quantities).

2. In the New Schedule dialog box, set the *Filter list* to **Piping**, set *Category* to **Plumbing Fixtures**, and name it **Plumbing Fixtures**. Click **OK**.

3. In the Schedule Properties dialog box, in the *Fields* tab, add the following fields:
   - *Family*
   - *Type*
   - *Manufacturer*
   - *Count*

4. In the *Sorting/Grouping* tab, sort by **Family**, and clear **Itemize every instance**.

5. Click **OK** to create the schedule. Stretch the columns such that all the words are visible, as shown in Figure 2–32.

Plumbing Fixture Schedule			
Family	Type	Manufacturer	Count
Drinking Fountain-Hi-Lo-3D	Drinking Fountain-Hi-Lo-3D		2
Shower Base-Round Corner	36" x 36"		1
Sink Kitchen-Double	42" x 21"		3
Sink Vanity-Round	19" x 19"		8
Toilet-Commercial-Wall-3D	15" Seat Height		6
Urinal-Wall-3D	Urinal-Wall-3D		2

Figure 2–32

6. Open the **P601- Plumbing Schedules** sheet. Drag and drop the schedule to this sheet. Modify the width of each field as required.

7. Save the project.

Task 3 - Create electrical-related schedules.

1. If time permits, create an electrical circuit schedule (as shown in Figure 2–33) and a lighting fixture schedule similar to the plumbing fixture schedule. Place these schedules on the **E601 - Electrical and Lighting Schedules** sheet.

Figure 2–33

2. Save and close the project.

Practice 2c	# Create Schedules for Structural Projects

Practice Objectives

- Create a structural schedule that includes all types of structural elements.
- Reorganize the schedule content by sorting and grouping.
- Place the schedule on a sheet.

In this practice, you will create a schedule displaying structural elements by category, You will then place it on a sheet and modify it to fit, as shown in Figure 2–34.

Structural Schedule		
Type Mark	Family and Type	Count
Structural Columns		
P-1	Concrete-Rectangular-Column: 24 x 24	22
	W-Wide Flange-Column: W10X33	1
	W-Wide Flange-Column: W10X49	22
Structural Foundations		
F-2	Footing-Rectangular: 14'x14'x2'-0"	1
F-1	Footing-Rectangular: 36" x 36" x 12"	21
	Foundation Slab: 6" Foundation Slab	1
	Step Footing: Step Footing	4
	Wall Foundation: Bearing Footing – 24" X 12"	6
	Wall Foundation: Bearing Footing – 36" X 12"	4
	Wall Foundation: Retaining Footing – 24" X 12" X 12"	1
Structural Framing		
	HSS-Hollow Structural Section: HSS6X6X .500	9
	K-Series Bar Joist-Rod Web: 16K5	65
	W-Wide Flange: W8X10	6
	W-Wide Flange: W12X26	63
	W-Wide Flange: W14X48	62
	W-Wide Flange: W16X45	1

Figure 2–34

Task 1 - Create a structural schedule.

1. In the practice files *Structural* folder, open **Axiom-Building-Create.rvt**.

2. In the *View* tab>Create panel, expand ▦ (Schedules) and click ▦ (Schedule/Quantities).

3. In the New Schedule dialog box, set *Filter list* to **Structure**, set *Category* to **<Multi-Category>**, and name it **Structural Schedule**. Click **OK**.

4. In the Schedule Properties dialog box, in the *Fields* tab, add the following fields:
   - *Type Mark*
   - *Family and Type*
   - *Count*
   - *Category*

5. Use ⬆E (Move Up) and ⬇E (Move Down) to change the order of the scheduled fields, if required, so they display as shown in Figure 2–35.

Scheduled fields (in order):

Type Mark
Family and Type
Count
Category

Figure 2–35

6. Click **OK**. The new schedule displays with all of the structural elements in the project in a long list, as shown in part in Figure 2–36.

<Structural Schedule>

A	B	C	D
Type Mark	Family and Type	Count	Category
	W-Wide Flange-Colum	1	Structural Columns
	W-Wide Flange-Colum	1	Structural Columns
	W-Wide Flange-Colum	1	Structural Columns
	W-Wide Flange-Colum	1	Structural Columns
	W-Wide Flange-Colum	1	Structural Columns
	W-Wide Flange-Colum	1	Structural Columns
	W-Wide Flange-Colum	1	Structural Columns
	W-Wide Flange-Colum	1	Structural Columns
	W-Wide Flange-Colum	1	Structural Columns
	W-Wide Flange-Colum	1	Structural Columns
	W-Wide Flange-Colum	1	Structural Columns
	W-Wide Flange-Colum	1	Structural Columns
	W-Wide Flange-Colum	1	Structural Columns
	W-Wide Flange-Colum	1	Structural Columns
	W-Wide Flange-Colum	1	Structural Columns
	W-Wide Flange-Colum	1	Structural Columns
	W-Wide Flange-Colum	1	Structural Columns
	W-Wide Flange-Colum	1	Structural Columns
	Wall Foundation: Beari	1	Structural Foundati
	Wall Foundation: Beari	1	Structural Foundati
	Wall Foundation: Beari	1	Structural Foundati

Figure 2–36

7. Save the project.

Task 2 - Add filtering, sorting, and grouping to the schedule.

1. In Properties, in the *Other* category, next to **Sorting/ Grouping**, click **Edit....** The Schedule Properties dialog box opens with the *Sorting/Grouping* tab selected.

2. In the *Sorting/Grouping* tab, sort by **Category**, and select **Header**. Then sort by **Family and Type** with no header. Clear **Itemize every instance**, as shown in Figure 2–37.

Figure 2–37

3. In the Schedule Properties dialog box, in the *Filter* tab, add the *Filter* **Category does not equal Structural Rebar**, as shown in Figure 2–38.

Figure 2–38

4. Click **OK** to update the schedule.

5. Resize the columns to see the information. Right-click on the *Category* column and select **Hide Columns**. The schedule displays as shown in Figure 2–39.

A	B	C
	<Structural Schedule>	
Type Mark	Family and Type	Count
Structural Columns		
P-1	Concrete-Rectangular-Column: 24 x 24	22
	W-Wide Flange-Column: W10X33	1
	W-Wide Flange-Column: W10X49	22
Structural Foundations		
F-2	Footing-Rectangular: 14'x14'x2'-0"	1
F-1	Footing-Rectangular: 36" x 36" x 12"	21
	Foundation Slab: 6" Foundation Slab	1
	Step Footing: Step Footing	4
	Wall Foundation: Bearing Footing - 24" x 12"	6
	Wall Foundation: Bearing Footing - 36" x 12"	4
	Wall Foundation: Retaining Footing - 24" x 12" x 12"	1
Structural Framing		
	HSS-Hollow Structural Section: HSS6X6X.500	9
	K-Series Bar Joist-Rod Web: 16K6	65
	W-Wide Flange: W8X10	6
	W-Wide Flange: W12X26	63
	W-Wide Flange: W14X48	62
	W-Wide Flange: W16X45	1

Figure 2–39

6. Open the **S601- Schedules** sheet. Drag and drop the schedule to this sheet. Modify the width of each field as required.

7. Save the project.

Task 3 - (Optional) Additional Schedules.

---

1. If time permits, create schedules that incorporate the information shown in Figure 2–40 and Figure 2–41.

A	B	C	D	E
		<Structural Foundation Schedule>		
Type Mark	Count	Type	Width	Length
F-1	21	36" x 36" x 12"	3' - 0"	3' - 0"
F-2	1	14'x14'x2'-0"	14' - 0"	14' - 0"
Grand total: 22				

Figure 2–40

Hint: Filter by **Type Mark begins with "F"** so that only the individual footing foundations display and sort by Type Mark.

<Structural Foundation Column Schedule>				
A	B	C	D	E
Type Mark	Count	Type	Top Level	Base Level
P-1	22	24 x 24	Level 1	T.O. Footing

Figure 2–41

- **Hint:** Create a Structural Column Schedule, change the name and Filter by **Type Mark begins with "P"** so that only the foundation columns display.

2. Save and close the project.

2.3 Modifying Schedule Appearance

While you assign global appearance settings in the Schedule Properties dialog box, you can also modify the appearance of each cell in a schedule and add other rows and columns. Title and Heading cells can include both text and parameter values and have different text formatting, as shown in Figure 2–42. You can also add images to title cells and to individual rows in a schedule.

<Window Schedule>						
<Toronto Towers>				Project No. <1234-5678>		
A	B	C	D	E	F	G
Type	Count	Height	Width	Manufacturer	Model	Comments
36 x 36	72	3' - 0"	3' - 0"	Anderson	FX3636	
36" x 48"	84	4' - 0"	3' - 0"	Anderson	FX3648	
Grand total: 156						

Figure 2–42

- These modifications work with all types of schedules.

- Most of these modifications can be accessed in the *Modify Schedule/Quantities* tab (as shown in Figure 2–43), which is available when you are in a schedule view.

Figure 2–43

- Many of these options are also found in the shortcut menu.

Setting up Parameter Values

Parameter values and options can be set up by cells. The type of cell determines the options you can use.

- **Title Cells:** Select either **Schedule** or **Project Information**, as shown in Figure 2–44. Then, choose from the parameters available, as shown in Figure 2–45.

Figure 2–44

Figure 2–45

- **Header or Data Cells:** Select options based on the type of element the schedule is made for, as shown in Figure 2–46. Then, choose from the parameters available, as shown in Figure 2–47. Changing this information also changes the field specified for the selected column.

Figure 2–46

Figure 2–47

- Parameter values in titles display in the schedule view with **<>** at either end of the value. This does not display on the sheet view.

- Additional options for modifying the parameters include ▣ (Format Unit), f_x (Calculated), and ▣ (Combine Parameters). These are covered in more depth in the *Advanced Schedule Options* topic.

Modifying Columns and Rows

Be careful about making changes in the ribbon when you are in a data cell because any changes you make apply to the entire row or column.

The options for Columns and Rows (as shown in Figure 2–48), vary according to the type of cell selected. You can **Insert**, **Delete**, and **Resize** title columns and rows. If you select a header column you can insert, delete, resize, and hide the column.

Figure 2–48

How To: Hide a Column

1. Select any cell in the column that you want to hide.
2. In the *Modify Schedule/Quantities* tab>Columns panel, click
   (Hide). Alternatively, if you have selected the header cell, right-click and select **Hide Columns**.
3. The column is hidden.

- If you have hidden any columns and no longer want them hidden, you can click (Unhide All) or right-click and select **Unhide All Columns** at any time.

- Hiding columns is typically used when you want to sort or filter and do not want them to display in the final schedule.

How To: Resize a Row or Column

1. Select a cell. If the cell is a title cell you can resize both the row and column
2. In the *Modify Schedule/Quantities* tab>Columns panel, click
   (Resize) or in the Rows panel, click (Resize).
3. In the Resize Column (or Row) dialog box (as shown in Figure 2–49), type a size and click **OK**.

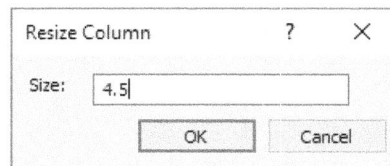

Figure 2–49

4. The column or row is resized in the schedule view and sheet.

Modifying Titles and Headers

The more complex and extensive a schedule, the more it can help to modify the title and header cells, using the commands shown in Figure 2–50. The title cells can be merged or unmerged. You can also insert images and delete the contents of title cells. Header cells can be grouped and ungrouped.

Merge Unmerge   Insert Image   Clear Cell   Group Ungroup

Titles & Headers

Figure 2–50

How To: Add and Merge Title Cells

1. Click inside a title cell.
2. In the *Modify Schedule/Quantities* tab>Rows panel, expand ⌐⌐ (Insert) and click ⌐⌐ (Above Selected) or ⌐⌐ (Below Selected). When inserting below the primary cell it typically comes in matching the number of header cells as shown in Figure 2–51.

<Door Schedule>						
A	B	C	D	E	F	G
Mark	Family and Type	Height	Width	Fire Rating	Frame Material	Frame Type

Before

<Door Schedule>						
A	B	C	D	E	F	G
Mark	Family and Type	Height	Width	Fire Rating	Frame Material	Frame Type

After

Figure 2–51

3. Pick and drag across the cells that you want to merge.

4. Click ▢ (Merge Unmerge).

5. The cells are now merged together, as shown in Figure 2–52.

<Door Schedule>						
A	B	C	D	E	F	G
Mark	Family and Type	Height	Width	Fire Rating	Frame Material	Frame Type

Figure 2–52

6. Add a parameter, text, or image in the newly merged cell.

• If you no longer want the cells to be merged, select the cell and click ▢ (Merge Unmerge).

• To insert an image file (such as a .BMP, .JPG, or .PNG) in a title cell, select the title cell and click ▧ (Insert Image) and select the image from the list.

• Use ▧ (Clear Cell) to delete the text, image, or parameter used in that cell (Titles only).

How To: Group Sub-headers

1. In the Schedule view, drag the cursor over the headers you want to group.
2. In the *Modify Schedule/Quantities* tab>Titles & Headers panel, click ▢ (Group).
3. A new header area is created above the selected columns. Enter a new name, as shown in Figure 2–53.

A	B	C	D	E
		Window Dimensions		
Window Type	Count	Height	Width	Sill Height
36 x 36	72	3' - 0"	3' - 0"	3' - 0"
36" x 48"	84	4' - 0"	3' - 0"	3' - 0"
Grand total: 156				

Figure 2–53

• If you no longer need the grouped header cell, select the grouped cell and click ▧ (Ungroup).

Setting the Appearance

The overall appearance of a schedule, including the text types used in the various cells, is set up in the Schedule Properties. You can also modify individual title and header cells using the options in the Appearance panel, as shown in Figure 2–54.

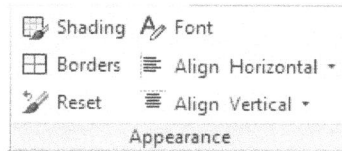

Figure 2–54

(Shading)	Opens the Color dialog box in which you can select a background color for the selected cells.
(Borders)	Opens the Edit Borders dialog box in which you can specify the line style and locations of borders around the selected cells.
(Reset)	Returns the formatting of selected cells to the original specified in the schedule properties.
(Font)	Opens the Edit Font dialog box in which you can specify the **Font**, **Font size**, **Font Style** (**Bold**, **Italic**, or **Underline**) and **Font Color** for the selected cells.
(Align Horizontal)	Aligns the text in the selected cells to the **Left**, **Center**, or **Right** justification.
(Align Vertical)	Aligns the text in the selected cells to the **Top**, **Middle**, or **Bottom** justification.

- The changes you make the tools in the Appearance panel, are not included in a schedule view template.

Adding Image Fields and Images

In addition to adding images in the title cells of a schedule you can assign images to elements and have them display in the schedule on a sheet, as shown in Figure 2–55.

Lighting Fixture Types			
Type Mark	Image	Family	Count
A		Troffer Light - 2x2 Parabolic	17
B		Troffer Light - 2x4 Parabolic	48
C		Pendant Light - Hemisphere	10

Figure 2–55

- Images can be set by instance or by type.

How To: Add Images to Schedules

1. In the schedule view, open the Schedule Properties dialog box in the *Fields* tab.
2. Add the *Image* (or *Type Image*) field to the scheduled fields, as shown in Figure 2–56.

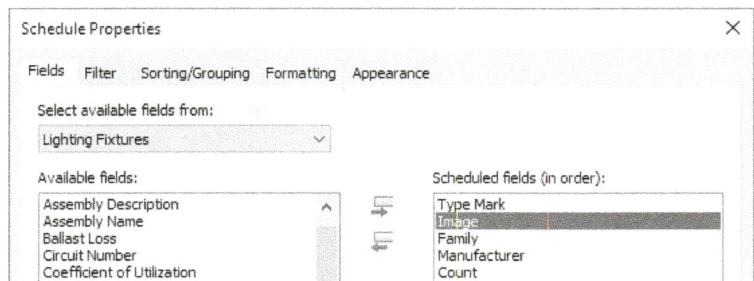

Figure 2–56

3. Complete the rest of your schedule design and click **OK**.

4. In the schedule view, the *Image* (or *Type Image*) column displays as part of the schedules, as shown in Figure 2–57.

<Lighting Fixture Types>			
A	B	C	D
Type Mark	Image	Family	Count
A	<None>	Troffer Light - 2x2 Parabolic	17
B	<None>	Troffer Light - 2x4 Parabolic	48
C	<None>	Pendant Light - Hemisphere	10

Figure 2–57

5. Assign the appropriate image file to the instances or types.

- Type images for component families (such as light fixtures) are assigned directly in the family file and are read-only in the project. Type images for system families (such as walls) are assigned in the Type Properties.
- Instance images are assigned in Properties for each instance of the element.

6. To display the images, place the schedule on a sheet.

How To: Assign Image Files

1. In Properties, next to the *Image* parameter (as shown in Figure 2–58) or in Type Properties, next to the *Type Image* parameter, click ⬚ (Browse).

Identity Data	≫
Image	⬚
Comments	
Mark	

Figure 2–58

- Type Images for component families are assigned in the family file, not the project.

2. In the Manage Images dialog box, select the image that you want to use, as shown in Figure 2–59.

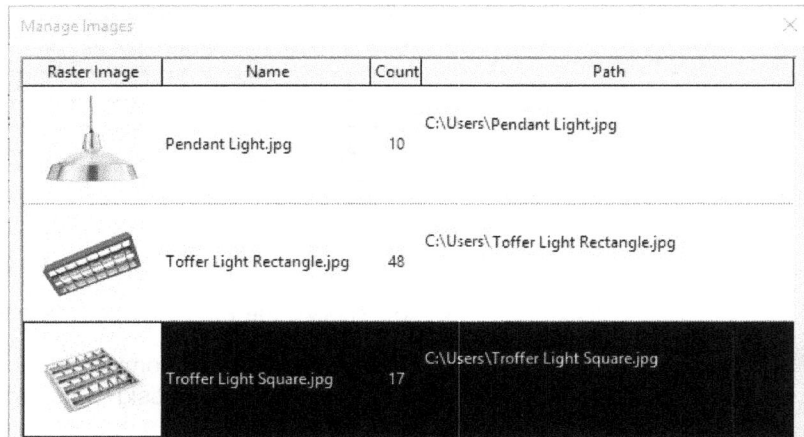

Raster Image	Name	Count	Path
	Pendant Light.jpg	10	C:\Users\Pendant Light.jpg
	Toffer Light Rectangle.jpg	48	C:\Users\Toffer Light Rectangle.jpg
	Troffer Light Square.jpg	17	C:\Users\Troffer Light Square.jpg

Figure 2–59

3. Click **OK**

• To add images to the Manage Image dialog box, click **Add...** and navigate to the location in which the images are stored.

• You can also delete and reload images as you would reload linked files.

• Image file formats include BMP, JPG, JPEG, PNG, and TIF.

Practice 2d

Modify Schedules for Architectural Projects

Practice Objectives

- Modify the look of the schedule using parameters, and by merging and grouping cells.
- Add images to a schedule.

In this practice, you will modify the appearance of a schedule by adding parameters and text to the title and by merging group headers, as shown in Figure 2–60 (on a sheet). You will also add an image field (column) and assign images to a schedule.

Door Schedule - Level 1							
Clark Hall Performing Arts Building				Project Number: 1234.56			
	Door Size			Frame Information			
Mark	Height	Width	Fire Rating	Frame Type	Frame Material	Finish	Comments

Figure 2–60

Task 1 - Modify the appearance of the schedule.

1. In the practice files *Architectural* folder, open **Clark-Hall-Schedules-Modify.rvt**.

2. Open the **Door Schedule-Level 1** view.

3. Select the top title row of the schedule.

4. In the *Modify Schedule/Quantities* tab>Row panel, expand ⌐┲ (Insert) and click ⌐╪ (Below Selected).

5. Drag the cursor over approximately half of the new heading columns on the left and, in the Titles & Headers panel, click ▦ (Merge Unmerge). The cells are merged as shown in Figure 2–61.

<Door Schedule - Level 1>							
A	B	C	D	E	F	G	H
Mark	Height	Width	Fire Rating	Frame Type	Frame Material	Finish	Comments

Figure 2–61

The name of the project displays in brackets indicating that it is a parameter rather than text.

6. Select the newly merged cell. In the Parameters panel, expand **Category** and select **Project Information**. Expand **Parameter** and select **Project Name**.

7. Merge the other cells and add text (**Project Number**) and another parameter (**Project Number**), as shown in Figure 2–62.

<Door Schedule - Level 1>							
<Clark Hall>				Project Number:		<1234.56>	
A	B	C	D	E	F	G	H
Mark	Height	Width	Fire Rating	Frame Type	Frame Material	Finish	Comments

Figure 2–62

8. In the *Manage* tab>Settings Panel, click (Project Information).

9. In the Project Properties dialog box, update the *Project Name* to **Clark Hall Performing Arts Building**. Click **OK**. The *Project Name* updates, as shown in Figure 2–63.

<Door Schedule - Level 1>							
<Clark Hall Performing Arts Building>				Project Number:		<1234.56>	
A	B	C	D	E	F	G	H
Mark	Height	Width	Fire Rating	Frame Type	Frame Material	Finish	Comments

Figure 2–63

10. Drag the cursor over the *Height* and *Width* header cells.

11. In the *Modify Schedule/Quantities* tab> Titles & Headers panel, click (Group).

12. Select the new cell and type **Door Size**.

13. Repeat for *Frame Type*, *Frame Material*, and *Finish* and enter **Frame Information**, as shown in Figure 2–64.

A	B	C	D	E	F	G	H
	Door Size			Frame Information			
Mark	Height	Width	Fire Rating	Frame Type	Frame Material	Finish	Comments

Figure 2–64

14. Save the project.

Task 2 - Modify the Appearance of the Title

1. Select the title cell and, in the *Schedules/Quantities* tab> Appearance panel, click $^{A\!\!/}$ (Font).

2. In the Edit Font dialog box, change the *Font size* to **1/4"** and set the *Font style* to **Bold**.

3. Modify the other title and header cells as required. In the example shown in Figure 2–65, in addition to changing the font appearance, the Project Number text and parameter have been aligned horizontally to be closer to each other and the border between the two of them has been removed.

\<Door Schedule - Level 1>							
\<Clark Hall Performing Arts Building>				**Project Number: \<1234.56>**			
A	B	C	D	E	F	G	H
	Door Size				Frame Information		
Mark	Height	Width	Fire Rating	Frame Type	Frame Material	Finish	Comments

Figure 2–65

4. Open the **A601-Schedules** view to display the images and adjust it as required.

5. Save the project.

Task 3 - Add Images to a schedule.

1. Open the **Window Schedule** view.

2. In the Schedule Properties dialog box, in the *Fields* tab add the **Type Mark** and **Image** parameters to the *Scheduled Fields* above the **Type** parameter, as shown in Figure 2–66. Move the **Count** parameter to the bottom of the list and click **OK**.

In this situation the Type Image is only accessible by opening and adjusting the family file. Therefore, you can use the instance Image parameter.

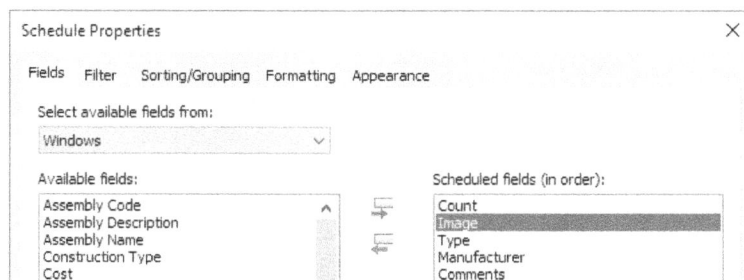

Figure 2–66

3. In the **Window Schedule** view, select the *Image* cell for the first type and click ⌊...⌋.

4. In the Manage Images dialog box, click **Add...**.

5. In the Import Image dialog box, navigate to the practice files *Architectural>Images* folder, select the two window images, and click **Open**.

6. In the Manage Images dialog box, select the image that matches the window row in which you are working and click **OK**.

7. Repeat the process with the other window image. The schedule should look similar to Figure 2–67.

<Window Schedule>					
A	B	C	D	E	F
Type Mark	Image	Type	Manufacturer	Comments	Count
18	Window Rectangle.png	36" x 72"			3
19	Window Square.png	48" x 48"			36
Grand total: 39					

Figure 2–67

8. Open the **Sheets (all): A601 - Schedules** view. The images should display as shown in Figure 2–68.

Figure 2–68

9. If time permits, modify the schedule appearance to match the Door schedule.

10. Save and close the project.

Practice 2e

Modify Schedules for MEP Projects

Practice Objectives

- Modify the look of the schedule using parameters and by merging and grouping cells.
- Add images to a schedule.

In this practice, you will modify the appearance of a schedule by adding parameters and text to the title and by merging headers. You will also add an image field (column) and assign images to a schedule, as shown on a sheet in Figure 2–69.

Lighting Fixture Types			
Type Mark	Image	Family	Count
A		Troffer Light - 2x2 Parabolic	17
B		Troffer Light - 2x4 Parabolic	48
C		Pendant Light - Hemisphere	10

Figure 2–69

Task 1 - Modify the appearance of the schedule.

1. In the practice files *MEP* folder, open **Freel-Office-Modify.rvt**.

2. Open the **Plumbing Fixtures** schedule view.

3. Select the top title row of the schedule.

4. In the *Modify Schedule/Quantities* tab>Row panel, expand ⌐ᵗᵗ (Insert) and click ⌐ᶠ (Below Selected).

5. Drag the cursor over half of the new heading columns on the left. In the Titles & Headers panel, click 🔲 (Merge Unmerge). The cells are merged, as shown in Figure 2–70.

<Plumbing Fixtures>			
A	B	C	D
Family	Type	Manufacturer	Count

Figure 2–70

6. Select the newly merged cell. In the Parameters panel, expand **Category** and select **Project Information**. Then expand **Parameter** and select **Project Name**. The name of the project displays in brackets, indicating that it is a parameter

7. In the other cells and add text (**Project Number:**) and another parameter (**Project Number**), as shown in Figure 2–71.

<Plumbing Fixtures>			
<Project Name>		Project Number:	<Project Number>
A	B	C	D
Family	Type	Manufacturer	Count

Figure 2–71

8. In the *Manage* tab>Settings Panel, click 🗔 (Project Information).

9. In the Project Information dialog box, update *Project Name* to **Freel Office Building** and *Project Number* to **1234.56**. Click **OK**. The parameters update as shown in Figure 2–72.

<Plumbing Fixtures>			
<Freel Office Building>		Project Number:	<1234.56>
A	B	C	D
Family	Type	Manufacturer	Count

Figure 2–72

10. Save the project.

Task 2 - Modify the Appearance of the Title

1. Select the title cell and, in the Schedules/Quantities tab> Appearance panel, click $A_\mathscr{D}$ (Font).

2. In the Edit Font dialog box change the *Font size* to **1/4"** and set the *Font style* to **Bold**.

3. Modify the other title and header cells, as required. In the example shown in Figure 2–73, besides changing the font appearance, the **Project Number** text and parameter have been aligned horizontally so they are closer to each other and the border between the two of them has been removed.

<Plumbing Fixtures>			
<Freel Office Building>		Project Number: <1234.56>	
A	B	C	D
Family	Type	Manufacturer	Count

Figure 2–73

4. Save the project.

Task 3 - Add Images to a schedule.

1. Open the **Lighting Fixture Types** view.

2. In the Schedule Properties dialog box, in the *Fields* tab, add the **Image** parameter to the Scheduled Fields after the **Type Mark** parameter, as shown in Figure 2–74. Then, click **OK**.

In this situation the Type Image is only accessible by opening and adjusting the family file. Therefore, you can use the instance Image parameter.

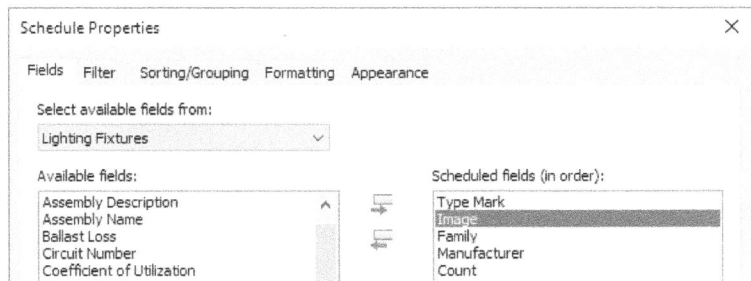

Figure 2–74

3. In the **Lighting Fixture Types** view, select the *Image* cell for the first type and click ⬚.

4. In the Manage Images dialog box, click **Add...**

5. In the Import Image dialog box, navigate to the practice files *MEP>Images* folder, select the three light images, and click **Open**.

6. In the Manage Images dialog box, select the image that matches the row in which you are working and click **OK**.

7. Repeat the process with the other lighting fixture images. The schedule should look similar to the one shown in Figure 2–75.

		<Lighting Fixture Types>		
A	**B**	**C**	**D**
Type Mark	Image	Family	Count
A	Troffer Light Square.jpg	Troffer Light - 2x2 Parabolic	17
B	Toffer Light rectangle.jpg	Troffer Light - 2x4 Parabolic	48
C	Pendant Light.jpg	Pendant Light - Hemisphere	10

Figure 2–75

8. Open the **Sheets (all): E601 - Electrical and Lighting Schedules** view. The images should display as shown in Figure 2–76.

Figure 2–76

9. If time permits, modify the schedule appearance to match the other schedule.

10. Save and close the project.

Practice 2f

Modify Schedules for Structural Projects

Practice Objective

• Modify the look of the schedule using parameters, and merging and grouping cells.

In this practice, you will modify the appearance of a schedule by adding parameters and text to the title and by merging cells, as shown in Figure 2–77.

<Structural Schedule>		
<Axiom Building>		Project Number: <1234.56>
A	B	C
Type Mark	Family and Type	Count

Figure 2–77

Task 1 - Modify the appearance of the schedule.

1. In the practice files *Structural* folder, open **Axiom-Building-Modify.rvt**.

2. Open the **Structural Schedule** view.

3. Select the top title row of the schedule.

4. In the *Modify Schedule/Quantities* tab>Row panel, expand ⬓ (Insert) and click ⬓ (Below Selected).

5. If there are more than three new cells, drag the cursor over half of the new heading columns on the left and, in the Titles & Headers panel, click ▢ (Merge Unmerge). The cells are merged as shown in Figure 2–78.

<Structural Schedule>		
A	B	C
Type Mark	Family and Type	Count

Figure 2–78

6. Select the newly merged cell. In the Parameters panel, expand **Category** and select **Project Information**. Then expand **Parameter** and select **Project Name**. The name of the project displays in brackets indicating that it is a parameter rather than text, as shown in Figure 2–79.

7. Add text (**Project Number:**) and another parameter (**Project Number**) as shown in Figure 2–79.

<Structural Schedule>		
<Project Name>	Project Number:	<Project Number>
A	B	C
Type Mark	Family and Type	Count

Figure 2–79

8. In the *Manage* tab>Settings Panel, click 🗒 (Project Information).

9. In the Project Information dialog box, update *Project Name* to **Axiom Building** and *Project Number* to **1234.56**. Click **OK**. The project name and number update as shown in Figure 2–80.

<Structural Schedule>		
<Axiom Building>	Project Number:	<1234.56>
A	B	C
Type Mark	Family and Type	Count

Figure 2–80

10. Save the project.

Task 2 - Modify the appearance of the title.

1. Select the title cell. In the *Schedules/Quantities* tab>Appearance panel, click ᴬ (Font).

2. In the Edit Font dialog box, change the *Font size* to **1/4"** and set the *Font style* to **Bold**.

3. Modify the other title and header cells as required. In the example shown in Figure 2–81, in addition to changing the font appearance, the **Project Number** text and parameter have been aligned horizontally to be closer to each other and the border between them has been removed.

A	B	C
<Axiom Building>	Project Number: <1234.56>	
Type Mark	Family and Type	Count

<Structural Schedule>

Figure 2–81

4. Modify the other two schedules to match the appearance.

5. Save and close the project.

2.4 Additional Schedule Types

Two important types of schedules are used in construction documents to help clarify information that is not included in a standard building component schedule.

- *Key schedules* lists provide information that is not automatically included in an element, such as the finish or frame type of a door. By grouping this information into keys, you can enter it more quickly.

- *Material Takeoff* schedules gather information about the materials in a project (such as the area and volume) so you can calculate the amount and price of the material, as shown in Figure 2–82.

Brick - Material Takeoff

A	B	C	D	E	F
Material: Name	Material: Area	Material: Manufacturer	Material: Cost	Total Cost Per SF	Total Units of Brick
Masonry - Brick			3.00		
Masonry - Brick: 11					

<Brick - Material Takeoff>

Figure 2–82

Creating Key Schedules

Schedule key styles are useful when you have a large number of elements that need to have the same finish information, as shown in Figure 2–83. Fields in key styles are typically controlled by instance rather than by type. Grouping styles together makes it easier to apply this information to large numbers of instances.

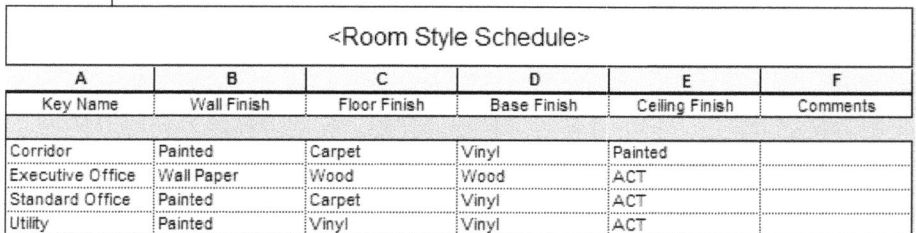

<Room Style Schedule>

A	B	C	D	E	F
Key Name	Wall Finish	Floor Finish	Base Finish	Ceiling Finish	Comments
Corridor	Painted	Carpet	Vinyl	Painted	
Executive Office	Wall Paper	Wood	Wood	ACT	
Standard Office	Painted	Carpet	Vinyl	ACT	
Utility	Painted	Vinyl	Vinyl	ACT	

Figure 2–83

How To: Create a Schedule Key Style

1. Start a new schedule.
2. In the New Schedule dialog box, select a category.
3. Select the **Schedule keys** option and type a *Name* for the key, as shown in Figure 2–84. This adds an **Instance** parameter in the Properties dialog box for the selected category and adds a field to the schedule properties.

Use the Filter list to limit the number of categories with which you can work.

Figure 2–84

4. Click **OK**.
5. In the Schedule Properties dialog box, the *Fields* tab displays the new **Key Name** that has already been added to the *Scheduled fields*, as shown in Figure 2–85.
6. Add other fields from the list of *Available fields*, as shown in Figure 2–85.

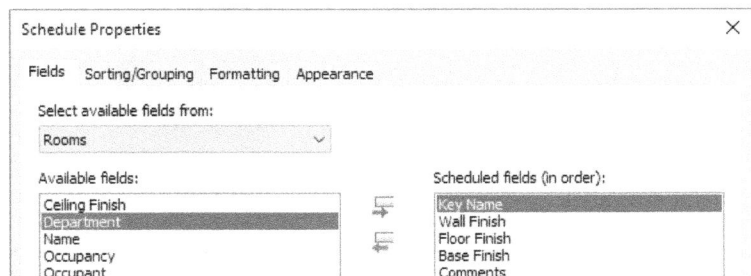

Figure 2–85

7. Fill out the rest of the tabs as required and click **OK**. The new schedule opens with only the fields displayed, as shown in Figure 2–86.

<Room Style Schedule>					
A	B	C	D	E	F
Key Name	Wall Finish	Floor Finish	Base Finish	Ceiling Finish	Comments

Figure 2–86

8. In the *Modify | Schedule/Quantities* tab>Rows panel, click (Insert Data Row) or right-click on the schedule and select **Insert Data Row**. A new row with the default label **1** displays, as shown in Figure 2–87. Type a new name for the row.

<Room Style Schedule>					
A	B	C	D	E	F
Key Name	Wall Finish	Floor Finish	Base Finish	Ceiling Finish	Comments
1					

Figure 2–87

9. Continue adding rows and names as shown in Figure 2–88.

<Room Style Schedule>					
A	B	C	D	E	F
Key Name	Wall Finish	Floor Finish	Base Finish	Ceiling Finish	Comments
Corridor					
Executive Office					
Standard Office					
Utility					

Figure 2–88

10. Fill in the values for the rows as shown in Figure 2–89.

<Room Style Schedule>					
A	B	C	D	E	F
Key Name	Wall Finish	Floor Finish	Base Finish	Ceiling Finish	Comments
Corridor	Painted	Carpet	Vinyl	Painted	
Executive Office	Wall Paper	Wood	Wood	ACT	
Standard Office	Painted	Carpet	Vinyl	ACT	
Utility	Painted	Vinyl	Vinyl	ACT	

Figure 2–89

11. To assign the key style, add a column to the schedule (such as the *Room Style* column in a Room Schedule shown in Figure 2–90).

Figure 2–90

You can also modify the properties of various instances in the project as shown in Figure 2–91.

Figure 2–91

Creating Material Takeoff Schedules

Creating material takeoff schedules follows the same procedure as when creating building component schedules, except that it uses a different command. In the *View* tab>Create panel, expand ▦ (Schedules) and click ▦ (Material Takeoff) or in the Project Browser, right-click on the **Schedule/Quantities** node and select **New Material Takeoff**.

- The options for fields include all of the material parameters, as shown in Figure 2–92.

Figure 2–92

- When creating a Material Takeoff Schedule, it can help to modify the unit settings for the various fields. In the *Formatting* tab, select a field and click **Field Format...**. In the Format dialog box, clear the **Use project settings** option and modify the options, as shown in Figure 2–93. This is only available for numerical fields.

Figure 2–93

- A numerical value can be assigned a currency. Zeros can be suppressed. Spaces can be suppressed and large numbers can include commas as separators.

Hint: Material Properties

Most material properties used in material takeoff schedules can be set by material. In the *Manage* tab>Settings panel, click

(Materials). In the Material Browser, select the material that you want to modify. In the *Identity* tab, you can add information, such as **Manufacturer** and **Cost** as shown in Figure 2–94.

Figure 2–94

2.5 Advanced Schedule Options

An important use of schedules, in addition to showing quantities and other information for construction documents, is to analyze and modify the information stored in the elements in the project. You can add conditional formatting that add a background color to schedule cells that meet the condition. For schedules based on rooms or spaces, you can also create nested schedules to show information such as the number of casework elements in a room or if the supply airflow to a space meets the expected setting.

Conditional Formatting

Conditional formatting can be applied to any field where you need to display some specific information that can easily be seen at a glance. For example, in Figure 2–95, the *Area* field is highlighted according to a conditional test for any size over 10000 SF.

Conditional formatting is typically used for testing and does not carry over when placed on a sheet.

Area Schedule Over 10000 SF			
A	B	C	D
Number	Name	Area Type	Area
1	Office	Building Common Area	2657 SF
2	Auditorium	Building Common Area	9694 SF
3	Classrooms	Building Common Area	13533 SF
4	Area	Building Common Area	3682 SF

Figure 2–95

How To: Add Conditional Formatting in a schedule

1. Open the schedule you want to work in and select the *Formatting* tab.
2. Select the field to which you want to apply the conditional formatting.
3. Click **Conditional Format...**.

4. In the Conditional Formatting dialog box, select the *Field*, *Test*, and specify a *Value*, as shown in Figure 2–96.

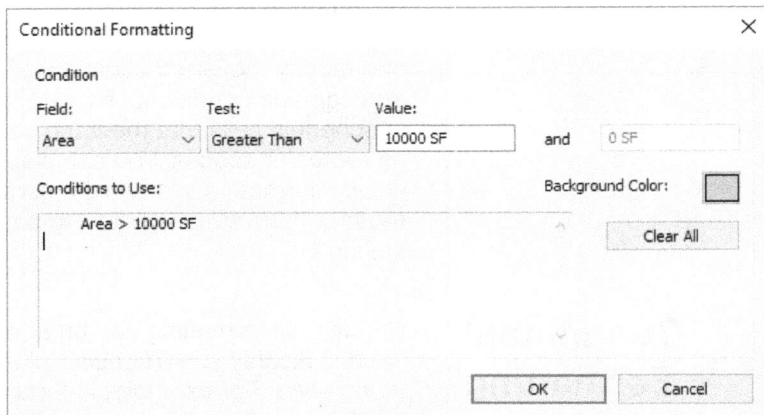

Figure 2–96

5. Click the **Background Color** button and select a color to display in the schedule when the conditions are met.
6. You can select additional fields, test, and values to further refine the conditional statements.
7. When you are finished, click **OK** to close the dialog box and continue working on the Schedule Properties as required.

Embedded Schedules

When working with schedules that refer to spaces or rooms, you can use embedded schedules. For example, in Figure 2–97, a space schedule that is displaying the **Space Number** and **Name**, also has an embedded schedule displaying information about the air terminals in each space.

- This is most frequently used with MEP schedules but also works with any elements that you may want to group by room or space.

A	B
SPACE NO.	NAME
DIFFUSER ID	DIFFUSER TYPE
1501	CLASSROOM
29	Supply Diffuser - Perforated - Round Neck - Ceiling Mounted:
30	Supply Diffuser - Perforated - Round Neck - Ceiling Mounted:
31	Supply Diffuser - Perforated - Round Neck - Ceiling Mounted:
32	Supply Diffuser - Perforated - Round Neck - Ceiling Mounted:
1502	CLASSROOM
45	Supply Diffuser - Perforated - Round Neck - Ceiling Mounted:
46	Supply Diffuser - Perforated - Round Neck - Ceiling Mounted:
47	Supply Diffuser - Perforated - Round Neck - Ceiling Mounted:
48	Supply Diffuser - Perforated - Round Neck - Ceiling Mounted:

Figure 2–97

How To: Add an Embedded Schedule

1. Create the base Space or Room schedule.
2. In the Schedule Properties dialog box, select the *Embedded Schedule* tab.
3. Select **Embedded Schedule** and then select a category type from the Category list, as shown in Figure 2–98.

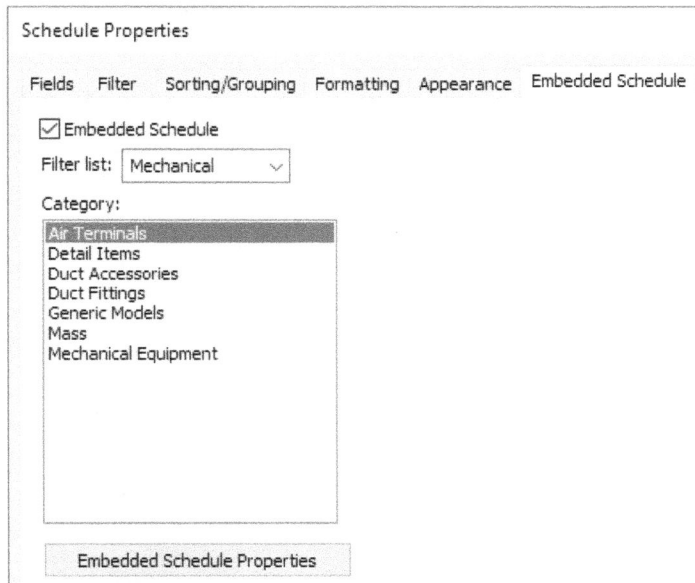

Schedule Properties

Fields   Filter   Sorting/Grouping   Formatting   Appearance   Embedded Schedule

☑ Embedded Schedule

Filter list: Mechanical   ⌄

Category:

Air Terminals
Detail Items
Duct Accessories
Duct Fittings
Generic Models
Mass
Mechanical Equipment

Embedded Schedule Properties

Figure 2–98

4. Click **Embedded Schedule Properties**.
5. In the Schedule Properties dialog box, in the *Field* tab, add the required fields and then add any filters, sorting, and formatting as required.
6. Click **OK** until the schedule displays. The fields display in order directly under the base schedule columns, as shown in Figure 2–99.

Base Schedule Fields
Embedded Schedule Fields   <SPACE AIRFLOW CHECK>

A	B	C	D
SPACE NO.	NAME	Condition Type	ACTUAL SUPPLY AIRFLOW
DIFFUSER ID	DIFFUSER TYPE	DIFFUSER AIRFLOW	

Figure 2–99

2.6 Working with Project Parameters

When you are working in a variety of schedules, you might want to include additional parameters, create fields that include formulas, as shown for a rounded area in Figure 2–100, or combine parameters.

<Room Schedule>			
A	B	C	D
Number	Name	Area	Floor Area
101	Office	280.49 SF	280 SF
102	Conference	337.38 SF	340 SF
103	Office	199.63 SF	200 SF
104	Office	199.63 SF	200 SF
105	Office	193.17 SF	190 SF
106	Office	243.22 SF	240 SF
107	Work Room	154.77 SF	150 SF
108	Reception	327.48 SF	330 SF
109	Library	404.78 SF	400 SF

Figure 2–100

- Project Parameters can be added to building elements and items, such as model groups, RVT Links, and Schedules.

- Project parameters can be created in a schedule or through a separate command.

- Project parameters can be used in schedules, but not in tags.

- To add parameters used in schedules and tags, you must create shared parameters. Shared parameters can also be used in other projects and exported to a database. For more information, see *6.4 Working with Shared Parameters*.

How To: Create a Project Parameter in a Schedule

1. In the Schedule Properties dialog box, in the *Fields* tab, click

   (New parameter) (or other Project Parameter access).
2. In the Parameter Properties dialog box, select **Project parameter**, as shown in Figure 2–101.

Parameter Properties ✕

Parameter Type

⦿ Project parameter

(Can appear in schedules but not in tags)

○ Shared parameter

(Can be shared by multiple projects and families, exported to ODBC, and appear in schedules and tags)

Select... Export...

Figure 2–101

3. In the *Parameter Data* area shown in Figure 2–102, Set the value as an **Instance** or a **Type**. and then specify a new *Name* for the parameter and select the *Discipline*, *Type of Parameter*, and *Group* from the drop-down lists. You can also add a custom tooltip.

Parameter Data

Name:

Material   ○ Type

Discipline: ⦿ Instance

Common

Type of Parameter: ⦿ Values are aligned per group type

Material   ○ Values can vary by group instance

Group parameter under:

Materials and Finishes

Tooltip Description:

<No tooltip description. Edit this parameter to write a custom tooltip. Custom tooltips hav...

Edit Tooltip...

Figure 2–102

- **Type:** Modify all instances of a specific type. For example, if you create a **Material** parameter for a furniture component, changing the material for one component changes all of them.

- **Instance:** Set for each instance of the associated element. For example, if you create a **Material** parameter when you are creating a furniture schedule, you can assign a different material to each instance of the component.

- **Values are aligned per group type:** (Instance Parameters only.) If an element that includes this parameter is part of multiple groups, the value remains the same for all of the groups. Changing the value in one group changes the value in all of the groups.

- **Values can vary by group instance:** (Instance Parameters only.) If an element that includes this parameter is part of multiple groups, the value can vary according to the group. Changing the value in one group changes the value for all other instances of that group, but does not change the value for instances of other groups that also include the element.

- The *Discipline* can be set to **Common**, **Structural**, **HVAC**, **Electrical**, **Piping**, or **Energy**.

- The *Type of Parameter* specifies how the parameter value is stored, The options available for Discipline impact the types of parameters in the list, as shown in Figure 2–103.

Figure 2–103

Common Parameter Types

Text	A text parameter can host any type of information that consists of both numbers and letters. Examples could be the fabric color or part number of the element.
Integer	Any value that is always represented by a whole number. Examples could be the number of chairs that fit around a conference table or the number of shelves in a bookcase.
Number	Any numeric value: whole, decimal, or fraction. You can use formulas with **Number** parameters.
Length	When you label dimensions, you create **Length** parameters. You can use formulas with **Length** parameters.
Area	Establishes the area of an element. It is numeric and can have formulas applied to it.

Volume	Establishes the volume of an element. It is numeric and can have formulas applied to it.
Angle	Establishes the angle of an element. It is numeric and can have formulas applied to it.
Slope	Displays a slope, as set up in the Field Format.
Currency	Displays the amount in dollars or other currencies, as set up in the Field Format.
Mass Density	Displays the mass per unit volume of material.
URL	Specifies a link to a web site.
Material	Provides a place to assign a material from the list of materials that are set up in the project.
Image	Creates a parameter in which you can add a raster image connected to the family.
Yes/No	Used with instance parameters where you need a **Yes** or **No** answer to a question listed in the name. The default is **Yes**.
<Family Type>	Opens a dialog box where you can select from the list of family types, such as doors, furniture, or tags.

The Group parameter under drop-down list lists groups that categorize parameters in the Properties and Family Types dialog boxes, as shown in Figure 2–104.

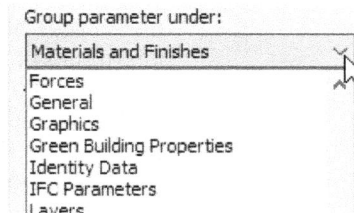

Group parameter under:

Materials and Finishes

Forces
General
Graphics
Green Building Properties
Identity Data
IFC Parameters
Layers

Figure 2–104

To add information to display when you hover the cursor over the new parameter in Properties (as shown in Figure 2–105), click **Edit Tooltip...**.

Figure 2–105

How To: Create Parameters Outside of Schedules

1. In the *Manage* tab>Settings panel, click ⬛ (Project Parameters).
2. In the Project Parameters dialog box, click **Add**.
3. In the Parameter Properties dialog box, select **Project parameter** and set up the Parameter Data (i.e., the same information that is in the Parameter Properties dialog box for the schedule).
4. In the *Categories* area, select one or more related categories, as shown in Figure 2–106. Use the Filter list drop-down box to specify the discipline to limit the number of items that display.

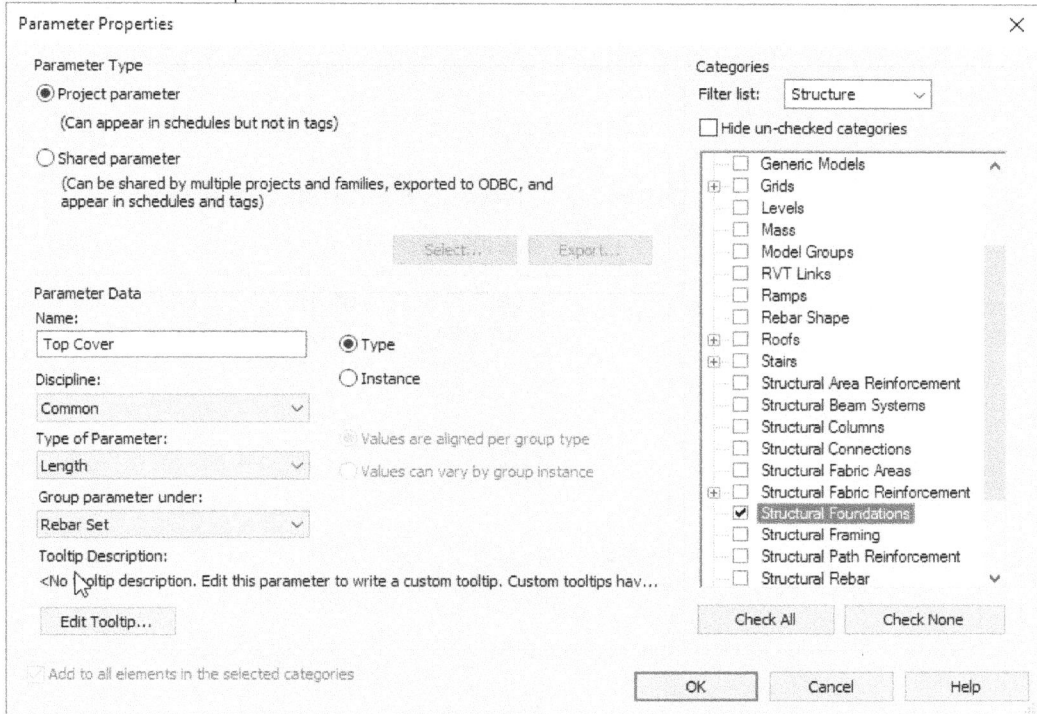

Figure 2–106

5. Click **OK**. The parameter is now available in the properties of the selected categories.

Creating Fields from Formulas

In a variety of schedules, you need to gather numerical information and apply formulas to it for a new parameter. For example, you can include cost and quantity information in a Material Takeoff, as shown in the schedule in Figure 2–107.

\<Brick - Material Takeoff\>					
A	B	C	D	E	F
Material: Name	Material: Area	Material: Manufacturer	Material: Cost	Total Cost	Total Units of Brick
Masonry - Brick	22160 SF	XYZ Masonry	3.00	$66480	155123
Masonry - Brick: 14	22160 SF			$66480	155123

Figure 2–107

- You can create calculated value fields to add formulas to a schedule, or create a percentage field using values in the schedule.

- Gather the information you need to use to create formulas, including the exact name of any fields, before you start the process of creating the calculated value.

- Formula outcomes can be rounded off.

How To: Create a Calculated Value Field

*A formula has been added for this figure: (Material: Area / 1 SF) * Material: Cost.*

1. In the Schedule Properties dialog box, in the *Fields* tab, click f_x (Add calculated parameter). The Calculated Value dialog box opens, as shown in Figure 2–108.

Figure 2–108

2. Type a *Name* for the new field.
3. Specify **Formula** as the type of field.
4. Select the *Discipline* and *Type*, as required.
5. Type the formula you want to use in the *Formula* field.

   - If a warning displays about inconsistent units, clarify the units by adding ***1** or **/1** to a formula. After doing this, the software should then apply the correct units.

   - To ensure you get the exact field name, click [...] (Browse) to select from a list of fields, as shown in Figure 2–109.

Formulas can only reference fields that are already included in the schedule.

Figure 2–109

6. Click **OK**.

Percentage Fields

Percentage fields can be used with area schedules, as shown in Figure 2–110.

<Area Schedule (Rentable)>		
A	B	C
Name	Area	Percent of Total Area
Office	2657 SF	9%
Auditorium	9694 SF	33%
Classrooms	13533 SF	46%
Area	3682 SF	12%

Figure 2–110

How To: Create a Percentage Field

1. In the Schedule Properties dialog box, in the *Fields* tab, click

   f_x (Add calculate parameter). The Calculated Value dialog box opens, as shown in Figure 2–111.

Figure 2–111

2. Type a *Name* for the new field.
3. Specify **Percentage** as the type of field.
4. Select the field you want to take a percentage *Of.*

5. Select the field you want to take a percentage *By*.
   - The default option is **<Grand total>**, which calculates the percentage based on the total of the entire schedule.
   - If you have created groups in the *Sorting/Grouping* tab, they are also available. For example, if Fields are sorted by **Level**.
6. Click **OK**.

Combining Parameters

Parameters can be combined into a new parameter. For example, you might want to include the height, width and depth of casework in one **Size** parameter, as shown in Figure 2–112.

<Casework Schedule>

A	B	C	D	E
Family	Size	Cost	Count	Comments
Base Cabinet-2 Bin	2' - 10 1/2" x 1' - 6" x 2' - 0"		1	
Base Cabinet-4 Drawers	2' - 10 1/2" x 2' - 0"		2	
Base Cabinet-Double Door Sink Unit	2' - 10 1/2" x 3' - 0" x 2' - 0"		1	
Base Cabinet-Single Door & Drawer	2' - 10 1/2" x 2' - 0" x 2' - 0"		1	

Figure 2–112

- Combined parameters are schedule-specific and need to be created for each schedule.

How To: Create Combined Parameters

1. In the Schedule Properties dialog box, in the *Fields* tab, click ⬚ (Combine Parameters).
2. In the Combine Parameters dialog box, in the *Combined Parameter Name* text box, type a new name for the parameter.
3. Select two or more *Schedule Parameters* from the list on the left and click ⬚ (Add parameter(s)) to add it to the *Combined Parameter* list on the right.

4. Modify the Separator between each parameter, as shown in Figure 2–113.

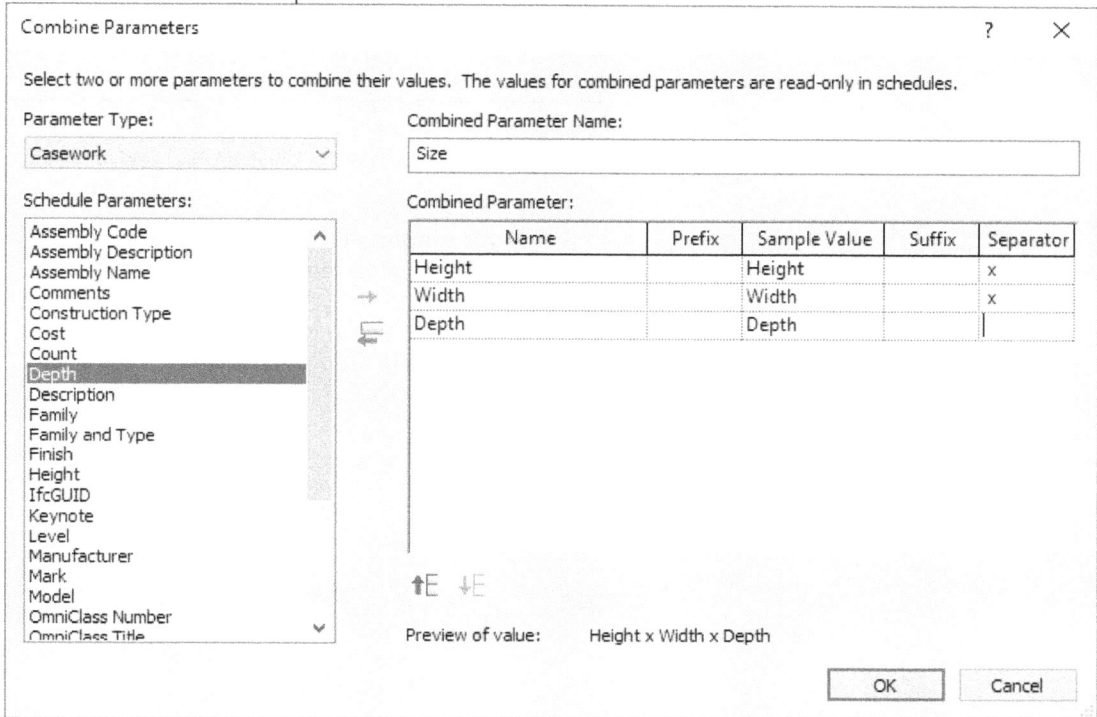

Figure 2–113

- Check the preview of the value that displays at the bottom of the dialog box.
- You can also add a Prefix or Suffix and modify the *Sample Value* name.

5. Click **OK**.

Practice 2g	# Create Complex Schedules for Architectural Projects

Practice Objectives

- Create material takeoff schedules.
- (Optional) Create a percentage-based calculated value field for use in a schedule.

In this practice, you will create a material takeoff schedule that includes several calculated value formulas. You will then add it to a sheet, as shown in Figure 2–114, and test it and other material takeoff schedules by modifying the wall type and material properties. As an optional task, you will create a percentage-based field for an area schedule.

Brick - Material Takeoff					
Material: Name	Material: Area	Material: Manufacturer	Material: Cost	Total Cost per SF	Total Units of Brick
Masonry - Brick	2749 SF	XYZ Masonry	3.00	$8250	19242
Masonry - Brick: 11	2749 SF			$8250	19242

Figure 2–114

Task 1 - Create a material takeoff schedule.

1. In the practice files *Architecture* folder, open **Mall-Addition.rvt**.

2. In the *View* tab>Create panel, expand (Schedules) and click (Material Takeoff).

3. In the New Material Takeoff dialog box, in the *Filter* list, select **Architecture**, and in the *Category* list, select **Walls**. Name the schedule **Brick – Material Takeoff** and select **New Construction** from the *Phase* list.

4. Click **OK**.

5. In the *Fields* tab of the Material Takeoff Properties dialog box, add the fields **Material: Name**, **Material: Area**, **Material: Manufacturer**, and **Material: Cost**, as shown in Figure 2–115.

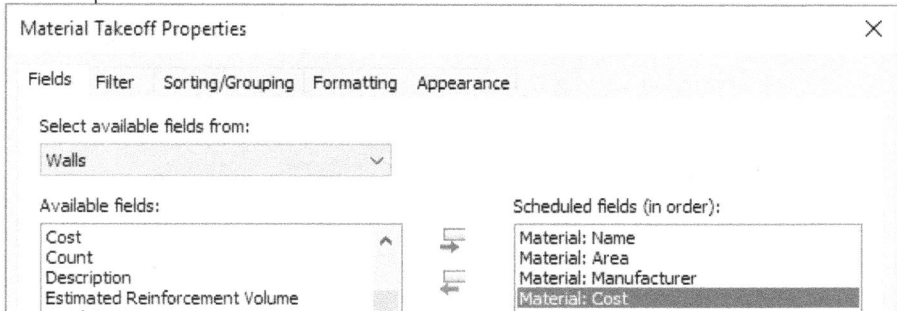

Figure 2–115

*Area and Cost are two different types of parameters. Therefore, in this practice, you need to divide the **Material: Area** parameter by 1 to get the correct result.*

6. Click f_x (Add calculated value) and set the following parameters, as shown in Figure 2–116. (Ensure that you account for the spaces in the field names when typing the formulas. There should be a space after the colon for the software to recognize **Material: Area** as a field.)

- *Name:* **Total Cost per SF**
- *Discipline:* **Common**
- *Type:* **Number**
- *Formula:* **(Material: Area / 1) * Material: Cost**

You can click [...] (Browse) to select from a list of fields as you are creating the formula to prevent you from misspelling parameter names.

Figure 2–116

7. Create another calculated value field using the following parameters. (There are seven standard bricks in a square foot. The type and size of bricks being used might vary and that can affect the number of bricks.)

- *Name:* **Total Units of Brick**
- *Discipline:* **Common**
- *Type:* **Number**
- *Formula:* **(Material: Area / 1) *7**

8. In the *Filter* tab, filter the schedule using **Material: Name equals Masonry - Brick**, as shown in Figure 2–117.

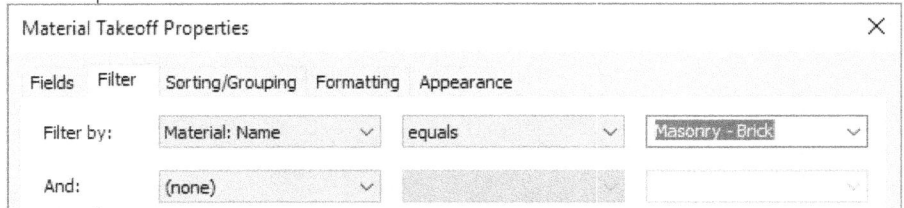

Material Takeoff Properties ✕

Fields Filter Sorting/Grouping Formatting Appearance

Filter by: | Material: Name ∨ | equals ∨ | Masonry - Brick ∨

And: | (none) ∨ | ∨ |

Figure 2–117

9. In the *Sorting/Grouping* tab, sort by **Material: Name** and select **Footer**, as shown in Figure 2–118.

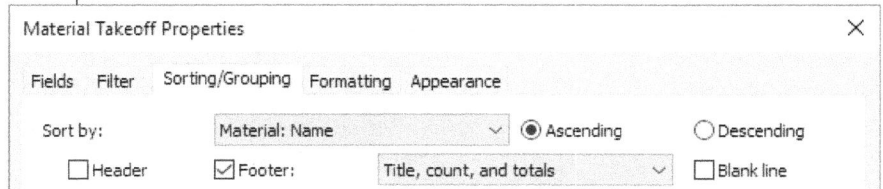

Material Takeoff Properties ✕

Fields Filter Sorting/Grouping Formatting Appearance

Sort by: | Material: Name ∨ | ◉ Ascending | ◯ Descending

☐ Header ☑ Footer: | Title, count, and totals ∨ | ☐ Blank line

Figure 2–118

10. In the *Formatting* tab, in the *Fields* list, select **Material: Area**, **Total Cost per SF**, and **Total Units of Brick**. In the *Field formatting* area, select **Calculate totals** from the drop-down list, as shown in Figure 2–119.

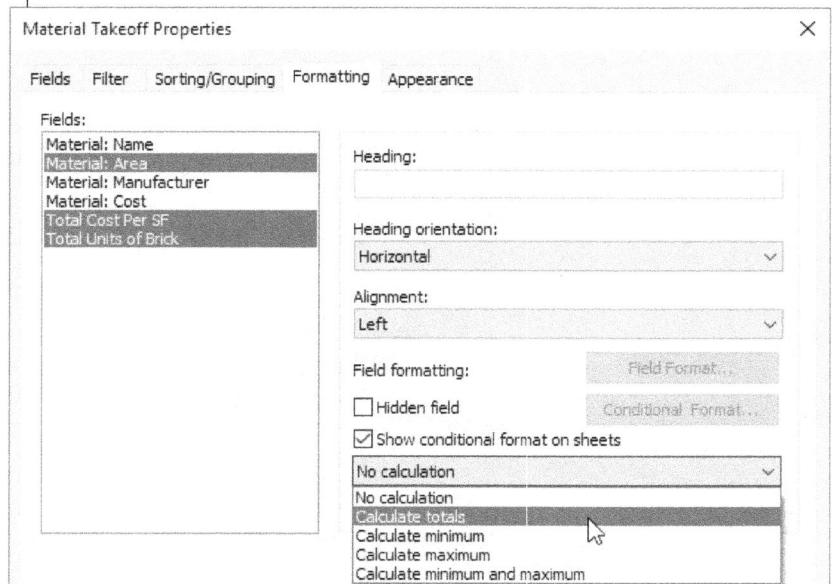

Material Takeoff Properties ✕

Fields Filter Sorting/Grouping Formatting Appearance

Fields:

Material: Name
Material: Area
Material: Manufacturer
Material: Cost
Total Cost Per SF
Total Units of Brick

Heading:

Heading orientation:
Horizontal ∨

Alignment:
Left ∨

Field formatting: | Field Format...
☐ Hidden field | Conditional Format...
☑ Show conditional format on sheets

No calculation ∨
No calculation
Calculate totals
Calculate minimum
Calculate maximum
Calculate minimum and maximum

Figure 2–119

11. In the *Appearance* tab, modify the grid lines or text fonts as required and click **OK**.

Task 2 - Modify the material takeoff schedule.

1. The units for the *Total Cost per SF* and *Total Units of Brick* fields have six decimal places, as shown in Figure 2–120. This is more than required.

\<Brick - Material Takeoff\>					
A	B	C	D	E	F
Material: Name	Material: Area	Material: Manufact	Material: Cost	Total Cost per SF	Total Units of Brick
Masonry - Brick	192 SF		4.00	769.675167	1346.931543
Masonry - Brick	756 SF		4.00	3023.630924	5291.354117

Figure 2–120

2. In Properties, next to *Formatting*, click **Edit...**. The Material Takeoff Properties dialog box opens with the *Formatting* tab selected.

3. Select the *Total Cost per SF* field and click **Field Format...**.

4. In the Format dialog box, clear the **Use default settings** option. Set the *Units* to **Currency**, *Rounding* to **To the nearest 10** and *Unit symbol* to **$**, as shown in Figure 2–121. Click **OK**.

Figure 2–121

5. Select the *Total Units of Brick* field and click **Field Format...**.

6. In the Format dialog box, clear the **Use default settings** option. Set the *Units* to **Fixed** and *Rounding* to **0 decimal places**. Click **OK**.

7. Click **OK** to close the dialog box.

8. In the schedule view, add a manufacturer's name and change the *Material: Cost* of the Brick to **3.00**. The Total Cost updates, but the Total Units of Brick remains the same.

Task 3 - Test the material takeoff schedule.

1. Open the **A102 – Plan and Schedules** sheet.

2. Zoom in on the existing schedules to one side.

3. Add the new **Brick – Material Takeoff** schedule to the sheet. Use grips to modify the size of the schedule as required.

4. This schedule is different from other schedules because it includes all the instances of Brick. In the Project Browser, select the **Brick - Material Takeoff** schedule (you do not have to open it to change the properties).

5. In Properties, in the *Other* area, next to Sorting/Grouping, click **Edit...**.

6. In the Material Takeoff Properties dialog box, in the *Sorting/Grouping* tab, clear the **Itemize every instance** option and click **OK**. The schedule updates on the sheet.

7. Open the **3D Views: Front View**. Arrange the views so that you can see the 3D view and the top two schedules on the sheet, as shown in Figure 2–122.

Stone - Material Takeoff			
Material: Description	Material: Area	Material: Cost	Total Cost
Facestone	1164 SF	0.00	0
Facestone: 7	1164 SF		0

EIFS - Material Takeoff			
Material: Description	Material: Area	Material: Cost	Total Cost

Figure 2–122

8. In the 3D view, select one of the walls on the tower to the left and change its wall type to **Basic Wall: FCE – Exterior – EIFS on Mtl.Stud**, as shown in Figure 2–123.

EIFS on Mtl.Stud

Figure 2–123

9. The schedules change to display a smaller amount of the stone used and add to the EIFS schedule that was blank before, as shown in Figure 2–124.

Stone - Material Takeoff			
Material: Description	Material: Area	Material: Cost	Total Cost
Facestone	865 SF	0.00	0
Facestone: 6	865 SF		0

EIFS - Material Takeoff			
Material: Description	Material: Area	Material: Cost	Total Cost
EIFS	298 SF	12.00	3574
EIFS: 1	298 SF		3574

Figure 2–124

10. Double-click on the Stone - Material Takeoff schedule in the sheet to open the related schedule view.

11. Change the *Material: Cost* to **10**.

12. The *Material: Cost* and *Total Cost* fields update on the sheet as well.

13. Modify these fields so that they display as currency.

Task 4 - (Optional) Create a percentage-based Calculated Value field.

---

1. Using ▦ (Schedule/Quantities), create a new area schedule called **Area Schedule (Rentable)**.

2. Add the fields *Name* and *Area*.

3. Click f_x (Add calculated parameter) and add the new *Calculated Value* field, as shown in Figure 2–125.

Calculated Value	✕
Name:	Percent of Total Area
○ Formula	● Percentage
Of:	Area ⌄
By:	<Grand total> ⌄

Figure 2–125

4. Click **OK** twice to create the schedule.

5. Open the **A103 – Area Plans** sheet and add the new area schedule to the sheet next to the colored legend, as shown in Figure 2–126.

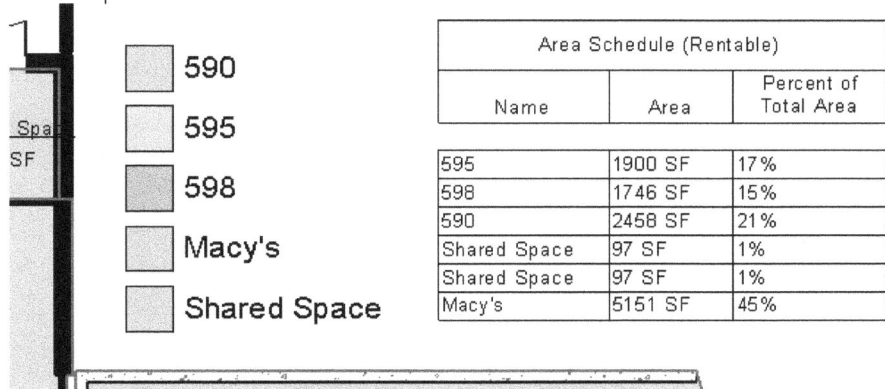

Area Schedule (Rentable)		
Name	Area	Percent of Total Area
595	1900 SF	17%
598	1746 SF	15%
590	2458 SF	21%
Shared Space	97 SF	1%
Shared Space	97 SF	1%
Macy's	5151 SF	45%

Figure 2–126

6. Save and close the project.

Practice 2h

Create Complex Schedules for MEP Projects

Practice Objectives

- Create a base schedule and add an embedded schedule into it.
- Test the scheduled information using conditional formatting.

In this practice, you will create a base schedule including a Calculated Value and Conditional Formatting. You will then add an embedded schedule to create an Space Air Flow Check schedule, as shown in Figure 2–127.

<Space Air Flow Check>					
A	B	C	D	E	F
Space Number	Name	Condition Type	Actual Supply Airfl	Calculated Supply	Airflow Check
Diffuser ID	Diffuser Type	Diffuser Airflow			
101	Office Area 1	Heated and cooled	0 CFM	2833 CFM	-2833 CFM
102	Office Area 2	Heated and cooled	0 CFM	2546 CFM	-2546 CFM
103	Vestuble 1	Heated and cooled	0 CFM	351 CFM	-351 CFM
104	Foyer 1	Heated and cooled	0 CFM	718 CFM	-718 CFM
105	Conf. Room	Heated and cooled	800 CFM	519 CFM	281 CFM
1	Supply Diffuser	400 CFM			
2	Supply Diffuser	400 CFM			
106	Women's 1	Heated and cooled	500 CFM	203 CFM	297 CFM
13	Supply Diffuser	500 CFM			
107	Mens 1	Heated and cooled	500 CFM	201 CFM	299 CFM
14	Supply Diffuser	500 CFM			
108	Hall 1	Heated and cooled	500 CFM	864 CFM	-364 CFM
8	Supply Diffuser	500 CFM			
109	Mech. Room	Heated and cooled	100 CFM	90 CFM	10 CFM
50	Supply Diffuser	100 CFM			
110	Elec. Room	Heated and cooled	100 CFM	168 CFM	-68 CFM
49	Supply Diffuser	100 CFM			
111	Utility	Heated and cooled	0 CFM	54 CFM	-54 CFM
112	Break Room 1	Heated and cooled	500 CFM	527 CFM	-27 CFM
9	Supply Diffuser	500 CFM			
113	Vestuble 2	Heated and cooled	0 CFM	150 CFM	-150 CFM
114	Stair	Heated and cooled	0 CFM	53 CFM	-53 CFM
115	Elev.	Heated and cooled	0 CFM	25 CFM	-25 CFM
201	Office Space 3	Heated and cooled	0 CFM	7327 CFM	-7327 CFM
202	Office Space 4	Heated and cooled	0 CFM	6196 CFM	-6196 CFM
203	Foyer 2	Heated and cooled	0 CFM	867 CFM	-867 CFM
204	Womens 2	Heated and cooled	0 CFM	203 CFM	-203 CFM
205	Mens 2	Heated and cooled	140 CFM	201 CFM	-81 CFM
37	Supply Diffuser	140 CFM			
206	Hall 2	Heated and cooled	0 CFM	1003 CFM	-1003 CFM
25	Supply Diffuser	500 CFM			
207	Stair	Heated and cooled	0 CFM	238 CFM	-238 CFM
208	Break Room 2	Heated and cooled	410 CFM	497 CFM	-87 CFM
24	Supply Diffuser	205 CFM			
34	Supply Diffuser	205 CFM			
209	Mechanical Ro	Heated and cooled	0 CFM	268 CFM	-268 CFM

Figure 2–127

Task 1 - Create a Base schedule.

1. In the practice files *MEP* folder, open **Office-Airflow.rvt**.

2. Create a new Schedules/Quantities schedule.

3. In the New Schedule dialog box, filter the list by *Mechanical*, if required, and select **Spaces**. Name the schedule **Space Air Flow Check** and click **OK**.

4. Add the following fields: **Number**, **Name**, **Condition Type**, **Actual Supply Airflow**, and **Calculated Supply Airflow**, as shown in Figure 2–128.

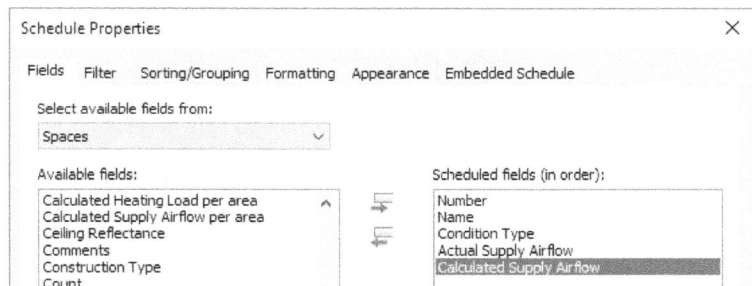

Figure 2–128

5. While still in the *Fields* tab, click f_x (Add calculated parameter).

6. In the Calculated Value dialog box, specify the *Name* as **Airflow Check**, *Discipline* as **HVAC**, and *Type* as **Air Flow**.

7. For the Formula, click ⌐…⌐ and select **Actual Supply Airflow** and click **OK**. Type a minus sign (-) and then click ⌐…⌐ again and select **Calculated Supply Airflow**. Click **OK**.

8. In the *Sorting/Grouping* tab, sort by **Number**.

By browsing for the fields, you save time by not misspelling or mis-capitalizing the field names.

9. In the *Formatting* tab, select **Airflow Check** and click **Conditional Format...**.

10. In the Conditional Formatting dialog box, specify the different fields (as shown in Figure 2–129), and click **OK**. You can select any color you want.

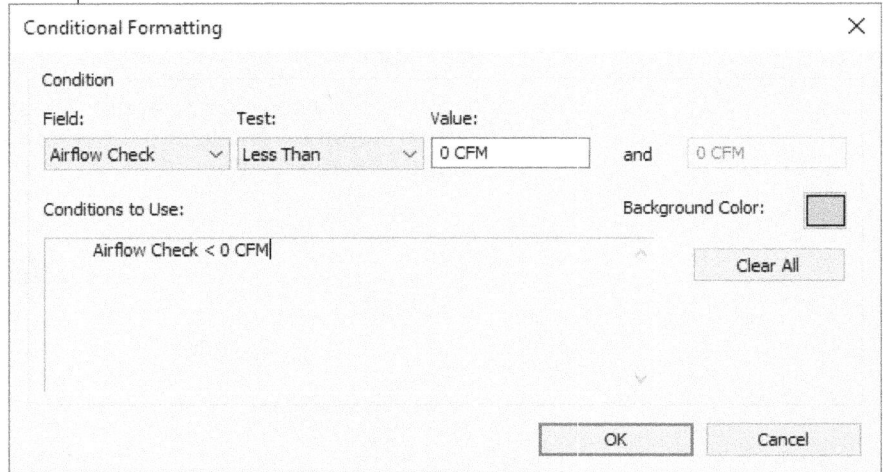

Figure 2–129

11. Click **OK** again to display the schedule (shown in part) up to this point. Expand the columns, as shown in Figure 2–130.

<Space Air Flow Check>					
A	B	C	D	E	F
Number	Name	Condition Type	Actual Supply Airfl	Calculated Supply	Airflow Check
101	Office Area 1	Heated and cooled	0 CFM	2833 CFM	-2833 CFM
102	Office Area 2	Heated and cooled	0 CFM	2546 CFM	-2546 CFM
103	Vestuble 1	Heated and cooled	0 CFM	351 CFM	-351 CFM
104	Foyer 1	Heated and cooled	0 CFM	718 CFM	-718 CFM
105	Conf. Room	Heated and cooled	800 CFM	519 CFM	281 CFM
106	Women's 1	Heated and cooled	500 CFM	203 CFM	297 CFM
107	Mens 1	Heated and cooled	500 CFM	201 CFM	299 CFM
108	Hall 1	Heated and cooled	500 CFM	864 CFM	-364 CFM

Figure 2–130

12. Click inside the **Number** heading and change it to **Space Number**.

13. Save the project.

Task 2 - Add an embedded schedule.

1. While still in the Space Air Flow Check schedule view, in Properties, beside *Embedded Schedule*, click **Edit...**.

2. In the Schedule Properties dialog box, in the *Embedded Schedule* tab, select **Embedded Schedule**.

3. In the Category list, select **Air Terminals**.

4. Click **Embedded Schedule Properties**.

5. In the Schedule Properties dialog box, in the *Fields* tab, add the following fields:

   - *System Classification*
   - *Mark*
   - *Family and Type*
   - *Flow*

6. In the *Filter* tab, filter by: **System Classification equals Supply Air**.

7. In the *Sorting/Grouping* tab, set *Sort by as* **Mark** and *Then by* as **Family and Type**, as shown in Figure 2–131.

Figure 2–131

8. In the *Formatting* tab, select the *Field* **System Classification** and select **Hidden field**.

9. Select **Mark** and set *Heading* as **Diffuser ID**. Set *Heading orientation* as **Horizontal** and *Alignment* as **Right**.

10. Select **Family and Type** and set *Heading* as **Diffuser Type**. Set *Heading orientation* as **Horizontal** and *Alignment* as **Left**.

11. Select **Flow** and set *Heading* as **Diffuser Airflow**. Set *Heading orientation* as **Horizontal** and *Alignment* as **Left**.

12. Click **OK** until the schedule displays, as shown in part in Figure 2–132.

<Space Air Flow Check>					
A	B	C	D	E	F
Space Number	Name	Condition Type	Actual Supply Airfl	Calculated Supply	Airflow Check
Diffuser ID	Diffuser Type	Diffuser Airflow			
101	Office Area 1	Heated and cooled	0 CFM	2833 CFM	-2833 CFM
102	Office Area 2	Heated and cooled	0 CFM	2546 CFM	-2546 CFM
103	Vestuble 1	Heated and cooled	0 CFM	351 CFM	-351 CFM
104	Foyer 1	Heated and cooled	0 CFM	718 CFM	-718 CFM
105	Conf. Room	Heated and cooled	800 CFM	519 CFM	281 CFM
1	Supply Diffuser	400 CFM			
2	Supply Diffuser	400 CFM			
106	Women's 1	Heated and cooled	500 CFM	203 CFM	297 CFM
13	Supply Diffuser	500 CFM			

Figure 2–132

13. If time permits, work with the project to establish the correct air flow for the various spaces.

14. Save and close the project.

Practice 2i

Create Complex Schedules for Structural Projects

Practice Objectives

- Create project parameters and modify an existing schedule using them.
- Modify and group headers in a schedule to graphically link the parameter types.

In this practice, you will create project parameters for structural footing types. Your will then add the new parameters to a schedule, add an additional parameter, add headers to the schedule, and fill in the schedule, as shown in Figure 2–133.

A	**B**	**C**	**D**	**E**	**F**	**G**	**H**	**I**	**J**
		Dimensions			Reinforcement				
					Cover		Bars		
Type	Length	Width	Thickness	Top Cover	Bottom Cover	Major Bars	Minor Bars	Count	Volume
FC3.0		3' - 0"	1' - 0"	0' - 3"	0' - 1 1/2"	#4 @ 1'-0"	#4 @ 1'-0"	4	715.22 CF
FC5.0	139' - 10"	5' - 0"	1' - 0"	0' - 3"	0' - 2"	#4 @ 0'-9"	#4 @ 0'-9"	1	553.47 CF
FS6.0	6' - 0"	6' - 0"	1' - 0"	0' - 3"	0' - 1 1/2"	#4 @ 1'-0"	#4 @ 1'-0"	27	972.00 CF
FS8.0	8' - 0"	8' - 0"	1' - 0"	0' - 3"	0' - 2"	#4 @ 0'-9"	#4 @ 1'-0"	3	192.00 CF
Grand total: 35								35	2432.69 CF

Figure 2–133

Task 1 - Add Project parameters.

1. In the practice files *Structural* folder, open **Century-Building.rvt**.

2. In the Project Browser, in the *Schedules/Quantities* area, open the **Structural Foundation Schedule**, as shown in Figure 2–134. This schedule is limited to existing parameters and does not include any rebar information. Also, the **Foundation Thickness** parameter is recorded for continuous footing (FC) types but not for spot footings (FS) types.

A	**B**	**C**	**D**	**E**	**F**
		Dimensions			
Type	Length	Width	Foundation Thickness	Count	Volume
FC3.0		3' - 0"	1' - 0"	4	715.22 CF
FC5.0	139' - 10"	5' - 0"	1' - 0"	1	553.47 CF
FS6.0	6' - 0"	6' - 0"		27	972.00 CF
FS8.0	8' - 0"	8' - 0"		3	192.00 CF
Grand total: 35				35	2432.69 CF

Figure 2–134

3. Open the **Structural Plans: T.O.F.** view.

4. Select one of the spot footings.

5. In Properties, click 🗗 (Edit Type).

You can see a
Thickness *parameter,*
but this does not link
into schedules.

6. In the Type Properties dialog box, there are parameter groups for *Dimensions* and *Identity Data*, as shown in Figure 2–135, but no information about the rebar that typically needs to be included in a foundation schedule.

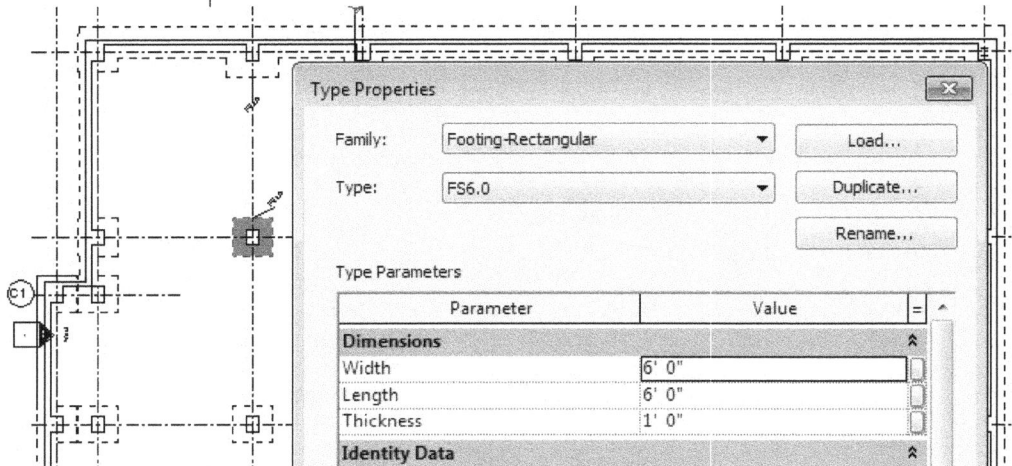

Figure 2–135

7. Click **Cancel** to close the dialog box and click in the view to clear the foundation selection.

8. In the *Manage* tab>Settings panel, click 🗗 (Project Parameters).

9. In the Project Parameters dialog box, click **Add**.

10. In the Parameter Properties dialog box, create a *Project parameter* named **Bottom Cover**. Make it a **Type** parameter and set *Discipline* to **Common**, *Type of Parameter* to **Length**, and *Group parameter under* to **Rebar Set**. In *Categories*, set the *Filter list* to **Structure**, and select **Structural Foundations**, as shown in Figure 2–136.

Figure 2–136

11. Click **OK**.

12. Add additional Type parameters. Set *Discipline* as **Common** and *Group parameter under* as **Rebar Set** with the following additional information:

Name	Type of Parameter	Categories
Top Cover	Length	Structural Foundations
Major Bars	Text	Structural Foundations and Walls
Minor Bars	Text	Structural Foundations and Walls

13. When you are finished, the four parameters display as shown in Figure 2–137. Click **OK**.

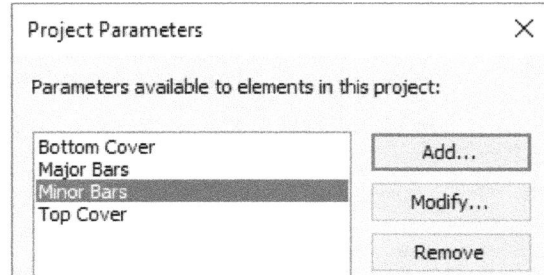

Figure 2–137

14. Select a footing again and open the Type Properties dialog box. This time the **Rebar Set** group of parameters is also displayed, as shown in Figure 2–138. Click **OK**.

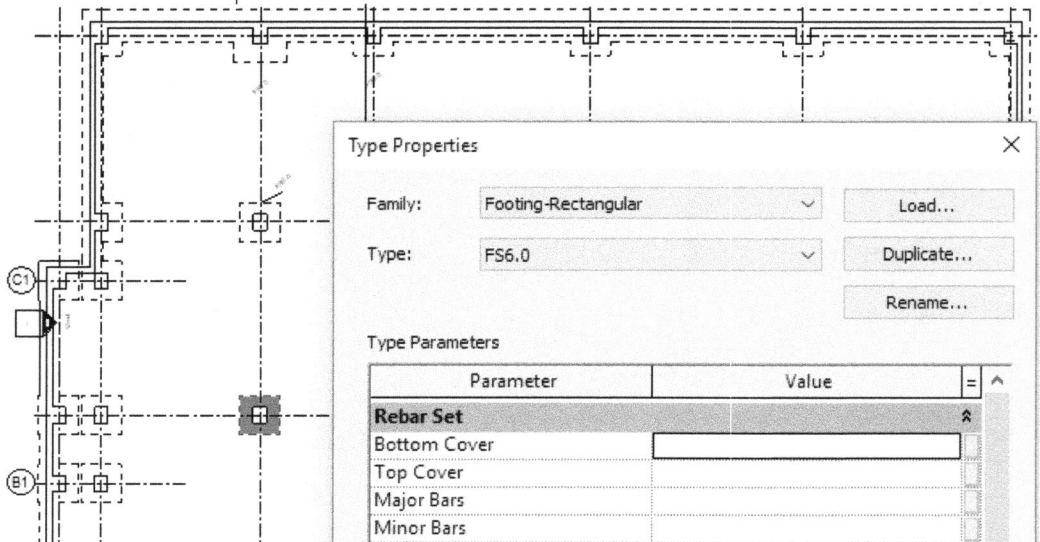

Figure 2–138

15. Save the project.

Task 2 - Modify a Foundation schedule.

1. Switch back to the Structural Foundation Schedule.

2. In Properties, in the *Other* area, next to *Fields*, click **Edit...**.

3. In the Schedule Properties dialog box, in the *Fields* tab, add the following fields: **Top Cover**, **Bottom Cover**, **Major Bars** and **Minor Bars**. Place them in the order shown in Figure 2–139.

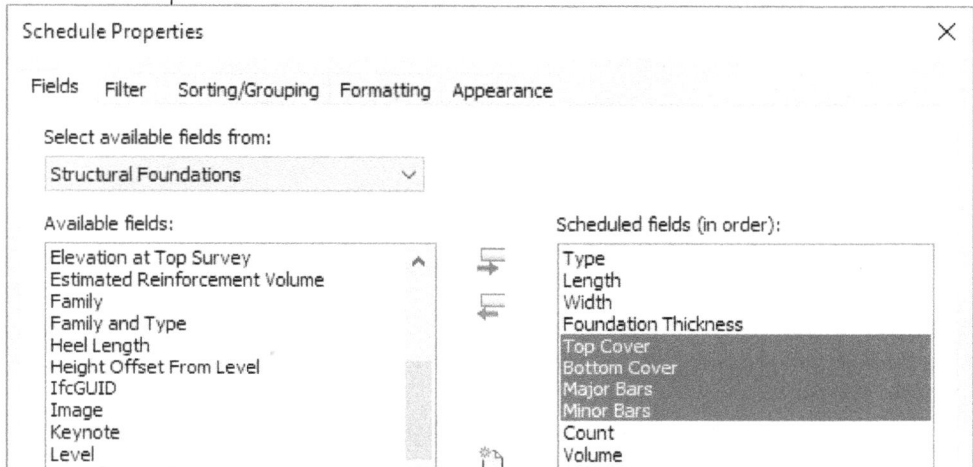

Figure 2–139

4. In the *Scheduled fields (in order)* area, remove the existing **Foundation Thickness** parameter.

5. In the *Fields* tab, click ⬜ (New parameter).

6. In the Parameter Properties dialog box, select **Project parameter**, and enter the *Name* **FS and FC Foundation Thickness**. Set it as a **Type** parameter with *Discipline* set to **Common**, *Type of Parameter* set to **Length**, and *Group* with **Dimensions**.

7. Click **OK**.

8. Click ↑E (Move parameter up) to place it below the existing **Width** parameter.

9. Select the new parameter and click ✎ (Edit parameter).

10. The full Parameter Properties dialog box opens. The **Structural Foundations** category is already selected because you are working in that type of schedule. Additionally, select the **Walls** category.

11. Click **OK** twice to close the dialog boxes.

12. The schedule displays as shown in Figure 2–140.

			<Structural Foundation Schedule>						
A	B	C	D	E	F	G	H	I	J
	Dimensions		FS and FC						
Type	Length	Width	Foundation	Top Cover	Bottom Cover	Major Bars	Minor Bars	Count	Volume
FC3.0		3' - 0"						4	715.22 CF
FC5.0	139' - 10"	5' - 0"						1	553.47 CF
FS6.0	6' - 0"	6' - 0"						27	972.00 CF
FS8.0	8' - 0"	8' - 0"						3	192.00 CF
Grand total: 35								35	2432.69 CF

Figure 2–140

13. Save the project.

Task 3 - Modify and apply headers.

A column cannot be added under an existing header. Therefore, delete the header and then remake it with the correct associations.

1. Click inside the header for FS and FC Foundation Thickness. Delete **FS and FC Foundation** so it displays as only *Thickness*.

2. In the schedule view, select the *Dimensions* header and in the *Modify Schedule/Quantities* tab>Titles & Headers panel, click ⬚ (Ungroup).

3. Press and drag the cursor over the columns from *Length* to *Thickness*.

4. In the Titles & Headers panel, click ⬚ (Group).

5. Type a header name of **Dimensions**.

6. Repeat the process to create a header from *Top Cover* to *Minor Bars* with the name **Reinforcement**.

7. Group *Top Cover* and *Bottom Cover* and name the header **Cover**.

8. Group *Major Bars* and *Minor Bars* and name the header **Bars**. The schedule displays as shown Figure 2–141.

				<Structural Foundation Schedule>					
A	B	C	D	E	F	G	H	I	J
	Dimensions			Reinforcement					
				Cover		Bars			
Type	Length	Width	Thickness	Top Cover	Bottom Cover	Major Bars	Minor Bars	Count	Volume
FC3.0		3' - 0"						4	715.22 CF
FC5.0	139' - 10"	5' - 0"						1	553.47 CF
FS6.0	6' - 0"	6' - 0"						27	972.00 CF
FS8.0	8' - 0"	8' - 0"						3	192.00 CF
Grand total: 35								35	2432.69 CF

Figure 2–141

9. Set the *Thickness* to **1'-0"** for each of the types.

10. Open the **Structural Plans: T.O.F.** view and select one of the larger **FS8.0** spot footings.

11. In Properties, click ⊞ (Edit Type). The **FS and FC Foundation Thickness** parameter has been added and set to **1'-0"**. Fill out the rest of the information for the *Cover* and *Bars*, as shown in Figure 2–142, and close the Type Properties dialog box.

Type Properties		✕
Family:	Footing-Rectangular ⌄	Load...
Type:	FS8.0 ⌄	Duplicate...
		Rename...

Type Parameters

Parameter	Value	=
Rebar Set		☆
Bottom Cover	0' 2"	
Top Cover	0' 3"	
Major Bars	#4 @ 0'-9"	
Minor Bars	#4 @ 1'-0"	
Dimensions		☆
Width	8' 0"	
Length	8' 0"	
Thickness	1' 0"	
FS and FC Foundation Thickness	1' 0"	

Figure 2–142

12. In the Type Properties of each foundation type or in the schedule view, fill out the rest of the information as shown in the schedule in Figure 2–143.

<Structural Foundation Schedule>

A	B	C	D	E	F	G	H	I	J
		Dimensions			Reinforcement				
				Cover		Bars			
Type	Length	Width	Thickness	Top Cover	Bottom Cover	Major Bars	Minor Bars	Count	Volume
FC3.0		3' - 0"	1' - 0"	0' - 3"	0' - 1 1/2"	#4 @ 1'-0"	#4 @ 1'-0"	4	715.22 CF
FC5.0	139' - 10"	5' - 0"	1' - 0"	0' - 3"	0' - 2"	#4 @ 0'-9"	#4 @ 0'-9"	1	553.47 CF
FS6.0	6' - 0"	6' - 0"	1' - 0"	0' - 3"	0' - 1 1/2"	#4 @ 1'-0"	#4 @ 1'-0"	27	972.00 CF
FS8.0	8' - 0"	8' - 0"	1' - 0"	0' - 3"	0' - 2"	#4 @ 0'-9"	#4 @ 1'-0"	3	192.00 CF
Grand total: 35								35	2432.69 CF

Figure 2–143

13. Save and close the project.

Chapter Review Questions

1. In the Schedule Properties dialog box (shown in Figure 2–144), in which tab do you define the order of the list of elements?

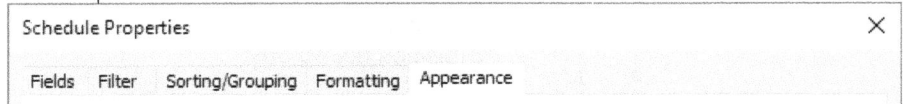

Schedule Properties   ✕

Fields   Filter   Sorting/Grouping   Formatting   Appearance

Figure 2–144

   a. *Fields*

   b. *Filter*

   c. *Sorting/Grouping*

   d. *Formatting*

   e. *Appearance*

2. Which type of schedule lists style information that is not automatically included in an element, such as the finish or frame type of a door?

   a. Material Takeoff

   b. Quantities

   c. Key

   d. Building Component

3. When creating *Calculated Value* fields (such as shown in Figure 2–145), the parameters you use must first be added to the list of fields in the schedule.

Figure 2–145

a. True

b. False

4. When creating a Material takeoff schedule, where do you modify information about the material, such as the cost or manufacturer, as shown in Figure 2–146? (Select all that apply.)

Stone - Material Takeoff			
Material: Description	Material: Area	Material: Cost	Total Cost
Stone	865 SF	0.00	0
Stone: 6	865 SF		0

EIFS - Material Takeoff			
Material: Description	Material: Area	Material: Cost	Total Cost
EIFS	298 SF	12.00	3574
EIFS: 1	298 SF		3574

Figure 2–146

a. In the Type Properties dialog box.

b. In the schedule, fill out the columns related to the type information.

c. In the Material Editor.

d. In the Material Browser.

5. (MEP only) Which of the following should be created before you can create an embedded schedule, as shown in Figure 2–147?

A	B
SPACE NO.	NAME
DIFFUSER ID	DIFFUSER TYPE
1501	CLASSROOM
29	Supply Diffuser - Perforated - Round Neck - Ceiling Mounted:
30	Supply Diffuser - Perforated - Round Neck - Ceiling Mounted:
31	Supply Diffuser - Perforated - Round Neck - Ceiling Mounted:
32	Supply Diffuser - Perforated - Round Neck - Ceiling Mounted:
1502	CLASSROOM
45	Supply Diffuser - Perforated - Round Neck - Ceiling Mounted:
46	Supply Diffuser - Perforated - Round Neck - Ceiling Mounted:
47	Supply Diffuser - Perforated - Round Neck - Ceiling Mounted:
48	Supply Diffuser - Perforated - Round Neck - Ceiling Mounted:

Figure 2–147

a. Rooms or Spaces.

b. Elements covered in the schedule.

c. The schedule that you want to embed.

d. A key schedule.

Command Summary

Button	Command	Location
Schedule Types		
NA	Graphical Column Schedule	• **Ribbon:** *View* tab>Create panel> expand Schedules (*Structural Columns only*)
	Material Takeoff Schedule	• **Ribbon:** *View* tab>Create panel> expand Schedules
	Note Block	• **Ribbon:** *View* tab>Create panel> expand Schedules
	Schedule/ Quantities	• **Ribbon:** *View* tab>Create panel> expand Schedules
	Sheet List	• **Ribbon:** *View* tab>Create panel> expand Schedules
	View List	• **Ribbon:** *View* tab>Create panel> expand Schedules
Schedule Appearance		
	Align Horizontal	• **Ribbon:** *Modify Schedule/Quantities* tab>Appearance panel
	Align Vertical	• **Ribbon:** *Modify Schedule/Quantities* tab>Appearance panel
	Borders	• **Ribbon:** *Modify Schedule/Quantities* tab>Appearance panel
	Font	• **Ribbon:** *Modify Schedule/Quantities* tab>Appearance panel
	Reset	• **Ribbon:** *Modify Schedule/Quantities* tab>Appearance panel
	Shading	• **Ribbon:** *Modify Schedule/Quantities* tab>Appearance panel
	Delete (Columns)	• **Ribbon:** *Modify Schedule/Quantities* tab>Columns panel
	Hide (Columns)	• **Ribbon:** *Modify Schedule/Quantities* tab>Columns panel
	Insert (Columns)	• **Ribbon:** *Modify Schedule/Quantities* tab>Columns panel
	Resize (Columns)	• **Ribbon:** *Modify Schedule/Quantities* tab>Columns panel
	Unhide All (Columns)	• **Ribbon:** *Modify Schedule/Quantities* tab>Columns panel
	Calculated	• **Ribbon:** *Modify Schedule/Quantities* tab>Parameters panel
	Combine Parameters	• **Ribbon:** *Modify Schedule/Quantities* tab>Parameters panel

	Format Unit	• **Ribbon:** *Modify Schedule/Quantities* tab>Parameters panel
	Delete (Rows)	• **Ribbon:** *Modify Schedule/Quantities* tab>Rows panel
	Insert (Rows)	• **Ribbon:** *Modify Schedule/Quantities* tab>Rows panel
	Insert Data Row	• **Ribbon:** *Modify Schedule/Quantities* tab>Rows panel
	Resize (Rows)	• **Ribbon:** *Modify Schedule/Quantities* tab>Rows panel
	Clear Cell	• **Ribbon:** *Modify Schedule/Quantities* tab>Titles & Headers panel
	Group	• **Ribbon:** *Modify Schedule/Quantities* tab>Titles & Headers panel
	Insert Image	• **Ribbon:** *Modify Schedule/Quantities* tab>Titles & Headers panel
	Merge Unmerge	• **Ribbon:** *Modify Schedule/Quantities* tab>Titles & Headers panel
	Ungroup	• **Ribbon:** *Modify Schedule/Quantities* tab>Titles & Headers panel

Introduction to Revit Families

Families are the backbone of Autodesk Revit. They are the elements you add as you model a building and its services, as well as the tools you use as you are annotating views. There are three types of families all of which are customizable.

- *System Families* are preset in the templates used to create projects (e.g., walls, roofs, slabs, ducts, pipes, and conduit, as well as text and dimensions). You create new types by duplicating and existing type and modifying type parameters. System Families are covered in *Chapter 3: Custom System Families*.

- *Component Families* (e.g., doors, air handling units, columns, as well as tags and symbols, etc.) are defined in the Family Editor and loaded into a project. One family can have many types. Component families can be stand-alone or hosted to elements such as walls, floors, or ceilings. Component Families are the most complicated elements to create. Component Families are covered in *Chapter 4: Component Family Concepts*, *Chapter 5: Advanced Family Techniques*, and *Chapter 6: Additional Family Types*.

- *In-Place Families* are component families created directly in a project and are dependent on the model geometry (e.g., custom gutters, special trim, or built-in columns). Use these only for unique situations where a component family does not work. In-Place Families are covered in *Chapter 6: Additional Family Types*, *6.3 Creating In-Place Families*.

There are also three additional chapters of discipline-specific family creation practices:

- *Chapter 7: Creating Architectural Specific Families*
- *Chapter 8: Creating MEP Specific Families*
- *Chapter 9: Creating Structural Specific Families*

Chapter

3

Custom System Families

System families are embedded in an Autodesk® Revit® project or template file. Walls, roofs, floors, and compound ceiling types each have an assembly of layers that can be modified along with other parameters by editing the type properties of the family. MEP system families include duct, pipe, conduit, cable tray, and wire type families.

Learning Objectives in this Chapter

- Create system family types for walls, roofs, floors, and ceilings.
- Modify wall types vertically to include split materials, profiles, and reveals.
- Create a vertically stacked wall type from two or more wall types.
- Create duct and pipe types using routing preferences.
- Create cable tray, conduit, and wire types using type properties.

3.1 Creating Wall, Roof, Floor, and Ceiling Types

System families are created and modified in a project or template file by duplicating an existing element type. Some of these system families (such as walls, roofs, floors, and some ceilings) are compound or layer-based. For example, to modify a compound wall, you edit the type and select the **Structure** parameter. This opens the Edit Assembly dialog box (as shown in Figure 3–1) which enables you to specify each layer of the assembly.

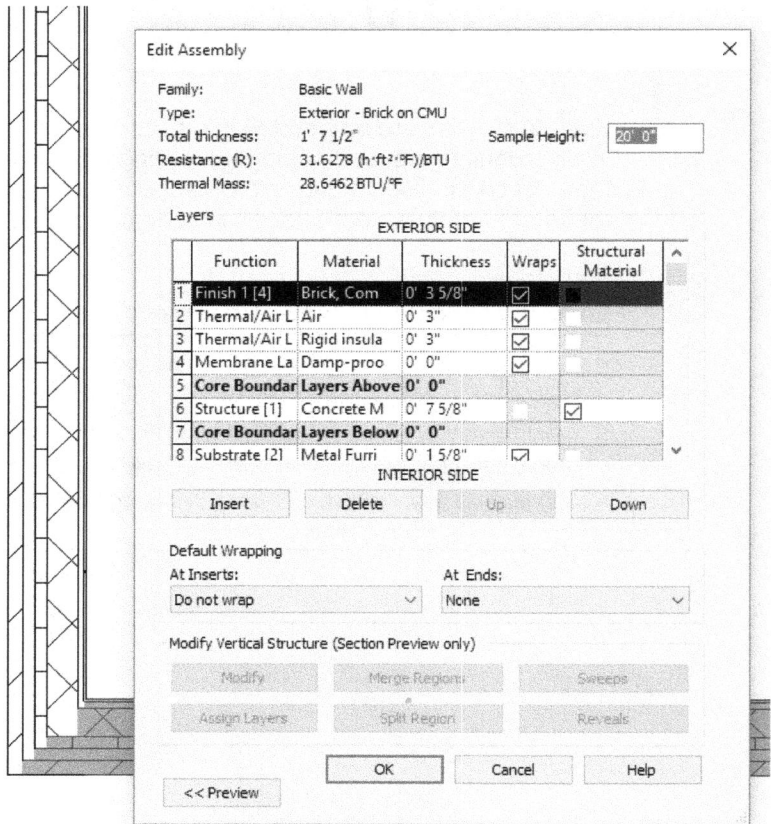

Figure 3–1

- Walls are used as the primary example, but floors, roofs, and compound ceilings follow the same pattern.

- Structural Floors often use profiles for metal decking. Creating this type of floor is covered in the profile families topic.

How To: Create a Compound Wall, Floor, Roof, or Ceiling

1. Start the wall, floor, roof or ceiling command.
2. In Properties, select a type similar to the one you want to create and click ⊞ (Edit Type).
3. In the Type Properties dialog box, click **Duplicate...**.
4. In the Name dialog box, enter a name for the new type and click **OK**.
5. Next to the **Structure** parameter, click **Edit...**.
6. In the Edit Assembly dialog box, modify the layers of the assembly as required, and then click **OK**.
7. Modify any Type Parameters in the Type Properties dialog box.
8. Click **OK** to close the dialog box.

Hint: Basic Ceilings

The basic ceiling system family does not include a structure parameter. Instead, modify the Type by specifying a *Material* for the entire thickness of the ceiling.

Editing Wall, Roof, and Floor Assemblies

In the Edit Assembly dialog box, you can define the layers that make up the compound structure, as shown in Figure 3–2.

Figure 3–2

- To better visualize the wall, click **<< Preview** to open a view of the layers in the structure. You can preview the structure in a plan or section view, and zoom or pan in the preview screen.

Assembly Information

The top of the dialog box lists the *Family* (such as **Basic Wall** or **Floor**), the *Type* that you gave to the new type, and the *Total thickness* (which is the sum of the layers defined in the wall), as shown in Figure 3–3. It also includes *Resistance (R)* and *Thermal Mass* which are automatically calculated from the materials assigned to the layers. You can also set a *Sample Height* for your wall design.

Family: Basic Wall
Type: Exterior - Brick on CMU
Total thickness: 1' 7 1/2"   Sample Height: | 20' 0" |
Resistance (R): 31.6278 (h·ft²·°F)/BTU
Thermal Mass: 28.6462 BTU/°F

Figure 3–3

Layers

When you specify the layers for the compound element, you assign them a *Function*, *Material*, and *Thickness*, as shown in Figure 3–4.

Layers
	Function	Material	Thickness	Wraps	Structural Material
1	Finish 1 [4]	Brick, Com	0' 3 5/8"	☑	■
2	Thermal/Air L	Air	0' 3"	☑	
3	Thermal/Air L	Rigid insula	0' 3"	☑	
4	Membrane La	Damp-proo	0' 0"	☑	
5	**Core Boundar**	**Layers Above**	**0' 0"**		
6	Structure [1]	Concrete M	0' 7 5/8"		☑
7	**Core Boundar**	**Layers Below**	**0' 0"**		
8	Substrate [2]	Metal Furri	0' 1 5/8"	☑	
9	Finish 2 [5]	Gypsum W	0' 0 5/8"	☑	

EXTERIOR SIDE / INTERIOR SIDE

| Insert | Delete | Up | Down |

Figure 3–4

- Use the buttons to insert additional layers and to rearrange them in the layer list. You can also delete layers from the list.

- The *Core Boundary* function defines the layers above and below the wrapping; a heavier line displays when a plan or section view is cut.

- Editing a wall assembly works from the exterior side at the top of the list to the interior side at the bottom. For floors and roofs, you work around the layers above and below the wrap of the *Core Boundary*.

Options

Function		Select from a set list of functions in the drop-down list with a priority of highest (1) to lowest (5). High priority layers connect before low priority layers.
	Structure [1]	The structural support for the wall, floor, or roof.
	Substrate [2]	A material that acts as a foundation for another material, such as plywood or gypsum board.
	Thermal/ Air Layer [3]	An open layer for air space.
	Finish 1 [4]	The exterior finish layer, such as brick for a wall.
	Finish 2 [5]	The interior finish layer, such as drywall for a wall.
	Membrane Layer	A vapor barrier. Typically, this is set to a zero thickness. Therefore, it does not have a priority code.
	Structural Deck (1)	(Floors only) A structural support based on a Deck Profile. You can also specify the Deck Usage with a Bound Layer Above or a Standalone Deck.

Structural Deck Properties

Deck Profile	Deck Usage
Form Deck_Non-Composite : 2" x 6 ∨	Bound Layer Above ∨

Material		Select from a list of available materials. Layers clean up if they share the same material. If they do not, a line displays at the join.
Thickness		Set the thickness of the particular layer.

Wall Only Options

Sample Height	Displays the height of a wall in section when you are creating it. It does not impact the height of the wall in the project.
Default Wrapping	Set up how the heavy line style wraps around openings in walls: *at Inserts* (**Do not wrap**, **Interior**, **Exterior**, or **Both**), and *at Ends* (**None**, **Exterior**, or **Interior**). Wrapping is only visible in plan view.
Wraps	Set up individual layers to wrap—select the Wraps option at the end of each layer.

- Wall wrapping can be set in the assembly or in the Type Properties, as shown in Figure 3–5.

Wrapping at Inserts	Do not wrap
Wrapping at Ends	None

Figure 3–5

- Roofs, floors, and structural slabs have an additional parameter that relates to sloping for drains. When *Variable* is not selected, the slab is set to a constant thickness and the entire element slopes, as shown on the top in Figure 3–6. When *Variable* is selected, only the top layer slopes, as shown on the bottom in Figure 3–6.

Variable not checked

Variable checked

Figure 3–6

Practice 3a | Create an Architectural Wall Type

Practice Objective

- Create an exterior wall type with multiple of layers on the interior and the exterior of a core structural layer.

In this practice, you will create a custom exterior wall type, as shown in Figure 3–7.

Figure 3–7

Task 1 - Create a custom wall type.

1. Start a new project based on the default architectural template and save it as **Custom Wall Types.rvt**.

2. In the *Architecture* tab>Build panel, click ⬚ (Wall).

3. In Properties, click ▦ (Edit Type).

4. In the Type Properties dialog box, select **Generic - 8"**, click **Duplicate...**.

5. In the Name dialog box, type **Exterior - Custom** and click **OK**.

6. Next to the **Structure** parameter, click **Edit....** The simple wall type without any layers displays as shown in Figure 3–8.

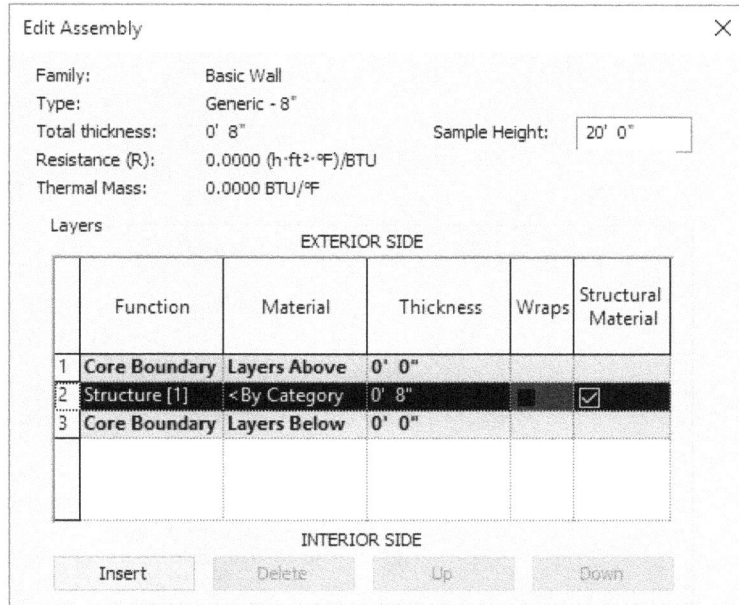

Figure 3–8

7. Click **<<Preview** and set the *View:* to **Floor Plan: Modify type attributes**.

8. Click **Insert** and then **Up** so a new layer is placed on the Exterior side as shown in Figure 3–9.

Figure 3–9

9. Click **Insert** three more times for a total of four layers above the structure. and then add two layers below the structure. At the moment, they all have a *Function* of Structure and no materials or thicknesses.

10. Set the *Function* and *Thickness* as shown in Figure 3–10.

Layers

EXTERIOR SIDE

	Function	Material	Thickness	Wraps	Structural Material
1	Finish 1 [4]	<By Categor	0' 3 5/8"	☑	
2	Thermal/Air Layer	<By Categor	0' 3"	☑	
3	Membrane Layer	<By Categor	0' 0"	☑	
4	Substrate [2]	<By Categor	0' 0 3/4"	☑	
5	**Core Boundary**	**Layers Above**	**0' 0"**		
6	Structure [1]	<By Categor	0' 8"		☑
7	**Core Boundary**	**Layers Below**	**0' 0"**		
8	Membrane Layer	<By Categor	0' 0"	☑	
9	Finish 2 [5]	<By Categor	1/2"	☑	

INTERIOR SIDE

Insert	Delete	Up	Down

Figure 3–10

11. Next to the **Structure [1]** layer, select the *Material* column and click ⋯ (Browse).

12. In the Material Browser, select **Metal Stud Layer**. You can limit the numbers of materials you see by typing stud in the search box, as shown in Figure 3–11. Click **OK**.

Material Browser - Metal Stud Layer   ?   ✕

stud	✕

Identity | Graphics | Appearance | Physical | Thermal

Project Materials: All ▼ ▷   ▢ »

Search results for "stud"

Name

Metal Stud Layer

▼ **Shading**

☐ Use Render Appearance

Color   RGB 199 199 199

Transparency   0

▼ **Surface Pattern**

▼ **Foreground**

Pattern <none>

Figure 3–11

13. In the Edit Assembly dialog box, in the *Thickness* column, type **6"** and verify that **Structural Material** is selected, as shown in Figure 3–12.

14. Add the materials show in Figure 3–12 to the other layers.

Edit Assembly   ✕

Family:	Basic Wall
Type:	Exterior - Custom
Total thickness:	1' 1 7/8"	Sample Height:	20' 0"
Resistance (R):	53.4556 (h·ft²·°F)/BTU
Thermal Mass:	8.1284 BTU/°F

Layers

EXTERIOR SIDE

	Function	Material	Thickness	Wraps	Struct Mat
1	Finish 1 [4]	Concrete Masonry Unit	0' 3 5/8"	☑	
2	Thermal/Air L	Air	0' 3"	☑	
3	Membrane La	Air Infiltration Barrier	0' 0"	☑	
4	Substrate [2]	Plywood, Sheathing	0' 0 3/4"	☑	
5	**Core Boundar**	**Layers Above Wrap**	**0' 0"**		
6	Structure [1]	Metal Stud Layer	0' 6"	■	☑
7	**Core Boundar**	**Layers Below Wrap**	**0' 0"**		
8	Membrane La	Vapor Retarder	0' 0"	☑	
9	Finish 2 [5]	Gypsum Wall Board	0' 0 1/2"	☑	

Figure 3–12

15. Click **OK** twice to close the dialog boxes.

16. Add a couple of walls to the project to see how the new wall functions.

17. Save and close the project.

Practice 3b | Create a Structural Floor Type

Practice Objectives

- Load a custom profile into a project.
- Create a new structural floor type using the profile.

In this practice, you will load the profile into a project, use it to create a new Metal Deck Floor type, as shown in Figure 3–13, and test the new floor type.

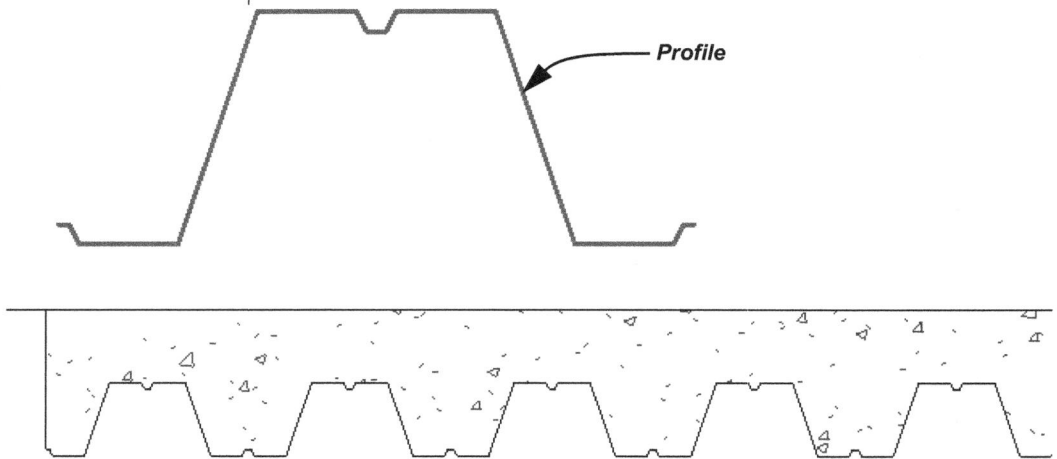

Figure 3–13

Task 1 - Load the a profile and create a structural floor.

1. Start a new project based on the default Structural template. You should be in the **Structural Plans: Level 2** view of the new project.

2. Save the project as **Custom Floor Types.rvt**.

3. In the *Insert* tab>Load from Library panel, click 🔲 (Load Family).

4. Navigate to the practice files>Structural folder, select **Custom-Metal-Deck-Profile.rfa**, and click **Open**.

5. In the *Structure* tab>Structure panel, click ⌒ (Floor: Structural).

6. in the Type Selector, verify that **Floor: 3"LW Concrete on 2" Metal Deck** is selected.

7. In the *Modify | Create Floor Boundary* tab>Draw panel, use the **Line** or **Rectangle** tool to draw a slab of any type or size, as shown in Figure 3–14.

Figure 3–14

- If the span direction is not horizontal, in the *Modify | Edit Boundary* tab> Draw panel, click (Span Direction) and select a horizontal sketch line.

8. Click (Finish Edit Mode).

9. In the Quick Access Toolbar or *View* tab>Create panel, click (Section) and place a section vertically through the slab from north to south.

10. Open the new section view and change the *Scale* to **3/4"=1'-0"** and the *Detail Level* to **Fine**. You might need to adjust the crop region and/or zoom in on the slab section. It should look similar to the one shown in Figure 3–15.

Figure 3–15

11. Save the project.

Task 2 - Create a new floor type.

1. Select the slab.

2. In Properties, click (Edit Type).

3. Duplicate the existing type. Name the duplicated type **6" Concrete on 3" Comp Metal Deck**.

4. In the Type Properties dialog box, next to the **Structure** parameter, click **Edit...**.

5. Modify the **Structure [1], Concrete, Lightweight - 4 ksi** layer to a *Thickness* of **6"**, as shown in Figure 3–16.

Layers

	Function	Material	Thickness	Wraps	Struct Mate
1	Core Bounda	Layers Above Wrap	0' 0"		
2	Structure [1]	Concrete, Lightweight - 4	0' 6"		☑
3	Structural Dec	Metal Deck	0' 0"		☐
4	Core Bounda	Layers Below Wrap	0' 0"		

Figure 3–16

6. In the *Layers* area, select the **Structural Deck** layer.

7. In the *Structural Deck Properties* area, select **Custom-Metal-Deck-Profile: 3"** from drop-down list, as shown in Figure 3–17.

Structural Deck Properties

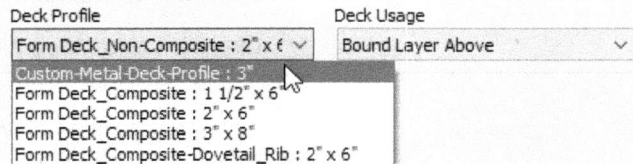

Deck Profile   Deck Usage

Form Deck_Non-Composite : 2" x 6 ∨	Bound Layer Above ∨

Custom-Metal-Deck-Profile : 3"
Form Deck_Composite : 1 1/2" x 6"
Form Deck_Composite : 2" x 6"
Form Deck_Composite : 3" x 8"
Form Deck_Composite-Dovetail_Rib : 2" x 6"

Figure 3–17

8. Click **OK** to close all of the dialog boxes. The section should display the metal deck profile that was previously created, as shown in Figure 3–18.

Figure 3–18

9. Save and close the project.

3.2 Vertically Compound Walls

Vertically Compound walls are made of regions of different materials, as well as optional permanent sweeps or reveals, as shown in Figure 3–19. Several options help you create these walls: **Modify**, **Split Region**, **Merge Regions**, **Assign Layers**, **Wall Sweeps**, and **Reveals**.

Figure 3–19

You must have the *View:* set to **Section: Modify Type Attributes** to work with the **Modify Vertical Structure** tools, as shown in Figure 3–20.

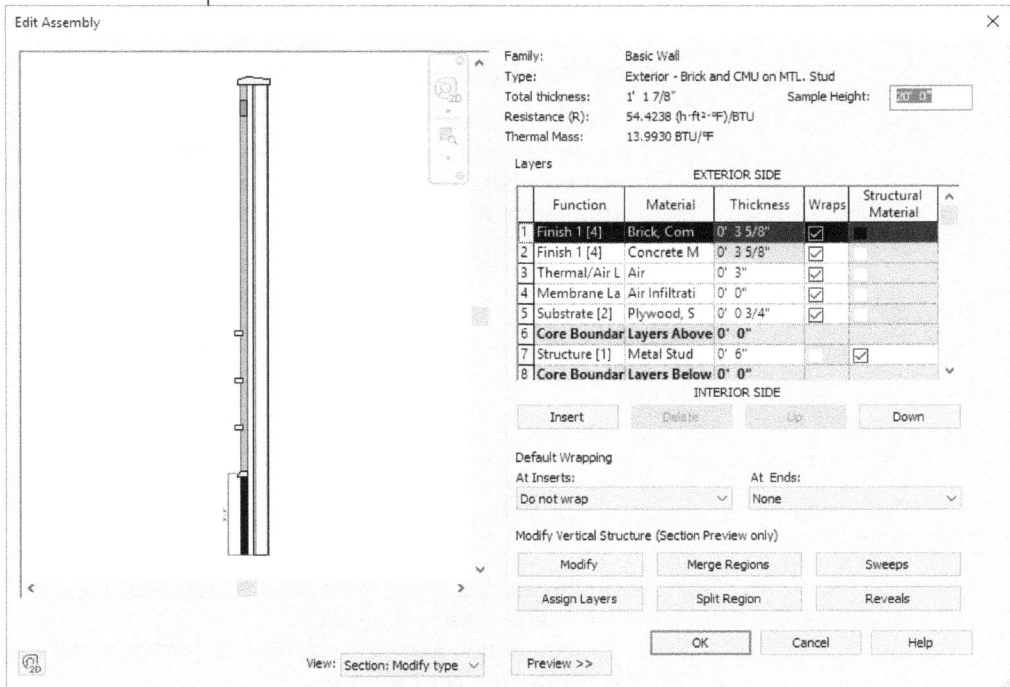

Figure 3–20

How To: Modify the Vertical Structure of a Wall Type

1. Open the wall type you want to modify and edit the structure.
2. Create any additional layers that might be required.
3. In the Edit Assembly dialog box, open the preview and set the *View:* to **Section: Modify Type Attributes**. This activates the *Modify Vertical Structure* tools, as shown in Figure 3–21.

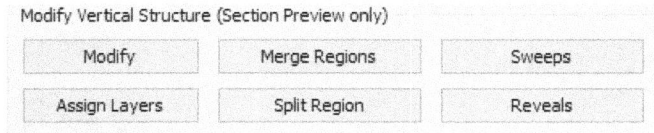

Modify Vertical Structure (Section Preview only)

Modify	Merge Regions	Sweeps
Assign Layers	Split Region	Reveals

Figure 3–21

4. Zoom in as required to see the various layers.
5. In the Layers list, select the layer you want to work with.
6. Use the various tools that are outlined below.
7. Click **OK** until all of the dialog boxes are closed to save the wall type.

• When making changes to the vertical structure of a wall type it helps to have the *Sample Height* set to the shortest expected height for the wall type so the changes display more clearly.

How To: Split Regions and Assign Layers

1. In the Edit Assembly dialog box, click **Split Region**.
2. In the section preview, move the cursor up the wall to the place where you want the region to be cut. Select the wall at that point and a dimension displays as shown in Figure 3–22.

Figure 3–22

3. In the *Layers* area, highlight the layer that you want to use and click **Assign Layers**.
4. In the section view, select the wall part that you want to change and click **Modify**.

- You can create as many split regions as required in one layer.

- To change the dimension, click **Modify** and select the border between the two regions that have been split. Then type a new distance using the temporary dimension.

- You can modify the width of the layer in the section view or in the *Thickness* column in the *Layers* area.

- You can add additional functions as required. In the example shown in Figure 3–23, two layers have the function **Finish 1**, and each layer has a different material. The *Thickness* is set by the selected layer and cannot be modified.

*Do not select more than you need. There is no **Undo** option in this dialog box.*

Layers

			EXTERIOR SIDE			
	Function	Material	Thickness	Wraps	Structural Material	^
1	Finish 1 [4]	Brick, Com	0' 3 5/8"	☑	■	
2	Finish 1 [4]	Concrete M	0' 3 5/8"	☑		
3	Thermal/Air L	Air	0' 3"	☑		

Figure 3–23

Merging Regions

To link regions together, click **Merge Regions** and select the line between the layers you want to merge, as shown in Figure 3–24. Watch the arrow cursor. It tells you which way the merge takes place. The tooltip also tells you names of the layers that are being merged. You can only merge layers that are next to each other.

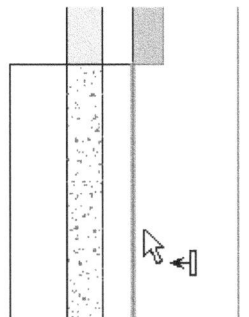

Figure 3–24

- You can merge layers vertically or horizontally. For example, to create the situation shown in Figure 3–24, you need to split the regions horizontally before merging some of the vertical lines.

Wall Sweeps and Reveals

When you split regions, the parts you create cannot have different widths. To create a protrusion or a reveal, add a wall sweep, as shown in Figure 3–25.

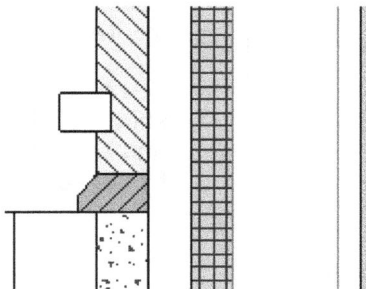

Figure 3–25

How To: Add a Sweep

1. In the Edit Assembly dialog box, click **Sweeps** to open the Wall Sweeps dialog box.
2. In the Wall Sweeps dialog box, click **Add**. A default row is added.
3. Select the *Profile* column and select from the list of the existing profiles in the project. Click **Load Profile** to add a profile.
4. Continue setting up the profile by selecting a *Material* and setting the *Distance* from the top or bottom, interior or exterior *Side*, and the *Offset* from that side, as shown in Figure 3–26. If required, place a checkmark in the *Flip* column to flip the profile.

Wall Sweeps

Wall Sweeps

	Profile	Material	Distance	From	Side	Offset	Flip	Setback	Cuts Wall	Cuttable	
1	Parapet Cap-	Concrete,	0' 0"	Top	Exterior	0' 0"	☐	0' 0"	☑	☐	
2	Wall Sweep-	Brick, Soldi	-1' 4"	Top	Exterior	-0' 3 5/	☐	0' 0"	☑	☐	
3	Sill-Precast :	Concrete,	3' 4"	Base	Exterior	0' 0"	☐	0' 0"	☑	☐	

Figure 3–26

5. Click **Apply** to see the addition before you click **OK** to finish.

• Reveals work the same way, except that you do not assign a material to a reveal. The whole shape of the reveal profile is visible in the section view, but you only see the cut in the project.

Practice 3c

Create a Vertically Compound Wall

Practice Objective

- Create a vertically compound wall.

In this practice, you will modify the vertical structure of a wall type using **Split Region** and **Assign Layers**. You will then add wall sweeps and reveals, as shown in Figure 3–27.

Figure 3–27

Task 1 - Add Materials to the project.

1. In the practice files *Architectural* folder, open **Custom Wall Types-Vertical.rvt**.

2. In the *Manage* tab>Settings panel, click ⊛ (Materials)

3. In the Material Browser, limit the *Project Materials* to **Masonry**, as shown in Figure 3–28.

4. If you do not see the AEC Materials library at the bottom of the dialog box, click **Shows/Hides Library panel**, as shown in Figure 3–28.

Figure 3–28

5. In the AEC Material library, select the *Masonry* folder.

6. In the *Name* list scroll down and select **Brick, Common, Grey** and click **Adds material to document**, as shown in Figure 3–29.

Figure 3–29

7. Repeat the process and add the **CMU, Split Face** material to the project and click **OK**.

8. Save the project.

Task 2 - Split regions in the wall type section

1. Select the existing wall and in Properties, verify that it is set to **Exterior - Custom** and click ⊞ (Edit Type).

2. Edit the *Structure* parameter.

3. Set the *Sample Height* to **30'-0"**

4. Click **<< Preview** and set the *View:* to **Section: Modify type attributes**.

5. In the *Layers* area, insert two additional layers with the *Function* **Finish1 [4]** on the exterior side of the structure. Set the materials as shown in Figure 3–30. Do not specify a thickness. Once you apply it to part of the split region, it takes on the appropriate thickness.

Layers

EXTERIOR SIDE

	Function	Material	Thickness	Wraps
1	Finish 1 [4]	CMU, Split Face	0' 0"	☑
2	Finish 1 [4]	Brick, Common, Grey	0' 0"	☑
3	Finish 1 [4]	Concrete Masonry Units	0' 3 5/8"	☑
4	Thermal/Air Layer	Air	0' 3"	☑
5	Membrane Layer	Air Infiltration Barrier	0' 0"	☑
6	Substrate [2]	Plywood, Sheathing	0' 0 3/4"	☑
7	**Core Boundary**	**Layers Above Wrap**	**0' 0"**	
8	Structure [1]	Metal Stud Layer	0' 6"	☑
9	**Core Boundary**	**Layers Below Wrap**	**0' 0"**	
10	Membrane Layer	Vapor Retarder	0' 0"	☑
11	Finish 2 [5]	Gypsum Wall Board	0' 0 1/2"	☑

Figure 3–30

6. In the *Modify Vertical Structure* area, click **Split Region**.

7. In the Section view, move the cursor to a point **3'-6"** above the base. Zoom in to ensure that you split the finish layer and not the central structural layer. Add the three additional splits to the same layers, as shown in Figure 3–31.

4'-0"

2'-0"

4'-0"

3'-6"

Figure 3–31

Task 3 - Assign layers in a wall type.

1. Zoom in so you can see the areas that have been split, as shown in Figure 3–32.

2. In the *Layers* area, select the **Brick, Common, Gray** layer on the Exterior Side.

3. In the *Modify Vertical Structure* area, click **Assign Layers**.

4. In the preview, select the **2'-0"** part of the exterior wall where you want the finish applied. The section should highlight as shown in Figure 3–32.

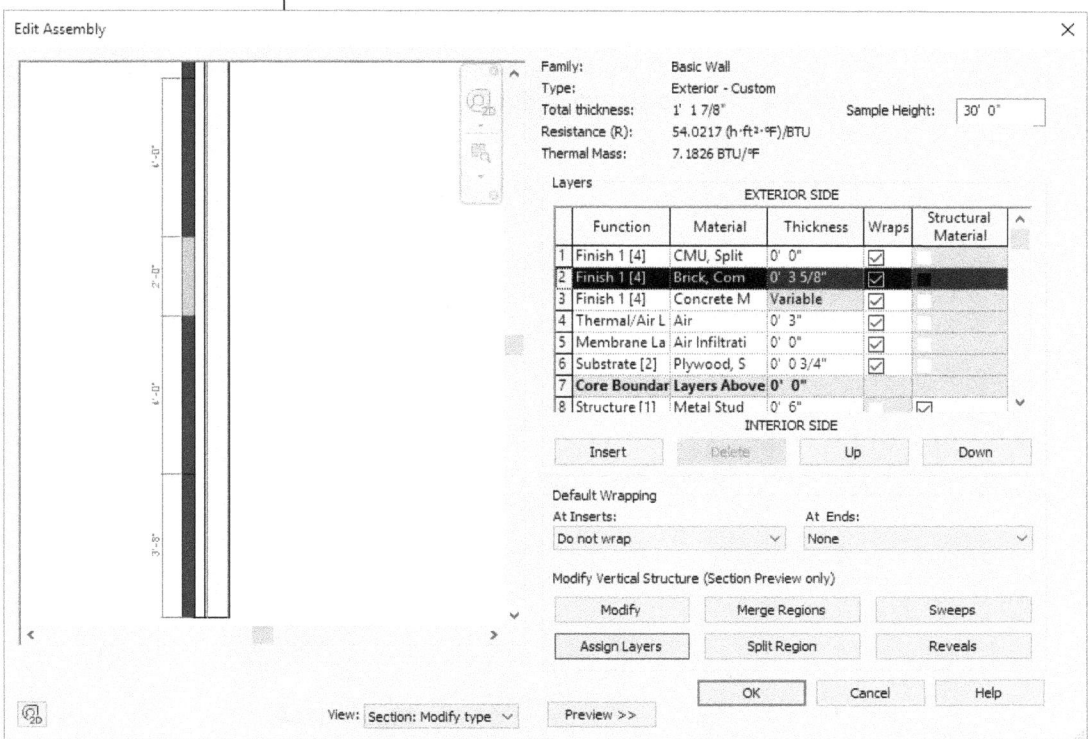

Figure 3–32

5. Repeat with the **CMU, Split face** material in each of the 4'-0"
   sections. The top and bottom of the wall remain using the
   Concrete Masonry Units material.

6. Click **Modify** to finish the process. The list of layers displays
   as shown in Figure 3–33.

Layers

EXTERIOR SIDE

	Function	Material	Thickness	Wraps	Structural Material
1	Finish 1 [4]	CMU, Split	Variable	☑	
2	Finish 1 [4]	Brick, Com	0' 3 5/8"	☑	
3	Finish 1 [4]	Concrete M	Variable	☑	
4	Thermal/Air L	Air	0' 3"	☑	
5	Membrane La	Air Infiltrati	0' 0"	☑	
6	Substrate [2]	Plywood, S	0' 0 3/4"	☑	
7	Core Boundar	Layers Above	0' 0"		
8	Structure [1]	Metal Stud	0' 6"		☑

INTERIOR SIDE

Insert   Delete   Up   Down

Figure 3–33

7. Click **OK** twice to close the dialog boxes.

8. Set the *Visual Style* of the 3D view to **Realistic** or **Ray Trace**, as shown in Figure 3–34, to see the layout of the materials.

Figure 3–34

9. Save the project.

Task 4 - Add sweeps and reveals to the wall type.

---

1. Edit the structure of the same wall type.

2. In the Edit Assembly dialog box, *Modify Vertical Structure* area, click **Sweeps**.

3. In the Wall Sweeps dialog box, click **Add** and set up two wall sweeps using the following information, as shown in Figure 3–35.

	Profile	Material	Distance	From	Side	Offset
1	Parapet Cap-Precast : 16" Wide	Concrete, Cast-in-Place gray	0' 0"	Top	Exterior	0' 0"
2	Sill-Precast : 5" Wide	Concrete, Cast-in-Place gray	3' 4"	Base	Exterior	0' 0"

Figure 3–35

4. Click **OK** to exit the Wall Sweeps dialog box.

5. In the preview of the Edit Assembly dialog box, you should see the two sweeps when you zoom in, as shown for the sill in Figure 3–36 and the cap in Figure 3–37.

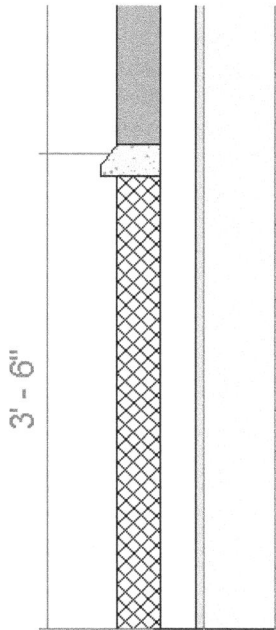

3' - 6"

Figure 3–36   **Figure 3–37**

6. In the Edit Assembly dialog box, *Modify Vertical Structure* area, click **Reveals**.

7. In the Reveals dialog box click **Add** and setup three reveals as shown in Figure 3–38. Click **OK**.

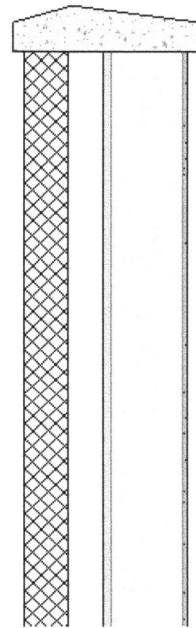

	Profile	Distance	From	Side	Offset	Flip	Setback	
1	Reveal-Brick Course : 1 Brick	13' 5"	Base	Exterior	0' 0"	☐	0' 0"	
2	Reveal-Brick Course : 1 Brick	9' 5"	Base	Exterior	0' 0"	☐	0' 0"	
3	Reveal-Brick Course : 1 Brick	7' 5"	Base	Exterior	0' 0"	☐	0' 0"	

Figure 3–38

8. Click **OK** twice to close the dialog boxes. The wall displays complete with sweeps and reveals.

9. Save and close the project.

3.3 Stacked and Embedded Walls

A vertically stacked wall is a specific system family that takes two or more existing basic walls and stacks them on top of each other at specific heights, as shown in Figure 3–39. One wall must be variable in height. The basic wall types have to be in place before you create the stacked wall. These walls are created by copying and editing an existing Vertically Stacked Wall type.

Figure 3–39

How To: Create a Vertically Stacked Wall

1. Start the **Wall** command.
2. In Properties, select an existing stacked wall type and click

   ☐ (Edit Type).
3. Duplicate the wall type and give it a new name.
4. In the Type Properties dialog box, next to the **Structure** parameter, click **Edit...**.
5. In the Edit Assembly dialog box, set the *Offset* for how the walls are stacked, and a *Sample Height* for the preview, as shown in Figure 3–40.

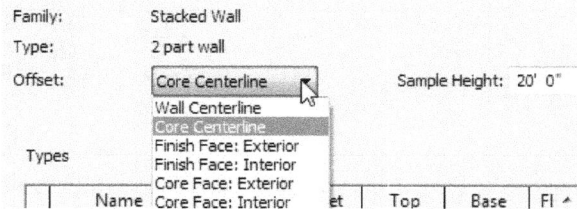

Figure 3–40

6. In the *Name* column, select the basic wall types you want to add to the stacked wall, as shown in Figure 3–41.

Types

	Name	Height	Offset	Top	Base	
				TOP		
1	Exterior - Brick on ▾	Variable	0' 0"	0' 0"	0' 0"	
2	Exterior - CMU on	3' 0"	0' 0"	0' 0"	0' 0"	

Figure 3–41

7. For each wall type, set the appropriate height and location (Up or Down) in the list. One height must be variable. Set the *Offset* of the wall as required.
8. Click **<< Preview** to see the wall, as shown in Figure 3–42.

Edit Assembly   ×

Family: Stacked Wall
Type: Exterior - Brick Over CMU w Metal Stud
Offset: Core Centerline ∨   Sample Height: 20' 0"

Types

	Name	Height	Offset	Top	Base	Flip
				TOP		
1	Exterior - Brick o	Variable	0' 0"	0' 0"	0' 0"	☐
2	Exterior - CMU o	3' 0"	0' 0"	0' 0"	0' 0"	☐
				BASE		

Variable   Insert   Delete   Up   Down

View: Section: Modify type ∨   Preview >>   OK   Cancel   Help

Figure 3–42

9. Click **OK** until all of the dialog boxes are closed.

Hint: Embedding a Wall Inside Another Wall

Another way of creating a compound wall is to embed one wall inside another wall, as shown in Figure 3–43. When you have drawn a host wall, draw another wall on top of, or parallel to it near the host. A warning box opens and recommends that you use **Cut Geometry** to embed the wall in the host wall.

Figure 3–43

1. Add the embedded wall to the host wall.
2. Close the warning box.

3. In the *Modify* tab>Geometry panel, click ⌖ (Cut).
4. Select the host wall.
5. Select the wall that cuts the host wall.

- Embedded walls work similar to windows. You can modify the embedded wall with controls.

- Some curtain wall types are created to be automatically embedded in another wall. The type **Curtain Wall: Storefront** is an example. The Type Parameter *Automatically Embed* is available for all curtain wall types.

- You can separate embedded walls. In the *Modify* tab> Geometry panel, expand ⌖ (Cut) and click ⌖ (Uncut Geometry).

Practice 3d

Create Stacked and Embedded Walls

Practice Objectives

- Create a vertically stacked wall type.
- Embed a wall into a stacked wall.

In this practice, you will create a vertically stacked wall and use it in a project. You will also embed a curtain wall and another wall type into a host wall, as shown in Figure 3–44.

Figure 3–44

Task 1 - Create a stacked wall.

1. Start a new project based on the default architectural or structural template and save it as **Warehouse.rvt**.

2. Start the **Wall** command and select the **Stacked Wall: Exterior – Brick Over CMU w Metal Stud** type.

3. Edit the type and duplicate it to create a new wall type named **Exterior – EIFS over Brick/CMU**.

4. Edit the structure of the new wall.

5. For the top wall, select **Exterior – EIFS on Mtl. Stud**. Leave the *Height* as **Variable** and set the *Offset* to **4"**.

6. For the bottom wall, select **Exterior – Brick on CMU** and set the *Height* to **6'-0"**.

7. Click **OK** to close all of the open dialog boxes.

8. Draw a rectangular building **50'-0" x 30'-0"** using the new wall style.

9. Display the walls in 3D to verify that the Brick/EIFS display on the exterior.

10. Save the project.

Task 2 - Create an embedded wall.

1. Open the **Floor Plans: Level 1** view.

2. On the south face of the building, add a wall using **Curtain Wall: Storefront** at an *Unconnected Height* of **8'-0"**. Place it directly on the center line of the existing wall along only a portion of the wall. It automatically cuts the existing wall.

3. Open the **Floor Plans: Level 2** view.

4. Add another wall on the same face using **Basic Wall: Exterior – Brick on Mtl. Stud**. This time a warning box opens.

5. Close the warning box.

6. In the *Modify|Place Wall* tab>Geometry panel, click (Cut).

7. Select the host wall.

8. Select the wall that cuts the host wall.

9. In the *Elevations* area, open the **South** view.

10. Flip the orientation of the brick insert as required.

11. Change the size of the embedded wall using the controls, but do not move it down into the lower brick wall.

12. Save and close the project.

3.4 Creating MEP System Families

Autodesk Revit templates for mechanical, electrical, and plumbing are preloaded with system families for Ducts, Pipes, Cable Trays, Conduits and Wire types. You can also duplicate and modify these families to create new family types. Ducts (as shown in Figure 3–45) and Pipes are set using Routing Preferences. Flex Ducts and Flex Pipes as well as Cable Tray Conduit, and Wire types are set up by defining fittings in the Type Properties.

Figure 3–45

How To: Create Duct Types

1. Start the **Duct** command, select one of the existing types, and click ⊞ (Edit Type).
2. In the Type Properties dialog box, click **Duplicate...**, type a new name in the Name dialog box, and click **OK**.
3. Next to the **Routing Preferences** parameter, click **Edit....**

4. The Routing Preferences dialog box displays as shown in Figure 3–46.

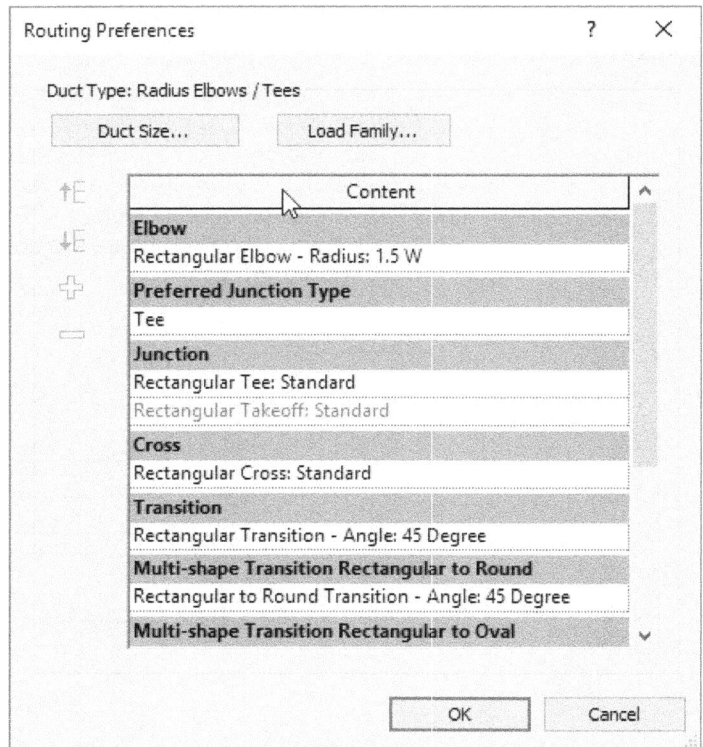

Figure 3–46

5. Click **Duct Size...** to open the Mechanical Settings dialog box to the Duct Settings so that you can add or remove the typical sizes used in the project.
6. Click **Load Family...** to add any duct fittings that you want to use in the type that are not already loaded in the project.
7. For each of the fittings, expand the drop-down list and select the size that you want use, as shown in Figure 3–47.

Figure 3–47

8. If you want to include more than one option for a fitting, click

   ✛ (Add row) and select the secondary option for the fitting.

   You can also use ↑E (Move row up) or ↓E (Move row down) to specify the order in which the fittings are applied by

   default or click ⊟ (Remove Row) to delete the ones you do not need to use.

9. When you have finished assigning fittings, click **OK** to close the Routing Preference dialog box.

10. Fill in the other Parameters for the Type Properties as required and click **OK** to finish the new duct type.

   • Flex ducts do not have routing preferences; the Fitting selection takes place directly in the Type Properties, as shown in Figure 3–48.

Parameter	Value	=
Construction		⊼
Roughness	0.0003'	
Fittings		⊼
Preferred Junction Type	Tap	
Tee	Round Tee: Standard	
Tap	Round Takeoff: Standard	
Transition	Round Transition - Angle: 45 Degre	
Multi Shape Transition Rect to R	Rectangular to Round Transition -	
Multi Shape Transition Rect to O	None	
Multi Shape Transition Oval to R	None	
Union	Round Union: Standard	
Identity Data		⊼

Type Properties ✕

Family: System Family: Flex Duct Round ⌄ Load...

Type: Flex - Round ⌄ Duplicate...

Rename...

Type Parameters

Figure 3–48

How To: Create Pipe Types

1. Start the **Pipe** command, select one of the existing types, and click ⊞ (Edit Type).
2. In the Type Properties dialog box, click **Duplicate...**, type a new name in the Name dialog box, and click **OK**.
3. Next to the **Routing Preferences** parameter, click **Edit...**.
4. The Routing Preferences dialog box opens, as shown in Figure 3–49.

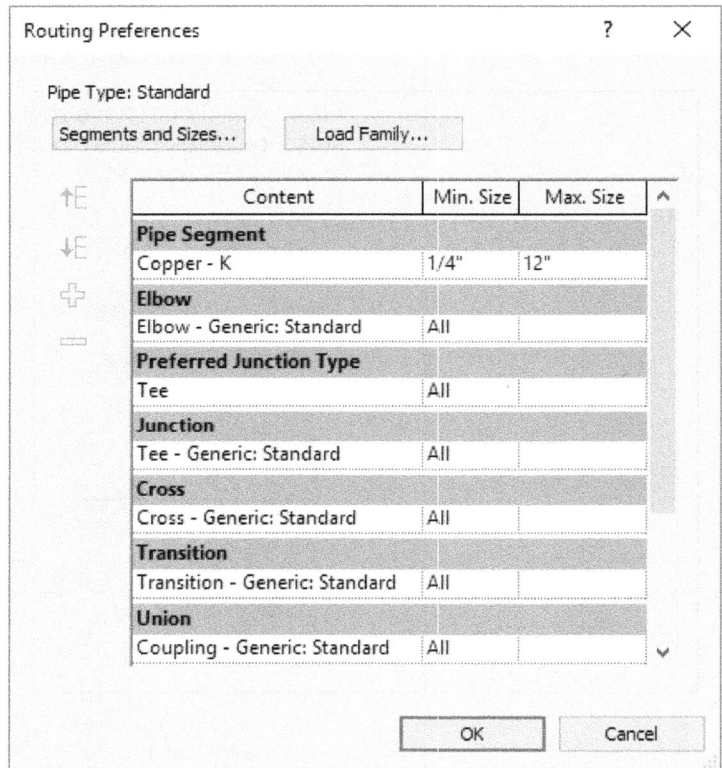

Figure 3–49

5. Click **Segments and Sizes...** to open the Mechanical Settings dialog box to the Pipe Settings. In this dialog box, specify the Segment types and sizes for the various types of pipe as shown in Figure 3–50.

*Segment types can be
added or removed here.*

Figure 3–50

6. Click **Load Family...** to add any pipe fittings that you want to
   use in the type that have not already been loaded in the
   project.
7. For the Pipe Segment type and each of the fittings, expand
   the drop-down list and select the size that you want to use as
   shown in Figure 3–51.

Figure 3–51

8. If you want to include more than one option for a fitting, click

   (Add row) and select the secondary option for the fitting.

   You can also use ⬆E (Move row up) or ⬇E (Move row
   down) to specify the order in which the fittings are applied by

   default or ⬛ (Remove Row) to delete the ones you do not
   need to use.

9. When you have finished assigning fittings, click **OK** to close the Routing Preference dialog box.

10. Fill in the other Parameters for the Type Properties as required and click **OK** to finish the new pipe type.

- Flex pipes do not have routing preferences; the Fitting selection takes place directly in the Type Properties, as shown in Figure 3–52.

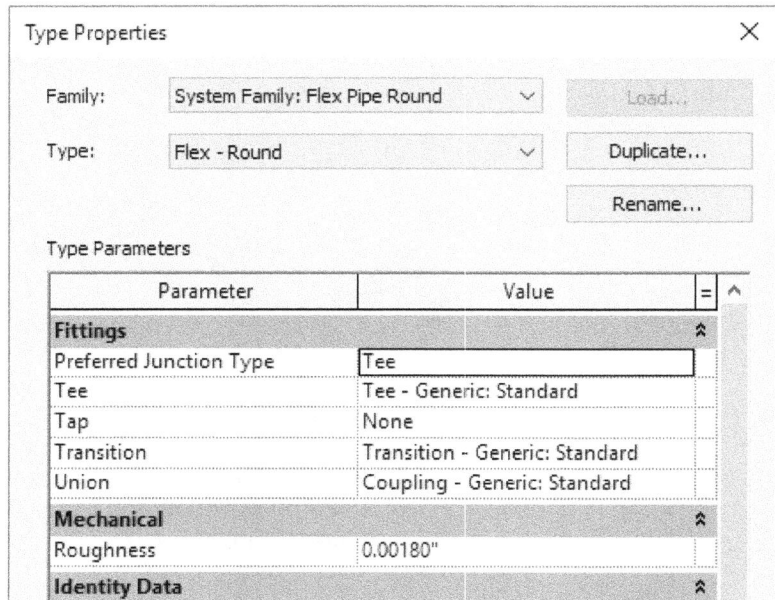

Figure 3–52

How To: Set up Cable Tray and Conduit Types

1. Start the **Cable Tray** or **Conduit** command, select one of the existing types, and click ⊞ (Edit Type).

2. In the Type Properties dialog box, click **Duplicate**, type a new name in the Name dialog box, and click **OK**.

3. Select the fittings that you want to use as shown in Figure 3–53. For example, you may want to specify a more specific type of coupler for the *Union* parameter.

Most of the Cable Tray types you need are preloaded in the default electrical and systems templates. You can only change some of the options such as the radius size.

Figure 3–53

•   For Conduit you first need to specify the Electrical Standard that you are using, as shown in Figure 3–54.

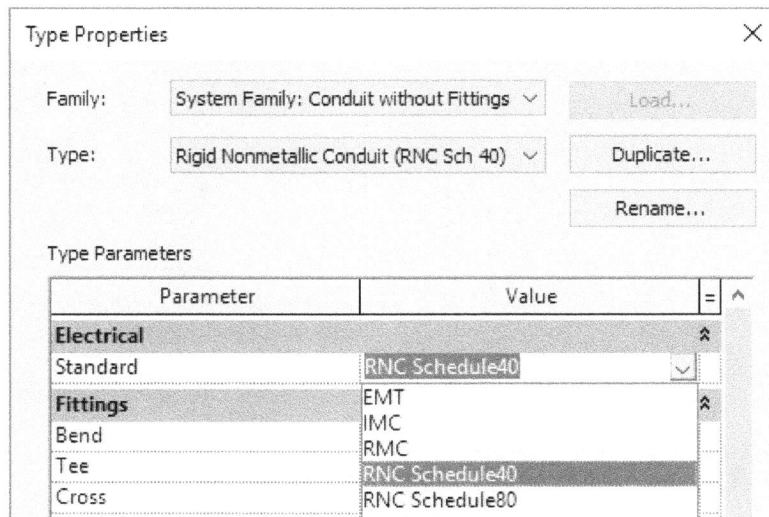

Figure 3–54

4. Fill in the values for any of the Identity Data information you might have and click **OK** to finish.

How To: Set up Wire Types

1. Start the **Wire** command, select one of the existing types, and click ⊞ (Edit Type).
2. In the Type Properties dialog box, click **Duplicate**, type a new name in the Name dialog box, and click **OK**.
3. Select the information that you want to use, as shown in Figure 3–55.

Type Properties		X
Family:	System Family: Wire Types ⌄	Load...
Type:	THWN ⌄	Duplicate...
		Rename...

Type Parameters

Parameter	Value	= ^
Electrical - Loads		⌃
Share Neutral Conductor	☑	
Share Ground Conductor	☑	
Material	Copper	
Temperature Rating	60	
Insulation	THWN	
Max Size	2000	
Neutral Multiplier	1.000000	
Neutral Included in Balanced Lo	☑	
Neutral Size	Hot Conductor Size	
Conduit Type	Non-Magnetic	

Figure 3–55

- Wire Types for THWN and XHHW are preset in the default electrical and systems templates.

- Another use of wire types is to show wire differently based on certain conditions. For example, create a type called **THWN - Above Ceiling** that is an exact duplicate of the basic **THWN** type. Then, create a view filter using this type name and change the line style to hidden or dashed.

Practice 3e

Create MEP System Families - Duct

Practice Objective

- Create a new duct system family.

In this practice, you will sketch ducts that show the various fittings that come with the default information. You will then duplicate and modify a duct system family, by loading additional fittings and assigning them to the system family, as shown in Figure 3–56.

Rectangular Duct: Radius Elbow / Tees

Rectangular Duct: Radius Elbow / Taps - DTL

Figure 3–56

Task 1 - Create a new duct type.

1. In the practice files *MEP* folder, open **Midrise-Template-MEP-Systems.rte**.

2. Open the Mechanical>HVAC>Floor Plans>**1 - Mech** view.

3. Start the **Duct** command and using the **Rectangular Duct: Radius Elbows / Tees** type, add some ducts in an arrangement similar to Figure 3–57. The exact size and length does not matter.

Cap this open end

Figure 3–57

4. Right-click on the end of the far right open pipe and select **Cap Open End.**

5. Make a copy of the entire duct system below the original making sure they don't touch.

6. Select one of the new ducts and in Properties, click ⊞ (Edit Type).

7. In the Type Properties dialog box, click **Duplicate...**.

8. In the Name dialog box, type **Radius Elbows / Taps - DTL** and click **OK**.

9. Next to the **Routing Preferences** parameter, click **Edit...**.

10. In the Routing Preferences dialog box, click **Load Family...**.

11. In the Load Family dialog box in the Autodesk Revit Library, navigate to the *Duct>Fittings>Rectangular>Caps* folder and select **Rectangular Endcap - DTL.rfa**, as shown in Figure 3–58. Then, click **Open**.

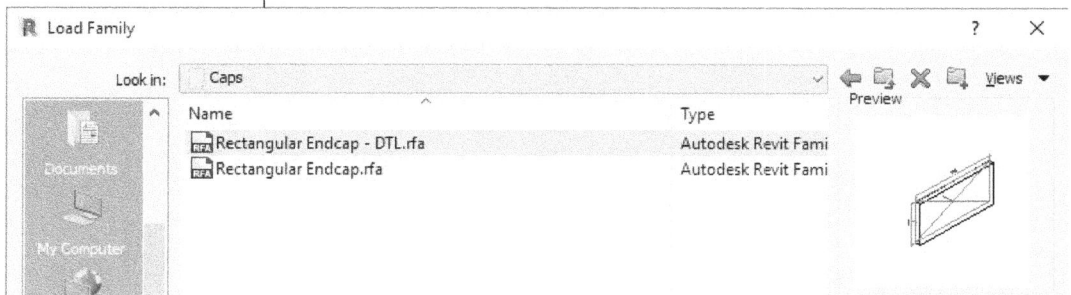

Figure 3–58

12. Load the following additional families from the following folders:

   - Elbows: **Rectangular Elbow Eccentric Radius - DTL.rfa**
   - Taps: **Rectangular Radius Tap - DTL.rfa**
   - Transitions: **Rectangular Length Eccentric Transition - DTL.rfa**

13. Assign the families to the appropriate section as shown in Figure 3–59.

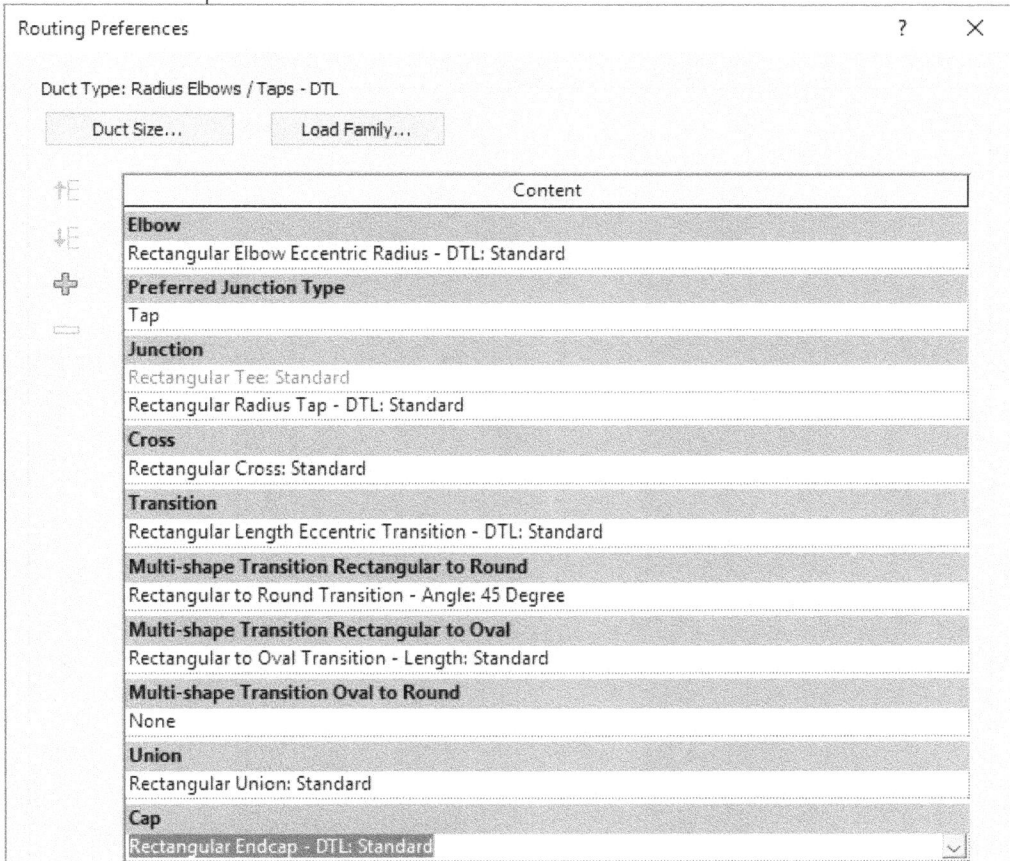

Routing Preferences   ?   ✕

Duct Type: Radius Elbows / Taps - DTL

Duct Size...   Load Family...

Content
Elbow
Rectangular Elbow Eccentric Radius - DTL: Standard
Preferred Junction Type
Tap
Junction
Rectangular Tee: Standard
Rectangular Radius Tap - DTL: Standard
Cross
Rectangular Cross: Standard
Transition
Rectangular Length Eccentric Transition - DTL: Standard
Multi-shape Transition Rectangular to Round
Rectangular to Round Transition - Angle: 45 Degree
Multi-shape Transition Rectangular to Oval
Rectangular to Oval Transition - Length: Standard
Multi-shape Transition Oval to Round
None
Union
Rectangular Union: Standard
Cap
Rectangular Endcap - DTL: Standard

Figure 3–59

14. Click **OK** twice to close the dialog boxes.

15. Highlight the new system and, in the *Modify | Multi-Select*

    tab>Edit panel, click ⊞ (Change Type).

16. In Properties, select one of the other types to see the change
    and then select **Rectangular Duct: Radius Elbow /Taps -
    DTL**. The duct updates as shown in Figure 3–60.

Figure 3–60

• Sometimes, the first selection does not update as
   expected, so select a different one before trying to apply
   the new type.

17. Save and close the template.

Practice 3f

Create MEP System Families - Pipe

Practice Objective

- Create a new pipe system family.

In this practice, you will sketch pipes that show the various fittings that come with the default information as shown on the top in Figure 3–61. You will then duplicate and modify a pipe system family, by loading additional fittings and assigning them to the new system family, as shown on the bottom in Figure 3–61.

Pipe Types: Standard

Pipe Types: Ductile Iron - Flanged - 250lb

Figure 3–61

Task 1 - Create a new Pipe Type

1. In the practice files *MEP* folder, open **Midrise-Template-MEP-Systems.rte.**

2. Open the Plumbing>Plumbing>Floor Plans>**1 - Plumbing** view.

3. Start the **Pipe** command.

4. In Properties, under the *Mechanical* section, set the *System Type* parameter to **Domestic Cold Water.**

5. Using the **Pipe Types: Standard** type, add some pipes in an arrangement similar to Figure 3–62. The exact size and length does not matter.

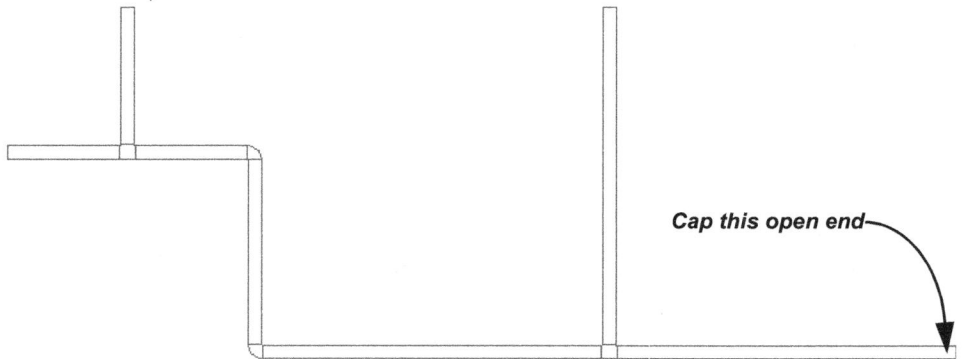

Cap this open end

Figure 3–62

6. Right-click on the end of the far right open pipe and select **Cap Open End.**

7. Make a copy of the entire system below the original ensuring that they do not touch.

8. Select one of the pipes in the new system.

9. In Properties, click (Edit Type).

10. In the Type Properties dialog box, click **Duplicate....**

11. In the Name dialog box, type **Ductile Iron - Flanged - 250lb** and click **OK**.

12. Next to the **Routing Preferences** parameter, click **Edit...**.

13. In the Routing Preferences dialog box, under *Pipe Segment* select **Iron, Ductile - 22** from the list and set the *Min. Size* to **3"** and the *Max. Size* to **30"**, as shown in Figure 3–63.

Figure 3–63

14. Click **Load Family...**.

15. In the Load Family dialog box, in the Autodesk Revit Library, navigate to the *Pipe>Fittings>Gray Iron Flanges>Class 250* folder and select both Flange families. as shown in Figure 3–64. Then, click **Open**.

Figure 3–64

16. Load the following additional families from the *Gray Iron> Class 250>Flanged* folder:

- **Cross - Flanged - GI - Class 250.rfa**
- **Elbow - Flanged - GI - Class 250.rfa**
- **Reducer - Flanged - GI - Class 250.rfa**
- **Tee Reducing - Flanged - GI - Class 250.rfa**

17. Assign the families to the appropriate section as shown in Figure 3–65. In the *Min. Size* column, select **All** for all the options except the Pipe Segment.

Routing Preferences

Pipe Type: Ductile Iron - Flanged - 250lb

Segments and Sizes...   Load Family...

Content	Min. Size	Max. Size
Pipe Segment		
Iron, Ductile - 22	3"	30"
Elbow		
Elbow - Flanged - GI - Class 250: Standard	All	
Preferred Junction Type		
Tee	All	
Junction		
Tee Reducing - Flanged - GI - Class 250: Standard	All	
Cross		
Cross - Flanged - GI - Class 250: Standard	All	
Transition		
Reducer - Flanged - GI - Class 250: Standard	All	
Union		
None	All	
Flange		
Flange - Threaded - GI - Class 250: Standard	All	
Cap		
Flange - Blind - GI - Class 250: Standard	All	

OK   Cancel

Figure 3–65

18. Click **OK** twice to close the dialog boxes.

19. Highlight the new system and in the *Modify | Multi-Select* tab>Edit panel, click ⊞ (Change Type).

20. In Properties, select **Pipe Types: Ductile Iron - Flanged - 250lb**. The pipe updates as shown in Figure 3–66.

Figure 3–66

21. Save and close the template.

Chapter Review Questions

1. When creating a compound wall, you assign a Function for each layer. The numbers after the function names is the priority of the layers when they are joined together with other walls, as shown in Figure 3–67. Which of the following function connects first?

    Figure 3–67

    a. Membrane Layer

    b. Substrate

    c. Structure

    d. Thermal/Air Layer

    e. Finish

2. How do you create a wall type that has more than one finish material on the vertical plane in the one type, as shown for stone and stucco in Figure 3–68?

    Figure 3–68

    a. Create separate wall types for the stone and stucco. Duplicate an existing Stacked Wall type and set the wall types to stone and stucco.

    b. Draw two walls on top of each other and use 🖉 (Join Geometry) to link them.

    c. Duplicate an existing Basic Wall type and use **Split Region** and **Assign Layers** to apply the stone and stucco materials to separate parts of the wall.

    d. Draw the first wall, draw the other wall on top of the first, and use 🖉 (Cut Geometry) to cut the second wall out of the first wall.

3. Which command do you need to use to embed a wall inside another wall?

   a. **Wall Joins**

   b. **Cut Geometry**

   c. **Cope**

   d. **Split Face**

4. (MEP only.) When setting up a new duct or pipe type, which of the following items can be set by type?

   a. System Type

   b. Width and Height

   c. Preferred Junction Type

   d. Justification

5. (MEP only.) When creating a new conduit or cable tray type you need to assign Routing Preferences.

   a. True

   b. False

Command Summary

Button	Command	Location
	Cable Tray	• **Ribbon:** *Systems* tab>Electrical panel • **Shortcut:** CT
	Conduit	• **Ribbon:** *Systems* tab>Electrical panel • **Shortcut:** CN
	Cut Geometry	• **Ribbon:** *Modify* tab>Geometry panel
	Duct	• **Ribbon:** *Systems* tab>HVAC panel • **Shortcut:** DT
	Edit Type	• **Ribbon:** *Modify* tab>Properties panel • **Properties Palette**
	Pipe	• **Ribbon:** *Systems* tab>Plumbing & Piping panel • **Shortcut:** PI
	Uncut Geometry	• **Ribbon:** *Modify* tab>Geometry panel> expand Cut
	Wall: Architectural	• **Ribbon:** *Architecture* tab>Build panel or *Structure* tab>Structure panel>expand Wall • **Shortcut:** WA
	Wall: Structural	• **Ribbon:** *Architecture* tab>Build panel or *Structure* tab>Structure panel>expand Wall • **Shortcut:** WA
	Wire	• **Ribbon:** *Systems* tab>Electrical panel • **Shortcut:** EW

Component Family Concepts

Component (or loadable) families are the heart of the Autodesk® Revit® software. They include furniture; doors and windows; mechanical, electrical, and plumbing equipment; and structural framing. While some families are included with the software, it is important to know how to create custom families yourself. The basics include creating a parametric framework, adding solid geometry, and creating family types.

Learning Objectives in this Chapter

- Understand the different types of families that can be created in the software.
- Set up a parametric framework using reference planes, dimensions, and labels.
- Flex the framework to test all of the parameters.
- Create solid/void forms including extrusions, blends, revolves, sweeps, and swept blends.
- Create family types.
- Load and test families in a project.

4.1 Creating Component Families

Loadable component families are model or annotation elements that have been grouped together and set up with dimensions and other parameters. Families are parametric, meaning that they can be changed without having to recreate the elements. For example, when you change the *Width* and *Depth* of the base cabinet shown in Figure 4–1, other parts move as well.

Figure 4–1

Families are created in the Family Editor that has a slightly different set of ribbon tabs from the standard interface, as shown in Figure 4–2.

Figure 4–2

- *Component Families* (e.g., doors, air handling units, columns, etc.) are defined in the Family Editor and loaded into a project. One family can have many types.

- Many families are complex and time-consuming to create, but creating them all follows the same basic process.

- Sometimes, it is easier to modify an existing component family than to create a family from scratch.

How To: Create a Component Family (Overview)

1. On the Home page, under *Families*, click **New...** or (if a project file is already open) in the *File* tab, expand ☐ (New) and click ☐ (Family).
2. In the New Family - Select Template File dialog box, select the template you want to use and click **Open**.
3. Set the parametric framework by adding reference planes/lines in plan and elevation views. This is a very important step when working with parametric families.
4. Label and dimension the reference planes/lines to control the movement of the elements and create parameters.
5. Flex the model to ensure the parameters change as expected.
6. Use the Forms tools (shown in Figure 4–3) to draw the elements.

Flexing a model: Changing the dimensions of a model to test its parametric features.

Figure 4–3

7. Lock the elements to the reference planes/lines.
8. Flex the elements again by changing the parameters to ensure that they are working.
9. Create family types with different parameters, as required.
10. Save the family.

11. Click 📤 (Load into Project) to test the family in a project.

Preparing to Create Families

As you create component families, you should plan ahead by asking a variety of questions, including:

- Is this family going to be used by one project (in-place) or by many projects (component)?

- Do you need different 2D representations in different views? What about 3D elements?

- Is this going to be a host-based or stand-alone family?

- Do you need various sizes of this family component?

> **Hint: Host-based vs. Stand-alone Families**
>
> *Host-based* families are dependent on a host. Examples include downlights (which require a ceiling) and sconces (which require a wall), as shown in Figure 4–4.
>
> *Stand-alone* families do not need a host. Examples include the desk and table lamp shown in Figure 4–4.
>
> Ceiling-based family   Stand-alone family   Wall-based family
>
>
>
> Figure 4–4

Saving Custom Family Files

When you create custom family files, you should save them to a location shared by the entire company, similar to the Autodesk Revit library. For easy access, set the custom library as the primary or secondary library available when you load a family.

How To: Specify the File Location for Custom Libraries

1. In the *File* tab, click **Options**.
2. In the Options dialog box, select the *File Locations* tab.
3. Click **Places...**.

4. In the Places dialog box, click ✛ (Add Value). A new *Library Name* is added to the list. Specify the name and path for the library, as shown in Figure 4–5.

	Library Name	Library Path
	Imperial Library	C:\ProgramData\Autodesk\RVT 2019\Libraries\US Imperial\
	Imperial Detail Library	C:\ProgramData\Autodesk\RVT 2019\Libraries\US Imperial...
	Metric Library	C:\ProgramData\Autodesk\RVT 2019\Libraries\US Metric\
	Metric Detail Library	C:\ProgramData\Autodesk\RVT 2019\Libraries\US Metric\...
	Custom Library	

Places — ⊗ — OK — Cancel — Help

Figure 4–5

5. Click ⬆E (Move Rows Up) and ⬇E (Move Rows Down) to reorder the list of library names.
6. Click **OK** to close the dialog boxes.

- The library at the top of the list will be the default location when loading families.

4.2 Creating the Parametric Framework

Autodesk Revit families can be parametric (i.e., controlled by parameters). These parameters are the framework for creating family elements. They are based on reference planes that are dimensioned and labeled, as shown in Figure 4–6.

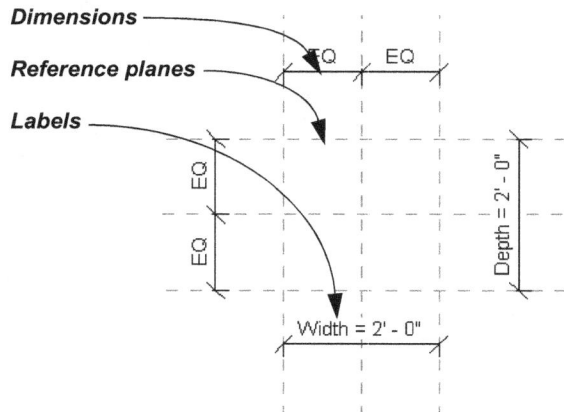

Figure 4–6

Before you draw any elements in a family, set up the parametric framework:

1. Place reference planes at critical locations.
2. Dimension the reference planes and label some of them so they can be manipulated.
3. Flex the dimensioned and labeled reference planes to ensure that they function as expected.

How To: Draw Reference Planes

1. In the Family Editor, in the *Create* tab>Datum panel, click

   (Reference Plane).
2. In the *Modify | Place Reference Plane* tab>Draw panel, click

   (Line) or   (Pick Lines).
3. Draw or select the lines that define the location of the plane.
4. Draw or select other lines as required.

- The number of reference planes you need depends on what you are drawing.

- Reference planes display in plan and elevation views, but not in 3D views.

Reference Plane Options

- By default, the origin of a family is the center of the space where you create the family. In most templates, this is located at the intersection of the existing reference planes. You can also specify your own origin by modifying the properties of two intersecting reference planes to specify that they define the origin, as shown in Figure 4–7.

Figure 4–7

- Reference planes do not display in the project when you insert the family type, but might impact snap and alignment behavior.
    - In Properties, under *Other*, set the **Is Reference** parameter to the plane you want to use, as shown in Figure 4–8.
    - If you do not want a reference plane to be a snap or an alignment, set the **Is Reference** parameter to **Not a Reference**.

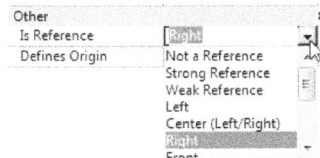

Figure 4–8

- After placing a reference plane, you can name it by clicking on **<Click to name>** and typing in the text box, as shown in Figure 4–9, or in Properties.

Figure 4–9

- Naming a reference plane enables you to use it to set the work plane when you are ready to add geometry to the family.

Reference Lines

Reference Lines, as shown in Figure 4–10, are similar to reference planes, but have distinct start and end points. They can be drawn using a wide variety of geometry, such as rectangles, circles, or arcs. Typically, they are used for angled elements.

Figure 4–10

- In the Family Editor, in the *Create* tab>Datum panel, click
  (Reference Line).

- Reference lines cannot be named.

Adding Dimensions and Labels

Add dimensions and labels to reference planes to start the constraining process, as shown in Figure 4–11. For example, you might want to run a string of dimensions and then set the distances to be equal by clicking on the associated **EQ** symbol. This moves the reference planes into place. Labeling a dimension creates a parameter that can be modified in the Family Types dialog box.

Figure 4–11

How To: Label a Dimension

1. Select the dimension you want to label.
2. In the *Modify | Dimensions* tab>Label Dimension panel, select an existing label from the drop-down list, as show in Figure 4–12. You can also right-click on the dimension text, select **Label**, and choose from the list as shown in Figure 4–13.

Figure 4–12

Figure 4–13

How To: Add a Label

1. Select the dimension you want to label.
2. In the *Modify | Dimensions* tab>Label Dimension panel, click

   (Create Parameter).

Shared parameters are covered in 6.4 Working with Shared Parameters.

3. In the Parameter Properties dialog box, in the *Parameter Type* area, select **Family parameter**, as shown in Figure 4–14.

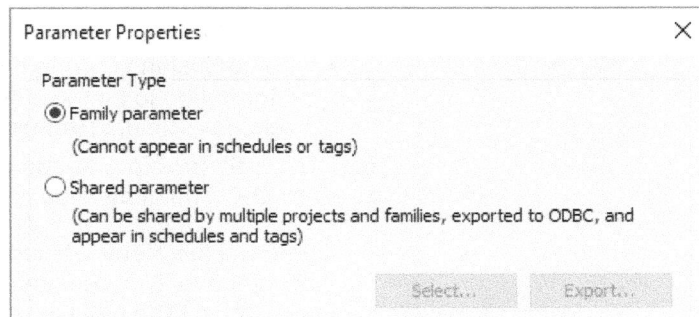

Figure 4–14

4. In the *Parameter Data* area, specify the *Name*, as shown in Figure 4–15. The *Type of Parameter* is automatically set to **Length** and the *Group parameter under* is set to **Dimensions**, because the parameter is a dimension.

Parameter Data

Name:

TrimWidth

⦿ Type

Discipline:

Common

◯ Instance

Type of parameter:

☐ Reporting Parameter

Length

(Can be used to extract value from a geometric condition and report it in a formula or as a schedulable parameter)

Group parameter under:

Dimensions

Tooltip description:

<No tooltip description. Edit this parameter to write a custom tooltip. Custom t...

Edit Tooltip...

How do I create family parameters?

OK   Cancel

Figure 4–15

5. Select **Type** or **Instance**.

- **Type** applies it to all instances of a family when it is inserted into a project. To modify it, you need to change the Type Properties.

- **Instance** applies it to individual instance when inserted into a project. It can be modified directly in Properties.

- For an instance property, if you want the dimension information to be used in a formula or placed in a schedule, select **Reporting Parameter**.

6. Click **Edit Tooltip...** to add a tooltip description, if required.

7. Click **OK**. The dimension is labeled and ready to be flexed.

- If you add too many labeled dimensions, the software warns that you have over-constrained the sketch. You cannot ignore this warning. The label is not created in this case.

- You can change the *Type* or *Instance* setting of a label parameter. Select the related dimension and in the *Modify Dimension* tab>Label Dimension panel, select (or clear) **Instance Parameter**, as shown in Figure 4–16.

Label:

TrimWidth = 4' - 0"

✓ Instance Parameter

Label Dimension

Figure 4–16

Flexing Geometry

Once you have established dimensions and labeled them, you need to verify that the parameters work correctly with each other. To do this, flex the geometry by changing the value of a label (as shown in Figure 4–17), or using the Family Types dialog box.

Width = 3' - 0"

3' 0"

Figure 4–17

- Select the labeled dimension and then the dimension text to change the value.

- To see all of the values you can flex at one time and to add formulas and non-dimension parameters, you need to work in the Family Types dialog box.

How To: Flex the Geometry in the Family Types Dialog box

1. In the *Create* or *Modify* tab>Properties panel, click

   (Family Types). The Family Types dialog box displays as shown in Figure 4–18.

You might have to move the dialog box to display the elements you are adjusting.

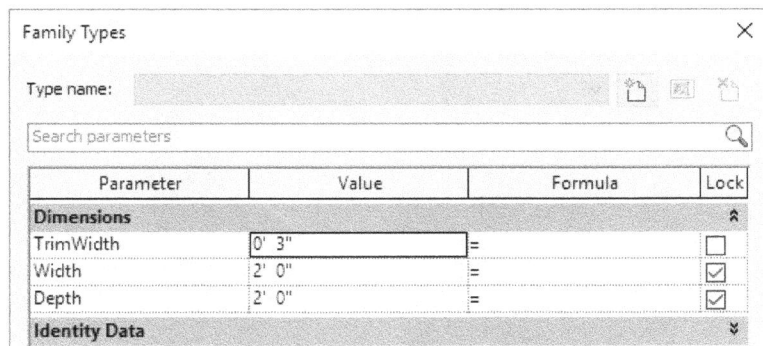

Family Types   ✕

Type name:

Search parameters   🔍

Parameter	Value	Formula	Lock
Dimensions			☆
TrimWidth	0' 3"	=	☐
Width	2' 0"	=	☑
Depth	2' 0"	=	☑
Identity Data			☟

Figure 4–18

2. Change the labeled parameters and click **Apply**.
3. Do the elements move correctly? Try several modifications.
4. Set the parameters as required and click **OK** to finish the command.

- When you open a family file, the Autodesk Revit software automatically checks the constraints in the family. If there are any issues, a dialog box offers information.

Creating and Modifying Parameters

In addition to creating labels (parameters specifically for dimensions), you can add parameters that store other information (such as the material of the element, as shown in Figure 4–19, the wattage of a light fixture, or the reinforcement cover setting in concrete). You can also add formulas to parameters so that they change when a related parameter changes.

Figure 4–19

- Instance parameters include (default) after the name, as shown in Figure 4–19. The assigned value is then used when the component is inserted into a project. It can be changed in Properties when the component is selected.

- The Family Types dialog box contains options for editing, creating, and organizing parameters, as shown in Figure 4–20.

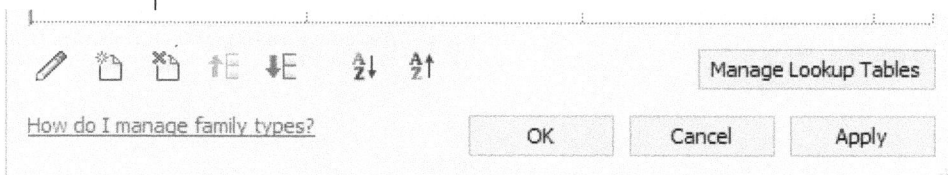

How do I manage family types?   OK   Cancel   Apply

Figure 4–20

✎	**Edit Parameter**	Displays the Parameter Properties dialog box, where you can change the name, group, or tooltip, or switch between **Type** and **Instance**. You can also change the parameter to reference a shared parameter.
◻	**New Parameter**	Opens the Parameter Properties dialog box, where you can setup a new parameter.
⬆E , ⬇E	**Move parameter up/down**	Enables you to organize the parameters in each group.
✗◻	**Delete parameter**	Removes the selected parameter.
A↓ , A↑	**Sort parameters in ascending/ descending order**	Sets the order of the parameters to alphabetical order and removes any changes you might have made.

How To: Create Parameters

1. In the Family Editor, in the *Create or Modify* tab>Properties panel, click ▦ (Family Types).

2. In the Family Types dialog box click ◻ (New Parameter).

3. In the Parameter Properties dialog box, set up the Parameter Data, as shown in Figure 4–21.

*The Discipline can be set to **Common**, **Structural**, **HVAC**, **Electrical**, **Piping**, or **Energy**. The Type of Parameter list changes according to the discipline.*

Figure 4–21

4. Click **OK**.

Common Parameter Types

Text	A text parameter can host any type of information that consists of both numbers and letters. Examples could be the fabric color or part number of the element.
Integer	Any value that is always represented by a whole number. Examples could be the number of chairs that fit around a conference table or the number of shelves in a bookcase.
Number	Any numeric value: whole, decimal, or fraction. You can use formulas with **Number** parameters.

Length	When you label dimensions, you create **Length** parameters. You can use formulas with **Length** parameters.
Area	Establishes the area of an element. It is numeric and can have formulas applied to it.
Volume	Establishes the volume of an element. It is numeric and can have formulas applied to it.
Angle	Establishes the angle of an element. It is numeric and can have formulas applied to it.
Slope	Displays a slope, as set in the Field Format.
Currency	Displays the amount in dollars or other currencies, as set up in the Field Format.
Mass Density	Displays the mass per unit volume of material.
URL	Specifies a link to a web site.
Material	Provides a place to assign a material from the list of materials that are set up in the project.
Image	Creates a parameter at which you can add a raster image connected to the family.
Yes/No	Used with instance parameters where you need a **Yes** or **No** answer to a question listed in the name. The default is **Yes**.
<Family Type>	Opens a dialog box where you can select from the list of family types, such as doors, furniture, or tags.

How To: Add Formulas to Parameters

1. In the *Create* or *Modify* tab>Properties panel, click
   ⊞ (Family Types).
2. In the Family Types dialog box, in the *Formula* column, add formulas to the parameters. In the example shown in Figure 4–22, the *Shelf Height* is defined as the **Height** divided by **4**. When you change the *Shelf Height* or *Height*, the other value updates according to the formula.

Dimensions			⌃
Depth	2' 0"	=	☑
Height	6' 0"	=	☑
ShelfHeight	1' 6"	= Height / 4	☑
TrimWidth	0' 2"	=	☐
Width	4' 0"	=	☑

Figure 4–22

You can use several types of formulas with families:

Arithmetic	Basic arithmetic operations in formulas include addition (+), subtraction (-), multiplication (*), division (/), exponentiation, logarithms, and square roots.
Trigonometric	Trigonometric functions include sine, cosine, tangent, arcsine, arccosine, and arctangent.
Conditional	Conditional functions include comparisons in a condition (e.g., <, >, =, etc.) and Boolean operators with a conditional statement (e.g., AND, OR, NOT, etc.). See the Autodesk Revit Help files for more information about creating conditional statements.

- You can enter numbers as integers, decimals, or fractions. Conditional statements can include numeric values, numeric parameter names, or **Yes/No** parameters.

- Formulas are case-sensitive. Therefore, if you have created a dimension label named **Height**, ensure that the formula that uses this label also has the H capitalized (e.g., **Height * 2**).

Hint: Formulas in Projects

You can use a formula to specify the length of a wall by typing it in the temporary dimension. Start with an equal sign (e.g., =12 / 3 + 4). The example shown in Figure 4–23 returns the number 8 (interpreted as 8'-0") in the dimension. Formulas also work with numerical values in Properties.

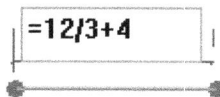

$$=12/3+4$$

Figure 4–23

Practice 4a

Set up a Bookcase Family

Practice Objectives

- Add reference planes.
- Dimension and label reference planes.
- Add a formula to a parameter.
- Flex the framework.

In this practice, you will create a family file based on a template and view the existing reference planes. You will also create reference planes, dimension them, and label the dimensions, as shown in Figure 4–24. You will add a formula to control a parameter and then test the framework by changing parameter values.

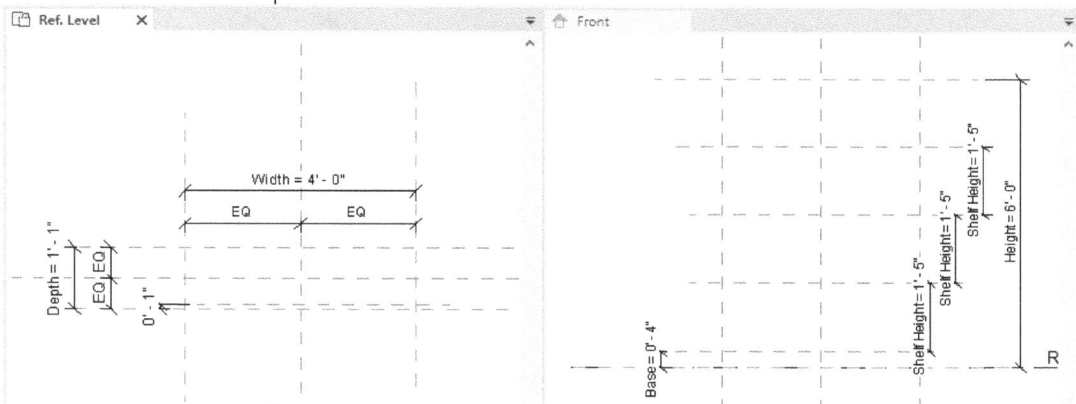

Figure 4–24

Task 1 - Open a family template.

1. Close all open projects.

2. On the Home page, under the *Families* area, click **New...**.

3. In the New Family - Select Template File dialog box, select the template **Furniture.rft** from the Revit Library and click **Open**.

4. In the *View* tab>Windows panel, click (Tile) (or type **WT**).

5. The four open views display so you can see each of them. Type **ZA** (the shortcut for **Zoom All to Fit**) to fit the view in all of the windows.

6. Two existing reference planes are included in the file, as well as **Ref.Level**.

7. Save the family in the practice files *Architectural* folder as **Barrister Bookcase.rfa**.

Task 2 - Create plan view reference planes.

---

1. Click inside the **Ref. Level** view and type **TW** to maximize the view.

2. Create four new reference planes, one on each side of the existing planes, as shown in Figure 4–25. Do not worry about the exact location yet.

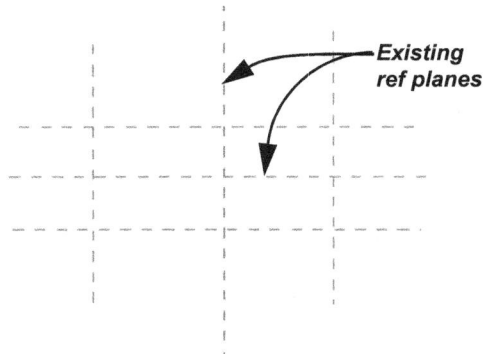

Figure 4–25

3. Add dimensions between each reference plane and across the top and side, as shown in Figure 4–26. Set the interior dimensions to **Equal**.

Your dimensions might vary depending on where you originally placed the reference planes.

Figure 4–26

4. Select the overall horizontal dimension. In the *Modify |*

Dimensions tab>Label Dimension panel, click ⬚ (Create Parameter).

5. In the Parameter Properties dialog box, in the *Parameter Data* area, ensure that **Type** is selected and then type the name **Width**. Click **OK**.

6. Repeat the process for the overall vertical dimension and name the parameter **Depth**.

7. Select the *Width* dimension and click on the text. Change it to **3'-0"**. Repeat the process and set the *Depth* to **1-'4"**, as shown in Figure 4–27.

Figure 4–27

8. Create one more horizontal reference plane **1"** inside the front reference plane and name the reference plane **Door Face**. Dimension and lock the dimension in place, as shown in Figure 4–28.

Figure 4–28

9. Flex the framework by changing the *Width* dimension to **3'-6"** and the *Depth* dimension to **1'-1"**.

10. Verify that the other reference planes have remained in place.

11. Save the family file.

Task 3 - Create front view reference planes.

1. Open the **Elevations: Front** view.

2. Create the reference planes and dimensions and label them, as shown in Figure 4–29.

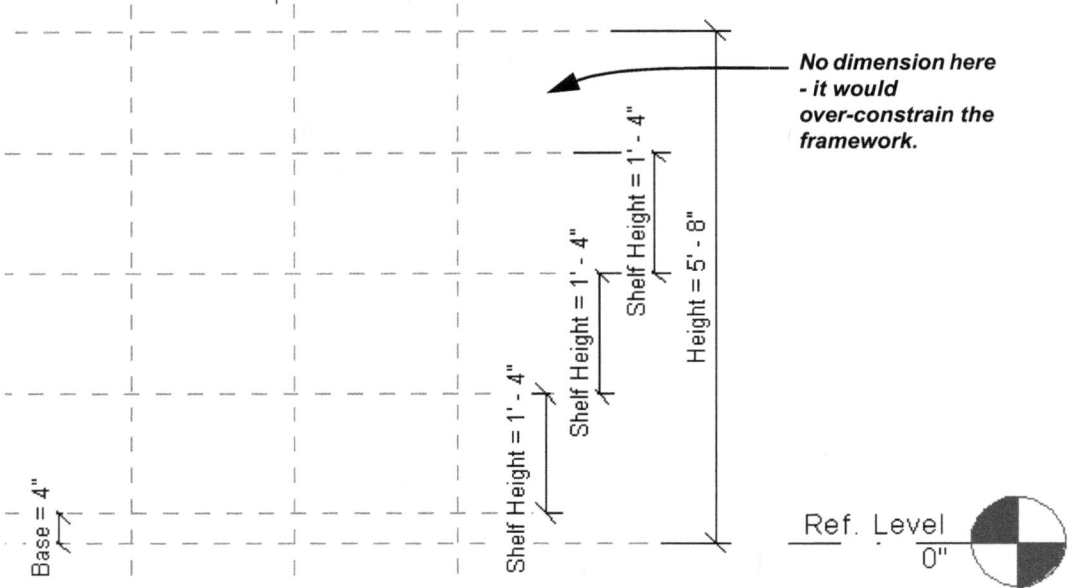

Figure 4–29

- Each of the shelf height dimensions must be separate. Once you have created one shelf height parameter, you can apply the same label to the other dimensions.

3. In the *Modify* (or *Create*) tab>Properties panel, click

   (Family Types).

The parameters automatically display in alphabetical order. You can reorganize them as required.

4. In the Family Types dialog box, set up a formula for the *Shelf Height*, as shown in Figure 4–30. Lock the **Height** parameter and the related **Base** and **Shelf Height** parameters also lock.

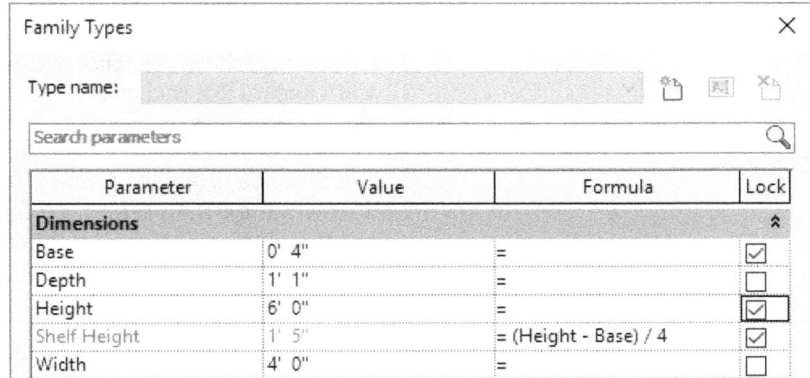

Family Types   ✕

Type name:

Search parameters 🔍

Parameter	Value	Formula	Lock
Dimensions			☆
Base	0' 4"	=	☑
Depth	1' 1"	=	☐
Height	6' 0"	=	☑
Shelf Height	1' 5"	= (Height - Base) / 4	☑
Width	4' 0"	=	☐

Figure 4–30

5. Move the dialog box to one side and try several different values. Click **Apply** to apply the changes to the family. Verify that all of the reference planes move together. Click **OK**.

6. Save and close the family file.

Practice 4b

Set up a Heat Pump Family

Practice Objectives

- Add reference planes.
- Dimension and label reference planes.
- Add a formula to a parameter.
- Flex the framework.

In this practice, you will create a family file based on a template and view the existing reference planes. You will also create reference planes, dimension them, label the dimensions, as shown in Figure 4–31, and use a formula in parameters, as shown in Figure 4–32.

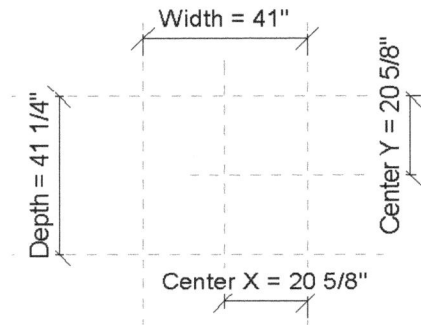

Figure 4–31

Figure 4–32

Task 1 - Open a family template.

1. Close all open projects.

2. On the Home page, under the *Families* area, click **New...**.

3. In the New Family - Select Template File dialog box, select the template **Mechanical Equipment.rft** from the Revit Library and click **Open**.

4. In the *View* tab>Windows panel, click ⊟ (Tile) or type **WT**.

5. The four open views display. Type **ZA** (the shortcut for **Zoom All to Fit**) to fit the view in all of the windows.

6. Two existing reference planes are included in the file, as well as **Ref.Level**.

7. Type **UN** to open the Project Units dialog box. Click the button under *Format* for *Length* and change the *Units* to **Fractional inches**. Then, set the *Rounding* **To the nearest 1/8"**.

Changing the units so that they display as inches makes it easier to work with the dimensions.

8. Click **OK** until all of the dialog boxes are closed. Save the family in the practice files *MEP* folder as **Heat Pump.rfa**.

Task 2 - Create plan view reference planes.

1. Click inside the **Ref. Level** view and type **TW** to maximize the view.

2. Create two new reference planes, above and to the right of the existing planes, as shown in Figure 4–33. Do not worry about the exact location yet.

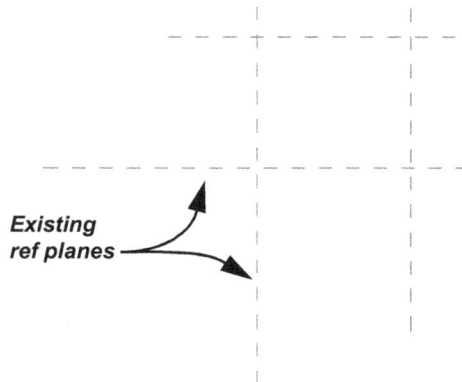

Existing ref planes

Figure 4–33

3. Add the dimensions shown in Figure 4–34.

Your dimensions might vary depending on where you originally placed the reference planes.

43 3/32"

35 7/8"

Figure 4–34

The scale in the graphics have been changed to display the dimensions more clearly.

4. Select the horizontal dimension. In the *Modify | Dimensions* tab>Label Dimension panel, click (New Parameter).

5. In the Parameter Properties dialog box, in the *Parameter Data* area, ensure that **Type** is selected and then type the name **Width**. Click **OK**.

6. Repeat the process for the overall vertical dimension and name the parameter **Depth**.

7. Add two more reference planes inside the other reference planes. Dimension and label them, as shown in Figure 4–35.

These new dimensions are not at the center of the unit but a specific distance from the right side and the top reference planes. The exact distance is not required at this time.

Width = 38 7/8"
CenterY = 17 9/16"
Depth = 34 3/4"
CenterX = 19"

Figure 4–35

8. Open the Elevations**: Front** view.

9. Create the reference planes and dimensions shown in Figure 4–36. Name the **Top of Unit** and **Top of Base** reference planes. Label the *Height* dimension and lock the **1"** and **EQ** dimensions into place.
   - Note that you might need to zoom in to do this.

1"
EQ
Height = 44 3/4"

Name: Top of Unit
(lowest of the three
reference planes)

Name: Top of Base

Ref. Level
0"

1"

Figure 4–36

10. Save the family.

Task 3 - Flex the parameters.

1. Remain in elevation view.

2. Select the **Height** parameter and change it to a different height. Verify that the top dimensions moves with the height and the bottom one stays in place.

3. Try a different height to fully check it.

4. Return to the **Floor Plans: Ref. Level** view.

5. In the *Modify* (or *Create*) tab>Properties panel, click ⊞ (Family Types).

6. In the Family Types dialog box, set up a formula for *CenterY* and *CenterX*, as shown in Figure 4–37. Lock one of the center parameters and the related parameters also lock.

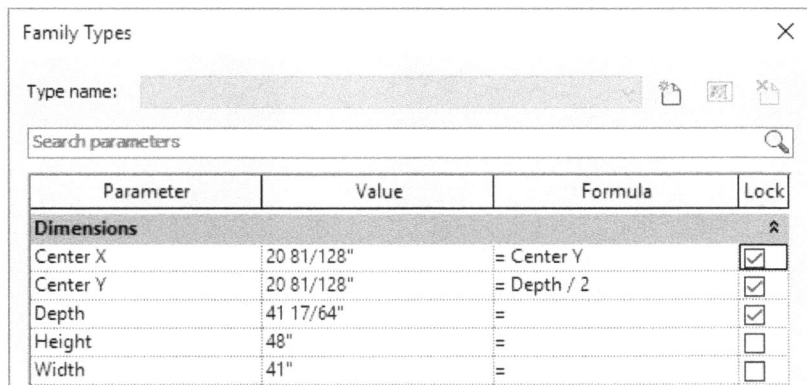

Family Types   ×

Type name: _____

Search parameters   🔍

Parameter	Value	Formula	Lock
Dimensions			☆
Center X	20 81/128"	= Center Y	☑
Center Y	20 81/128"	= Depth / 2	☑
Depth	41 17/64"	=	☑
Height	48"	=	☐
Width	41"	=	☐

Figure 4–37

7. Move the dialog box to one side and try several different values. Click **Apply** to apply the changes to the family. Verify that all of the reference planes move together. Click **OK**.

8. Save and close the family file.

Practice 4c

Set up a Structural Column Family

Practice Objectives

- Add reference planes and reference lines.
- Add dimensions and labels.
- Add a formula to a parameter.

In this practice, you will create a family file based on a template and view the existing reference planes. You will also create reference lines and reference planes, dimension them, label the dimensions, as shown in Figure 4–38, and use a formula in parameters.

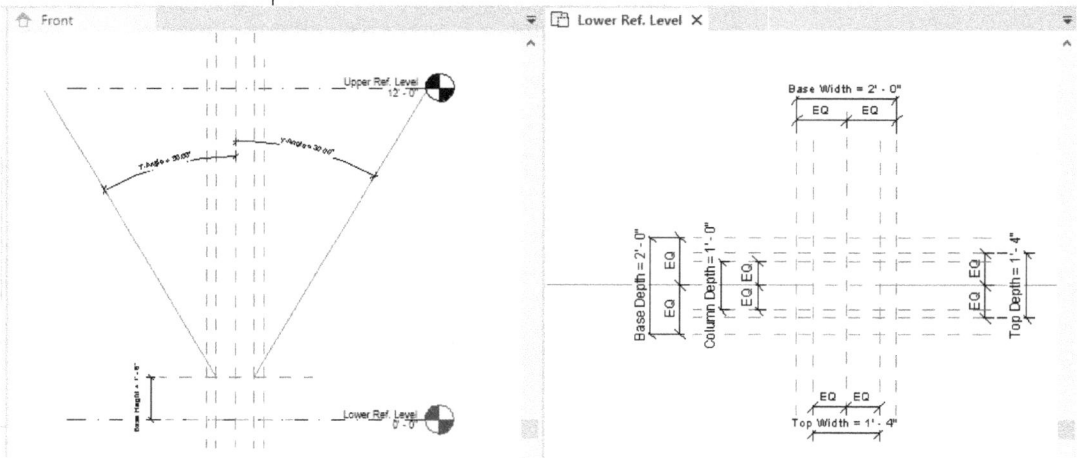

Figure 4–38

Task 1 - Open a family template.

1. Close all open projects.

2. On the Home page, under the *Families* area, click **New...**.

3. In the New Family - Select Template File dialog box, select the template **Structural Column.rft** from the Revit Library and click **Open**.

4. Open a 3D view and the **Elevations: Front** views.

5. In the *View* tab>Windows panel, click ⊟ (Tile) or type **WT**. The three open views display so you can see each of them. Type **ZA** (the shortcut for **Zoom All to Fit**) to fit the view in all of the windows.

6. Several existing reference planes and some dimensions are included in the file, as well as **Lower Ref.Level** and **Upper Ref. Level**, which set the height of the column once it is used in a project.

7. Save the family in the practice files>*Structural* folder as **Y-Column.rfa**.

Task 2 - Create reference planes.
---

1. Click inside the **Lower Ref. Level** view and type **TW** to maximize the view.

2. Add dimensions across the top and side, as shown in Figure 4–39.

Figure 4–39

3. Select the overall horizontal dimension. In the *Modify |*
   Dimensions tab>Label Dimension panel, click 🗋 (Create
   Parameter).

4. In the Parameter Properties dialog box, in the *Parameter*
   Data area, ensure that **Type** is selected and then type the
   name **Base Width**. Click **OK**.

5. Repeat the process for the overall vertical dimension and
   name the parameter **Base Depth**. The labels display as
   shown in Figure 4–40.

Figure 4–40

6. Add the additional reference planes and labeled dimensions
   shown in Figure 4–41.

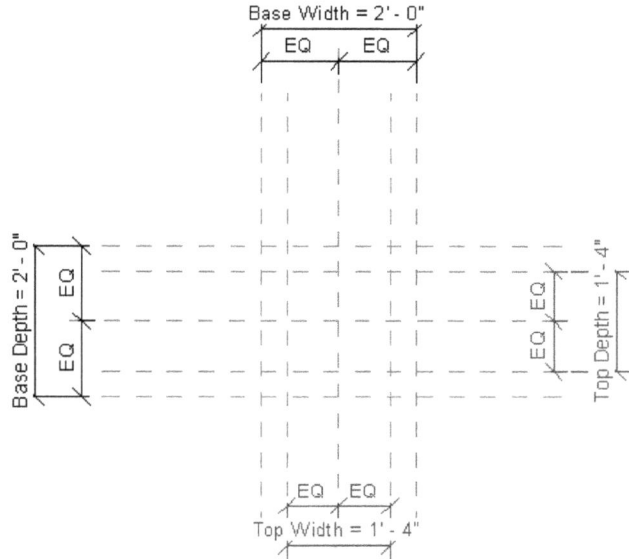

Base Width = 2' - 0"
EQ   EQ

Base Depth = 2' - 0"
EQ   EQ

Top Depth = 1' - 4"
EQ   EQ

EQ   EQ
Top Width = 1' - 4"

Figure 4–41

7. Add two more reference planes along with the dimensions and label for *Column Depth,* as shown in Figure 4–42.

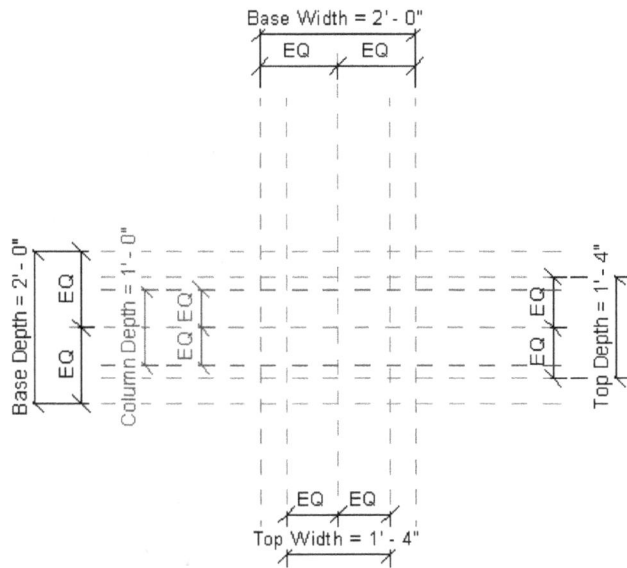

Base Width = 2' - 0"
EQ   EQ

Base Depth = 2' - 0"
EQ   EQ

Column Depth = 1' - 0"
EQ EQ

Top Depth = 1' - 4"
EQ EQ

EQ   EQ
Top Width = 1' - 4"

Figure 4–42

8. Save the family file.

Task 3 - Set up Formulas and Flex the Parametric Framework.

1. In *Create* or *Modify* tab>Properties panel, click ⊞ (Family Types).

2. In the Family Types dialog box, set the formulas as shown in Figure 4–43 and click **Apply**.

Family Types   ✕

Type name: 📄 🖼 ✕

Search parameters   🔍

Parameter	Value	Formula	Lock
Materials and Finishes			⌃
Structural Material (default)		=	
Dimensions			⌃
Base Depth	2' 0"	=	☐
Base Width	2' 0"	= Base Depth	☐
Column Depth	1' 0"	=	☐
Top Depth	1' 4"	= Base Depth / 1.5	☐
Top Width	1' 4"	= Top Depth	☐

Figure 4–43

3. Change the *Base Depth* to *3'-0"* and click **Apply**. Verify that all of the reference planes update as expected.

4. Test other sizes.

5. Change the *Base Depth* back to **2'-0"** and click **OK**.

6. Save the family.

Task 4 - Add a Parametric Framework to the Elevation view.

1. Switch to the **Elevations: Front** view.

2. Change the *Upper Ref. Level* to **12'-0"**.

3. Extend the reference planes past the upper level marker.

   - If required, to modify the **Center (Left/Right)** reference plane, click the **Prevent or allow change of element position** icon. Once you have moved it, click the icon shown in Figure 4–44 to repin it.

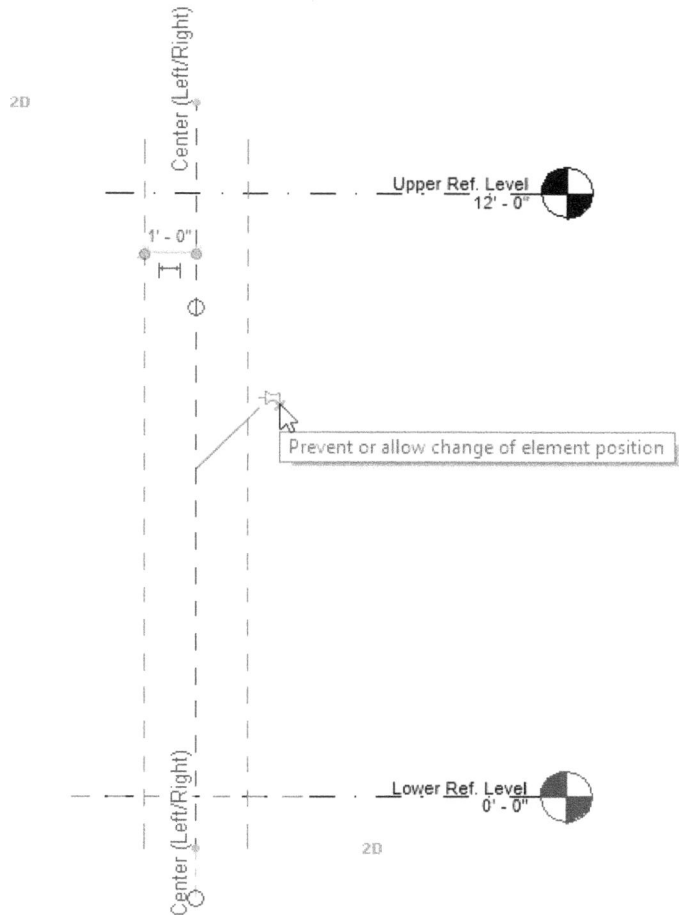

2D

Center (Left/Right)

Upper Ref. Level
12' - 0"

1' - 0"

Prevent or allow change of element position

Center (Left/Right)

Lower Ref. Level
0' - 0"

2D

Figure 4–44

4. Add a reference plane and name it **Top of Base.**

5. Dimension and label the dimension as shown in Figure 4–45.

Top of Base

Base Height = 1'- 6"

Lower Ref. Level
0' - 0"

Figure 4–45

6. In the *Create* tab>Datum panel, click ⌐ (Reference Line).

7. Draw reference line from the intersection shown in Figure 4–46 past the **Upper Ref. Level**. The exact angle does not matter at this point. Ensure that you snap to the intersections of the reference planes and lock them in place.

Upper Ref. Level
12' - 0"

Reference Line

Lock the Reference Line

Make sure you select the intersection of the ref planes

12' - 0"

Base Height= 1'- 6"

19.00°   0' - 4"

Lower Ref. Level
0' - 0"

Figure 4–46

8. Repeat the process on the other side of the center line and add angular dimensions and labels, as shown in Figure 4–47.

9. Flex the *Y-Angle* parameter and end on **30.00 (d)**.

Figure 4–47

10. Save and close the family file.

4.3 Creating Family Elements

Once parametric framework has been created, it is recommended to add actual geometry to the family file, as shown in Figure 4–48. The components in a family can include 3D solids and voids as well as 2D symbolic lines. You can also include model lines, model text, and annotation text.

Figure 4–48

Creating 3D Elements

There are five methods of creating solid forms, as shown in Figure 4–49. Each method uses a sketched 2D profile as the basis of the 3D shape.

Figure 4–49

Void forms use the same creation methods.

- **Extrusion** pushes the profile out in one direction.
- **Blend** links two profiles together.
- **Revolve** rotates the profile around an axis.
- **Sweep** extends a profile along a path.
- **Swept Blend** connects two different profiles along a path.

Hint: Selecting Void Forms

Solids and voids are considered separate categories. You can use the **Filter** command to select them separately, as shown in Figure 4–50.

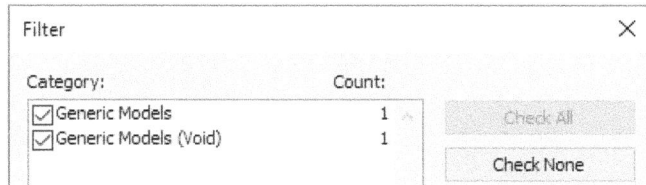

Figure 4–50

Extrusions

Extrusions are the simplest elements to create. All you need to do is draw a closed profile using Autodesk Revit sketch tools and assign a depth for the extrusion, as shown in Figure 4–51.

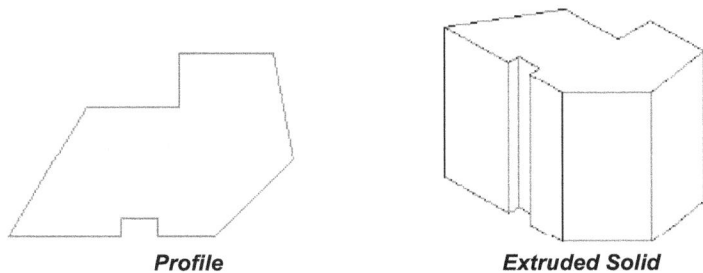

Profile   *Extruded Solid*

Figure 4–51

How To: Create Solid Extrusions

1. In the *Create* tab>Forms panel, click ⬜ (Extrusion).
2. In the Options Bar, set the *Depth* for the extrusion, as shown in Figure 4–52.

Figure 4–52

- A positive value for the depth extrudes up or toward you depending on the work plane. A negative value extrudes down or away from you.

---

3. In the *Modify | Create Extrusion* tab>Draw panel, use the sketch tools to create the profile for the extrusion. You can add dimensions and reference planes as required, to create the profile. They will not display when the extrusion is finished.

4. In the Mode panel, click ✓ (Finish Edit Mode) to create the extrusion.

5. In the *Modify | Extrusion* tab, make changes to the extrusion as required.

*By default, **Start** is at the work plane and **End** is at the depth.*

6. In Properties, you can adjust the *Extrusion Start* and *Extrusion End*, the *Visible* and *Visibility/Graphics Overrides*, and *Material.* You can also change it from a **Solid** to a **Void** or vice versa, and place it in the *Subcategory* of **Hidden Lines** or **Overhead Lines**.

- In the *Create* tab>Work Plane panel, click ⊞ (Set) to select the plane on which you want to draw a profile (e.g., on top of another extrusion).

Blends

Blends are defined by two profiles: one for the base (bottom) and one for the top. The two profiles are connected by the solid element. If the base and top do not have the same number of corners, adjust the vertex connection, as shown in Figure 4–53.

If the entire blended element is not displayed in plan view, select the View name in the Project Browser, and then in Properties, modify the View Range Cut Plane.

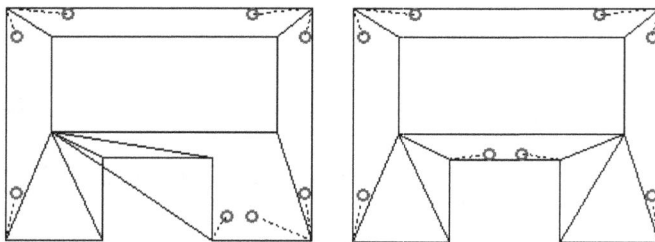

Figure 4–53

How To: Create Solid Blends

1. In the *Create* tab>Forms panel, click ⬚ (Blend).

2. In the *Modify | Create Blend Base Boundary* tab>Draw panel, use the sketch tools to draw the base profile.

3. In the Mode panel, click ⬚ (Edit Top).

4. In the Options Bar, set the *Depth* for the top.

5. Draw the top profile using the sketch tools.

6. If the intersections are complex, click 🗗 (Edit Vertices) and ensure that all of the connections work correctly.

7. Click ✓ (Finish Edit Mode) to create the blend.

8. The *Modify | Blend* tab displays, where you can edit the base or the top. You also have access to the Properties of the blend.

- When you click 🗗 (Edit Vertices), open blue dots display on the dotted lines. These lines are suggested connections. Select the dot to toggle the connection on or off, and repeat with other corners to obtain the required connections. Use the tools in the *Edit Vertices* tab>Vertex Connect panel, as shown in Figure 4–54, to modify the vertices.

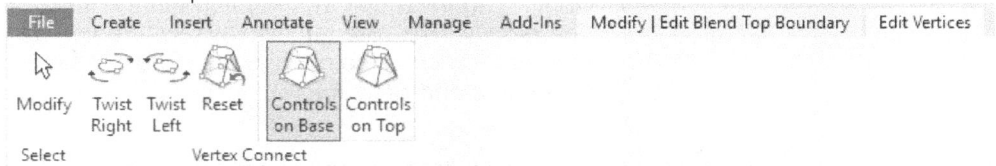

Figure 4–54

Revolves

A revolved solid form requires a profile and an axis around which it is revolved, as shown in Figure 4–55. The profile often needs to be sketched in a work plane perpendicular to the *ground*. Before sketching the profile, create a reference plane that you can use for the work plane. For example, if you are creating a dome, create two intersecting reference planes at the center of the dome and name them. Then, when you start the revolution, you can select one reference plane for your work plane and the other for your axis.

You can name a reference plane in Properties.

Profile with axis   **Revolved solid**

Figure 4–55

How To: Create Solid Revolves

1. In the *Create* tab>Forms panel, click ⬚ (Revolve).
2. In the *Modify | Create Revolve* tab>Work Plane panel, click

   ⬚ (Set). In the Work Plane dialog box, select the plane on which you want to draw the profile. A prompt warns you if you need to change views to draw in that work plane.

3. In the Draw panel, click ⬚ (Boundary Line) and draw the profile.

The axis can be an edge of the profile or some distance away if there is an opening.

4. In the Draw panel, click ⬚ (Axis Line) and draw or select the axis about which the profile will rotate.

5. Click ⬚ (Finish Edit Mode) to create the solid.
6. The *Modify | Revolve* tab displays, where you can edit the revolve. You can also change the Properties (such as the *End Angle* and *Start Angle*).

Sweeps

A sweep is similar to an extrusion. However, instead of only extruding in one direction, it follows a path that can have multiple segments, as shown in Figure 4–56. You define the path first and then create the profile on the path.

Figure 4–56

How To: Create Solid Sweeps

1. In the *Create* tab>Forms panel, click ⬚ (Sweep).

2. In the *Modify | Sweep* tab>Sweep panel, click ⬚ (Sketch Path) or ⬚ (Pick Path). Draw or select the path you want the sweep to follow.

3. Click ⬚ (Finish Edit Mode).

Click ✎ (Load Profile) to load additional profiles into the family file for use with the sweep.

4. In the Sweep panel, select a profile from the list or click ⬚ (Select Profile), and then click ✎ (Edit Profile) to sketch a profile.
   • The Go To View dialog box opens if you need to change views to draw the profile. Select the view in which you want to draw the profile and click **Open View**.
5. Draw the profile for the sweep on the profile plane, as shown in Figure 4–57.

The profile plane is automatically drawn on the first line of the path. It is the red dot with the green line through it, as shown in a 3D view in Figure 4–57. The red dot is the place where the profile and path intersect.

Figure 4–57

6. Click ✔ (Finish Edit Mode) twice to complete the process.
7. The *Modify | Sweep* tab displays, where you can edit the sweep. In Properties, you can change several options of the profile along with the other standard options.

Swept Blends

Swept blends consist of a path and two profiles, as shown in Figure 4–58. The profiles can have different shapes. The path must be one segment, which can be a line, an arc, or a spline.

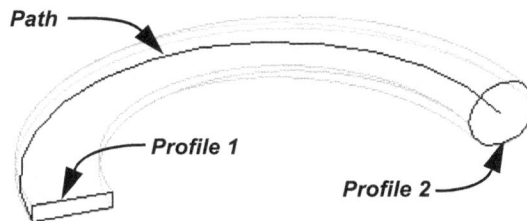

Figure 4–58

How To: Create Solid Swept Blends

1. In the *Create* tab>Forms panel, click ▱ (Swept Blend).
2. In the *Modify | Swept Blend* tab>Swept Blend panel, click ✎ (Sketch Path) or ⬚ (Pick Path). Draw or select the path you want the swept blend to follow. You can only have one segment in the path.

3. Click ✓ (Finish Edit Mode).

4. In the Swept Blend panel, click ▧ (Select Profile 1).

5. Select a profile from the list or create a new profile using

   ▧ (Edit Profile).

6. Click ▧ (Select Profile 2) and repeat the process. It does not need to be the same size or shape as the first profile.

7. In the Swept Blend panel, click ▱ (Edit Vertices) and align the vertices. This controls the twist of the swept blend.

8. Click ✓ (Finish Edit Mode).

9. In the *Modify | Swept Blend* tab, make any changes as required.

10. In Properties, set any options as required.

Aligning and Locking

It is important to lock and align sketches to reference planes (rather than other family elements) so that they can be flexed parametrically. The padlock symbol displays when you snap to reference planes while drawing. Select the padlock to lock the element to the reference plane, as shown in Figure 4–59.

Figure 4–59

- When using the ✎ (Pick Line) option, in the Options Bar, you can select **Lock** to automatically lock the sketch line to the selected reference plane.

- You can also use the **Align** command to align and lock elements to reference planes.

- You can temporarily hide other elements before sketching to ensure that you only work with the reference planes.

- Tangency Locks display when you add arcs that are tangent to other lines, as shown in Figure 4–60. Close the padlock to keep the tangency as the element is flexed.

Figure 4–60

Practice 4d

Create Family Geometry for the Bookcase

Practice Objectives

- Create solid extrusion elements.
- Align and lock the elements to reference planes.
- Join the geometry of elements.

In this practice, you will create extruded solids for the base, frame, shelves, and back of a bookcase, and lock them in place with dimensions. You will also join the solid elements together to form one unit, as shown in Figure 4–61.

Figure 4–61

Task 1 - Create a base for the bookcase.

1. In the practice files *Architectural* folder, open **Barrister-Bookcase-Geometry.rfa**.

2. Open the **Floor Plans: Ref. Level** view.

3. In the *Create* tab>Forms panel, click ▢ (Extrusion). In the Options Bar, set the *Depth* to **4"**.

4. In the *Modify | Create Extrusion* tab>Draw panel, use the sketch tools to draw a rectangle across the outside intersections of the reference planes. Lock all four lines to the reference planes, as shown in Figure 4–62.

Figure 4–62

5. Click (Finish Edit Mode).

6. Open the **Elevations: Front** view.

7. In the *Modify* tab>Modify panel, click (Align). Align the top of the extrusion to the *Base* reference plane and lock it.

8. Save the family.

Task 2 - Create the frame and shelves for the bookcase.

---

1. Continue working in the **Front** view.

2. In the *Create* tab>Work Plane panel, click (Set).

3. In the Work Plane dialog box, set the *Name* to **Reference Plane : Door Face** and click **OK**.

4. Start the **Extrusion** command.

5. Draw four reference planes inside the existing reference planes. Dimension and label them as shown in Figure 4–63.

Drawing the reference planes inside the extrusion helps to keep the primary views from getting cluttered.

Figure 4–63

- Ensure that you dimension to the reference planes and not any existing geometry.

6. In the Family Types dialog box, flex the *Height* and *Width* of the overall bookcase to verify that the new **Frame Width** parameters move as expected.

7. Return to the *Modify | Create Extrusion* tab>Draw panel and select **Rectangle**.

8. In the Options Bar, set the *Depth* to **1'-0"**.

*Hint: type **SI** to force
the snap to the
intersection of the
reference planes.*

9. Draw and lock two rectangular sketches to the reference planes, as shown in Figure 4–64.

Figure 4–64

10. Click ✓ (Finish Edit Mode).

11. Start the **Extrusion** command again.

12. Draw two reference planes on either side of the shelf height reference plane. Dimension and label them as shown in Figure 4–65. Repeat with the other two shelf height locations.

Figure 4–65

- To make the labels more readable, change the scale to **1"=1'-0"**. You can also create an additional dimension type with the *Read Convention* set to **Horizontal** and use it for the **Shelf** parameters, as shown in Figure 4–65.

13. In the *Modify | Create Extrusion* tab>Draw panel, select **Rectangle**.

14. In the Options Bar, ensure that the *Depth* is set to **1'-0"**.

15. Draw the sketch around each shelf, as shown in Figure 4–66. Ensure that you lock the sketches to the reference planes.

Figure 4–66

16. Click ✓ (Finish Edit Mode).

17. Open the Family Types dialog box and move the *Height*, *Width*, and *Depth* to the top of the parameters list.

18. Flex the *Height* and *Width* of the overall bookcase to verify the new **Shelf Thickness** parameters move as expected. Finish the flexing with the *Height* set to **5'-0"** and the *Width* to **3'-0"**.

19. Save the family.

Task 3 - Create the back of the bookcase.

1. Open the **Elevations: Left** view.

2. Align and lock the back of the frame and shelf extrusions to the back reference plane (on the left).

3. Open the **Floor Plans: Ref. Level** view.

4. Start the **Extrusion** command again.

5. Add a reference plane **1/4"** from the back of the bookcase. Dimension it as shown in Figure 4–67 and lock the dimension in place.

Create a label if you want to change the size of the back.

Figure 4–67

6. Return to the *Modify | Create Extrusion* tab and select **Rectangle**.

7. In the Options Bar, set the *Depth* to **2'-6"**. (This is less than the bookcase height. You will adjust it later.)

8. Draw a rectangular sketch across the back and lock it to the reference planes., as shown in Figure 4–68.

Figure 4–68

9. Click ✓ (Finish Edit Mode).

10. Open the **Elevations: Left** view. Switch the **Visual Style** to
    ⬡ (Hidden Line). The back extrusion is shown in
    Figure 4–69.

11. Align and lock the top of the back panel with the top reference
    plane, as shown in Figure 4–70.

Figure 4–69

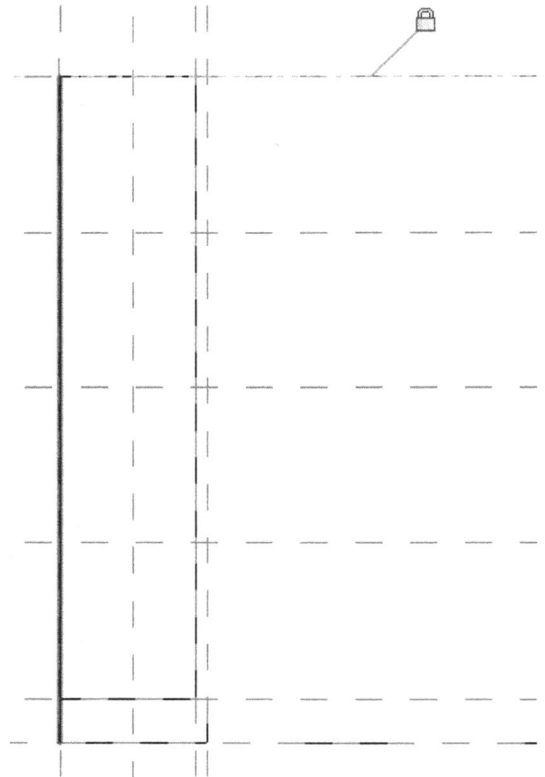

Figure 4–70

12. Switch to a 3D view. Set the *Visual Style* to **Hidden Lines** and rotate it as required. The base, frame, shelves, and back are all separate elements, as shown in Figure 4–71.

13. In the *Modify* tab>Geometry panel, click ⬚ (Join) and join the four elements. The bookcase should display as shown in Figure 4–72.

Figure 4–71

Figure 4–72

14. Save and close the family.

Practice 4e

Create Family Geometry for the Heat Pump

Practice Objective

- Create extrusions and blends.

In this practice, you will create extruded and blended solids for the base, cabinet, top, and fan unit of a heat pump, as shown in Figure 4–73.

Figure 4–73

Task 1 - Create the main cabinet of a heat pump.

1. In the practice files *MEP* folder, open **Heat-Pump-Geometry.rfa.**

2. Ensure that the **Floor Plans: Ref. Level** view is open.

3. Add four reference planes 3" to the inside of each exterior reference plane. Dimension and lock the dimensions into place, as shown in Figure 4–74.

4. In the *Create* tab>Datum panel, click (Reference Line).

5. In the Options Bar, toggle off **Chain**, if required.

6. Draw a reference line at each of the four corners, as shown in Figure 4–74. Ensure that you lock any open padlocks that display as you draw each line.

Figure 4–74

7. Flex the framework by changing the *Width* and *Depth*.

8. In the *Create* tab>Work Plane panel, click ⬚ (Set).

9. In the Work Plane dialog box, set *Name* as **Reference Plane : Top of Base** and click **OK**.

10. In the *Create* tab>Forms panel, click ⬚ (Extrusion). In the Options Bar, set the *Depth* to **30"**.

11. Sketch and lock the shape to the reference lines shown in Figure 4–75. (**Hint:** Use **Pick Lines** with the **Lock** option set and then trim the excess, as required.)

Figure 4–75

12. Click ✔ (Finish Edit Mode).

13. Open the **Elevations: Front** view. Align and lock the top of the unit extrusion to the **Top of Unit** reference plane, as shown in Figure 4–76.

Figure 4–76

14. Save the family.

Task 2 - Create the top and base of the heat pump.

1. Return to the **Floor Plans: Ref. Level** view.

2. Use **Temporary Hide/Isolate** to hide the existing extrusion.

3. Set the Work Plane to the **Top of Unit** reference plane.

4. In the *Create* tab>Forms panel, click ⬙ (Blend).

5. In the *Modify | Create Blend Base Boundary* tab>Draw panel, click ⬩ (Pick Lines).

6. In the Options Bar, set the *Depth* to **1/2"**, and the *Offset* to **1"**.

7. Position the offset inside the reference planes and click on the outer-most reference planes and reference lines. Use **Trim/Extend to Corner** to clean up the sketch for the base, as shown in Figure 4–77.

8. Click ⬙ (Edit Top). Select **Pick Lines**, and then set the *Depth* to **1/2"** and the *Offset* to **1-1/2"**.

9. Use and trim the same reference planes and reference lines to create a sketch for the top, as shown in Figure 4–77.

Using reference planes to establish the sketch of the blend, rather than other elements, ensures the accuracy of the elements.

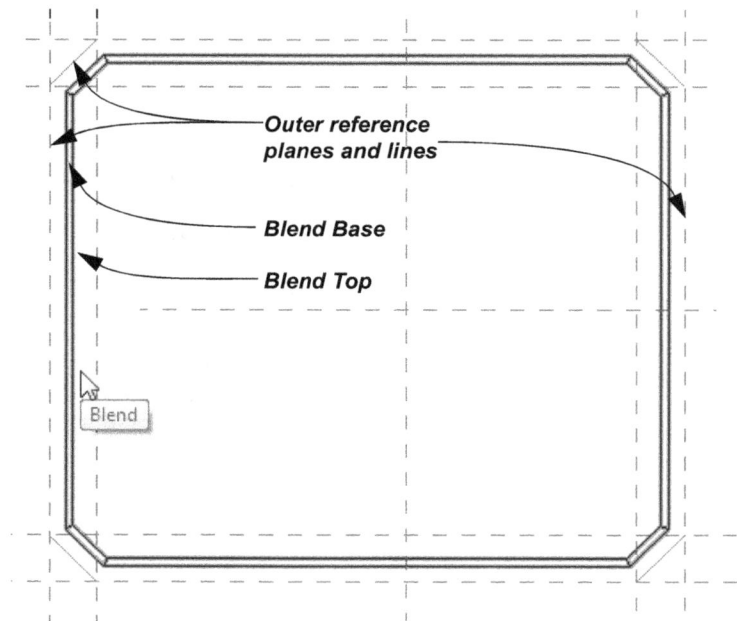

Outer reference planes and lines

Blend Base

Blend Top

Blend

Figure 4–77

10. Click ✔ (Finish Edit Mode).

11. Flex the framework to ensure that the blend is working.

12. Return to the **Floor Plans: Ref. Level** view, if you switched to a 3D view.

13. Use **Temporary Hide/Isolate** to hide the existing blend.

14. Set the *Work Plane* to **Level: Ref. Level**.

15. In the *Create* tab>Forms panel, click ⬚ (Extrusion). In the Options Bar, set the *Depth* to **1"**.

16. In the *Modify | Create Extrusion* tab>Draw panel, use the **Pick Lines** tool to draw a boundary at **1/2"** inside the unit reference planes, as shown in Figure 4–78.

Figure 4–78

17. Click ✔ (Finish Edit Mode).

18. Reset Temporary Hide/Isolate.

19. Open the **Elevations: Front** view.

20. Temporarily hide the main cabinet extrusion.

21. In the *Modify* tab>Modify panel, click ⬜ (Align) and align the top of the base extrusion to the *Top of Base* reference plane and lock it, as shown in Figure 4–79.

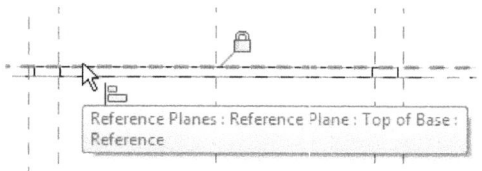

Reference Planes : Reference Plane : Top of Base : Reference

Figure 4–79

22. Reset Temporary Hide/Isolate.

23. Open a 3D view.

24. Open the Family Types dialog box and reorder the parameters so that *Width*, *Height,* and *Depth* are at the top.

25. Flex the dimensions to check that everything is working as expected. If one of the solid elements is not working as expected, check all of the alignments to ensure that they are locked in place.

26. Save the family.

Task 3 - Add the fan.

---

1. Return to the **Floor Plans: Ref. Level** view.

2. Set the Work Plane to the **Top of Unit** reference plane.

3. Start the **Extrusion** command and in the Options Bar, set the *Depth* to **1"**.

4. Draw a circle from the intersection of the CenterX and CenterY reference planes with a radius close to the outside, as shown in Figure 4–80. The exact dimension does not matter for this step.

Figure 4–80

5. Dimension the radius of the circle and create a new Label based on the dimension named **Radius of Fan**.

6. Open the Family Types dialog box and move the **Radius of Fan** parameter below all of the others.

7. Next to **Radius of Fan**, in the *Formula* area, type **Depth / 2 - 1"**.

8. Click **Apply**.

9. Flex the element by changing the *Depth*. When it works as expected, click **OK**.

10. Click ✓ (Finish Edit Mode).

11. Open the **Elevations: Front** view. Align and lock the top of the fan to the top reference plane (as shown in Figure 4–81), and the bottom of the fan to the **Top of Unit** reference plane.

Top reference plane   *Top of Unit reference plane*

Figure 4–81

12. In the *Modify* tab>Geometry panel, click (Join).

13. Join the unit and the beveled blend together. Then join the fan to the unit and the base to the unit.

14. View the unit in 3D, as shown in Figure 4–82.

Figure 4–82

15. Save and close the family file.

Practice 4f

Create Family Geometry for the Structural Column

Practice Objectives

- Create a blend and an extrusion.
- Add dimensions and labels.

In this practice, you will create a blended extruded solid for the base and an extruded Y-framework of the column. You will lock the geometry to the reference planes and lines and flex the parameters of the column. The final version is shown in Figure 4–83.

Figure 4–83

Task 1 - Create a base for the column.

1. In the practice files *Structural* folder, open **Y-Column-Geometry.rfa**.

2. Open the **Floor Plans: Lower Ref. Level** view.

3. In the *Create* tab>Forms panel, click ⬙ (Blend). In the Options Bar, set the *Depth* as **1'-0**.

4. Use the **Rectangle** option to add and lock the sketch based on the *Base Width* and *Depth*, as shown in Figure 4–84.

Figure 4–84

5. In the *Modify | Create Blend Base Boundary* tab>Mode panel, click (Edit Top).

6. In the Work Plane panel, click ⊞ (Set).

7. In the Work Plane dialog box, select **Reference Plane: Top of Base**, as shown in Figure 4–85. Click **OK**.

Figure 4–85

8. Sketch and lock a rectangle based on the *Top Depth* and *Width*, as shown in Figure 4–86.

Figure 4–86

9. Click ✓ (Finish Edit Mode).

10. Open the **Elevations: Front** view.

11. Set the *Visual Style* to **Shaded**.

12. In the *Modify* tab>Modify panel, click ⬜ (Align). Align the top of the blend to the **Top of Base** reference plane (as shown in Figure 4–87) and lock it.

Base Height = 1' - 6"

Reference Planes : Reference Plane : Top of Base : Reference

Figure 4–87

13. Save the family.

Task 2 - Create the Y-frame for the column.

1. Continue working in the **Elevations: Front** view.

2. Temporarily hide the base blend element.

3. Add two reference planes, as shown in Figure 4–88. To create the reference planes, select the **Pick Line** tool and in the Options Bar, set the *Offset* to **1'-0"** and select **Lock**. Then click on the angled reference lines.

4. Add the angled dimensions above the previous angled dimension. Then, apply labels as shown in Figure 4–88. Assign the labels one at a time. If you try to do both of them at the same time the ref planes will move unexpectedly. Undo and try again.

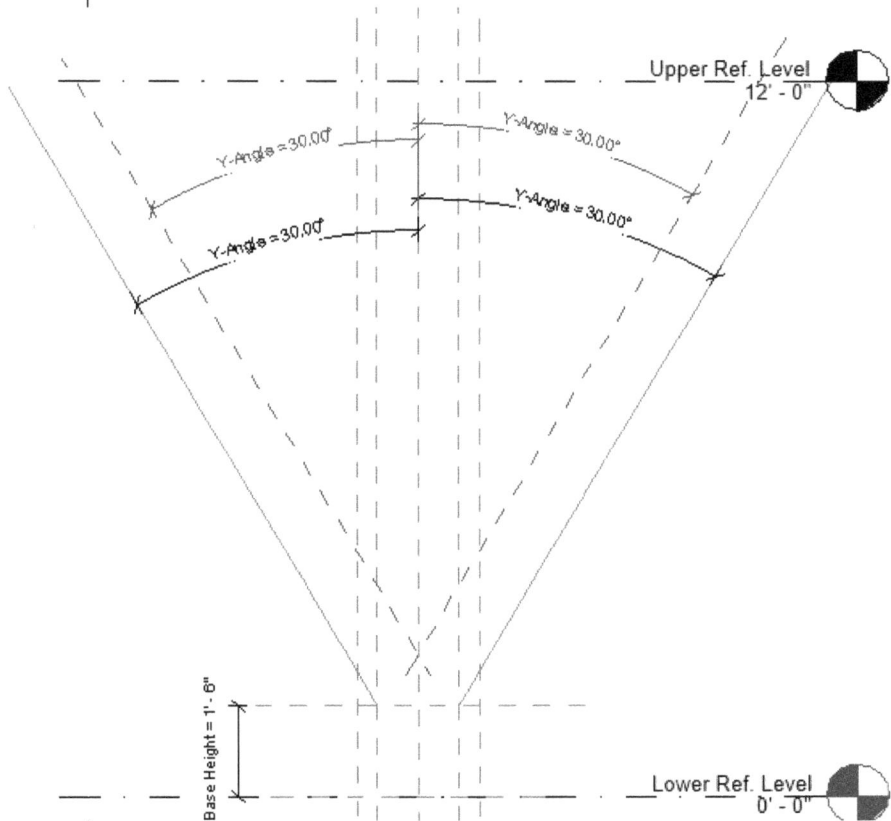

Figure 4–88

5. Flex the *Y-Angle* parameter and finish by setting the angle to **30.00°**.

6. Start the **Extrusion** command.

7. Draw the sketch shown in Figure 4–89 using the following instructions:

   - Use ⬉ (Pick Lines) and in the Options Bar, select **Lock**.

   - Use ⬌ (Split Element) and ⬚ (Trim Element) to create the lines, as required.
   - Ensure that the sketch is completely closed.

Figure 4–89

8. Click ✔ (Finish Edit Mode).

9. Flex the Y-Angle again to verify that the extrusion is moving with the angles.

10. Open the **Floor Plans: Lower Ref. Level** view.

11. Set the *Visual Style* to **Shaded**.

12. Align and lock the extrusion to the reference planes defined by the *Column Depth*, as shown in Figure 4–90.

Figure 4–90

13. Open the **3D Views: View 1** view.

14. Set the *Visual Style* to **Shaded**.

15. Rotate the view so you can see the Y framework.

16. Save and close the family.

4.4 Creating Family Types

An important aspect of Family Types is that it helps you *flex* or test the parametric dimensions you set up, as well as helps you create formulas for parameters. A further use for Family Types is the ability to create preset sizes for insertion into a project. When you select the related command, the types display in the Type Selector, as shown in Figure 4–91 for a desk component.

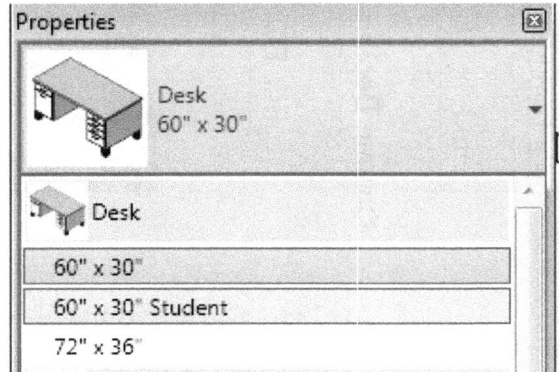

Figure 4–91

How To: Create Family Types

1. In the Family Editor, in the *Create* or *Modify* tab>Properties panel, click ⊞ (Family Types).

2. At the top of the Family Types dialog box, click 🗋 (New Type), as shown Figure 4–92.

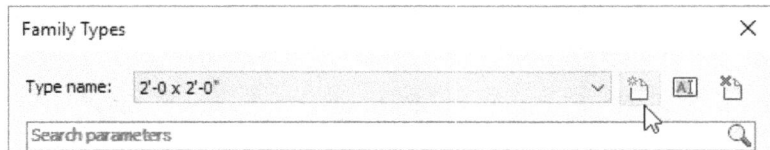

Figure 4–92

- You can type a part or all of a parameter's name to limit the number of parameters that display. This enables you to modify the values more quickly.

3. In the Name dialog box, type a name for the Family Type (as shown in Figure 4–93) and click **OK**.

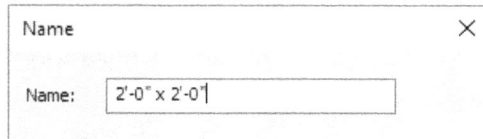

Name	×
Name:	2'-0" x 2'-0"

Figure 4–93

- Select a name that is useful for the entire set of types, typically a size.
- The name of the family always precedes the name of the type. Therefore, you do not need to re-enter that information.

4. In the Family Types dialog box, set the *Value(s)* for that size (as shown in Figure 4–94) and click **Apply**.

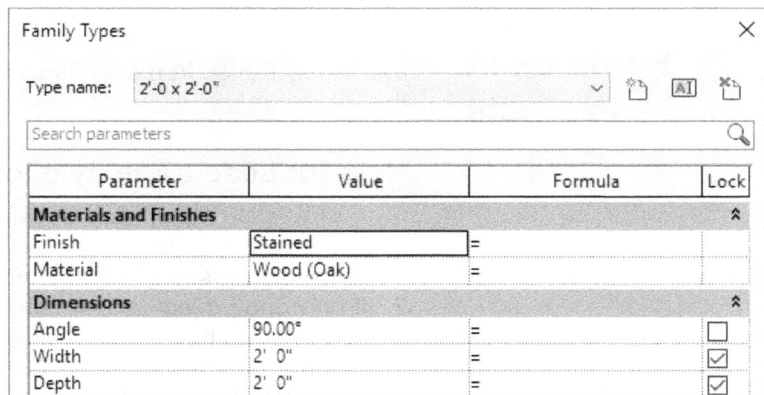

Family Types   ×

Type name: 2'-0 x 2'-0"   ⌄   ⊡ AI ⊠

Search parameters   ⚲

Parameter	Value	Formula	Lock
Materials and Finishes			☆
Finish	Stained	=	
Material	Wood (Oak)	=	
Dimensions			☆
Angle	90.00°	=	☐
Width	2' 0"	=	☑
Depth	2' 0"	=	☑

Figure 4–94

5. Repeat the process. You can create as many different types as you need.
6. Verify that all of the types are functioning correctly.
7. Click **OK** to finish the command.
8. Save the family.
9. Load the family into a test project and test the new types you have created.

- In the *Family Types* area, click AI (Rename Type) and ⊠ (Delete Type) as required, to modify the list.

- To edit a type, select the type name, change the value(s), and click **Apply**.

Hint: Exporting and Importing Family Types

Family Types can be exported to a text file and then imported into a related family. This can save you time when creating different versions of the same basic category.

- In the *File* tab, expand ⬒ (Export), scroll down and click ⊞ (Family Types). In the Export As dialog box, select a location and name. Click **Save**.

- In the *Insert* tab>Import panel, click ⊞ (Import Family Types). In the Import Family Types dialog box, select the required text file, and click **Open**.

Working with Families in Projects

To continue testing your family, it helps to see how it works in a project. You can load a family into one or more projects while in the Family Editor. You must have a project open before doing this.

How To: Load a Family into a Project

1. In the Family Editor panel, click 🗔 (Load into Project). The panel displays in all of the Family Editor tabs.
2. If only one project is open, the family is automatically loaded into it. If you have more than one project open, the Load into Projects dialog box opens. Select the project(s) to load into, as shown in Figure 4–95.

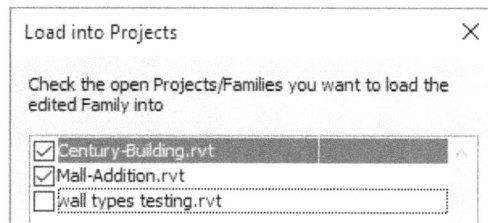

Load into Projects

Check the open Projects/Families you want to load the edited Family into

☑ Century-Building.rvt
☑ Mall-Addition.rvt
☐ wall types testing.rvt

Figure 4–95

3. The project opens with the family loaded. Often, the related command is started with the new family selected in the Type Selector.

- If you have finished working on the family you can click 🗔 (Load into Project and Close).

Practice 4g

Create Family Types for the Bookcase

Practice Objectives

- Create family types of different sizes.
- Test the family in a project.

In this practice, you will create Family Types for different sizes of the bookcase. Your will then test the bookcase family in a project by placing each of the different types, as shown in Figure 4–96.

Figure 4–96

Task 1 - Create Family Types.

1. In the practice files *Architectural* folder, open **Barristers-Bookcase-Types.rvt**.

2. In the *Create* or *Modify* tab>Properties panel, click (Family Types).

3. In the Family Types dialog box, click (New Type).

4. In the Name dialog box, type **3'-0" x 5'-0"** and click **OK**.

5. In the *Dimensions* area, verify or set the following values for the parameters as shown in Figure 4–97:

- *Width:* **3'-0"**
- *Height:* **5'-0"**
- *Depth:* **1'-1"**
- *Base:* **4"**

Figure 4–97

6. Click **Apply**.

7. Repeat these steps for the following sizes:

- **3'-0" x 6'-0"**
- **3'-6" x 5'-0"**
- **3'-6" x 6'-0"**

8. In the Family Types dialog box, test each of the new named types.

9. Click **OK**.

10. Save the family.

Task 2 - Use the family in a project.

1. In the practice files *Architectural* folder, open
   Barristers-Bookcase-Project.rvt.

2. Switch to one of the Bookcase family views.

3. In the Family Editor panel, click (Load into Project).
   - If there is only one project open, the family file is
     automatically loaded into that project.
   - If more than one project is open, the Load into Projects
     dialog box opens. Select the project you want to load and
     click **OK**.

4. The **Component** command is automatically started with the
   Barristers Bookcase family selected.

5. Place one of each type in the project.

6. Create a 3D view to see the differences.

7. Save and close the project and family files.

Practice 4h	# Create Family Types for the Heat Pump

Practice Objectives

- Create family types of different sizes.
- Test the family in a project.

In this practice, you will create and apply Family Types of different sizes to a heat pump and test the family in a project, as shown in Figure 4–98.

Figure 4–98

Task 1 - Create Family Types.

1. In the practice files *MEP* folder, open **Heat-Pump-Types.rfa**

2. In the *Create* tab>Properties panel, click ⊞ (Family Types).

3. In the Family Types dialog box, click ⬜ (New Type).

4. In the Name dialog box, type **HP060C** as the name.

5. In the *Dimensions* area, verify or set the following values for the parameters, as shown in Figure 4–99:

- *Width:* **38 7/8"**
- *Height:* **44 3/4"**
- *Depth:* **34 3/4"**

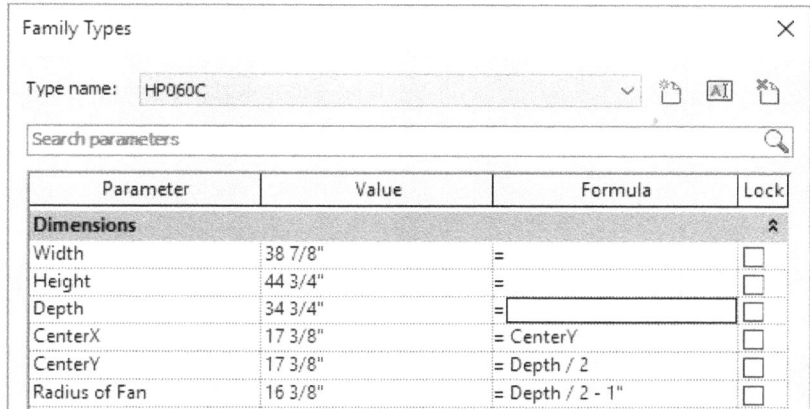

Figure 4–99

6. Click **Apply**. The family resizes to match the new information.

7. Create the other models as follows:

Model	Width	Height	Depth
HP048C	38 7/8"	37"	34 3/4"
HP030C	32 7/8"	32 3/4"	28 3/4"
HP024C	32 7/8"	28 5/8"	28 3/4"

8. In the Family Types dialog box, test the family types by selecting the *Name* and clicking **Apply** after each selection.

9. Click **OK**.

10. Save the family.

Task 2 - Use the family in a project.

1. In the practice files *MEP* folder, open **Heat-Pump-Project.rvt**.

2. Switch to one of the Heat Pump family views.

3. In the Family Editor panel, click (Load into Project).
   - If there is only one project open, the family file is automatically loaded into that project.
   - If more than one project is open, the Load into Projects dialog box opens. Select the project you want to load and click **OK**.

4. The **Component** command is automatically started with the new family selected.

5. Place one of each type in the project.

6. Create a 3D view to see the differences

7. Save and close the project and the family files.

Practice 4i

Create Family Types for the Structural Column

Practice Objectives

- Create family types.
- Use the family in a project.

In this practice, you will create and apply Family Types for the column. You will add the column family to a project and test the columns by modifying levels, as shown in Figure 4–100.

Figure 4–100

Task 1 - Create Family Types.

1. In the practice files *Structural* folder, open **Y-Column-Types.rfa**.

2. In the *Create* or *Modify* tab>Properties panel, click ⊞ (Family Types).

3. In the Family Types dialog box, click ▢ (New Type).

4. In the Name dialog box, set the name as **Over 12'-0"** and click **OK**.

5. In the *Dimensions* area, set the *Base Depth* to **3'-0"**.

6. Click **Apply**.

7. Create another new Family Type with the name **Under 12'-0"**.

8. In the *Dimensions* area, set the *Base Depth* to **2'-0"**.

9. Click **OK**.

10. Save the family.

Task 2 - Use the family in a project.

1. In the practice files *Structural* folder, open **Y-Column-Project.rvt**

2. Open the **Structural Plans: Level 2** view.

3. Switch to the Y-column family view.

4. In the Family Editor panel, click ⬆ (Load into Project).
   - If there is only one project open, the family file is automatically loaded into that project.
   - If more than one project is open, the Load into Projects dialog box opens. Select the project you want to load and click **OK**.

5. The **Structural Column** command is automatically started with the Y-Column family selected. Verify that

   ⬍ (Vertical Column) is selected.

6. Place one of each type in the project using the default information.

Change the Top Level first, so that the column does not go in the wrong direction.

7. Open the **Elevations: South** view.

8. Select the **Under 12'-0"** column. In Properties, set the *Top Level* to **Level 2,** the *Top Offset* to (negative) **-6",** and the *Base Level* to **Level 1** with no *Base Offset*.

9. Select the **Over 12'-0"** column. In Properties, set the *Top Level* to **Level 3**, the *Top Offset* to (negative) **-6"**, and the *Base Level* to **Level 1** with no *Base Offset*, as shown in Figure 4–101.

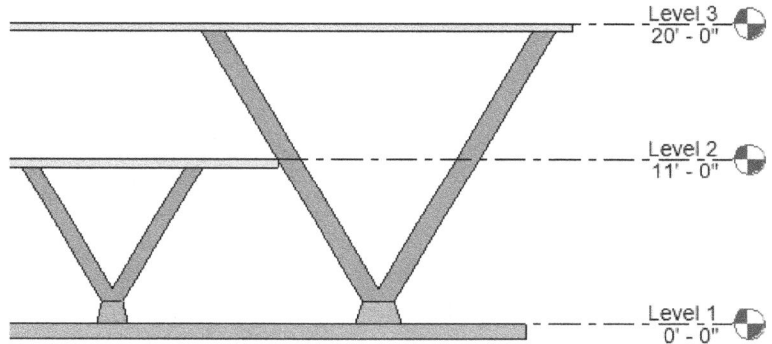

Figure 4–101

10. Change the height of the levels to see how the look of the column changes.

11. Save and close the project and the family files.

Chapter Review Questions

1. In which of the following views do the Reference planes, as shown in Figure 4–102, display? (Select all that apply.)

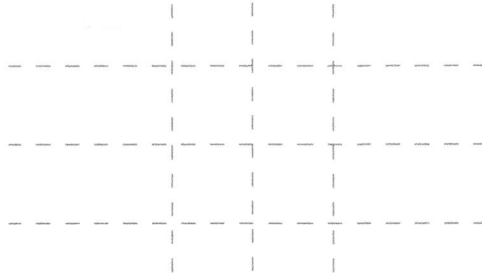

Figure 4–102

   a. Plan

   b. Elevation

   c. 3D

   d. Section

2. Which of the following is created when you label a dimension?

   a. Family

   b. Type

   c. Parameter

   d. Value

3. Which of the following commands, shown in Figure 4–103, require profiles instead of sketches? (Select all that apply.)

Extrusion Blend Revolve Sweep Swept Blend

Forms

Figure 4–103

   a. **Extrusion**

   b. **Blend**

   c. **Revolve**

   d. **Sweep**

   e. **Swept Blend**

4. Which of the following commands creates the element shown in Figure 4–104?

Figure 4–104

   a. **Extrusion**

   b. **Blend**

   c. **Revolve**

   d. **Sweep**

   e. **Swept Blend**

5. In which dialog box do you specify sizes for component types?

   a. Family Editor

   b. Family Types

   c. Family Categories

   d. Family Properties

Command Summary

Button	Command	Location
Forms		
	Blend	• **Ribbon**: *Create* tab>Forms panel
	Extrusion	• **Ribbon**: *Create* tab>Forms panel
	Revolve	• **Ribbon**: *Create* tab>Forms panel
	Sweep	• **Ribbon**: *Create* tab>Forms panel
	Swept Blend	• **Ribbon**: *Create* tab>Forms panel
	Void Forms	• **Ribbon**: *Create* tab>Forms panel
Other Tools		
	Align	• **Ribbon**: *Modify* tab>Modify panel
	Family Types	• **Ribbon**: *Create* or *Modify* tab> Properties panel
	Load Family	• **Ribbon**: *Insert* tab>Load from Library panel
	Load into Project	• **Ribbon**: *all tabs*>Family Editor panel
Reference and Work Plane		
	Reference Line	• **Ribbon**: *Create tab*>Datum panel
	Reference Plane	• **Ribbon**: *Create* tab>Datum panel
	Set	• **Ribbon**: *Create* tab>Work Plane panel

Advanced Family Techniques

Once you have created basic families with parametric framework, geometry, and family types, you can enhance the families with additional parameters, elements and settings. Possible enhancements include controls for flipping the family, or connectors for MEP system elements. You can also nest families into other families, and then coordinate the parameters between the two. Visibility Display settings enable you to specify the elements you want to display at various Detail Levels.

Learning Objectives in this Chapter

- Add controls, room calculation points, connectors, and openings.
- Insert components and associate the parameters.
- Control the display of elements in views at various detail levels using visibility settings.
- Create masking regions to block elements that would otherwise display through a family.
- Add Model and Symbolic lines.

5.1 Additional Tools for Families

Once you have created the basic framework of your family, added solid elements, established family types and tested it in a project, you can start to add items that will make the family even more powerful. Some family-specific functions include the following:

- Controls that flip and mirror the family.

- A room calculation point that makes a family room-aware.

- Connectors (MEP elements only) that contain information such as pipe or duct size and electrical currents.

- Openings in a host, such as a wall or ceiling.

- Nested families made of multiple families as shown in Figure 5–1.

Figure 5–1

Adding Controls

You can place control arrows to flip or mirror geometry in the family, as shown in Figure 5–2. The controls also display on doors and other elements. Some family templates already include controls and you can add others.

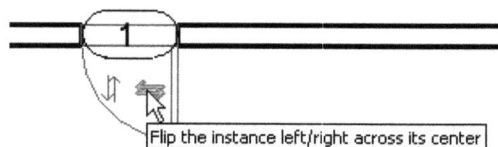

Figure 5–2

How To: Add Controls

1. In the *Create* tab>Control panel, click ⌖ (Control).
2. In the *Modify | Place Control* tab>Control Type panel, click one of the following controls:

    • ⌓ (Single Vertical)

    • ⌰ (Single Horizontal)

    • ⥮ (Double Vertical)

    • ⥃ (Double Horizontal)

3. Click on the screen to place the control in the view. Move the controls once you have placed them, as required.

Setting Room Calculation Points

Some families (e.g., lighting fixtures, specialty equipment, casework, furniture, etc.) can be placed so that the default center of the element is not in the room where it needs to be counted, as shown in Figure 5–3. You can adjust this by modifying the Room Calculation Point, making the family a room-aware family.

Before room calculation point

	<Furniture Schedule>		
A	B	C	D
Family and Type	Room: Number	Room: Name	Count
Sofa-Pensi	101	Lobby	1
Sofa-Pensi	102	Seating	1
Grand total: 2			

After room calculation point

	<Furniture Schedule>		
A	B	C	D
Family and Type	Room: Number	Room: Name	Count
Sofa-Pensi	102	Seating	2
Grand total: 2			

Figure 5–3

• Room Calculation Points must be set in the family.

How To: Set a Room Calculation Point

1. Open the Family file.
2. In Properties, select Room Calculation Point, as shown on the left in Figure 5–4.
3. Move the room calculation point to the required location, as shown on the right in Figure 5–5.

Figure 5–4

Figure 5–5

4. Save and load (or reload) the family file into the project.

Adding Connectors

In MEP families there is an additional option for creating connectors for the various systems. For example, you can add a duct connector to an air terminal where the duct element attaches to the air terminal, as shown in Figure 5–6.

Figure 5–6

- If you are using imported 3D shapes in a family, you can place connectors on the geometry.

These tools are found on the *Create* tab>Connectors panel, as shown in Figure 5–7.

Figure 5–7

How To: Add a Connector

1. In the *Create* tab>Connectors panel, select the type of connector you want to use.
2. In the Options Bar, specify the type of connector (if applicable), as shown for an electrical connector in Figure 5–8.

Figure 5–8

3. In the *Modify | Place Connector* tab>Placement panel, click

   (Face) or (Work Plane).
4. Select a face or workplane that matches the location and direction of the connector.
5. Select the connector and make any required adjustments in Properties.

Adding Openings

The **Opening** command enables you to sketch an opening in a host element. You need to have started the family using one of the host-based templates.

How To: Add an Opening to a Host Element

1. In the *Create* tab>Model panel, click ▢ (Opening).
2. In the *Modify | Create Opening Boundary* tab>Draw panel, use the sketch tools to create the opening. Use reference planes and dimensions as required.

3. Click ✓ (Finish Edit Mode).
4. In the *Modify | Opening cut* tab, make changes as required.
5. In the Options Bar, select when you want the cut to display transparently (in **3D**, **Elevation**, or both), as shown in Figure 5–9.

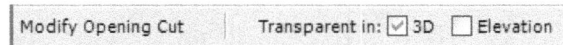

| Modify Opening Cut | Transparent in: ☑ 3D ☐ Elevation |

Figure 5–9

Adding Components

Adding a component to a family produces a nested family. In most cases, you want to do this with elements that are used multiple times in other families, such as the hardware shown in Figure 5–10.

Figure 5–10

- Nesting families increase the file size and can impact your computer's performance.

- There are two types of components:

  - ▱ **(Component):** In the *Create* tab>Model panel. places model components that display in all views.

  - ▱ **(Detail Component):** In the *Annotate* tab>Detail panel, places detail components that display only in the current view.

Associating Family Parameters

When you are working with nested families, you might need to associate parameters in the host family with the inserted family. Other types of parameters can also be associated.

How To: Associate Family Parameters

1. Select the element(s) whose parameters need to be associated.
2. In Properties, in the row where you want to connect the parameters, click ⬛ (Associate Family Parameter), as shown in Figure 5–11.

Figure 5–11

3. In the Associate Family Parameter dialog box, select the related parameter, as shown in Figure 5–12. Click **OK**.

Type part of the parameter name in the search box to speed up selection.

Figure 5–12

• The parameter is now grayed out and marked with the **=** sign, as shown in Figure 5–13.

Figure 5–13

Practice 5a

Add a Component to the Bookcase

Practice Objectives

- Add a component to a family.
- Associate parameters between the component and the family.
- Copy and align the component.

In this practice, you will insert a glass door component into the bookcase family. You will fit the component to the correct location on one shelf by aligning it and associating door width and height parameters with the related parameters in the family. You will then copy and align that door to other shelves, as shown in Figure 5–14. Optionally, you will add a Material parameter and test the options in a project.

Figure 5–14

Task 1 - Add door components.

1. In the practice files *Architectural* folder, open **Barrister-Bookcase-Component.rfa**.

2. Open the **Floor Plans: Ref. Level** view.

3. In the *Insert* tab>Load from Library panel, click (Load Family).

4. In the Load Family dialog box, in the practice files *Architectural* folder, select **Shelf-Door-Glass.rfa** and click **Open**.

5. In the *Create* tab>Model panel, click ⬛ (Component).

6. Place a copy of the door in the view aligned to the **Center L/R** reference plane, as shown in Figure 5–15. The width might not match the bookcase width.

Figure 5–15

7. Use ⬛ (Align) to lock the center of the bookcase with the center reference plane, as shown in Figure 5–16.

Figure 5–16

8. Use ⬛ (Align) to line up the back of the door with the **Door Face** reference plane and lock it, as shown in Figure 5–17.

Select the Door Face reference plane first when you are aligning.

Figure 5–17

9. Save the family.

Task 2 - Associate parameters.

1. Click (Modify) and select the door.

2. In Properties, scroll down to the *Other* heading.

3. Beside **Door Width**, at the end of the row. click (Associate Family Parameter).

4. In the Associate Family Parameter dialog box, select **Width**, as shown in Figure 5–18. Then, click **OK**.

Associate Family Parameter   ×

Family parameter: Door Width

Parameter type: Length

Existing family parameters of compatible type:

Search parameters

```
<none>
Base
Depth
Frame Width
Height
Shelf Height
Shelf Thickness
Width
```

How do I associate family parameters?

OK   Cancel

Figure 5–18

5. Repeat the process to associate **Door Height** with **Shelf Height**. The parameters in Properties gray out and an equal sign displays in the button, as shown in Figure 5–19. The door should now fit in the shelf, as shown in Figure 5–20.

Other		
Door Width	3' 0"	
Door Height	1' 3"	
Label	<None>	

Figure 5–19

Figure 5–20

6. Change the *Width* dimension to flex the model to ensure that it works correctly.

7. Save the family.

Task 3 - Align and copy the doors

1. Open the **Elevations: Front** view and set the *Visual Style* to ⬦ (Hidden Line). The door needs to be aligned vertically.

2. Align and lock the top of the door with the shelf height reference planes for the bottom shelf, as shown in Figure 5–21.

Figure 5–21

3. Copy the door to the other shelves.

Ensure that the **Multiple Alignment** option is not selected in the Options Bar.

4. Align and lock the top of each copied door with the associated reference plane, as shown in Figure 5–22.

Figure 5–22

5. Change the *Height* dimension to flex the model and check the door alignments.

6. Open the **Elevations: Left** view and align the back of the top three door faces with the **Door Face** reference plane.

7. Switch to a 3D view, as shown in Figure 5–23.

Figure 5–23

8. Use Family Types to flex the model again to ensure that everything is working together.

9. Save the family.

Task 4 - (Optional) Add and test a Material parameter.

1. In the *Create* tab>Properties panel, click ⊞ (Family Types).

2. In the Family Types dialog box, click ⬚ (New Parameter).

3. Create a family parameter with the *Parameter Data* set as shown in Figure 5–24. Click **OK**.

*Setting the type as an **Instance** makes modifying this parameter in the project file easier.*

Figure 5–24

4. In the Family Types dialog box, leave the **Material** parameter set to **<By category>**, as shown in Figure 5–25. Click **OK** to close the dialog box.

Parameter	Value	Formula
Materials and Finishes		
Material (default)	<By Category> ...	=

Figure 5–25

5. In the 3D view, select all of the bookcase components, but not the doors.

6. In Properties, a new instance parameter labeled **Material** displays under *Materials and Finishes*.

7. In the *Material* row, click ☐ (Associate Family Parameter), as shown in Figure 5–26.

Graphics		☆
Visibility/Graphics Over...	Edit...	
Visible	✓	
Materials and Finishes		☆
Material	<By Category>	
Identity Data		☆
Subcategory	None	

— **Click here**

Figure 5–26

8. In the Associate Family Parameter dialog box, select the **Material** parameter, as shown in Figure 5–27. Click **OK**.

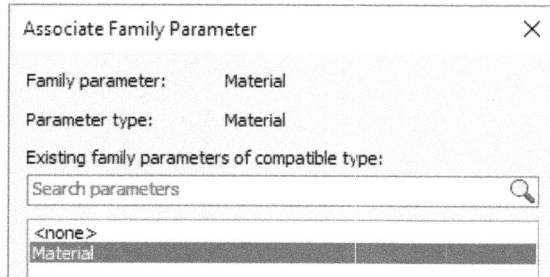

Associate Family Parameter   ✕

Family parameter: Material

Parameter type: Material

Existing family parameters of compatible type:

Search parameters   🔍

<none>
Material

Figure 5–27

• The Material is now marked with the **=** sign, as shown in Figure 5–28.

Materials and Finishes		☆
Material	<By Category>	🖹

Figure 5–28

9. Select one of the bookcase doors.

10. In Properties, click ⊞ (Edit Type).

11. In the Type Properties dialog box, associate the **Door Material** parameter with the **Material** parameter.

12. Click **OK**.

13. Save the family.

14. Open the **Barristers-Bookcase-Project.rvt** file.

15. Delete any existing bookcase elements.

16. Switch to the bookcase family and load it into the project.

17. Place one of each type in the project. Ensure that you are using the **Barristers-Bookcase-Component** family types. An older version of the family might also be in the project.

18. Create a 3D view to see the differences.

19. In the View Status Bar, set the *Visual Style* to ⬦ (Consistent Colors).

20. Select a bookcase. In Properties, in the *Materials and Finishes* area, next to the **Material** parameter, click **...** (Browse).

21. In the Material Browser, select a material and click **OK** to apply it to the bookcase. (Several materials starting with the word **Bookcase** are available for you to use.)

22. Repeat with the other bookcases using different materials, such as those shown in Figure 5–29.

Figure 5–29

23. Save and close the project and family files.

Practice 5b

Add a Component and Connectors to the Heat Pump

Practice Objectives

- Add a void element.
- Add a component to a family.
- Add electrical and piping connectors
- Associate parameters.

In this practice, you will add a void element to cut out part of the main unit of the heat pump. Your will then insert a panel component into that void. You will create additional extrusions and add connectors to these and other extrusions in the panel component. Finally, you will create and associate parameters to set pipe sizes. The completed family is shown in Figure 5–30.

Figure 5–30

Task 1 - Add a void.

1. In the practice files *MEP* folder, open **Heat-Pump-Connectors.rfa**.

2. Open the **3D**, **Ref. Level**, and **Front** views. Tile the views so that all three are visible on the screen.

3. In the **Front** elevation view, add two references planes to the lower left corner of the unit and dimension them as shown in Figure 5–31.

4. Select the lower reference plane and name it **Bottom of Void**, as shown in Figure 5–31.

Figure 5–31

5. Activate the **Ref. Level** view and zoom in on the lower left corner of the equipment.

6. Change the *Scale* to **1 1/2" =1'-0"**.

7. Draw and dimension the reference planes shown in Figure 5–32.

Existing 3" dimensions shown for clarity.

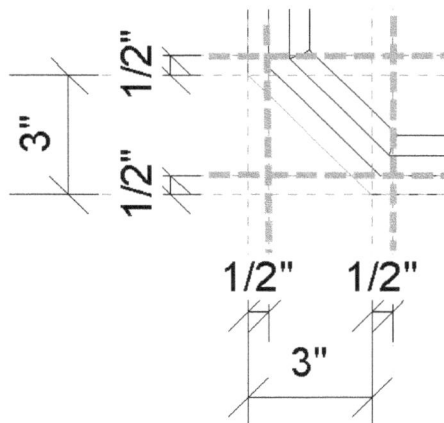

Figure 5–32

8. In the *Create* tab>Forms panel, expand ⬚ (Void Forms) and click ⬚ (Void Extrusion).

9. In the *Modify | Create Void Extrusion* tab>Work Plan panel, click ⊞ (Set).

10. In the Work Plane dialog box, select the *Name* **Reference Plane: Bottom of Void** and click **OK**.

11. Draw and lock the sketch, as shown in Figure 5–33.

Figure 5–33

12. In Properties, set the *Extrusion End* to **9"**.

13. Click ✓ (Finish Edit Mode) and click in empty space to release the selection.

14. In the **Elevation: Front** view, align and lock the extrusion end to the top reference plane.

15. Rotate the 3D view so you can see the new void, as shown in Figure 5–34.

Figure 5–34

16. Save the project.

Task 2 - Insert a component.

1. Activate the **Floor Plan: Ref. Level** view.

2. In the *Create* tab>Model panel, click ⬜ (Component).

3. When prompted to load a family, click **Yes**.

4. Navigate to the practice files *MEP* folder and open **Connector Panel.rfa**.

5. Insert the component, as shown in Figure 5–35.

Figure 5–35

6. Align and lock the back and side of the component to the reference planes.

7. In the **Elevations: Front** view, align and lock the top of the component to the top of the void reference plane, as shown in Figure 5–36.

Figure 5–36

8. Save the family.

Task 3 - Add extrusions for piping connections.

---

1. Activate the **Floor Plan: Ref. Level** view.

2. Draw a section in front of the angled reference line at 45 degrees and open it. (This section is not cutting anything, but acts similar to an elevation.)

3. Start the **Extrusion** command.

4. In the Work Plane dialog box, select **Pick a plane**, and then click **OK**. Select the edge of the plane shown in Figure 5–37.

5. Add the reference planes, dimensions, and the extrusion shown in Figure 5–37. Set the extrusion *Depth* to **1/4"**.

You might need to zoom in closer to place the smaller circle.

Figure 5–37

6. Click (Finish Edit Mode).

7. Join the extrusion to the rest of the unit.

8. Save the family.

Task 4 - Add connectors.

1. Open the 3D view and modify the view to display the corner of the unit where the connectors need to be applied.

2. In the *Create* tab>Connectors panel, click (Electrical Connector).

3. In the Options Bar, select **Power-Balanced**.

4. Select the face of the top circular extrusion, as shown in Figure 5–38.

5. Click **Modify** and select the new connector.

6. In Properties, in the *Identity Data* area, in the *Connector Description*, type **Electric Power Supply**.

7. Continue adding the other connectors as shown in Figure 5–38. For the Pipe Connectors, before selecting the location, in Properties, set the *Round Connector Dimension* to **Use Radius**.

Pipe Connector:
Other
Connector Description:
Gas Line

Pipe Connector:
Other
Connector Description:
Liquid Line

Electrical Connector:
Power-Balanced
Connector Description:
Electric Power Supply

Electrical Connector:
Power-Balanced
Connector Description:
Low Voltage

Figure 5–38

8. Save the family.

Task 5 - Create and assign new parameters for piping connectors.

1. In the Properties panel, click ⊞ (Family Types).

2. Add the following Type parameters:

Name	Discipline	Type	Group
Gas Line Service Valve	Piping	Pipe Size	Mechanical
Liquid Line Service Valve	Piping	Pipe Size	Mechanical
Gas Line Radius	Piping	Pipe Size	Dimensions
Liquid Line Radius	Piping	Pipe Size	Dimensions

- The **Radius** parameters are going to be linked to **Radius** parameters in the connectors. The Autodesk Revit software reads this and sets the correct diameter for the connector in the family when it is inserted into a project.

3. Assign the following values:
   - *Gas Line Service Valve:* **7/8"**
   - *Liquid Line Service Valve*: **3/8"**

4. Type in the following formulas:
   - *Gas Line Radius*: **Gas Line Service Valve / 2**
   - *Liquid Line Radius:* **Liquid Line Service Valve / 2**

5. Move the two radius parameters to the end of the Dimensions section. The final set of parameters is shown in Figure 5–39.

Parameter	Value	Formula	Lock
Dimensions			⌄
Width	38 7/8"	=	☐
Height	44 3/4"	=	☐
Depth	34 3/4"	=	☐
CenterX	17 3/8"	= CenterY	☐
CenterY	17 3/8"	= Depth / 2	☐
Radius of Fan	16 3/8"	= Depth / 2 - 1"	☐
Gas Line Radius	7/16"	= Gas Line Service Valve /	☐
Liquid Line Radius	3/16"	= Liquid Line Service Valve	☐
Mechanical			⌄
Gas Line Service Valve	7/8"	=	☐
Liquid Line Service Valve	3/8"	=	☐

Figure 5–39

6. Click **OK**.

7. In Properties, under the *Dimensions* heading, verify that the *Round Connector Dimension* is set to **Use Radius**.

8. Select the Gas Line connector.

9. In Properties, in the *Dimensions* area, in the **Radius** parameter, click ⌐ (Associate Family Parameter).

10. In the Associate Family Parameter dialog box, select **Gas Line Radius**, as shown in Figure 5–40. Then, click **OK**.

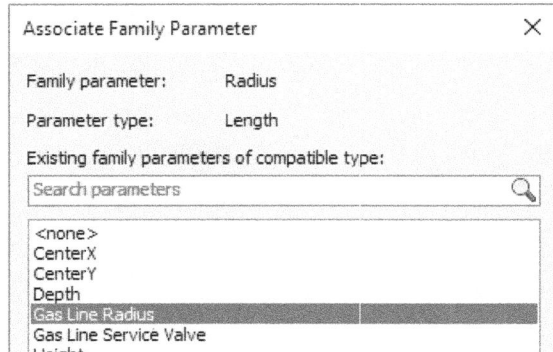

Figure 5–40

11. Repeat the process for the Liquid Line connector and associate the **Liquid Line Radius** to it.

12. When it is finished the connectors should be sized accordingly in the family, as shown in Figure 5–41.

Select the connector and click the Flip control if the Z-axis is pointing into the heat pump.

Figure 5–41

13. Save and close the family.

Practice 5c | Modify the Structural Column

Practice Objectives

- Add and test material parameters.
- Associate parameters.
- Add parameters to an existing extrusion.

In this practice, you will add a sweep element around the base of the column. You will then add a material parameter and test it in a project, as shown in Figure 5–42.

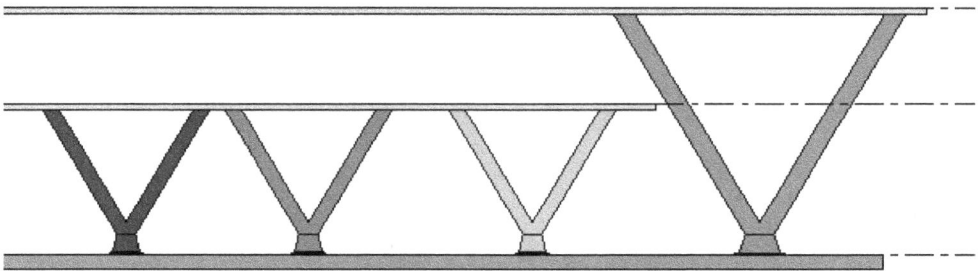

Figure 5–42

Task 1 - Add a Sweep around the Base of the column.

1. In the practice files *Structural* folder, open **Y-Column-Advanced.rfa.**

2. Open the **Floor Plans: Lower ref. Level** view.

3. Select the existing column and base elements and temporarily hide them.

4. In the *Create* tab>Forms panel, click 🕞 (Sweep).

5. In the *Modify | Sweep* tab>Sweep panel, click ✐ (Sketch Path).

6. Set the Work Plane to **Level: Lower Ref. Level.**

7. Add and lock the sketch as shown in Figure 5–43.

Figure 5–43

8. Click ✔ (Finish Edit Mode).

9. In the Sweep panel, click 📝 (Edit Profile).

10. In the Go To View dialog box, select **Elevation: Left** and click **Open View**.

11. Zoom in on the area near the red dot.

12. Use the sketch tools to add a profile similar to Figure 5–44. The exact size and design does not matter but ensure that you are locking the edges to the angled reference line and level reference plane.

Figure 5–44

13. Click ✓ (Finish Edit Mode) twice to apply the sweep.

14. Open the 3D view to see the sweep as shown in Figure 5–45.

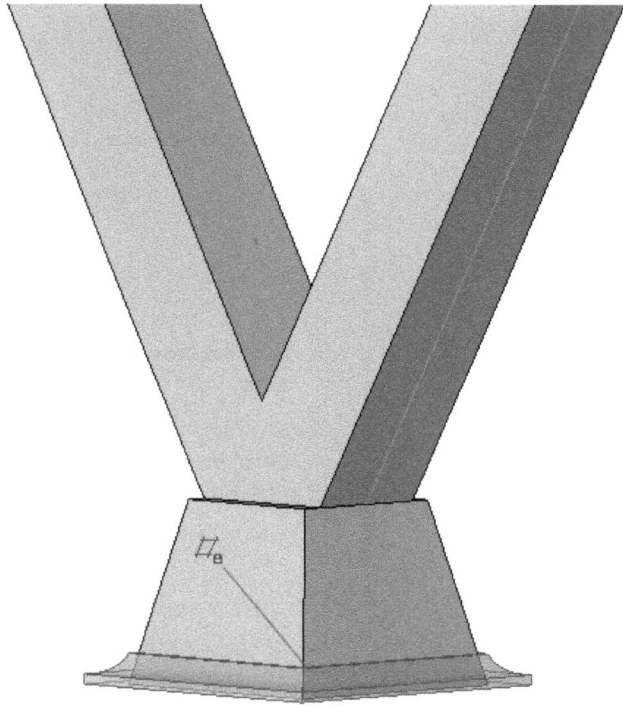

Figure 5–45

15. Save the family.

Task 2 - Add a material parameter.

---

1. In the *Create* tab>Properties panel, click 🔲 (Family Types).

2. Select the *Structural Material (default)* parameter and click

   ✎ (Edit Parameter).

3. In the Parameter Properties dialog box, you can see that this is a Built-in parameter and most of the information cannot be changed. Select **Type**, as shown in Figure 5–46. Click **OK**.

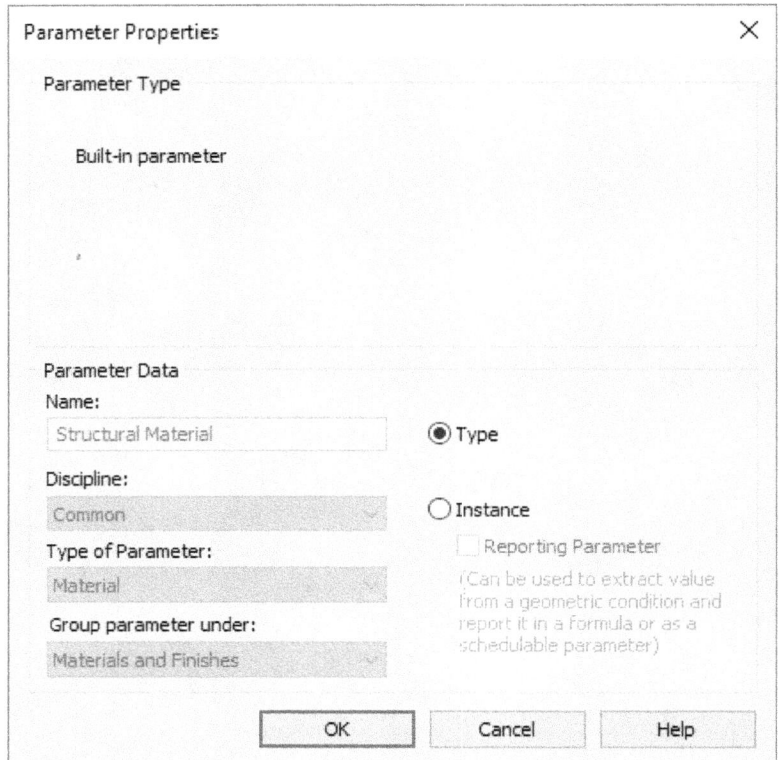

Figure 5–46

4. For the *Structural Material*, select one of the **Concrete, Cast-in-Place** materials. You will need to load it into the project from the AEC Materials library, as shown in Figure 5–47.

Figure 5–47

5. In the Family Types dialog box, click (New Parameter).

6. Create a **Family parameter** and set the *Parameter Data,* as shown in Figure 5–48. Click **OK**. Ensure that you select **Instance** so you can modify the parameter of each column individually.

Parameter Properties   ✕

Parameter Type

⦿ Family parameter

(Cannot appear in schedules or tags)

◯ Shared parameter

(Can be shared by multiple projects and families, exported to ODBC, and appear in schedules and tags)

Select...   Export...

Parameter Data

Name:

| Paint Color | ◯ Type |

Discipline:

| Common ∨ | ⦿ Instance |

Type of parameter:

| Material ∨ | ☐ Reporting Parameter |

Group parameter under:

(Can be used to extract value from a geometric condition and report it in a formula or as a schedulable parameter)

| Materials and Finishes ∨ |

Tooltip description:

<No tooltip description. Edit this parameter to write a custom tooltip. Custom t...

Edit Tooltip...

How do I create family parameters?

OK   Cancel

Figure 5–48

7. In the Family Types dialog box, ensure that the **Paint Color** parameter is set to **<By category>**, as shown in Figure 5–49.

8. Click **OK** to close the dialog box.

Parameter	Value	Formula	Lock
Materials and Finishes			⌃
Paint Color (default)	<By Category>	=	
Structural Material	Concrete, Cast-in-Place	=	

Figure 5–49

9. In Properties, in the *Structural* area, set the *Material for Model Behavior* to **Concrete**, as shown in Figure 5–50.

Figure 5–50

10. In the 3D view, select the three parts of the column.

11. In Properties, in the *Materials and Finishes* area, a parameter labeled **Material** displays.

12. In the *Material* row, click ⌐ (Associate Family Parameter), as shown in Figure 5–51.

13. In the Associate Family Parameter dialog box, select **Paint Color**, as shown in Figure 5–52. Click **OK**.

Figure 5–51

Figure 5–52

- The Material is now marked with the **=** sign, as shown in Figure 5–53.

Figure 5–53

14. Close all of the views except the 3D view.

15. Save the family.

Task 3 - Modify the material of the columns.

---

1. Open the **Y-Column-Project.rvt** file.

2. Open the **Structural Plans: Level 2** view.

3. Delete any existing columns from previous practices.

4. Switch to the column family and load it into the project.

5. Add several columns at different heights. Set the base and top of each column in properties.

6. Open the **Elevations: South** view.

7. In the View Status Bar, set the *Visual Style* to ⬜ (Consistent Colors).

8. Select one of the columns.

9. In Properties, in the *Materials and Finishes* area, beside *Paint Color,* in the <By Category> box, click ⬛ (Browse) to open the Material Browser.

10. In the Material Browser, select a paint material and click **OK** to apply it to the column.
    - Several materials of different colors (starting with the words **Metal - Paint Finish**) are available for you to use.

11. Repeat with the other columns using different materials.

12. Save and close the project and family files.

5.2 Visibility Display Settings

You can make families more versatile by controlling what displays in various views and at different detail levels. For example, you can set the Coarse view to display only 2D symbolic lines while the Fine detail view displays the full 3D model, as shown in Figure 5–54. To do this, change the visibility of the elements. You can also add Masking Regions to elements in a family to obscure other elements.

Fine detail level   *Coarse detail level*

Figure 5–54

How To: Control the Display of Elements

1. Select the elements that you want to modify.

2. In the *Modify* contextual tab>Mode panel, click (Visibility Settings).

3. In the Family Element Visibility Settings dialog box, specify the views and detail level in which you want the elements to display, as shown in Figure 5–55.

Family Element Visibility Settings   ✕

View Specific Display
  Display in 3D views and:
  ☑ Plan/RCP
  ☑ Front/Back
  ☑ Left/Right
  ☑ When cut in Plan/RCP (if category permits)

Detail Levels
  ☐ Coarse   ☐ Medium   ☑ Fine

[OK]   [Cancel]   [Default]   [Help]

Figure 5–55

4. Click **OK**.

• All model elements (not detail elements) typically display in 3D views. You can select how they display in plan and elevation views.

- The *Detail Levels* control whether or not the element displays at various scales. If you clear the checkmark from a level, the lines defining the element turn gray in the family file. They do not display at that detail level when inserted into the project.

- The plan is cut at the cut plane specified by the *View Range*. Some elements, such as furniture and mechanical equipment, cannot be cut in plan view, while structural columns can.

- To aid in assigning elements to various detail levels, you can preview the visibility. In the View Control Bar, expand

  ▣ (Preview Visibility Off) and select ▣ (Preview Visibility On). When the preview is on, you can change the *Detail Level* and only the elements assigned to that level display, as shown in Figure 5–56 and Figure 5–57.

Detail Level: Medium

Figure 5–56

Detail Level: Fine

Figure 5–57

- When the category permits, you can also set **Preview Visibility On (Not Cut)**, as shown in Figure 5–58.

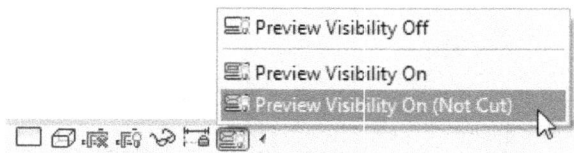

Figure 5–58

Adding Lines

Lines are often used to display the model elements in plan and elevation views at the **Coarse** (and sometimes **Medium**) detail level. There are two types of lines:

- ⌐⌐ (Model Line) in the *Create* tab>Model panel, shown in all views.

- ⌐ (Symbolic Line) in the *Annotate* tab>Detail panel, are visible in views parallel to the view in which they were drawn.

Lines can also be used in other situations. For example, you could use model lines to draw door hardware that is not three-dimensional, or use symbolic lines to draw the door swing (as shown in Figure 5–59) so that it does not display in 3D views.

Figure 5–59

- Use the standard sketch tools in the Draw panel to draw model and symbolic lines. You can also specify a subcategory with an associated line type (as shown in Figure 5–60) for a door family.

Figure 5–60

- You can create entire families of model and symbolic lines if they are only going to be used in a 2D view. For example, create a 2D family for a hospital bed, as shown in Figure 5–61, and use it in a large hospital layout where most of the instances do not need to be full 3D.

2D families can still be robust in the number and types of parameters they hold for use in schedules and quantity takeoffs.

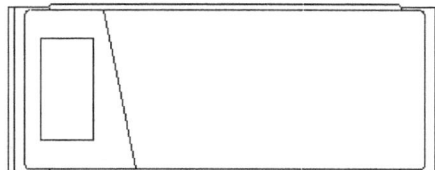

Figure 5–61

Creating Masking Regions

A masking region obscures other elements in a project. They can be placed in a family or project. For example, in the Desk family shown in Figure 5–62, a chair placed under the desk is masked but the lamp on top of the desk is not.

Figure 5–62

How To: Create Masking Regions

1. Open a plan or elevation view.

2. In the *Annotate tab*>Detail panel, click ⬚ (Masking Region).

3. In the *Modify | Create Masking Region Boundary* tab> Subcategory panel, select the subcategory you want to use for the boundary of the region.

4. In the Draw panel, select the tools to sketch the region. You can also use most of the Modify options as you draw.

5. Click ✓ (Finish Edit Mode) and click in empty space to finish the command.

Practice 5d | Modify the Visibility of Elements in the Bookcase

Practice Objectives

- Modify visibility settings.
- Create symbolic lines.

In this practice, you will modify the visibility settings of the main 3D elements so that they display at the **Medium** and **Fine** detail levels. You will also create a simple extrusion for 3D views and sketch symbolic lines for 2D views to display at the **Coarse** detail level. The elevation views of the three detail levels are shown in Figure 5–63.

Coarse   *Medium*   *Fine*

Figure 5–63

Task 1 - Modify the visibility settings of the 3D elements.

1. In the practice files *Architectural* folder, open **Barrister-Bookcase-Visibility.rfa**.

2. Open the **Floor Plans: Ref. Level** and **Elevation: Front** views. Tile the views so you see the 3D view along with the two opened views.

3. Activate the 3D view and set the *Visual Style* to ⬛ (Hidden Line).

4. In the View Control Bar, expand ▦ (Preview Visibility Off) and select ▦ (Preview Visibility On).

5. By default, the *Display Level* is set to **Medium** so all elements should be visible.

6. Hover the cursor over part of the bookcase element (but not the doors) and press <Tab> until the **Joined Solid Geometry** highlights, as shown in Figure 5–64. Click to select it.

Figure 5–64

7. In the *Modify | Joined Solid Geometry* tab>Visibility panel, click (Visibility Settings).

8. In the Family Element Visibility Settings dialog box, in the *Detail Levels* area, clear the **Coarse** option and select **Medium** and **Fine**, as shown in Figure 5–65. Then, click **OK**.

This has to be done in two steps because the doors are a different element (a nested family) from the rest of the elements.

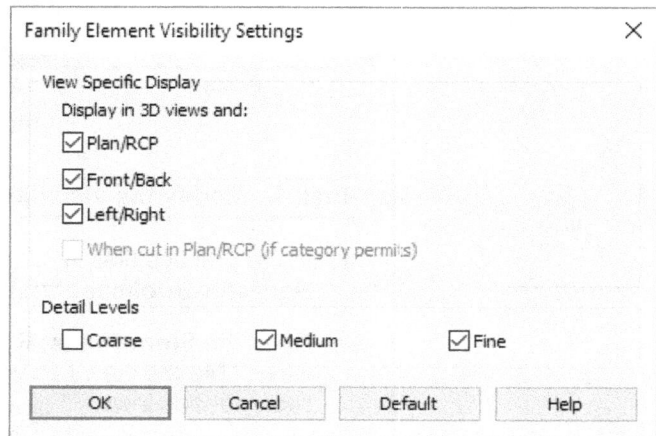

Figure 5–65

9. Select the door elements.

10. In the Family Element Visibility Settings dialog box, in the *Detail Levels* area, clear the **Coarse** and **Medium** options and select **Fine**. Click **OK**. The doors no longer display, as shown in Figure 5–66.

11. Change the *Detail Level* to **Fine**. The doors should display as shown in Figure 5–67.

Figure 5–66

Figure 5–67

12. Change the *Detail Level* to **Coarse**. Nothing should display in the 3D view.

13. Save the family.

Task 2 - Create an extrusion for coarse detail in 3D views.

1. In the **Elevation: Front** and **Floor Plans: Ref. Level** views, select 🖼 (Preview Visibility On).

2. The *Detail Level* is set to **Coarse** so none of the 3D elements display.

3. In the **Ref. Level** view, create a new extrusion with the footprint shown in Figure 5–68. Set the *Depth* to **2'-6"** and click ✓ (Finish Edit Mode).

Lock all sketch lines.

Preview Visibility

Figure 5–68

4. In the **Elevations: Front** view, align and lock the top of the new extrusion to the top reference plane, as shown in Figure 5–69. The simple extrusion also displays in the 3D view as shown in Figure 5–70.

Preview Visibility

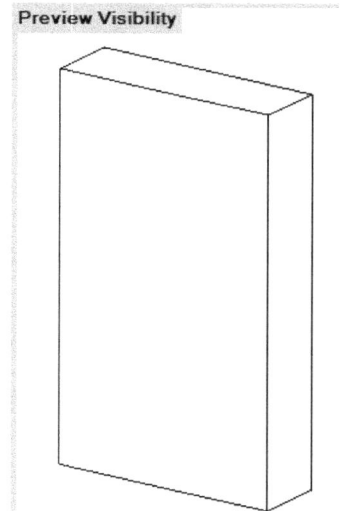

Figure 5–69   **Figure 5–70**

5. Select the new extrusion.

6. In the *Modify | Extrusion* tab>Mode panel, click 🔲 (Visibility Settings).

7. In the Family Element Visibility Settings dialog box, clear all of the options for the *View Specific Display* and all the *Detail Levels* except **Coarse**, as shown in Figure 5–71.

You do not want this element displaying in the 2D views at any detail level.

Family Element Visibility Settings ✕

View Specific Display
   Display in 3D views and:
   ☐ Plan/RCP
   ☐ Front/Back
   ☐ Left/Right
   ☐ When cut in Plan/RCP (if category permits)

Detail Levels
   ☑ Coarse   ☐ Medium   ☐ Fine

| OK | Cancel | Default | Help |

Figure 5–71

8. The simple extrusion should only display in the 3D view.

9. Save the family.

Task 3 - Add symbolic lines to elevation and plan views.

1. In the **Elevations: Front** view, verify that the *Detail Level* is set to **Coarse**.

2. In the *Annotate* tab>Detail panel, click ▢ (Symbolic Line).

3. Draw a rectangle around the outside of the bookcase and lock it to the reference planes, as shown in Figure 5–72.

Figure 5–72

4. Select all of the lines.

5. In the *Modify | Lines* tab>Visibility panel, click 🔲 (Visibility Settings).

6. In the Family Element Visibility Settings dialog box, in the *Detail Levels* area, select **Coarse** and clear the **Medium** and **Fine** options, as shown in Figure 5–73. Click **OK**.

*Symbolic lines display in views parallel to the view where they were drawn. Therefore, the lines in the **Front** view will automatically display in the **Back** view.*

Figure 5–73

7. Repeat the process in the **Floor Plans: Ref. Level** view, as shown in Figure 5–74.

Figure 5–74

8. Select all of the lines and set the *Visibility Settings* to **Coarse**.

9. Open the **Elevations: Left** view and repeat the process. (Toggle on **Preview Visibility** to hide the 3D elements at the **Coarse** detail level).

10. Check the detail levels in each of the views.

11. Save the family.

Task 4 - Load and test the family in a project.

1. Open the **Barristers-Bookcase-Project.rvt** file.

2. Delete any existing bookcases.

3. Switch to the bookcase family file and load it into the project.

4. Add at least one copy of the new bookcase.

5. In the View Status Bar, set the *Visual Style* to **Shaded**.

6. Change the detail levels to see the differences, as shown in Figure 5–75.

Detail Level: Coarse   *Detail Level: Medium*   *Detail Level: Fine*

Figure 5–75

7. Test in other views to ensure that the detail levels display the way you want them to.

8. Save and close the project and family files.

Practice 5e

Modify the Visibility of Elements in the Heat Pump

Practice Objectives

- Modify visibility settings.
- Create symbolic lines.

In this practice, you will modify the visibility settings of the 3D elements so that they display differently at various levels of detail, as shown in Figure 5–76. You will also create elements that display at a **Coarse** detail level, including a simple extrusion for 3D views and symbolic lines for plan and elevation views.

| *Coarse* | *Medium* | *Fine* |

Figure 5–76

- The electrical and piping connectors are hidden in these views for clarity.

Task 1 - Modify the visibility settings of the 3D elements.

1. In the practice files *MEP* folder, open
   Heat-Pump-Visibility.rfa

2. Open the **Floor Plans: Ref. Level** and **Elevation: Front** views. Tile the views so you see the 3D view along with the two opened views.

3. In each of the views, in the View Control Bar, expand
   ▭ (Preview Visibility Off) and select ▭ (Preview Visibility On).

4. Activate the 3D view and set the *Visual Style* to ▱ (Hidden Line), if required.

5. By default, the *Detail Level* is set to **Medium** so all elements should be visible, as shown in Figure 5–77.

6. Rotate the view as required and select the panel component.

7. In the *Modify | Joined Solid Geometry* tab>Visibility panel, click (Visibility Settings).

8. In the Family Element Visibility Settings dialog box in the *Detail Levels* area, clear the **Coarse** and **Medium** options and select **Fine**. Click **OK**.

9. Repeat the process with the connector extrusions. Neither of these elements should display in the **Medium** detail level, as shown in Figure 5–78, although the pipe connector elements still display.

Figure 5–77

Figure 5–78

10. Hover the cursor over part of the heat pump element and press <Tab> until the **Joined Solid Geometry** highlights, as shown in Figure 5–79. Click to select it.

Figure 5–79

11. In the Family Element Visibility Settings dialog box, in the *Detail Levels* area, clear the **Coarse** option and select **Medium** and **Fine**, as shown in Figure 5–80. Click **OK**.

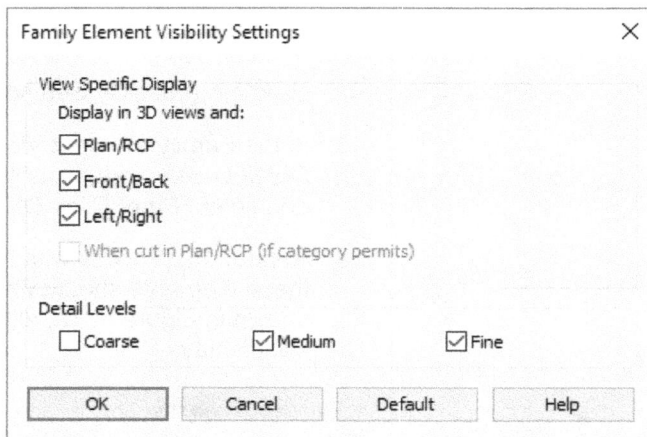

Family Element Visibility Settings   ✕

View Specific Display
  Display in 3D views and:
  ☑ Plan/RCP

  ☑ Front/Back

  ☑ Left/Right

  ☐ When cut in Plan/RCP (if category permits)

Detail Levels
  ☐ Coarse   ☑ Medium   ☑ Fine

    OK   Cancel   Default   Help

Figure 5–80

12. Change the *Detail Level* to **Fine**. The panel and connector extrusions should display.

13. Change the *Detail Level* to **Coarse**. No 3D elements should display in any of the views that are set to **Coarse**.

14. Save the family.

Task 2 - Add elements for the Coarse detail view.

1. Activate the **Floor Plans: Ref. Level** view.

2. Set the Workplane to **Ref. Level.**

3. Create a new extrusion with the footprint shown in

   Figure 5–81. Set the *Depth* to **40"** and click ✔ (Finish Edit Mode).

Figure 5–81

4. Switch to the **Elevations: Front** view.

5. Set the *Visual Style* to **Shaded** to display the extrusion.

6. Align and lock the top and bottom of the new extrusion to the reference planes, as shown in Figure 5–82.

Figure 5–82

7. Select the extrusion.

8. In the *Modify | Extrusion* tab>Mode panel, click (Visibility Settings).

9. In the Family Element Visibility Settings dialog box, clear all of the options except **Coarse**, as shown in Figure 5–83.

You do not want this element displaying in the 2D views at any detail level.

Family Element Visibility Settings ×

View Specific Display
Display in 3D views and:
☐ Plan/RCP
☐ Front/Back
☐ Left/Right
☐ When cut in Plan/RCP (if category permits)

Detail Levels
☑ Coarse   ☐ Medium   ☐ Fine

OK   Cancel   Default   Help

Figure 5–83

10. Activate the **Elevation: Front** view.

11. In the *Annotate* tab>Detail panel, click (Symbolic Line).

12. Draw a rectangle using the outermost reference planes of the heat pump and lock it to the reference planes.

13. Select all of the lines.

14. In the *Modify | Lines* tab>Visibility panel, click (Visibility Settings).

15. In the Family Element Visibility Settings dialog box, in the *Detail Levels* area, select **Coarse** and clear the **Medium** and **Fine** options, as shown in Figure 5–84. Click **OK**.

*Symbolic lines display in views parallel to the view where they were drawn. Therefore, the lines in the **Front** view will automatically display in the **Back** view.*

Family element visibility settings ×

Symbolic Element Visibility
Symbolic Elements are view direction specific: they show only in views parallel to their creation view.

☐ Show only if Instance is cut

Detail Levels
☑ Coarse   ☐ Medium   ☐ Fine

OK   Cancel   Default   Help

Figure 5–84

16. Return to the **Ref. Level** view and draw and lock symbolic lines to the outer reference planes using the same footprint as the extrusion. Set the visibility settings, as shown in Figure 5–84.

17. Open the **Elevations: Left** view and repeat the process. (Toggle on **Preview Visibility** to hide the 3D elements at the **Coarse** detail level).

18. Check the detail levels in each of the views.

19. Close all but one view of the family.

20. Save the family.

Task 3 - Load and test the family in a project.

---

1. Open the **Heat-Pump-Project.rvt** file.

2. Delete any existing Heat Pump components.

3. Open the Mechanical>HVAC>**Floor Plans: 1 - Mech** view.

4. Switch to the heat pump family file and load it into the project.

5. Add at least one copy of the new heat pump.

6. In the View Status Bar, set the *Visual Style* to **Shaded**.

7. Change the detail levels to display the differences, as shown in Figure 5–85.

Detail Level: Coarse   *Detail Level: Medium*   *Detail Level: Fine*

Figure 5–85

8. Open a 3D view, rotate it so that the connector locations display and test the detail levels.

9. Save and close the project and family files.

Practice 5f

Modify the Visibility of Elements in the Structural Column

Practice Objectives

- Modify visibility settings.
- Create a simple extrusion.
- Add symbolic lines.

In this practice, you will modify the visibility settings of the 3D elements so that they display differently at various levels of detail. You will also create elements that display at a **Coarse** detail level, including a simple extrusion for 3D views and symbolic lines for plan and elevation views, as shown in Figure 5–86.

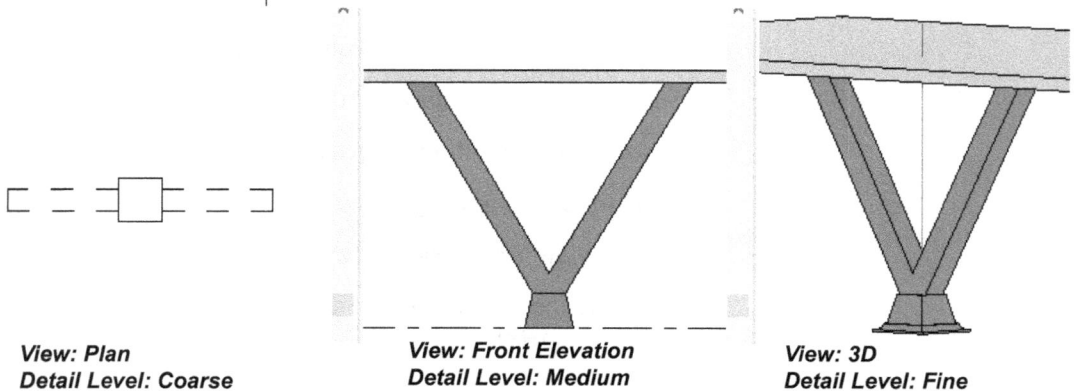

View: Plan
Detail Level: Coarse

View: Front Elevation
Detail Level: Medium

View: 3D
Detail Level: Fine

Figure 5–86

Task 1 - Modify the visibility settings of the 3D elements.

1. In the practice files *Structure* folder, open **Y-Column-Visibility.rfa**.

2. Close any other open files.

3. Open the **Floor Plans: Lower Ref. Level, Elevation: Front,** and **Elevation: Left** views. Tile the views so you see the 3D view along with the other opened views.

4. In each of the views, in the View Control Bar, expand

   (Preview Visibility Off) and select (Preview Visibility On).

5. Set the *Visual Style* to **Shaded** in each view.

6. Activate the 3D view. By default, the *Detail Level* is set to **Medium** and all elements should be visible, as shown in Figure 5–87.

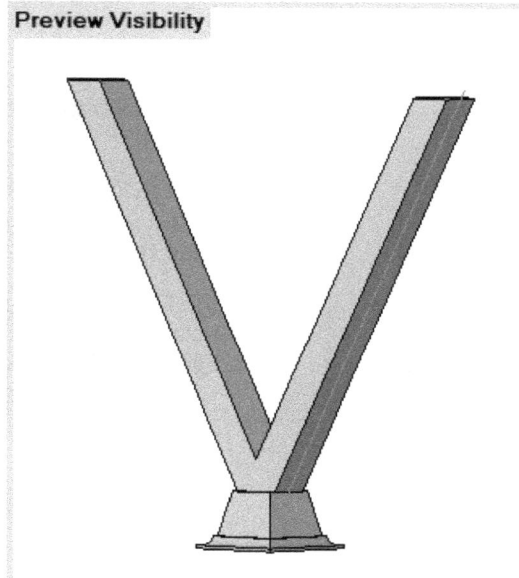

Figure 5–87

7. Select the curved part of the base element and in the Family Element Visibility Settings dialog box, in the *Detail Levels* area, clear the **Coarse** and **Medium** options and select **Fine**, as shown in Figure 5–88. Click **OK**. The curved base should be removed from the view.

Figure 5–88

8. Select the Y-column and Base elements. In the *Modify* tab> Clipboard panel, click ▢ (Copy to Clipboard).

9. In the *Modify* tab>Clipboard panel, expand **Paste** and click ▢ (Paste Aligned to Same Place). This creates duplicates of these two elements that will be used for Coarse 3D views only.

10. Select one of the Y-column elements and click ▢ (Visibility Settings).

   • Modifying the Visibility Settings for the elements must be done separately because the Y-column is an extrusion and the base is a blend.

11. In the Family Element Visibility Settings dialog box, clear the checkmarks from all of the options except **Coarse**, as shown in Figure 5–89. Click **OK**.

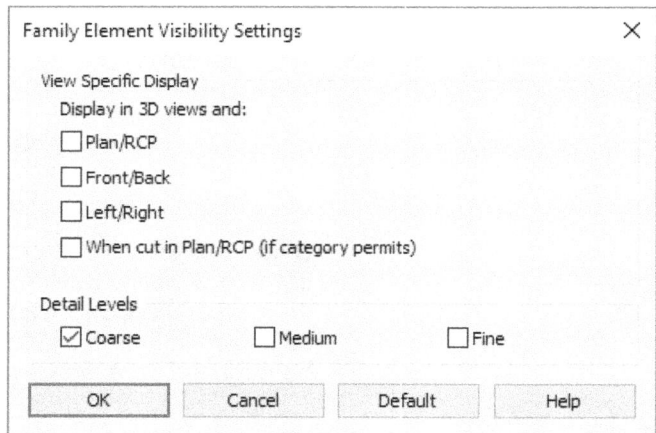

Figure 5–89

12. Repeat the process for one of the base elements. These elements should not longer display in the view but the copies of the elements continue to display.

13. Select the remaining Y-column element and set the Visibility Settings so that everything except **Coarse** is selected, as shown in Figure 5–90. Click **OK**.

Family Element Visibility Settings   ✕

View Specific Display
  Display in 3D views and:
    ☑ Plan/RCP
    ☑ Front/Back
    ☑ Left/Right
    ☑ When cut in Plan/RCP (if category permits)

Detail Levels
    ☐ Coarse   ☑ Medium   ☑ Fine

    OK   Cancel   Default   Help

Figure 5–90

14. Repeat the process with the remaining base element.

15. Save the family.

Task 2 - Add symbolic lines.

1. Activate the **Floor Plans: Lower Ref. Level** view.

2. In the View Control Bar, change the *Visibility Preview* to ▦ Preview Visibility On (Not Cut).

3. In the *Annotate* tab>Detail panel, click 🗗 (Symbolic Lines).

4. In the *Modify | Place Symbolic Lines* tab>Subcategory panel, expand the *Subcategory* list and select **Structural Columns (projection)**, if not already selected. Add symbolic lines around the edge of the base and lock them in place, as shown by the solid lines in Figure 5–91.

5. Set the *Subcategory* to **Hidden Line (projection)** and add the lines on either side of the base to show the area of the Y-Column above. The exact length of the lines is not important at this time. If you isolate the lines the display as shown in Figure 5–92.

Figure 5–91

Figure 5–92

6. Select all the symbolic lines and set the Visibility Settings to display only at the **Coarse** detail level, as shown in Figure 5–93.

Figure 5–93

7. Open the **Elevations: Front view** and **Elevations: Left** views add solid symbolic lines, as shown in Figure 5–94. Set the lines to display only at the **Coarse** Detail Level.

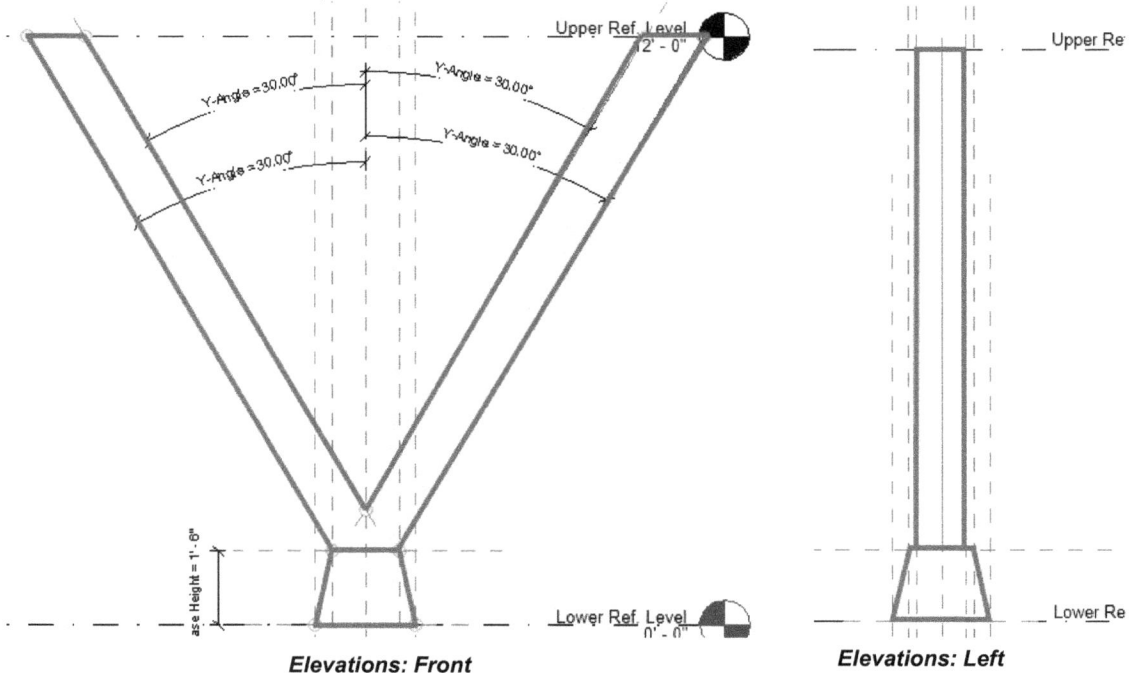

Elevations: Front   *Elevations: Left*

Figure 5–94

8. Check the detail levels in each of the views.

9. Close all but one open view.

10. Save the family.

Task 3 - Load and test the family in a project.

1. Open **Y-Column-Project.rvt**.

2. Switch to the Y-Column family file and load it into the project.

3. Select one of the existing columns and replace it with the new **Y-Column-Visibility** type of the same size.

   - The paint color is not retained because it is an instance parameter, not a type parameter.

4. Delete the other columns.

5. Open the **Structural Plans: Level 1** and **Elevations: South** views and tile the views.

6. Test the visibility settings in the different views including the **Elevations: Front** view shown in Figure 5–95.

Detail Level: Coarse   ***Detail Level: Medium***   ***Detail Level: Fine***

Figure 5–95

7. Save and close the project and family files.

Chapter Review Questions

1. If your family can be switched from one side to another (such as a door swing) which type of icon would you add?

   a. Mirror

   b. Connector

   c. Control

   d. Calculation

2. (MEP.) When adding an Electrical Connector, where do you specify the System Type (i.e, Power-Balanced or Security)?

   a. In the Options Bar

   b. In the shortcut menu

   c. In the expanded Connectors panel

   d. In the Type Properties

3. In which of the following situations would you use a nested family? (Select all that apply.)

   When the family is used multiple times...

   a. in one family

   b. in other families

   c. in one project

   d. in several projects

4. The main reason to associate a family parameter is when:

   a. The parameter will be shared in several projects.

   b. The parameter will be used in a schedule.

   c. You want a user-created parameter to control another parameter.

   d. You want the parameter to reference a project parameter.

5. For the elements in a family to display differently at Coarse and Fine detail levels (as shown in Figure 5–96), you must draw everything in 2D.

   Detail Level: Coarse *Detail Level: Fine*

   Figure 5–96

   a. True

   b. False

Command Summary

Button	Command	Location
Connectors		
	Cable Tray Connector	• **Ribbon**: *Create* tab>Connectors panel> expand Connector
	Conduit Connector	• **Ribbon**: *Create* tab>Connectors panel> expand Connector
	Duct Connector	• **Ribbon**: *Create* tab>Connectors panel> expand Connector
	Electrical Connector	• **Ribbon**: *Create* tab>Connectors panel> expand Connector
	Pipe Connector	• **Ribbon**: *Create* tab>Connectors panel> expand Connector
Other Tools		
	Component	• **Ribbon**: *Create* tab>Model panel
	Control	• **Ribbon**: *Create* tab>Control panel
	Detail Component	• **Ribbon**: *Annotate tab*>Detail panel
	Masking Region	• **Ribbon**: *Annotate tab*>Detail panel
	Model Line	• **Ribbon**: *Create* tab>Model panel
	Opening	• **Ribbon**: *Create* tab>Model panel
	Symbolic Line	• **Ribbon**: *Annotate* tab>Detail panel
	Visibility Settings	• **Ribbon**: Various contextual tabs> Mode panel

Chapter

6

Additional Family Types

Beyond the basics of family creation, there are several special cases. These include a variety of 2D detail and annotation families, 2D profiles used as the basis of other commands, line-based families that work with 2D and 3D elements, and in-place families that are only available in the current project. Shared parameters are frequently required when you create tags with information you want to include in schedules.

Learning Objectives in this Chapter

- Create 2D detail families.
- Create 2D profiles that are used to create 3D wall sweeps, reveals, railings, nosings, and other elements.
- Create 2D symbol families using drawing tools, filled regions, text, and labels.
- Create 2D and 3D Line-based families with and without arrays.
- Create in-place families directly in a project.
- Create shared parameters that can be used in both tags and schedules in multiple projects.

6.1 Creating 2D Families

2D elements can be inserted into views and families to give additional information and level of detail about a design, as shown in Figure 6–1. These families include Detail items, profiles, tags, and symbols.

Ceiling Tile

Recessed Fluorescent Light Fixture

Detail Items : Suspended Acoustic Ceiling-Square Edge- Section

Figure 6–1

Creating Detail Items

Detail components can be added into drafting views and nested into families. There are many sample files found in the Autodesk Revit library>*Detail Items* folder, divided by the way they are specified, as shown for a concrete joist section in Figure 6–2.

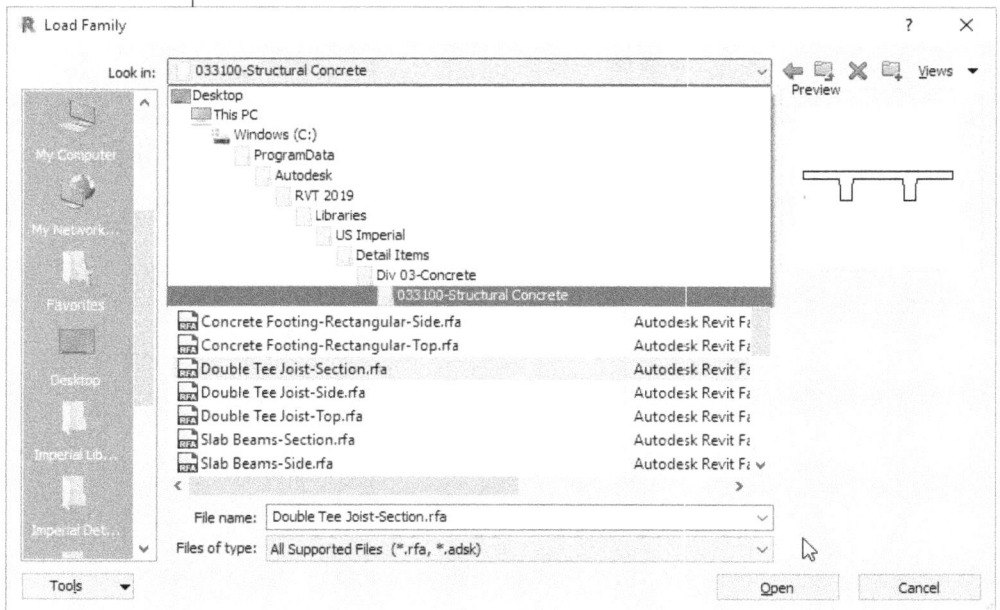

Figure 6–2

Detail families are created using the **Detail Item.rft** template, which only includes two reference planes used to define the insertion point. Then, you use the tools found on the *Create* tab>Detail panel to add elements such as lines and filled regions, as shown in Figure 6–3 for the front of a dock bumper, to create the detail.

Figure 6–3

- Standard family tools such as reference planes, dimensions, labels, controls, and family types also apply to detail families.

Creating Profiles

Profiles are 2D elements that are used in a variety of commands to create 3D elements. For example, you need a profile to create wall sweeps (as shown in the Base profile in Figure 6–4) and reveals, gutters, fascias, and floor slab edges. They are also used in families for curtain wall mullions, railings, stair nosings, and solid sweeps.

Profile   *Profile used in a Wall Sweep*
Figure 6–4

Several profile templates are supplied with the Autodesk® Revit® software: **Profile**, **Profile-Hosted**, **Profile-Mullion**, **Profile-Rail**, **Profile-Reveal**, and **Profile-Stair Nosing**. These are created with existing reference planes to help you place the elements correctly on the host element.

- All profiles must be closed shapes.

- Profile families can include detail components.

Creating Tags and Symbols

Tags and symbols are created using specific templates related to the type of element you want to tag, as shown in the Revit Library>*Annotations* folder in Figure 6–5. You can also create Generic and Multi-Category tags, as well as generic annotations such as a north arrow.

You can modify tags and symbols that are supplied with the Autodesk Revit software to fit your company standards.

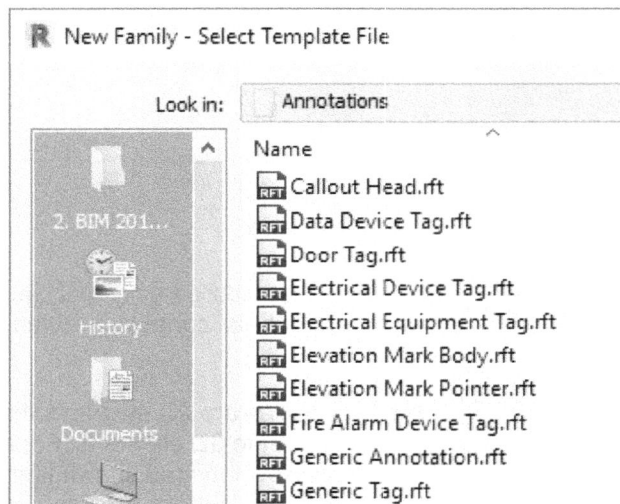

Annotation templates in

Figure 6–5

The drawing tools for annotation families include the standard line sketching tools, filled region, text, and label. You can also add existing symbols to the family.

- Most annotation symbols do not have family types. They are designed to change size according to the view scale.

Practices for creating tags are included with shared parameters practices.

- Some annotation family templates include notes to help you create the symbol. Delete them before using the family.

- Tags are frequently created using shared parameters that are both associated with elements and can be scheduled.

Adding Labels

Many tags (as well as title blocks) use Labels. Labels are not just text, but elements that are assigned to specific parameters. They can change without modifying the rest of the elements. For example, in a tag, you add a label (such as **Extension** shown in Figure 6–6) that can later be adjusted either by the type or instance parameter in the project.

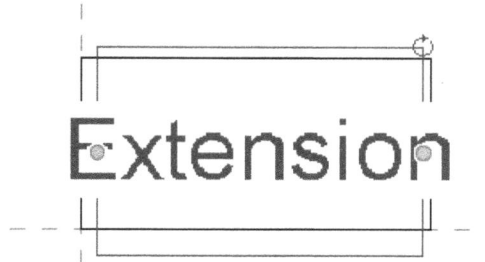

Figure 6–6

How To: Create a Label

1. In the *Create* tab>Text panel, click (Label).
2. In the *Modify | Place Label* tab>Format panel, specify the alignments: **Left**, **Center**, **Right**, **Top**, **Center Middle**, or **Bottom**, as shown in Figure 6–7.

Figure 6–7

3. Click in the view window to place the label, as shown in Figure 6–8.

Figure 6–8

4. In the Edit Label dialog box shown in Figure 6–9, select a label in the *Category Parameters* list and double-click, or click ⇥ (Add parameter(s) to label). You can select more than one by holding <Ctrl> or <Shift>.

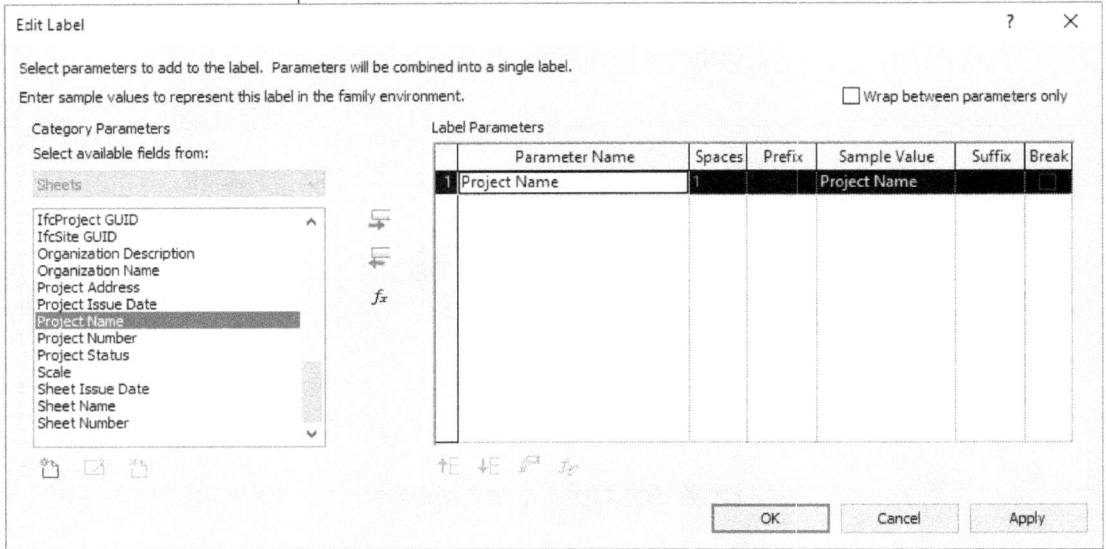

Edit Label   ? ✕

Select parameters to add to the label. Parameters will be combined into a single label.

Enter sample values to represent this label in the family environment.   ☐ Wrap between parameters only

Category Parameters   Label Parameters

Select available fields from:

Sheets

	Parameter Name	Spaces	Prefix	Sample Value	Suffix	Break
1	Project Name	1		Project Name		☐

IfcProject GUID
IfcSite GUID
Organization Description
Organization Name
Project Address
Project Issue Date
Project Name
Project Number
Project Status
Scale
Sheet Issue Date
Sheet Name
Sheet Number

⇥
⇤
f_x

↑E ↓E

OK   Cancel   Apply

Figure 6–9

5. Enter the *Sample Value* and specify any other options, as required.
6. Click **OK** when you have finished editing the label.

• While placing the label, you can rotate or stretch it (as shown in Figure 6–10), or select a point for an additional label.

•DRW

Figure 6–10

• You can also rotate or stretch a label once it has been placed in the family.

Hint: Modifying Labels

When you add labels, the length of the boundary box impacts the way the text word-wraps. For example, the Viewport: Title w Line tag that comes with the default metric template does not have enough room for a long title, as shown in Figure 6–11.

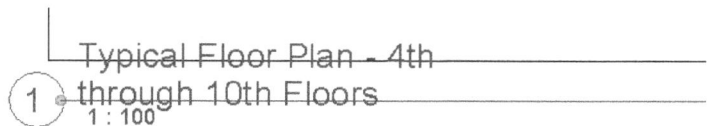

Typical Floor Plan - 4th
1 through 10th Floors
1 : 100

Figure 6–11

To modify it, open the related family file (in this case **M_View Title.rfa**) and stretch the length of the label boundary as shown in Figure 6–12.

1 View Name
View Scale

Figure 6–12

Save the annotation family and reload it into the project. The length of the title expands to fit the longer title as shown in Figure 6–13.

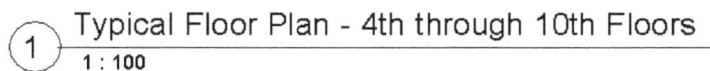

1 Typical Floor Plan - 4th through 10th Floors
1 : 100

Figure 6–13

Practice 6a

Create 2D Families: Arrow Symbol

Practice Objectives

- Create an annotation symbol.
- Add a Filled Region.
- Test the symbol in a project.

In this practice, you will create an annotation symbol and apply it to a project, as shown in Figure 6–14.

View Scale 1/2"=1'-0"   *View Scale 1/4"=1'=0"*

Figure 6–14

Task 1 - Create an annotation symbol.

1. Create a new annotation symbol family based on the **Generic Annotation.rft** template found in the Autodesk Revit Library in the *Annotations* folder.

2. Save the family to your practice folder as **Arrow.rfa**.

3. In the *Create* tab> Detail panel click ⌐ (Line) and sketch the arrow as shown in Figure 6–15. The dimensions are for reference only; do not add them to the sketch.

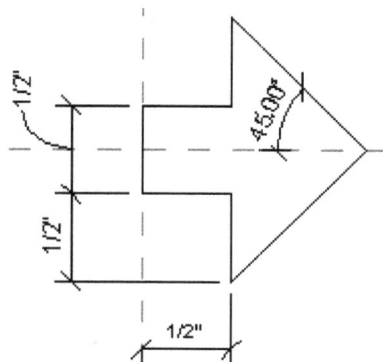

Figure 6–15

4. In the *Create* tab>Detail panel, click ▦ (Filled Region). Add a filled region to the arrow, as shown in Figure 6–16. You can use the default solid pattern or create a new pattern if time permits.

Figure 6–16

5. Delete the notes.

6. Save the family.

Task 2 - Add the symbol to a project.

1. Open a new project file.

2. Switch back to the arrow family and click 📥 (Load into Project and Close).

3. In the project, place the arrow symbol. (If required, in the *Annotate* tab>Symbol panel, click ⊕ (Symbol) to start the command if it is not automatically started and select the **Arrow** type.

4. Add some other full-scale elements near the arrow.

5. Change the *View Scale*, as shown in Figure 6–14. The arrow should resize according to the new view scale.

6. Close the project. You do not need to save it.

Practice 6b

Create 2D Families: Curtain Wall Mullion Profile

Learning Objectives

- Create a profile family including reference planes, dimensions, and a label.
- Insert a detail family.
- Modify the visibility of the detail family.

In this practice, you will create a mullion profile by creating a parametric framework of reference planes, dimensions, and a label, and then add lines, as shown in Figure 6–17. You will then insert an existing detail designed to work with the profile and modify it so it fits the new profile. Finally, you will set the visibility settings of the detail family so it only shows when the *Detail Level* is set to **Fine**, as shown in Figure 6–18.

Figure 6–17

Figure 6–18

Task 1 - Create a profile.

1. Close all open files.

2. In the Home page, in the *Families* area, click **New...**.

3. In the New Family - Select Template File dialog box, select **Profile-Mullion.rft** and click **Open**. The template includes some text and reference planes as shown in Figure 6–19.

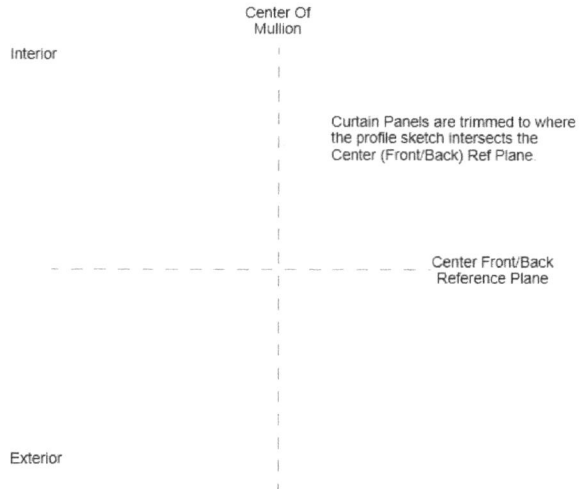

Figure 6–19

4. To make the information easier to read as you proceed, change the *Scale* to **3" = 1'-0"** and the *Units Format* to **Fractional Inches**.

5. Add the reference planes, dimensions, Depth label, and lines, as shown in Figure 6–20.

Figure 6–20

6. Save the family as **Mullion Profile.rfa.**

Task 2 - Add a Detail component to the profile.

1. In the practice files>*Architectural* folder, open **Mullion Detail Center.rfa**. This is a detail family that is based on the same shape as the mullion profile you just created., as shown in Figure 6–21.

2. In the *Modify* tab>Family Editor panel, click 📑 (Load into Project).

3. The **Detail Component** command automatically starts. Place the detail at the intersection of the original reference planes and click **Modify**. The detail does not fit with the profile yet, as shown in Figure 6–22.

Figure 6–21

Figure 6–22

4. Select the detail element and edit the type.

5. In the Type Properties dialog box, beside the **Depth** parameter, click the **Associate Family Parameter** button, as shown in Figure 6–23.

6. In the Associate Family Parameter dialog box, select **Depth** and click **OK**, as shown in Figure 6–23.

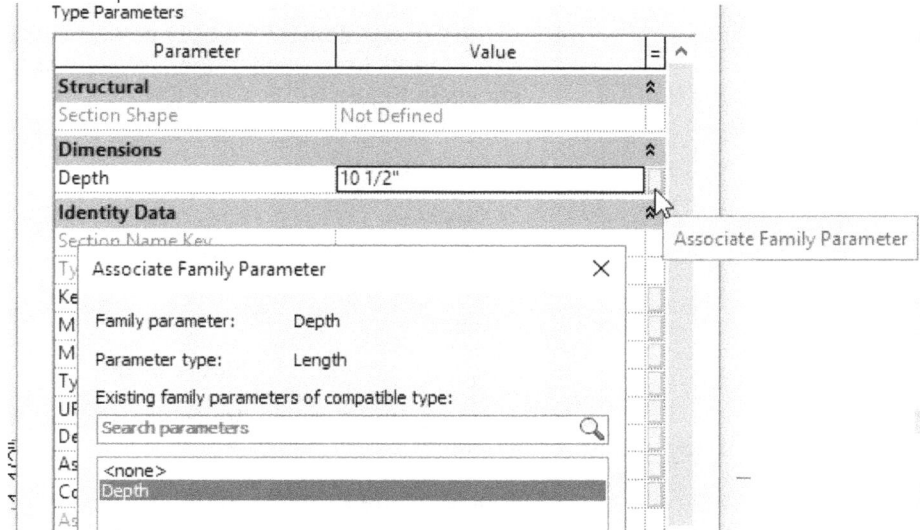

Figure 6–23

7. The mullion detail now matches the profile, as shown in Figure 6–24.

Figure 6–24

8. With the mullion detail still selected, in the *Modify | Detail Items* tab>Visibility panel, click ⬚ (Visibility Settings).

9. In the Family element visibility settings dialog box, clear the checkmarks from each of the *Detail Levels* except **Fine**, as shown in Figure 6–25. Click **OK**.

Figure 6–25

10. Toggle on the **Preview Visibility** and test the different detail levels.

11. Toggle off the **Preview Visibility**.

12. Save and close the family files.

• If time permits, you can add the mullion profile to a mullion type in a project (as shown in Figure 6–26) and test it in a curtain wall. Mullion types are system families.

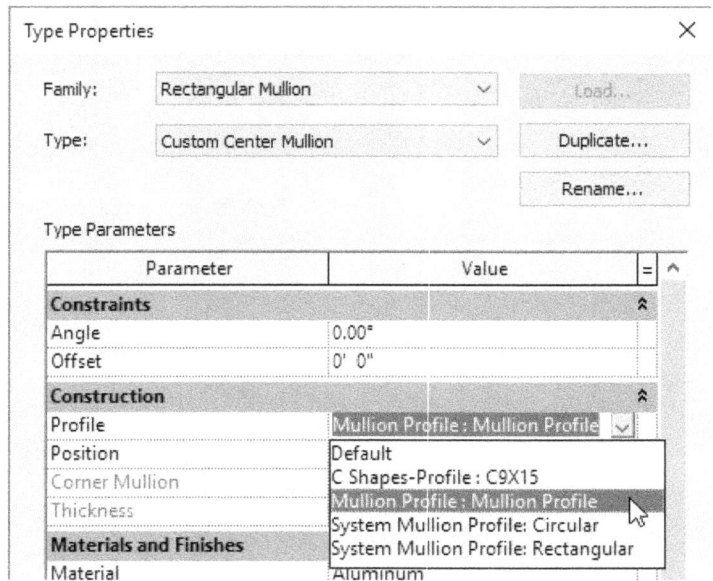

Figure 6–26

Practice 6c

Create 2D Families: Electrical Trunking Line Profile

Learning Objectives

- Create a profile family including reference planes, dimensions, and a label.
- Add a formula to parameters.

In this practice, you will create a profile by creating a parametric framework of reference planes, dimensions, and labels, and then add lines, as shown in Figure 6–27. You will also add a formula in the Family Types dialog box.

Land = 1"

Nominal Height = 4"

Land = 1"

Nominal Width = 4"

Figure 6–27

Task 1 - Create a profile.

1. Close all open files.

2. In the Home page, in the *Families* area, click **New...**.

3. In the New Family - Select Template File dialog box, select **Profile.rft** and click **Open**. The template includes two reference planes that define the insertion point of the profile.

4. Save the family as **Trunking Profile.rfa.**

5. To make the information easier to read as you proceed, change the *Scale* to **3" = 1'-0"** and the *Units Format* to **Fractional Inches**.

6. Add the reference planes, dimensions, labels, and lines, as shown in Figure 6–28.

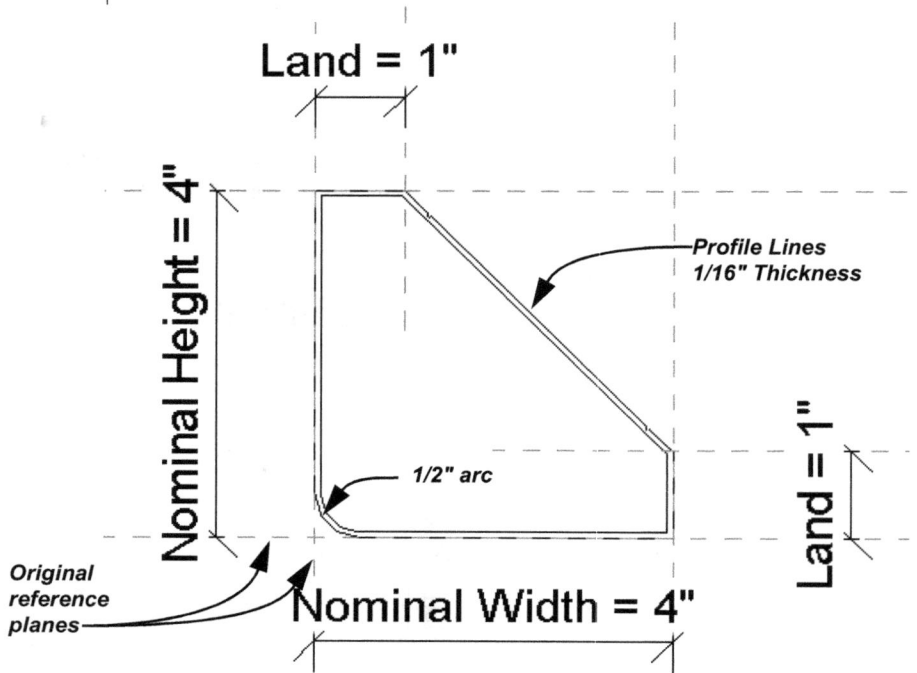

Figure 6–28

7. Open the Family Types dialog box and set the *Formula* for *Nominal Height* to **Nominal Width**, as shown in Figure 6–29. Click **OK**.

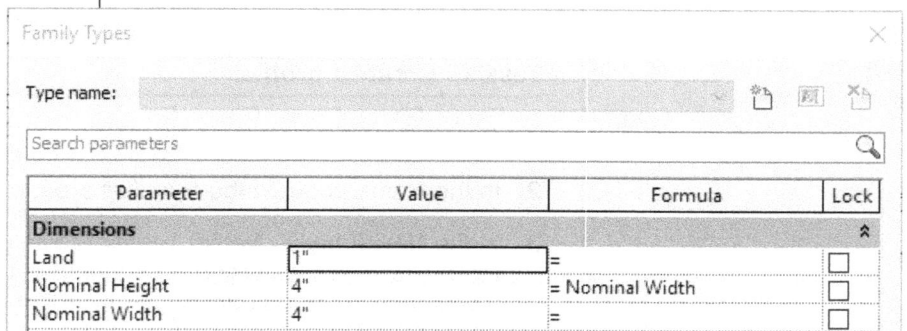

Figure 6–29

8. Zoom in on the top of the angled line and add a **1/32"** notch **3/8" off** each end of angled line, as shown in Figure 6–30.

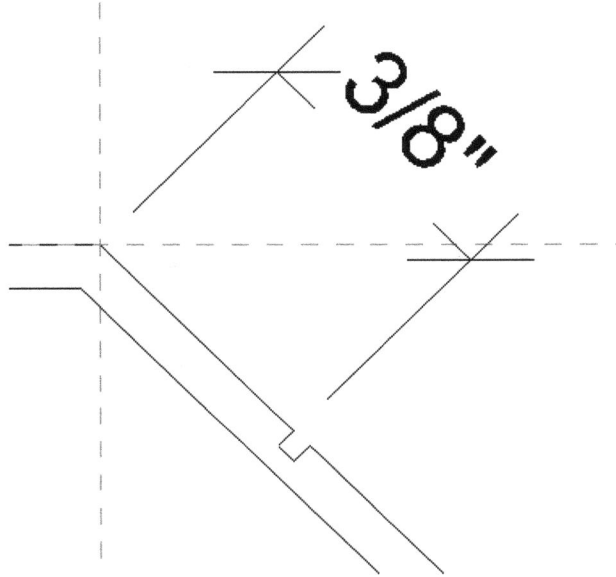

Figure 6–30

9. Mirror the notch to the other end of the angled line. Split and trim, as required.

10. Save and close the profile family.

Practice 6d	# Create 2D Families: Structural Floor Profile

Practice Objectives

- Create a profile to use in defining a composite metal deck.
- Load the profile into a project and create a new structural floor type using the profile.
- Test the new floor and change the span direction.

In this practice, you will create a profile for a composite metal deck and save it to a library. You will then load the profile into a project, use it to create a new Metal Deck Floor type, as shown in Figure 6–31, and test the new floor type.

Profile

Figure 6–31

Task 1 - Create a composite Metal Deck profile.

1. Close all open files.

2. In the Home page, in the *Families* area, click **New...**.

3. In the New Family - Select Template File dialog box, select **Profile.rft** and click **Open**.

4. Save the family to your practice folder as **Composite-Metal-Deck.rfa**.

5. Type **UN** to open the Project Units dialog box.

6. Next to *Length Units*, select **Format**.

7. In the Format dialog box, change the units to **Fractional inches**. (This makes the dimensions in the family read in inches only so that it is easier to create the profile.)

8. Click **OK** twice to close the dialog boxes.

9. Set the *Scale* to **3" = 1'-0"**.

10. In the *Create* tab>Datum panel, click (Reference Plane).

11. Add reference planes as shown in Figure 6–32. They help you draw the elements (the dimensions are shown for reference only).

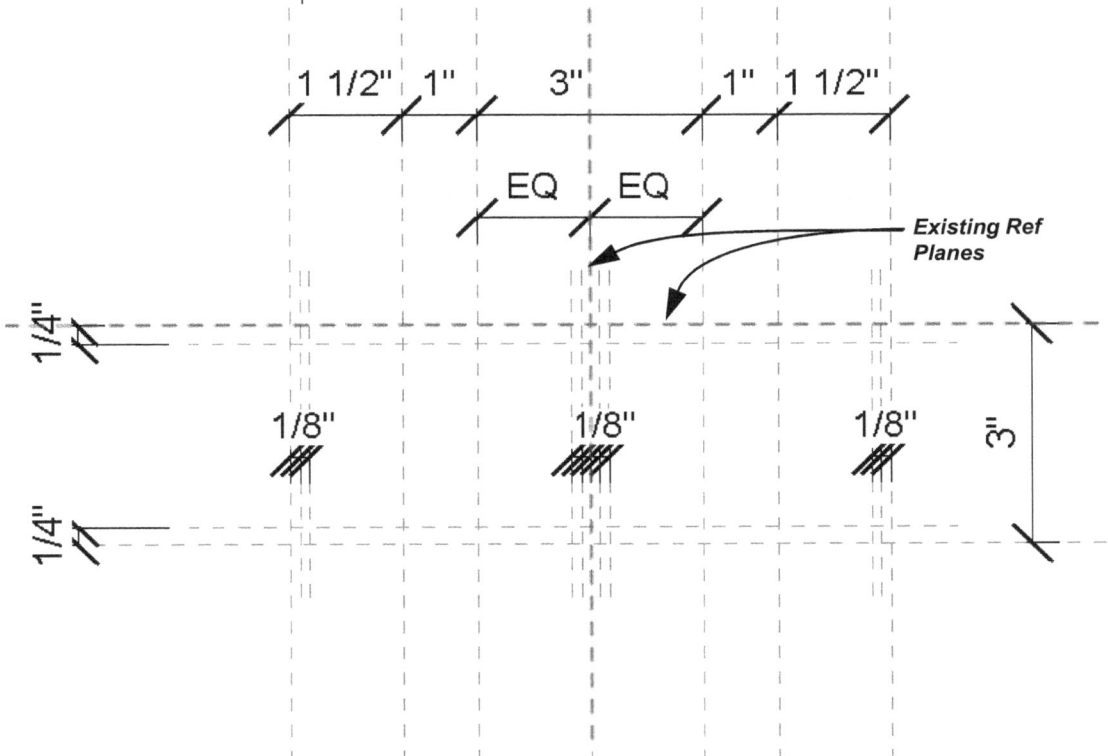

Figure 6–32

12. In the *Create* tab>Detail panel, click (Line). In the Options Bar, verify that the **Chain** option is selected.

13. Sketch the profile as shown in Figure 6–33.

Chain of walls or lines

Figure 6–33

14. Click (Modify) or press <Esc> when the profile is complete.

15. In the *Create* tab>Properties panel, click (Family Types).

16. At the top of Family Types dialog box, click (New Type).

17. In the Name dialog box, set the name to **3"**, and click **OK**.

18. Click **OK** again to close the dialog box.

19. Save the family without closing the file.

Task 2 - Load the composite Metal Deck profile.

1. Start a new project based on the default Structural template.

2. In the Quick Access Toolbar or *View* tab>Windows panel, expand (Switch Windows), and select **Composite-Metal-Deck.rfa** or press <Ctrl>+<Tab> to toggle back to the family file.

If more than one project is open, select the new one from the list that displays.

3. In the Family Editor panel, click (Load into Project) to insert the family into the new project. You should be in the **Structural Plans: Level 2** view of the new project.

4. In the *Structure* tab>Structure panel, click ⌒ (Floor: Structural).

5. in the Type Selector, verify that **Floor: 3"LW Concrete on 2" Metal Deck** is selected.

6. In the *Modify | Create Floor Boundary* tab>Draw panel, use the **Line** or **Rectangle** tool to draw a slab of any type or size. Set the *Span Direction* to **Horizontal**.

7. Click ✓ (Finish Edit Mode).

8. In the Quick Access Toolbar or *View* tab>Create panel, click
   ◗ (Section) and place a section vertically through the slab from north to south.

9. Open the new section view and change the *Scale* to **3/4"=1'-0"** and the *Detail Level* to **Fine**. You might need to adjust the crop region and/or zoom in on the slab section. It should look similar to the one shown in Figure 6–34.

Figure 6–34

10. Select the slab.

11. In Properties, click ⊞ (Edit Type).

12. Duplicate the existing type. Name the duplicated type **6" Concrete on 3" Comp Metal Deck**.

13. In the Type Properties dialog box, next to the **Structure** parameter, click **Edit...**.

14. Modify the **Structure [1], Concrete, Lightweight - 4 ksi** layer to a *Thickness* of **6"**, as shown in Figure 6–35.

Layers

	Function	Material	Thickness	Wraps	Structural Material	Variable
1	**Core Boundary**	**Layers Above Wrap**	0' 0"			
2	Structure [1]	Concrete, Lightweig	0' 6"		✓	
3	Structural Dec	Metal Deck	0' 0"			
4	**Core Boundary**	**Layers Below Wrap**	0' 0"			

Figure 6–35

15. For the **Structural Deck** layer, select **Composite-Metal-Deck: 3"** in the Deck Profile drop-down list, as shown in Figure 6–36.

Figure 6–36

16. Click **OK** to close all of the dialog boxes. The section should display the metal deck profile that was previously created, as shown in Figure 6–37.

Figure 6–37

Task 3 - Change the Flute Direction of a comp metal deck.

1. Return to the **Structural Plans: Level 2** view.

2. Select the **Span Direction Symbol**. Note that the **Direction Symbol** extends to the edges of the slab. The closed arrowheads represent the flute direction and the open arrowheads represent the extents of the slab in the perpendicular direction.

3. Start the **Rotate** command and rotate the span direction 90 degrees.

4. Return to the section view. The orientation of the composite metal deck has changed, as shown in Figure 6–38.

Figure 6–38

5. Save the project as **New Floor.rvt** and close the project.

6. Save and close the file **Composite-Metal-Deck.rfa**.

6.2 Creating Line-based Families

Line-based families enable you to add elements by selecting two points. These families can be made up of 2D detail elements (such as the filled region in Figure 6–39 that is used to show GWB in a wall section) or an array of 3D elements, such as the solar panels shown in Figure 6–40. The **Length** parameter, along with a reference line, is built in the family template and controls the start and end points of the family.

Figure 6–39

Figure 6–40

- When using a line based model component in a project, place the components on a face or on a work plane, as shown in Figure 6–41.

Figure 6–41

How To: Create a Simple Line-based Family

1. Start a new family based on the **Detail Item line Base.rft** or **Generic Model line Base.rft** template.
2. The new template includes several reference planes, a label, and a reference line, as shown in Figure 6–42.

Figure 6–42

3. Add any other framework information, as required.
4. Add elements that make up the family.

   - Detail elements include lines, detail components, symbols, masking regions, filled regions, text, and controls.

   - Model elements include all of the form tools along with components, model lines and text, connectors, and controls.

5. Flex the **Length** parameter to verify that what you have added works as expected.
6. Add parameters and family types, if required.
7. Load the family in a project to test it.

How To: Create Line-based Family with an Array

1. Start a new family based on the **Detail Item line Base.rft** or **Generic Model line Base.rft** template.
2. Add any other framework information, as required.
3. Insert a component or symbol you want to array.
4. Locate the element at the first point of the array. In the example shown in Figure 6–43, a label symbol (displaying **?**) is aligned and locked to the reference planes.

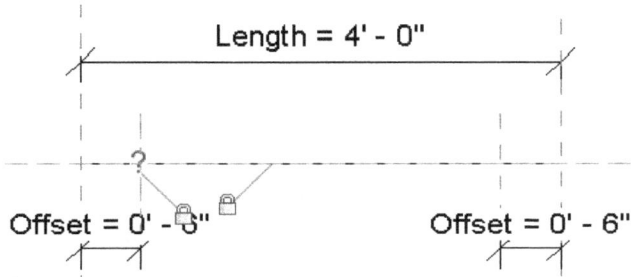

Figure 6–43

5. Select the element and in the Modify tab>Modify panel, click ⊞ (Array).
6. Setup the array and select the two points that define it.
7. Click **Modify** and select the array lines as shown in Figure 6–44.

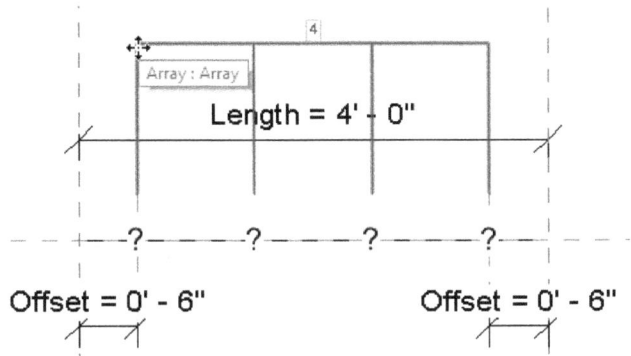

Figure 6–44

8. In the Options Bar, expand *Label* and select **<Add parameter...>**.
9. In the Parameter Properties dialog box, setup the parameter as required and click **OK**.
10. Flex the **Length** parameter to verify that it works as expected.
11. Add parameters and family types, if needed.
12. Load the family in a project to test it.

Practice 6e

Create Line-based Families - GWB Detail

Learning Objectives

- Create a line based detail family.
- Add family types.
- Test the family in a project.

In this practice, you will create a line-based detail family using a filled region to represent Gypsum Wall Board (GWB) in details. You will add reference planes, a label, and a flip control to help you create this family, as shown in Figure 6–45. You will create family types and test the family in a project.

Figure 6–45

Task 1 - Create a line-based detail family.

1. In the Home screen, in the *Families* area, click **New...**.

2. In the New Family dialog box, select **Detail Item line Base.rft** and click **Open**. The family template includes two reference planes, a reference line, and a labeled dimension, as shown in Figure 6–46.

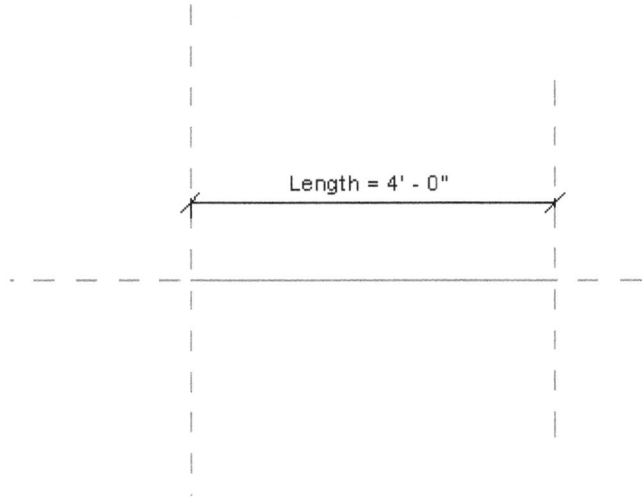

Length = 4' - 0"

Figure 6–46

3. Save the family as **Detail Component-GWB.rfa**.

4. In the *Create* tab>Datum panel, click (Reference Plane).

5. Add a horizontal reference plane above the existing and dimension it as shown in Figure 6–47.

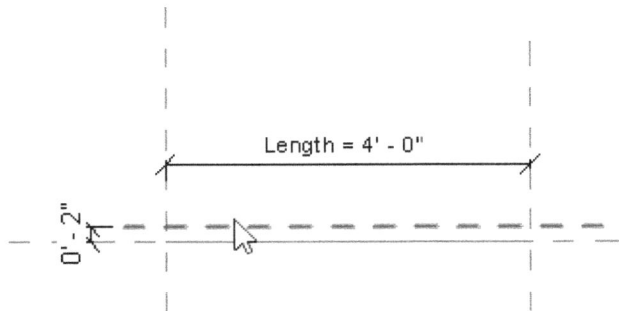

Length = 4' - 0"

0' - 2"

Figure 6–47

6. In the *Create* tab>Detail panel, click (Filled Region).

7. In the Draw panel, use the **Rectangle** tool to create the outline of the fill, snapping and locking the lines in place, as shown in Figure 6–48.

Figure 6–48

8. In the Type Selector, select **Filled region: Gypsum**.

9. Click ✔ (Finish Edit mode).

10. Flex the **Length** dimension to verify that the filled region moves as expected, as shown in Figure 6–49.

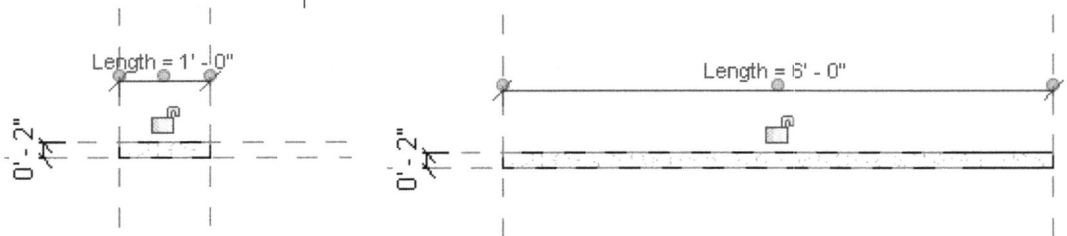

Figure 6–49

11. Finish with a Length of **4'-0"**.

12. Add a **Thickness** label (Type Parameter) to the **2"** dimension and change it to **5/8"**, as shown in Figure 6–50.

13. In the *Create* tab>Control panel, click ⊕ (Control).

14. In the *Modify | Place Control* tab>Control Type panel, click ⊹ (Double Vertical).

15. Place the control as shown in Figure 6–50.

Figure 6–50

16. Save the family.

Task 2 - Create Family Types and Test the Family in a project.

---

1. In the *Create* or *Modify* tab>Properties panel, click ⊞ (Family Types).

2. In the Family Types dialog box, click ⃞ (New Type).

3. Type in the *Name* **GWB 5/8"** and click **Apply**.

4. Create two additional types named **GWB 1/2" and GWB 1/4"** with the thickness modified to match.

5. Test each of the new types and click **OK**.

6. Save the family.

7. Open a new project.

8. In the *View* tab>Create panel, click ⊟ (Drafting View) and give it a generic name.

9. Switch back to the family file and load it into the project.

10. Switch to the drafting view and in the *Annotate* tab>Detail panel, click ⊟ (Detail Component) and select the new type if required.

11. Test each of the linear family types in the drafting view, as shown in Figure 6–51.

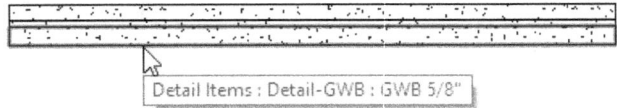

Detail Items : Detail-GWB : GWB 5/8"

Figure 6–51

12. Save and close the family file.

13. Close the project without saving.

Practice 6f

Create Line-based Families - Electrical Trunking

Learning Objectives

- Create a line based model family.
- Test the family in a project.

In this practice, you will create a line-based model family using a profile and a sweep for trunking, as shown in Figure 6–52. You will add a control and assign a family category and then use the new family in a project.

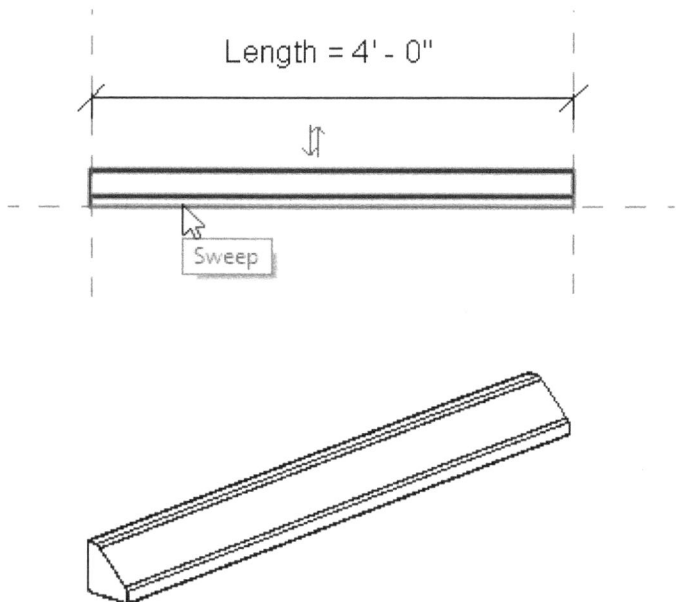

Figure 6–52

Task 1 - Create a line-based model family.

1. In the Home screen in the *Families* area click **New...**

2. In the New Family dialog box, select **Generic Model line Base.rft** and click **Open**. The family template includes two reference planes, a reference line, and a labeled dimension, as shown in Figure 6–53.

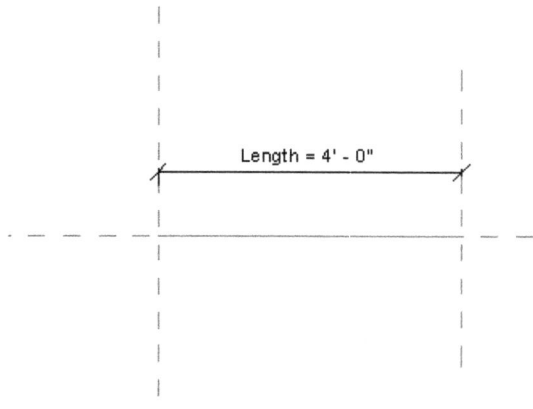

Figure 6–53

3. Save the family as **Trunking.rfa**.

4. In the *Create* tab>Forms panel, click 🖨 (Sweep).

5. In the *Modify | Sweep* tab>Sweep panel, click ✐ (Sketch Path).

6. Sketch the path from intersection to intersection of the reference planes and lock it. If required, use **Align** to help you lock it in place, as shown in Figure 6–54.

Figure 6–54

7. Click ✔ (Finish Edit mode).

8. In the *Modify | Sweep* tab>Sweep panel, click 🗔 (Load Profile).

9. In the practice files>*MEP* folder, select **Trunking Profile.rfa**

10. Select **Trunking Profile** from the Profile drop-down list, as shown in Figure 6–55.

Figure 6–55

11. Click ✓ (Finish Edit mode).

12. Flex the **Length** dimension to verify that the sweep moves as expected, as shown in Figure 6–56.

Figure 6–56

13. Finish with a Length of **4'-0"**.

14. In the *Create* tab>Control panel, click ⊹ (Control).

15. In the *Modify | Place Control* tab>Control Type panel, click ⊹ (Double Vertical).

16. Place the control as shown in Figure 6–57.

Figure 6–57

17. In the *Create or Modify* tab>Properties panel, click
    ⊟ (Family Categories).

18. In the Family Category and Parameters dialog box, set the
    Filter list to **Electrical**, and select **Electrical Fixtures**, as
    shown in Figure 6–58. Then, click **OK**.

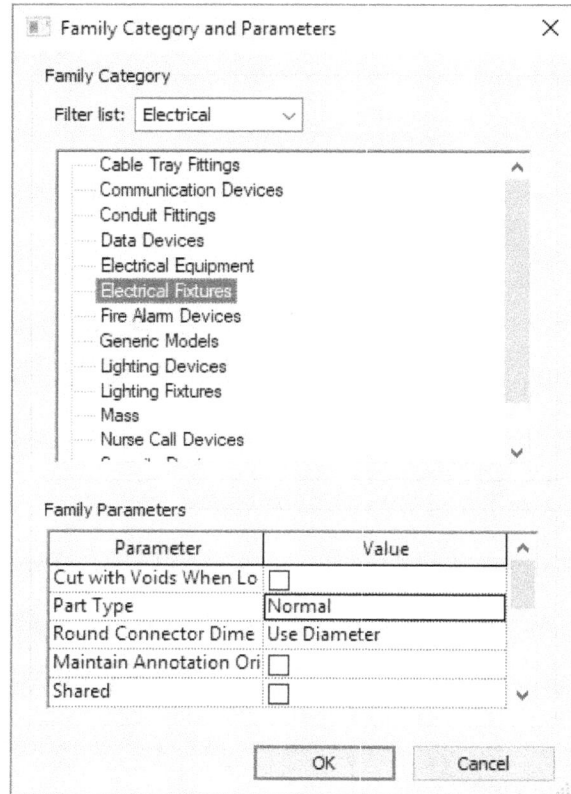

Figure 6–58

19. Save the family.

Task 2 - Test the Family in a project.

1. In the practice files>*MEP* folder, open **Fire Station-MEP.rvt**.

2. Open the Electrical>Power>Floor Plans>**1-Power** view and zoom on the training rooms.

3. Switch back to the family file and load it into the project.

4. If the command is not already started, in the *Systems* tab> Electrical panel, click ⌧ (Electrical Fixture) and in the Type Selector, select **Trunking**.

5. In the *Modify | Place Devices* tab>Placement panel, click ◇ (Place on Work Plane).

6. Add trunking to the training rooms as shown in Figure 6–59. Use the **Flip** control as required, to verify it is on the outside of the wall.

Electrical Fixtures : Trunking : Trunking

Figure 6–59

7. Save and close the project and family files.

Practice 6g

Create Line-based Families - Services Symbol Array

Learning Objectives

- Create a symbol family.
- Create a line based family.
- Add an array to the line-based family.
- Add family types.
- Test the family in a project.

In this practice, you will create an annotation symbol using a label that will be added to a line-based detail family. You will add parameters and create an array parameter. You will then associate a parameter in the label with a parameter in the line-based family and create a series of family types as shown in Figure 6–60. You will also test the family in a project.

Figure 6–60

Task 1 - Create an Annotation Symbol with a Label.

1. In the Home screen in the *Families* area click **New....**

2. In the New Family dialog box, navigate to the *Annotation* folder, select **Generic Annotation.rft**, and click **Open**.

3. Zoom in to read the red note and then delete it. The Family Category of this example does not matter at this time.

4. Save the family as **Services Symbol.rfa**.

5. In the *Create* tab>Text panel, click 🄰 (Label).

6. Click near the intersection of the reference planes to place the label.

7. In the Edit Label dialog box, click (Add Parameter).

8. In the Parameter Properties dialog box, create a type parameter with the *Name* of **Letter** and the *Type of parameter* set to **Text**, as shown in Figure 6–61.

Parameter Properties   ✕

Parameter Type

◉ Family parameter

(Cannot appear in schedules or tags)

◯ Shared parameter

(Can be shared by multiple projects and families, exported to ODBC, and appear in schedules and tags)

Select...   Export...

Parameter Data

Name:

| Letter | ◉ Type

Discipline:

| Common   ∨ | ◯ Instance

Type of parameter: ☐ Reporting Parameter

| Text   ∨ | (Can be used to extract value from a geometric condition and report it in a formula or as a schedulable parameter)

Group parameter under:

| Text   ∨ |

Tooltip description:

<No tooltip description. Edit this parameter to write a custom tooltip. Custom t...

| Edit Tooltip... |

How do I create family parameters?

OK   Cancel

Figure 6–61

9. Click ⬐ (Add parameter(s) to label), set the *Sample Value* to **A**, as shown in Figure 6–62. Click **OK**.

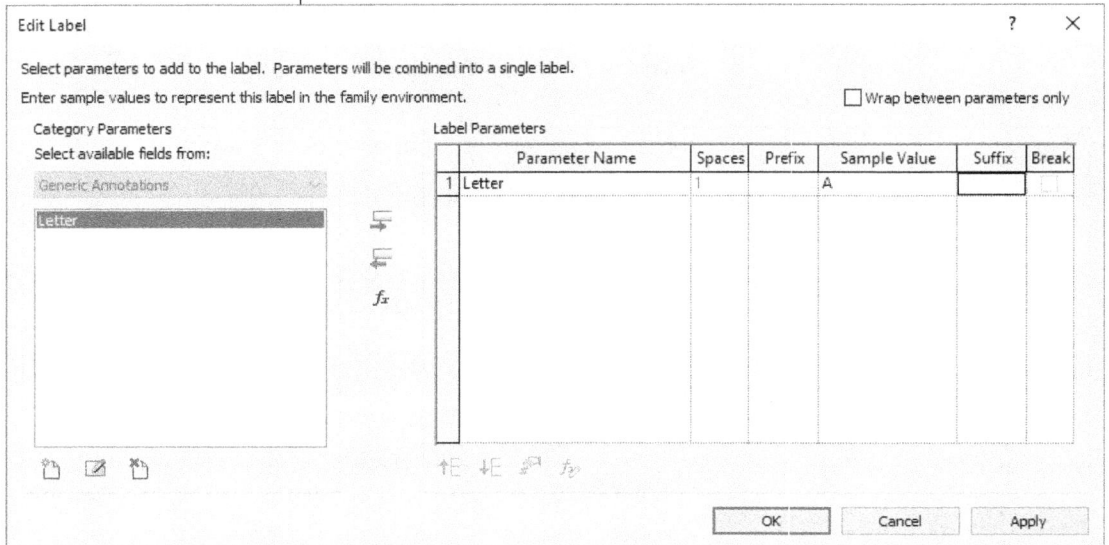

Edit Label   ?   ✕

Select parameters to add to the label. Parameters will be combined into a single label.

Enter sample values to represent this label in the family environment.   ☐ Wrap between parameters only

Category Parameters

Select available fields from:

Generic Annotations

Letter

	Parameter Name	Spaces	Prefix	Sample Value	Suffix	Break
1	Letter	1		A		

OK   Cancel   Apply

Figure 6–62

10. Move the label so it is at the intersection of the reference planes and resize boundary leaving some room on both size for longer text. Verify that the properties match what is shown in Figure 6–63.

Properties   ✕   🖻   -   ✕

Label
3/32"

Generic Annotations (1)   ⌄   🔳 Edit Type

Graphics   ☆

Sample Text	A
Label	Edit...
Wrap between param...	☐
Horizontal Align	Center
Vertical Align	Middle
Keep Readable	☑
Visible	☑

A

Figure 6–63

11. Click away from the label and in Properties, select **Keep Text readable**.

12. Save the family.

Task 2 - Create a line-based family.

1. Start a new family based on the **Detail Item line Base.rft**. The family template includes two reference planes, a reference line, and a labeled dimension, as shown in Figure 6–64.

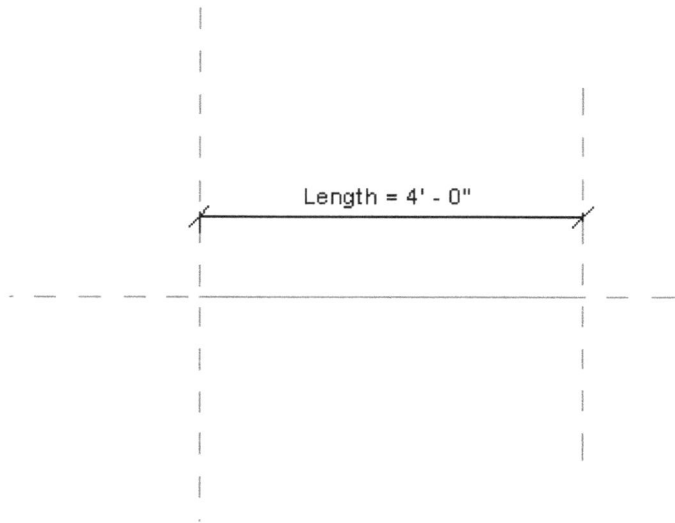

Length = 4' - 0"

Figure 6–64

2. Save the family as **Services Lines.rfa**.

3. In the *Create* tab>Detail panel, click (Line).

4. In the *Modify | Place Lines* tab>Subcategory panel, expand the Subcategory list and select **Light Lines**.

5. In the Options bar, toggle off **Chain**.

6. Sketch a line from the left intersection of the reference planes to the right intersection of the reference planes and lock it into place, as shown in Figure 6–65.

Length = 4' - 0"
4' - 0"

Figure 6–65

7. Add two reference planes, dimension and label them with a type parameter, as shown in Figure 6–66.

Figure 6–66

8. Save the family.

Task 3 - Add an array.

1. Switch to the Services Symbol family and load it into the Services Lines family.

2. Place the label, which displays as **?**, near the reference planes and then align and lock it into place, as shown in Figure 6–67.

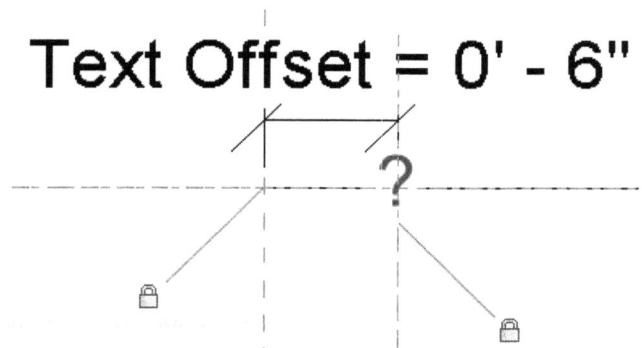

Figure 6–67

3. With the symbol selected, in the *Modify | Generic Annotations* tab>Modify panel, click ⊞ (Array).

4. In the Options Bar, verify that the **Group and Associate** option is selected, set the *Number* to **4** and *Move To:* to **Last**. Select the start point and end point as shown in Figure 6–68.

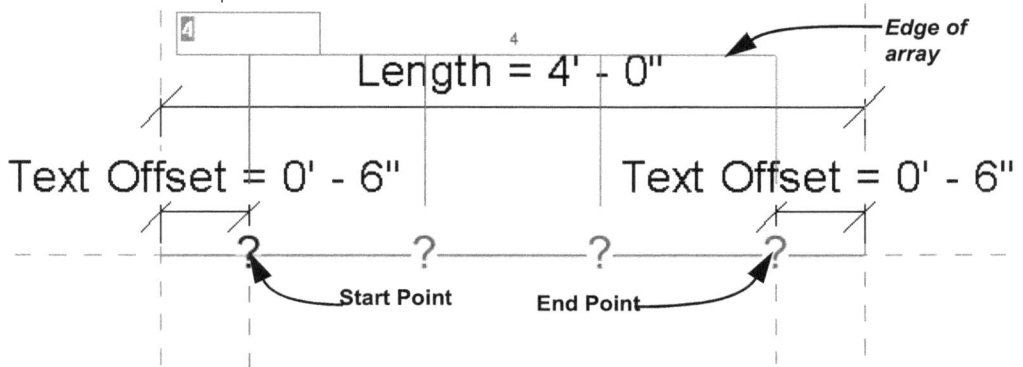

Length = 4' - 0"

Edge of array

Text Offset = 0' - 6"   Text Offset = 0' - 6"

Start Point   End Point

Figure 6–68

5. Align and lock the last label of the array to the right text offset lines.

6. Click on the edge of the array and in the Options Bar, expand the Label drop-down list and select **<Add parameter...>**.

7. In the Parameter Properties dialog box, *Name* the parameter **Number of Labels**, set it to **Type** and *Group* it under **Other**. Click **OK**.

8. Open the Family Types dialog box and flex the parameters to ensure that they are working as expected.

9. Save the family.

Task 4 - Create Family Types.

1. Open the Family Types dialog box.

2. Create a new type parameter named **Services** with the *Type of parameter* set to **Text**. Click **OK** twice to exit out of the dialog boxes.

3. Select one of the labels. Press <Tab> to ensure that you select the symbol, not the group.

4. Click **Edit Type**.

5. In the Type Properties dialog box, next to *Letter*, click

   (Associate Family Parameter).

6. In the Associate Family Parameter dialog box, select **Services**, as shown in Figure 6–69. Click **OK** twice to close the dialog boxes.

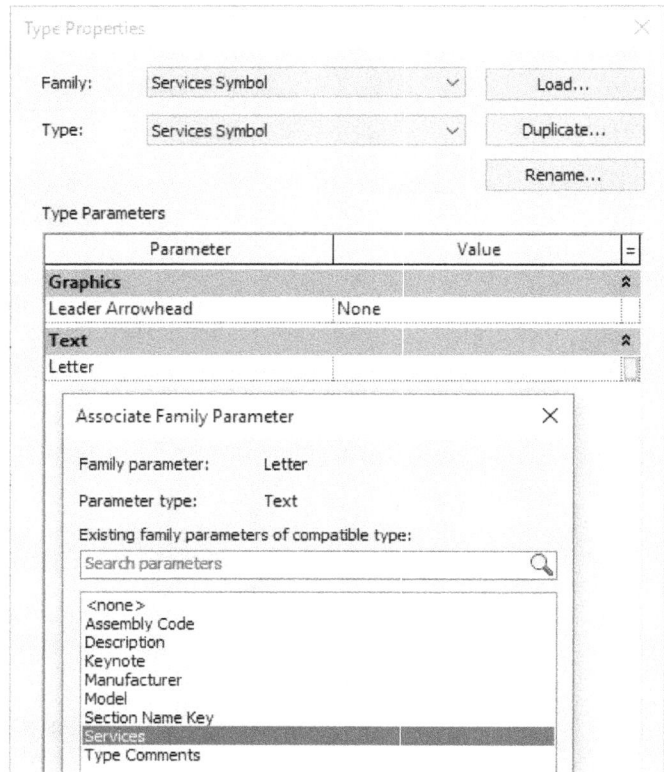

Figure 6–69

7. Open the Family Types dialog box again and set the *Value* for *Services* to **A**. Click **Apply**. The letters should update as shown in Figure 6–70.

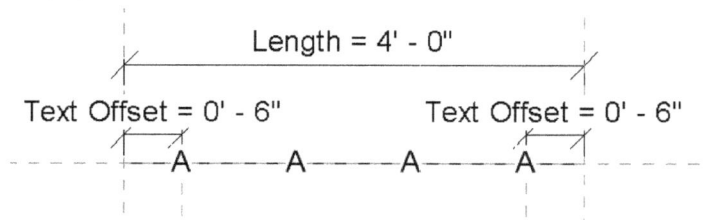

Figure 6–70

8. Remain in the Family Types dialog box and at the top, click

   (New Type). Name the *Type* **Compressed Air** and click **Apply**.

9. Create several other new types such as:

- Hot Water Heating Supply - **HW**
- Hot Water Heating Return - **HWR**
- High Pressure Steam - **HPS**
- Medium Pressure Steam - **MPS**
- Low Pressure Steam - **LPS**

10. Save the family.

11. In the practice files>*MEP* folder, open the project **Fire Station-MEP.rvt**.

If there are too many views open, in the View tab> Windows panel click ☐ (Close Inactive).*

12. Open the Coordination>All>Floor Plans>**Site** view.

13. Switch back to the Services Lines family and load it into the project.

14. In the *Annotate* tab>Detail panel, click ☐ (Detail Component), if required. Test several of the lines in the project as shown in Figure 6–71.

Figure 6–71

15. Save and close the project and families.

Practice 6h

Create Line-based Families: Solar Panel Array

Learning Objectives

- Create a line-based model family.
- Apply an array.
- Add parameters to define the interactions of the array.
- Test the family in a project.

In this practice, you will create a line-based model family using a solar panel component. You will array the component and then setup parameters to define the number of panels setup in an array. You will test the line-based solar panel family in a project, as shown in Figure 6–72.

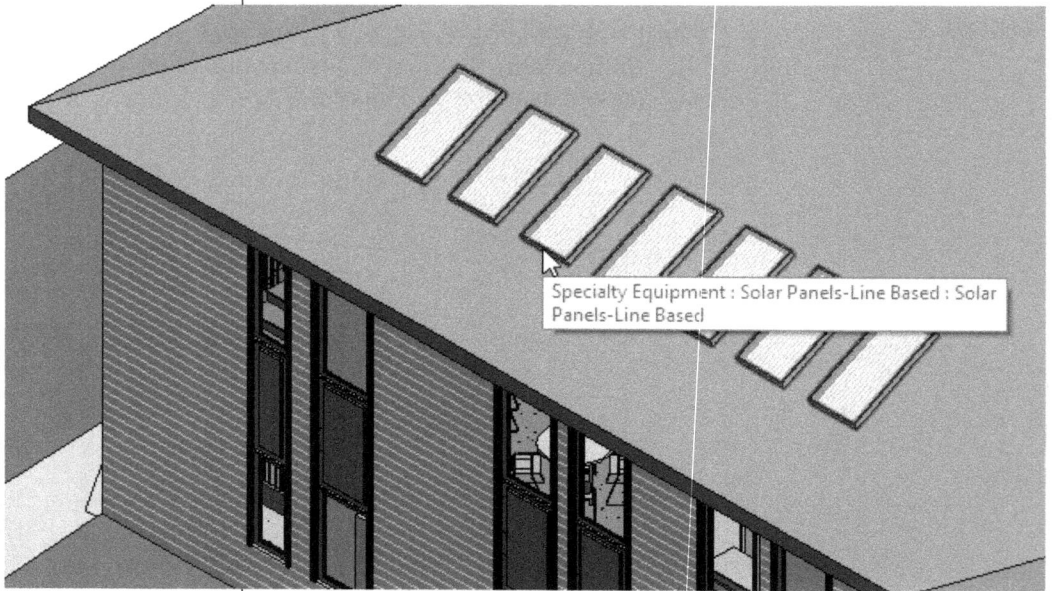

Specialty Equipment : Solar Panels-Line Based : Solar Panels-Line Based

Figure 6–72

Task 1 - Insert and array a component.

1. In the Home screen, in the *Families* area, click **New...**.

2. In the New Family dialog box, select **Generic Model line Base.rft** and click **Open**. The family template includes two reference planes, a reference line, and a labeled dimension, as shown in Figure 6–73.

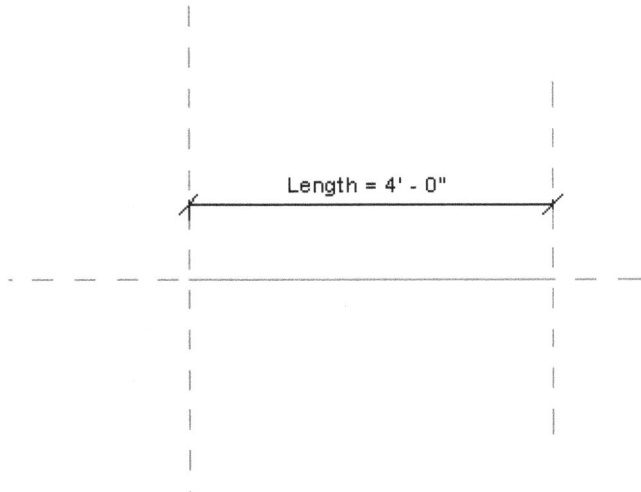

Length = 4' - 0"

Figure 6–73

3. Save the family as **Solar Panels - Line-based.rfa**.

4. Change the **Length** parameter to **9'-0"**.

5. In the *Create* tab>Model panel, click (Component).

6. An alert displays telling you that no component is loaded in the project. Click **Yes** to load one.

7. Navigate to the Revit library's *Sustainable Design* folder, select **Solar Panel.rfa**, and click **Open**.

8. In the *Modify | Place Component t*ab>Placement panel, click (Place on Workplane).

9. Place the component.

10. Align and lock it to the reference planes as shown in Figure 6–74.

Figure 6–74

11. Start the **Array** command and select the solar panel component. In the Options Bar set the *Number* to **2** and *Move To:* to **Last**. Place the array as shown in Figure 6–75. The exact distance does not matter at this time.

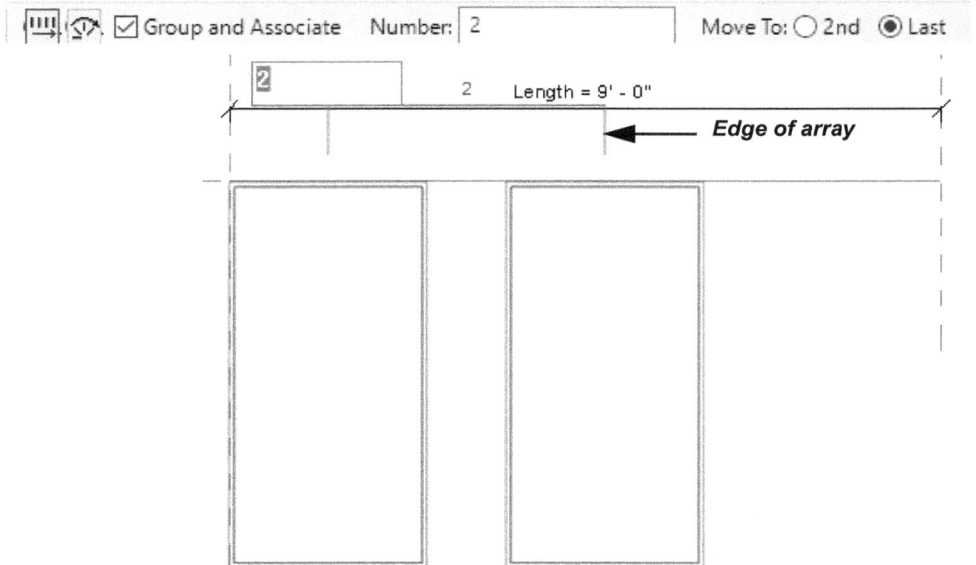

Figure 6–75

12. Align and lock the edge of the second solar panel to the right reference plane.

13. Save the family.

Task 2 - Add parameters.

1. Click **Modify**. Hover over the edge of one of the arrayed elements and press <Tab> until the edge of the array highlights. Select the edge of the array, as shown in Figure 6–76.

Figure 6–76

2. In the Options Bar, expand the Label drop-down list and select **<Add parameter...>**.

3. In the Parameter Properties dialog box, in the *Parameter Data* area, type **Number of Panels** for the *Name* type and select **Instance**. Group the parameter under **Constraints**, as shown in Figure 6–77.

Figure 6–77

4. Open the Family Type dialog box. Change the *Number of Panels* to **3** and click **Apply**.

5. Test other numbers and you can see that there is an issue with more than 3 panels when the Length is set to **9'-0"**.

6. In the Family Types dialog box, at the bottom, click (New Parameter).

7. In the Parameter Properties dialog box, create the parameter shown in Figure 6–78. Then, click **OK**.

Parameter Data

Name:

| Minimum Panel Distance | ○ Type |

Discipline:

| Common ∨ | ◉ Instance |

Type of parameter:

| Length ∨ | ☐ Reporting Parameter |

Group parameter under:

(Can be used to extract value from a geometric condition and report it in a formula or as a schedulable parameter)

| Constraints ∨ |

Tooltip description:

<No tooltip description. Edit this parameter to write a custom tooltip. Custom t...

Edit Tooltip...

Figure 6–78

8. Set the *Minimum Panel Distance* to **3'-6"**.

9. Set the formula for the *Number of Panels* to **Length / Minimum Panel Distance**. Then, click **Apply**.

10. Test out different lengths and distances to flex the family such as the example shown in Figure 6–79.

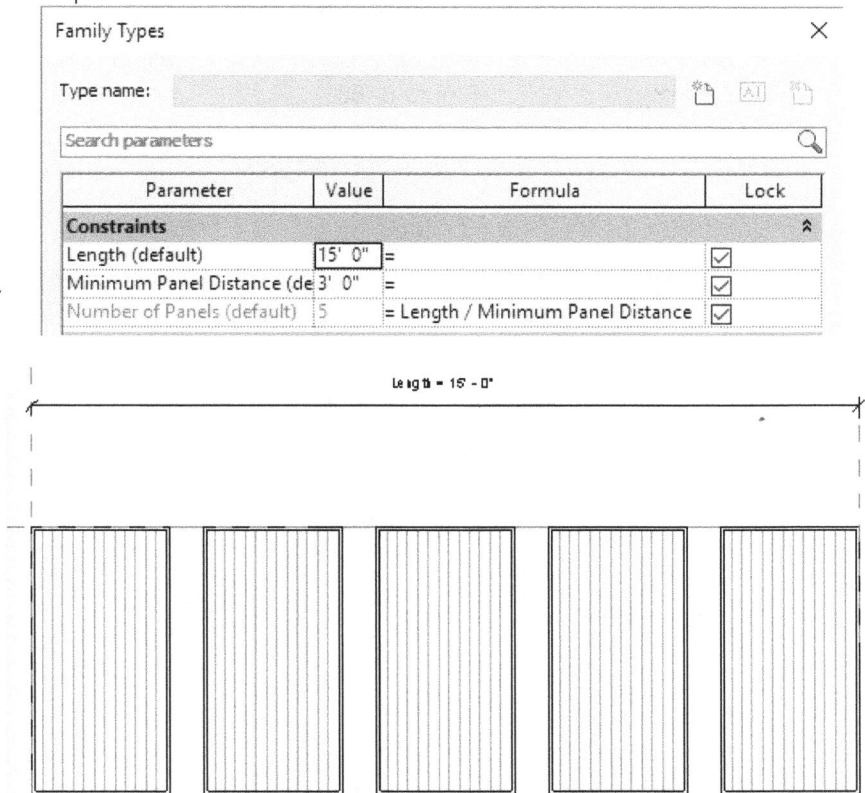

Figure 6–79

11. Finish the testing by setting the *Length* to **9'-0"** and the *Minimum Panel Distance* to **3'-0"**.

12. Save the family.

Task 3 - Test the Family in a project.

1. In the practice files>*Architectural* folder, open the **Fire Station.rvt** project.

2. Switch back to the family and load it into the project.

3. In the *Modify | Place Component* tab>Placement panel, click (Place on Face).

4. Select the south facing side of the roof.

5. Draw a string of solar panels across the roof, as shown in Figure 6–80.

Figure 6–80

6. Click **Modify** and select the solar panels.

7. In Properties, in the *Constraints* area, change the P*anel Distance* to **3'-6".** The number of panels changes with the new distance.

8. Save and close the project and family files.

6.3 Creating In-Place Families

In-place families use standard family tools to create elements that are specific to the project in which you create them. These might include built-in furniture, sloped walls (shown in Figure 6–81), custom door or window openings, and roofs.

Figure 6–81

In-place families should only be used if you are doing a one-time project specific modification. If you think a family might be used again, you should create a component family for it.

In-place family elements become the actual element you specify, such as a wall, door, roof, column, ceiling fixture, or floor.

- If the element is a host element, such as a wall, you can add elements to it, such as doors or windows.

- Elements, such as in-place doors and windows, can be copied and moved within their host.

- Complex stairs can be created as an in-place family.

- In-place family elements can be aligned and locked to project elements so they move together.

- Ensure that reference planes are drawn in the family. If you tie an in-place family to an external reference plane and delete the reference plane, you lose the family.

- In-place families are rarely used in the MEP disciplines.

How To: Create an In-Place Family

1. In a project, in the *Architecture* tab>Build panel, or *Structure* tab>Model panel, or *Systems* tab>Model panel, expand

   (Component) and click (Model In-Place).
2. In the Family Category and Parameters dialog box that opens (shown in Figure 6–82), you can filter the list to display only the disciplines, required.

Figure 6–82

3. Select a *Family Category* and click **OK**. In the Name dialog box, enter a name for the new family and click **OK**.
4. The Family Editor tabs display in the ribbon. Use the tools as required including reference planes, dimensions, labels and parameters, to create the elements you want to have in the family.
5. In the In-Place Editor panel, click (Finish Model) to create the in-place element.

Practice 6i

Create In-place Families: Door Opening

Learning Objectives

- Create an in-place door family and opening.
- Add trim for the in-place door family using a sweep based on a 2D profile.

In this practice, you will create a door in-place family and add an odd-shaped opening. Using a Sweep, you will add a profile for door trim, as shown in Figure 6–83.

Figure 6–83

Task 1 - Create an in-place door family.

1. Start a new project based on the default architectural template.

2. Open the **Floor Plan: Level 1** view and draw a **10'-0"** high wall in the project.

3. In the *Architecture* tab>Build panel, expand 🗔 (Component) and click 🗔 (Model In-Place).

4. In the Family Category and Parameters dialog box, Set the *Filter list* to **Architecture** and then set the *Family Category* to **Doors** and click **OK**.

5. Name the in-place family **Odd Shaped Opening**.

6. The Family Editor tools display in the ribbon. In the *Create* tab>Datum panel, click ✏ (Reference Plane) and draw a reference plane along the center of the wall. Name it **Center of Wall**, as shown in Figure 6–84.

The reference plane is used to specify the work plane. It does not impact the shape of the wall.

Center of Wall

Figure 6–84

7. Switch to the **Elevations :South** view and zoom in on the wall.

8. In the *Create* tab>Model panel, click ▢ (Opening).

9. If you have more than one wall in the project you are prompted to select a host for the opening. Click **OK** and select the wall.

10. Draw an opening similar to that shown in Figure 6–85.

The exact design does not matter; ensure that it is at least the width and height of a standard door opening. The sketch must be closed.

Figure 6–85

11. Click ✓ (Finish Edit Mode) but do not finish the model.

Task 2 - Add a sweep for the trim and sketch a profile.

---

1. In the *Create* tab>Work Plane panel, click ⊞ (Set).

2. In the Work Plane dialog box, set the *Name* to **Reference Plane: Center of Wall** and click **OK**.

3. In the *Create* tab>Forms panel, click ⟳ (Sweep).

4. In the *Modify | Sweep* tab>Sweep panel, click ↗ (Sketch Path).

5. Draw a path around the edge of the opening. Do not close this sketch.

- Click ⚡ (Pick Lines) and, in the Options Bar, select **Lock**. This locks the sketch to the existing geometry so the sketch updates if the opening is modified.

6. Click ✓ (Finish Edit Mode).

7. In the *Modify | Sweep* tab>Sweep panel, click ⬚ (Edit Profile).

8. In the Go To View dialog box, select **Floor Plan: Level 1** and click **Open View**.

9. Zoom in on the red dot. Draw the profile shown in Figure 6–86. The profile must be closed. You do not need to add the dimensions.

Drawing the profile in the in-place model keeps the size of the trim directly connected to the selected wall and opening.

Figure 6–86

10. Click ✓ (Finish Edit Mode) to finish the profile.

11. Click ✓ (Finish Edit Mode) again to finish the sweep.

12. Click ✓ (Finish Model).

13. View the new cased opening in several views.

14. Move the opening. You can see that the opening works just like a door.

15. Save the project as **Sample Opening.rvt**.

Practice 6j

Create In-Place Families: Concrete Corbeling

Practice Objectives

- Create a 2D profile and use it in an in-place family to create a concrete corbel.
- Join the corbeling to the wall.

In this practice, you will draw a profile of a corbel and then use it in an in-place family to create a sweep, as shown in Figure 6–87.

Walls : Wall Corbelling : Wall Corbelling

Figure 6–87

Corbel: A stepped bracket, designed to support a weight. It projects from a wall and is created from a building material, such as concrete, stone, or wood.

Task 1 - Create the profile.

1. Create a new family based on the **Profile-Hosted.rft** template found in the Autodesk Revit Library.

2. Save the family to your practice folder as **Corbel.rfa**.

3. Draw the four reference planes as shown in Figure 6–88.

The dimensions are for information only.

Figure 6–88

4. In the *Create* tab>Detail panel, click ⌐ (Line). Draw the profile shown in Figure 6–89.

The Family Editor does not display as many tabs or panels because fewer commands are required to create a 2D profile.

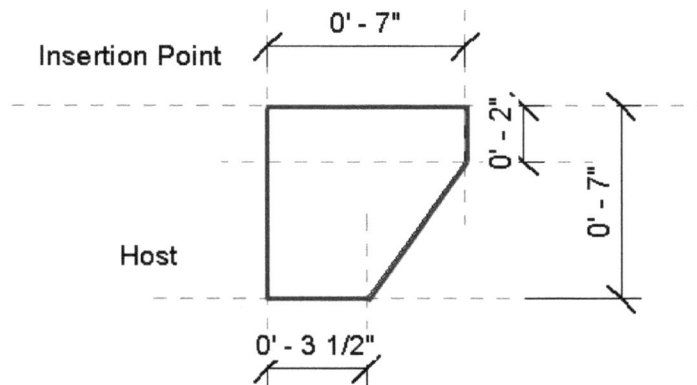

Figure 6–89

5. Save the family.

Task 2 - Add a new wall sweep using the profile.

1. In the practice files *Structural* folder, open **Concrete-Structure.rvt**.

2. Open the **Structural Plans: Level 1** view.

3. In the *Structure* tab>Model panel, expand ⬚ (Component) and click ⬚ (Model In-Place).

4. In the Family Category and Parameters dialog box, set the *Filter list* to **Structure** only, select **Walls**, and click **OK**.

5. In the Name dialog box, type **Wall Corbeling** and click **OK**.

6. In the In-Place Editor, in the *Create* tab>Forms panel, click ⬚ (Sweep).

7. In the *Modify | Sweep* tab>Sweep panel, click ⬚ (Sketch Path).

8. Use the Draw tools to sketch the lines shown in Figure 6–90.

Figure 6–90

9. Click ⬚ (Finish Edit Mode).

10. In the *Modify | Sweep* tab>Sweep panel, click ⬚ (Load Profile).

11. In the Load Family dialog box, navigate to the folder where you saved the **Crobel.rfa** profile created in the previous task. Select it and click **Open**.

12. In the Sweep panel, click ⬚ (Select Profile).

13. In the *Profile* list, select **Corbel**.

14. In the Quick Access Toolbar, click ⬚ (Default 3D View).

15. Zoom in on the profile location, it is facing into the wall as shown in Figure 6–91.

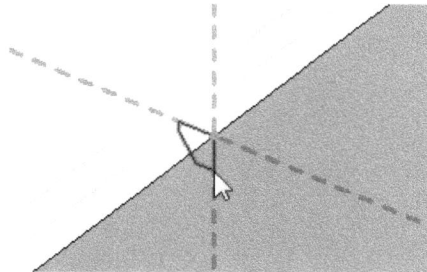

Figure 6–91

16. In the Options Bar, click **Flip**.

17. In the Options Bar or using the temporary dimension, lower the corbel (negative) **-6"** in the Y-direction, as shown in Figure 6–92.

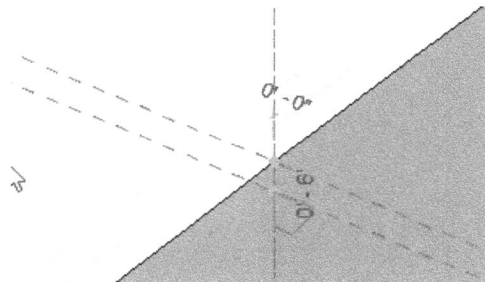

Figure 6–92

18. Click ✓ (Finish Edit Mode).

19. With the new Corbel sweep still selected, in Properties, in the *Materials and Finishes* area, next to Material, click
    … (Browse).

20. In the Materials Browser, select **Concrete - Cast-in-Place Concrete** and click **OK**.

21. In the *Modify* tab>In-Place Editor panel, click ✓ (Finish Model).

Task 3 - Join the corbel to the wall.

1. Open the **Structural Plans: Level 1** view.

2. Draw a Wall Section across the wall and corbel, as shown in Figure 6–93.

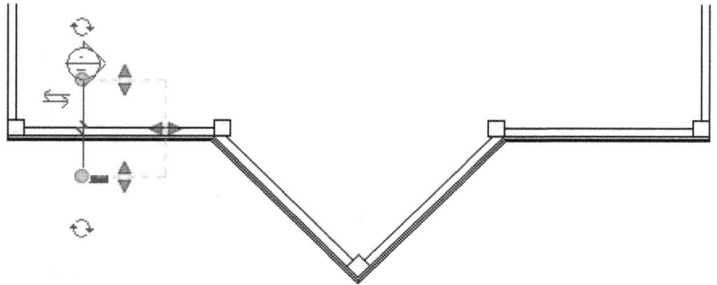

Figure 6–93

3. Open the section. You can see that the wall and corbel are still considered separate entities, as shown in Figure 6–94.

4. In the *Modify* tab>Geometry panel, click 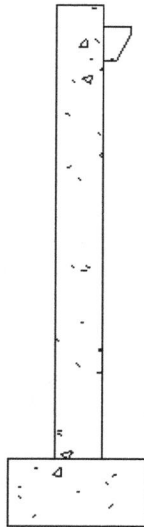 (Join). Select the wall and then the corbel. It becomes part of the existing wall, as shown in Figure 6–95.

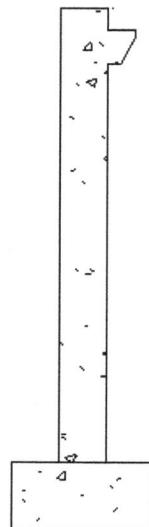

Figure 6–94   **Figure 6–95**

5. Save the project.

6.4 Working with Shared Parameters

The Autodesk Revit software includes many parameters used in families and schedules.

- **Family parameters:** Are specific to a family that constrain or flex geometry and assign attributes, such as material.
- **Project parameters:** Can be assigned to schedules and are available only in the current project.
- **Shared parameters:** Can be referenced in multiple locations, projects, families, tags, and schedules, and shared between projects.

Shared Parameters

Create shared parameters for custom information that needs to be displayed in both tags and schedules, used in multiple projects or families, or exported to ODBC to be put in a database.

- Shared parameters can be created wherever there is an option to create a parameter (as shown in Figure 6–96), including Schedule Properties (creating a Field) and the Family Types dialog box.

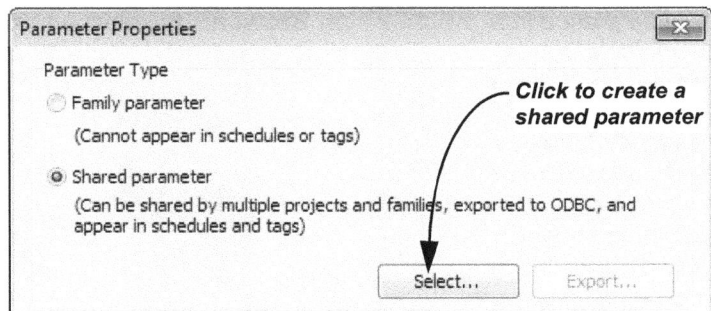

Figure 6–96

- You can also directly open the Edit Shared Parameters dialog box. In the *Manage* tab>Settings panel, click (Shared Parameters).

- If you are creating shared parameters in a family file, do it only for elements that constrain or flex the geometry and are used in a schedule.

How To: Create a Shared Parameter

1. Start the process of adding a parameter in Project Parameters, schedules, or family types.
2. Set the *Parameter Type* to **Shared parameter** in the Parameter Properties dialog box, as shown in Figure 6–97.

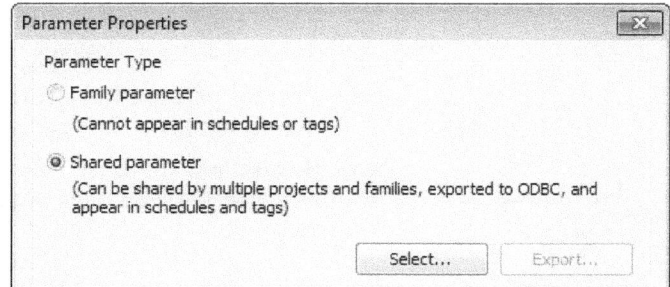

Figure 6–97

3. Click **Select...**.
4. In the Shared Parameters dialog box, you can select from groups and parameters that are already included in your project, or click **Edit...** to create a new shared parameter.

   - If no shared parameter file has been specified, an alert box opens. Click **Yes** to select a shared parameter file.

5. In the Edit Shared Parameters dialog box, as shown in Figure 6–98, click **Create...** to create a shared parameter file or **Browse...** to select an existing one.

Shared parameters are stored in a text file that should be placed in a network location available to everyone. This ensures consistency between projects and team members by maintaining naming standards and limiting typical typing errors with spaces and case sensitivity.

Figure 6–98

6. Creating groups for related parameters makes working with numerous names much easier. In the *Groups* area, click **New** to create a new parameter group.
7. In the New Parameter Group dialog box, as shown in Figure 6–99, type a new name and click **OK**.

Only one shared parameter file can be active in a project at a time. Therefore, create one main file with multiple groups instead of creating many files.

Figure 6–99

8. In the Edit Shared Parameters dialog box, in the *Parameters* area, click **New** to create a new shared parameter.
9. In the Parameter Properties dialog box, type a *Name* for the parameter, and set the *Discipline* (**Common**, **Structural**, or **Electrical**) and *Type of Parameter* in the drop-down lists. You can also add a Tooltip. The dialog box is shown in Figure 6–100.

Figure 6–100

10. Click **OK**.
11. In the Edit Shared Parameters dialog box, once you have the parameters in place, you can:
    • Click **Properties...** to display the contents of the Parameter Properties. You cannot modify them.
    • Click **Move...** to switch a parameter from one parameter group to another.

- Click **Delete** to remove a parameter. Be careful about using this because it might impact the current project and any other projects that use the parameter.

12. When you have finished creating the shared parameters, click **OK** to close the Edit Shared Parameters dialog box.

13. Continue with the other steps required to add the parameter to the project, family, or schedule.

How To: Add a Shared Project Parameter to a Project

1. In the *Manage* tab>Settings panel, click ⬚ (Project Parameters).

2. In the Project Parameters dialog box, as shown in Figure 6–101, click **Add**.

Figure 6–101

3. In the Parameter Properties dialog box, select **Shared parameter** and click **Select...**.

4. In the Shared Parameters dialog box, set the *Parameter group* and *Parameters* that you want to add to the project, as shown in Figure 6–102. Click **OK**.

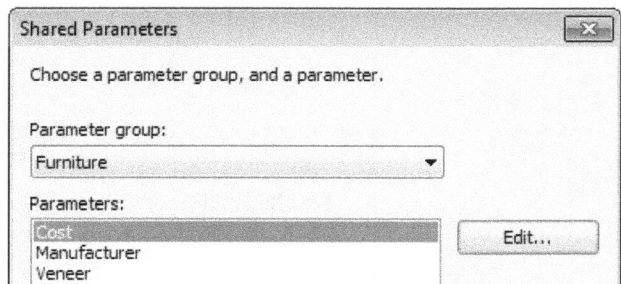

Figure 6–102

- If the parameter you want to use does not exist, click **Edit....** to create a new shared parameter.

5. In the Parameter Properties dialog box:

- In the *Categories* area, select the categories to which you want the parameter to apply, as shown in Figure 6–103.

Categories

Filter list: Architecture   ▼

☐ Hide un-checked categories

☐ Doors
☐ Electrical Equipment
☐ Electrical Fixtures
⊞ ☐ Floors
☑ Furniture
☑ Furniture Systems
☐ Generic Models
☐ Grids
☐ Levels
☐ Lighting Fixtures
⊟ ☐ Mass
  ☐ Mass Exterior Wall
  ☐ Mass Floor
  ☐ Mass Glazing

| Check All | Check None |

Figure 6–103

- In the *Parameter Data* area, the Name, Discipline, and Type of Parameter drop-down lists are grayed out, while the shared parameter you just selected is displayed.

6. Select an option from the Group parameter under drop-down list (this is where it displays in the Element Properties dialog box) and select **Instance** or **Type**, as shown in Figure 6–104. Add a tooltip description, if required.

Parameter Data

Name:

Cost   ○ Type

Discipline:

Common   ◉ Instance

Type of Parameter:

Currency

Group parameter under:

Other   ▼

Figure 6–104

7. Click **OK** twice to add the parameter to the project.

Practice 6k	# Work with Shared Parameters in Architectural Projects

Practice Objectives

- Create shared parameters in a project.
- Create an annotation tag family and link the shared parameters into the tag.
- Add the shared parameters to a family and insert them into the project along with the associated tags.
- Create a schedule using the shared parameters including the project, tag, and family.

In this practice, you will create shared parameters through project parameters and use them in a family, tag, and schedule, as shown in Figure 6–105.

Figure 6–105

Task 1 - Create shared parameters.

1. In the practice files *Architectural* folder, open **Office-Layout.rvt**.

2. In the *Manage* tab>Settings panel, click ▥ (Project Parameters).

3. In the Project Parameters dialog box, click **Add...**.

4. In the Parameter Properties dialog box, select **Shared parameter** and click **Select...**.

5. If there is no existing shared parameter file, an alert box displays prompting you to select a shared parameter file. Click **Yes**. If the Shared Parameters dialog box opens, click **Edit...**.

6. In the Edit Shared Parameters dialog box, click **Create...**.

7. Open the practice folder and save the new file as **Office-Parameters.txt**.

8. In the *Groups* area, click **New**. Type the name **Office Information** and click **OK**. This becomes the current group, as shown in Figure 6–106.

Figure 6–106

9. In the *Parameters* area, click **New...** and create three new shared parameters using the following information:

Name	Discipline	Type of Parameter
Extension	Common	Integer
Employee	Common	Text
Department	Common	Text

10. Click **OK**.

11. In the Shared Parameters dialog box, shown in Figure 6–107, select **Department** and click **OK**.

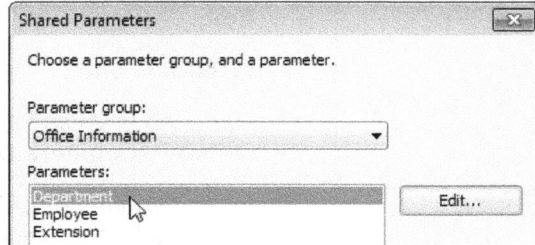

Figure 6–107

12. In the Parameter Properties dialog box, in the *Parameter Data* area, group the parameter under **Other** and make it an **Instance** parameter. In the *Categories* list, select **Furniture** and **Furniture Systems**, as shown in Figure 6–108.

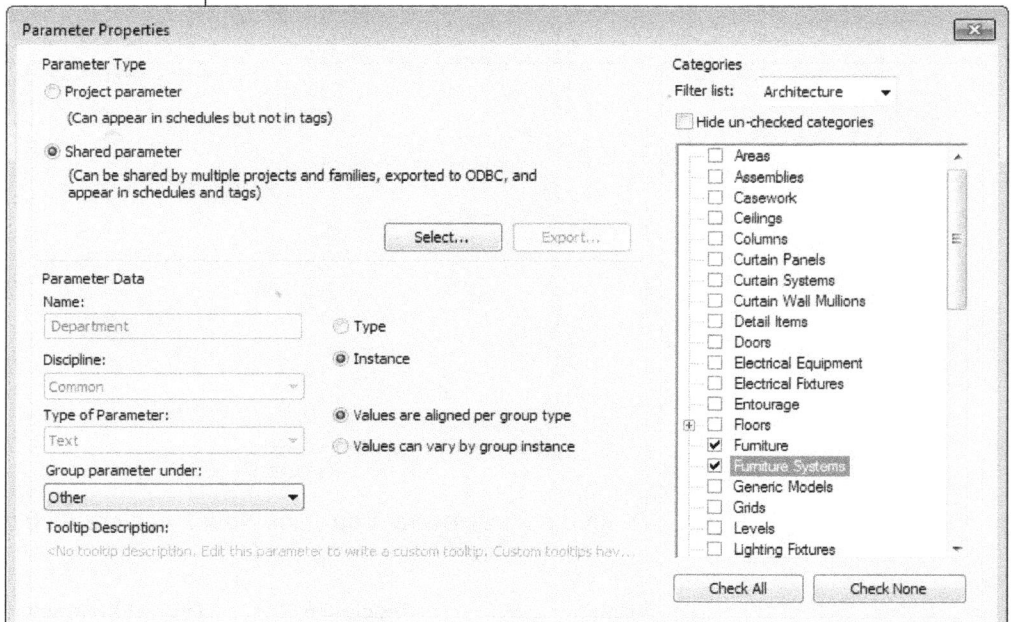

Figure 6–108

13. Click **OK**. **Department** is added to the shared parameters in the project.

14. Repeat the process for **Employee** and **Extension**.

15. Click **OK** to finish creating the project parameters.

16. Save the project.

Task 2 - Create a tag with shared parameters.

1. Create a new family based on the **Generic Tag.rft** template found in the *Annotation* folder of Autodesk Revit Library.

2. Save the family to the practice files folder as **Office-Information.rfa**.

3. Zoom in, read the information in red, and delete the note.

4. In the *Modify* tab>Properties panel, click ⬚ (Family Category and Parameters).

5. In the Family Category and Parameters dialog box, set the *Family Category* to **Furniture Systems Tags**, as shown in Figure 6–109. Click **OK**.

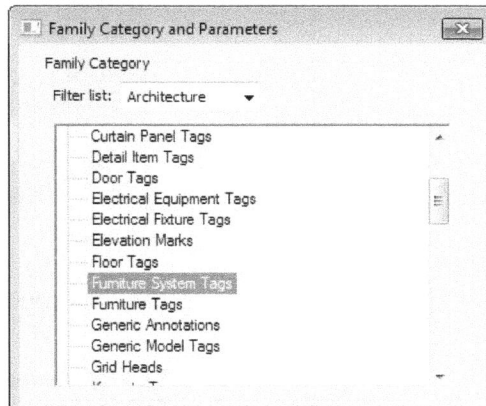

Figure 6–109

6. In the *Create* tab>Detail panel, click ⌐ (Line). Draw a box, starting at the crossing of the two reference lines, as shown in Figure 6–110. Do not add the dimensions; they are for reference only.

Figure 6–110

7. In the *Create* tab>Text panel, click ▦ (Label).

8. Use the default type, **Label: 3/32"**.

9. Click inside the box you just created.

10. In the Edit Label dialog box, which includes a list of the multi-category parameters supplied with the Autodesk Revit software, click 🗋 (Add Parameter).

In the Parameter Properties dialog box, you can only create shared parameters.

11. In the Parameter Properties dialog box, click **Select...**.

12. The shared parameters you created earlier should be available by default in the Shared Parameters dialog box. Select **Extension**, as shown in Figure 6–111. Then, click **OK**.

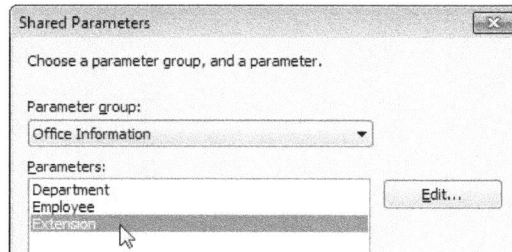

Figure 6–111

13. Click **OK** until you reach the Edit Label dialog box.

14. Select **Extension** and click ⇥ (Add parameter(s) to label). Click **OK** to insert the label into the family.

15. Click ▷ (Modify) and select the new label. Resize the outline of the text box to fit inside the box. Move the label so that it is centered in the box, as shown in Figure 6–112.

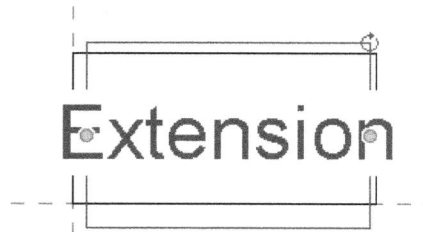

Figure 6–112

16. Save the family and load it into the project **Office-Layout.rvt**.

Task 3 - Add shared parameters to a furniture family.

1. Continue working in the project **Office-Layout.rvt**.

2. In the *Architecture* tab>Build panel, click (Component).

3. In the *Modify | Place Component* tab>Mode panel, click (Load Family).

4. In the practice files *Architectural* folder, open **Work-Station-Cubicle.rfa**.

5. Place a workstation in one of the rooms in the wing to the left of the main building.

6. Click (Modify) and select the new workstation.

7. In the *Modify | Furniture Systems* tab>Mode panel, click (Edit Family).

8. In the Properties panel, click (Family Types).

9. In the Family Types dialog box, click (New Parameter).

10. Select **Shared Parameter** and click **Select...**.

11. The shared parameters you created earlier are also available in this family file. Add each of the parameters from the *Office-Information* category into the family as an Instance parameter in the *Other* category.

12. In the Family Types dialog box, set the *Extension (default)* to **1234**, as shown in Figure 6–113. The other values can be left blank.

Other			⌃
Department (default)		=	
Employee (default)		=	
Extension (default)	1234	=	

Figure 6–113

13. Click **OK**.

14. Save the family file and load it into the **Office-Layout.rvt** project. Overwrite the existing version and its parameter values.

15. Add several other cubicles in various offices.

Task 4 - Add tags and create a schedule.

1. In the *Annotate* tab>Tag panel, click ⌂① (Tag by Category).

2. Select the workstations and tag each of them. The default **1234** extension number should display on each tag, as shown in Figure 6–114.

Figure 6–114

3. Select a workstation. In Properties, the **Extension**, **Employee**, and **Department** parameters should be available in the *Other* category, as shown in Figure 6–115.

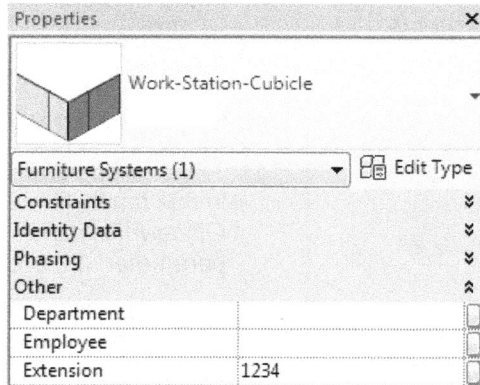

Figure 6–115

4. Change the *Extension*, and add an *Employee* name and *Department*.

5. Repeat with several other workstations.

6. In the *View* tab>Create panel, expand ▦ (Schedules) and click ▦ (Schedule/Quantities).

7. In the New Schedule dialog box, create a new Furniture Systems schedule and set the *Phase* is set to **Phase 1**, as shown in Figure 6–116.

Figure 6–116

8. In the *Fields* tab, add the **Family and Type** parameter and then add **Extension**, **Employee**, and **Department**, as shown in Figure 6–117.

Figure 6–117

9. At this point, you can modify the other schedule properties as required. Click **OK** when you are finished. The schedule should display the information you entered in the workstation's properties. Change the name of the schedule to **Office Information** and **Hide** the *Family and Type* column, as shown in Figure 6–118.

\<Office Information\>		
A	B	C
Employee	Extension	Department
Ronda	1234	Sales
Pual	1235	Engineering
Anne-Marie	1236	Sales
Kareen	1237	Marketing
Martha	1238	Engineering
Jen	1239	Enginering

Figure 6–118

10. Save the project.

11. If time permits, you can copy the Office Information tag and change the *Family Category* to **Furniture Tags**. Then you can use the new tag to tag the desks in the project. Furniture and Furniture Systems are different categories and cannot use the same tag.

Practice 6I

Work with Shared Parameters in MEP Projects

Practice Objectives

- Create a schedule that uses shared parameters.
- Add the shared parameters to a family file and note the impact on the schedule.

In this practice, you will create a mechanical equipment schedule and add shared parameters to the project through the schedule. You will then modify and add the shared parameters in a family file and update the family in the project. The shared parameters then populate the schedule, as shown in Figure 6–119.

Mechanical Equipment Schedule						
		Dimensions			Gas Line	Liquid Line
Mark	Type	Height	Width	Depth	Diameter	Diameter
1	HPD60C	44 3/4"	38 7/8"	34 3/4"	1"	1/2"
2	HPD60C	44 3/4"	38 7/8"	34 3/4"	1"	1/2"
3	HPD60C	44 3/4"	38 7/8"	34 3/4"	1"	1/2"
4	HPD60C	44 3/4"	38 7/8"	34 3/4"	1"	1/2"

Figure 6–119

Task 1 - Create a schedule and add shared parameters.

1. In the practice files *MEP* folder, open **Townhouse-Complex.rvt**. Note that four heat pumps have been added to serve the townhouses.

2. In the *View* tab>Create panel, expand ▦ (Schedules) and click ▦ (Schedule/Quantities).

3. In the New Schedule dialog box, set the *Filter list* to **Mechanical**, select the *Category* of **Mechanical Equipment**, and click **OK**.

4. In the Schedule Properties dialog box, in the *Fields* tab, select the following fields: **Mark** and **Type**. The rest of the parameters need to be shared parameters.

5. Click ▯ (New Parameter).

6. In the Parameter Properties dialog box, select **Shared parameter** and click **Select...**.

7. If there is no existing shared parameter file, an alert box displays prompting you to select a shared parameter file. Click **Yes**. If the Shared Parameters dialog box opens, click **Edit...**.

8. In the Edit Shared Parameters dialog box, click **Create...**.

9. In the Create Shared Parameter File dialog box, navigate to the practice files *MEP* folder and save the new file as **Townhouse-Parameters.txt**.

10. In the *Groups* area, click **New**. Set the name as **Heat Pump Information** and click **OK**. This becomes the current group, as shown in Figure 6–120.

Figure 6–120

11. In the *Parameters* area, click **New**. Create new shared type parameters using the following information:

Name	Discipline	Type of Parameter
Height	Common	Length
Width	Common	Length
Depth	Common	Length
Gas Line Diameter	Common	Length
Liquid Line Diameter	Common	Length

12. Click **OK**.

13. In the Shared Parameters dialog box, select **Height**, as shown in Figure 6–121. Then, click **OK**.

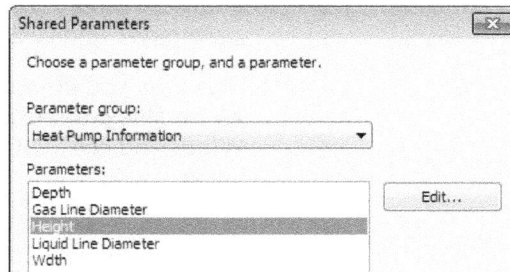

Figure 6–121

14. In the Parameter Properties dialog box, in the *Parameter Data* area, group the parameter under **Dimensions**, as shown in Figure 6–122.

Figure 6–122

15. Click **OK**. Height is added to the scheduled fields.

16. Click (New Parameter) again.

17. In the Parameter Properties dialog box, select **Shared parameter** and click **Select...**.

18. This time you do not have to create a shared parameter file, as the files created in the previous steps are available. Select **Width** and click **OK** to apply the parameter to the scheduled fields.

19. Repeat the process and add the rest of the new shared parameters in the order shown in Figure 6–123.

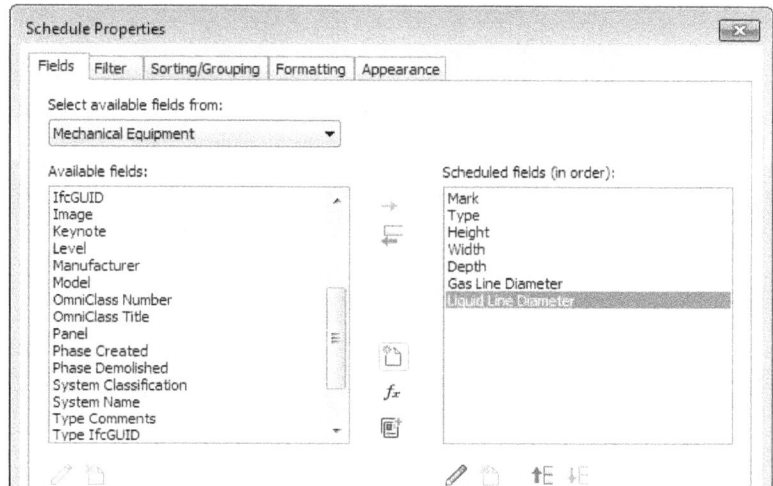

Figure 6–123

20. Click **OK**. The Mechanical Equipment Schedule displays but only includes values for the **Mark** and **Type**, as shown in Figure 6–124. The shared parameters are not yet identified in the Heat Pump family.

			<Mechanical Equipment Schedule>			
A	B	C	D	E	F	G
Mark	Type	Height	Width	Depth	Gas Line Diameter	Liquid Line Diamete
1	HP060C					
2	HP060C					
3	HP060C					
4	HP060C					

Figure 6–124

21. Save the project.

Task 2 - Add shared parameters to a family.

1. Open the Mechanical>HVAC>**Floor Plans: Ground-Mech** view and select one of the heat pumps.

2. In the *Modify | Mechanical Equipment* tab>Mode panel, click (Edit Family). The family file opens in the Family Editor.

3. In the Properties panel, click ⬚ (Family Types).

4. In the Family Types dialog box, several of the parameters that already exist in the family display, as shown in Figure 6–125, but they are not connected as shared parameters.

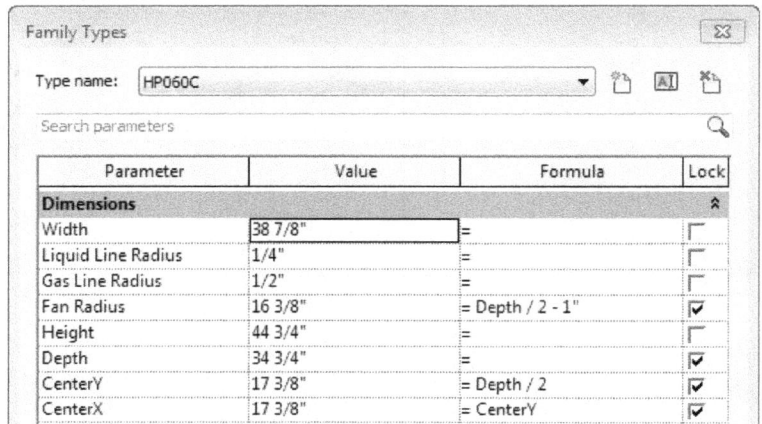

Figure 6–125

5. Select the **Width** parameter and in the *Parameters* area, click

   ✎ (Edit Parameter).

6. In the Parameter properties dialog box, select **Shared Parameter** and click **Select...**.

7. The shared parameters you created earlier are also available in this family file, as shown in Figure 6–126.

Figure 6–126

8. Select **Width** and click **OK** twice. The existing parameter is now connected with the shared parameter.

The information stored in the Heat Pump family for the Liquid Line and Gas Line are set to a radius, because it is required by the connectors. Therefore, you have to add Parameters and formulas for the diameters.

9. Repeat the process with the **Height** and **Depth** parameters.

10. In the Family Types dialog box, click ⬜ (New Parameter).

11. In the Parameter Properties dialog box, select **Shared parameter** and click **Select...**.

12. In the Shared Parameters dialog box, select **Gas Line Diameter** and click **OK**.

13. Set it as a **Type** parameter and group it with the **Dimensions** group. Click **OK**.

14. Repeat the process for **Liquid Line Diameter**.

15. Set the following formulas for the two diameter parameters, as shown in Figure 6–127.
    - Gas Line Diameter = **Gas Line Radius * 2**
    - Liquid Line Diameter = **Liquid Line Radius * 2**

Parameter	Value	Formula	Lock
Dimensions			⌄
Depth	34 3/4"	=	☑
Gas Line Diameter	1"	= Gas Line Radius * 2	☐
Height	44 3/4"	=	☐
Liquid Line Diameter	1/2"	= Liquid Line Radius * 2	☐
Liquid Line Radius	1/4"	=	☐
Gas Line Radius	1/2"	=	☐

Type name: HP060C

Figure 6–127

16. Click **OK** to close the Family Types dialog box.

17. Save the family to the practice folder.

Task 3 - Load the family and modify the schedule.

1. In the *Create* tab>Family Editor panel, click ⬆ (Load into Project).

2. Overwrite the existing version and its parameter values.

3. Open the Mechanical Equipment Schedule. The values for the parameters are now included. Add headers for the dimensions, as shown in Figure 6–128.

		Overall Dimensions			Pipe Dimensions	
A	B	C	D	E	F	G
Mark	Type	Height	Width	Depth	Gas Line Diameter	Liquid Line Diamete
1	HP060C	3' - 8 3/4"	3' - 2 7/8"	2' - 10 3/4"	0' - 1"	0' - 0 1/2"
2	HP060C	3' - 8 3/4"	3' - 2 7/8"	2' - 10 3/4"	0' - 1"	0' - 0 1/2"
3	HP060C	3' - 8 3/4"	3' - 2 7/8"	2' - 10 3/4"	0' - 1"	0' - 0 1/2"
4	HP060C	3' - 8 3/4"	3' - 2 7/8"	2' - 10 3/4"	0' - 1"	0' - 0 1/2"

<Mechanical Equipment Schedule>

Figure 6–128

4. Typically the values for these parameters should only be in inches. To fix this, in Properties next to **Formatting** parameter, click **Edit...**.

5. The Schedule Properties dialog box opens with the *Formatting* tab selected.

6. In the *Fields* area, select **Height** and click **Field Format...**.

7. Clear **Use project settings** and change the *Units* to **Fractional inches**. Click **OK**.

8. Repeat this for the rest of the length based parameters so that they display in inches and not in feet and inches.

9. Click **OK** to close the dialog box. The schedule updates as shown in Figure 6–129.

		Overall Dimensions			Pipe Dimensions	
A	B	C	D	E	F	G
Mark	Type	Height	Width	Depth	Gas Line Diameter	Liquid Line Diamete
1	HP060C	44 3/4"	38 7/8"	34 3/4"	1"	1/2"
2	HP060C	44 3/4"	38 7/8"	34 3/4"	1"	1/2"
3	HP060C	44 3/4"	38 7/8"	34 3/4"	1"	1/2"
4	HP060C	44 3/4"	38 7/8"	34 3/4"	1"	1/2"

<Mechanical Equipment Schedule>

Figure 6–129

10. Save the project.

Practice 6m

Work with Shared Parameters in Structural Projects

Practice Objectives

- Create shared parameters in a project.
- Use the shared parameters in a family, associated tag, and a schedule.

In this practice, you will create shared parameters through project parameters and use them in family, tag, and schedule, as shown in Figure 6–130. The context here is a public plaza with columns, some free-standing and some supporting canopies and roofs. Each column will have custom brackets for banners, flags, etc.

Figure 6–130

Task 1 - Create shared parameters.

1. In the practice files *Structural* folder, open **Events-Plaza.rvt**.

2. In the *Manage* tab>Project Settings panel, click 📄 (Project Parameters).

3. In the Project Parameters dialog box, click **Add...**.

4. In the Parameter Properties dialog box, select **Shared parameter** and click **Select...**.

5. If there is no existing shared parameter file, an alert box displays prompting you to select a shared parameter file. Click **Yes**. If the Shared Parameters dialog box opens, click **Edit...**.

6. In the Edit Shared Parameters dialog box, click **Create...**.

7. Save the new file as **Plaza-Parameters.txt** in the practice files folder.

8. Create a new parameter group. In the *Groups* area, click **New...**. Set the name as **Columns** and click **OK**. This becomes the current group, as shown in Figure 6–131.

Figure 6–131

9. In the *Parameters* area, click **New...** and create three new shared parameters using the following information:

Name	Discipline	Type of Parameter
Bracket Type	Common	Text
Bracket Offset from Base	Common	Length
Bracket Finish	Common	Material

10. Click **OK**.

11. In the Shared Parameters dialog box, select **Bracket Type**, as shown in Figure 6–132. Then, click **OK**.

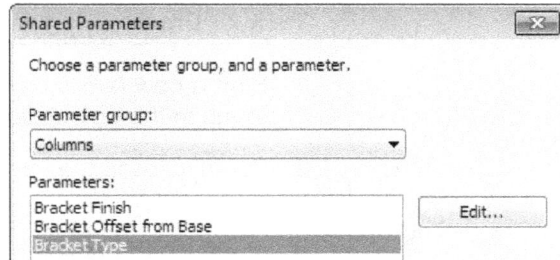

Figure 6–132

12. In the Parameter Properties dialog box, in the *Parameter Data* area, group the parameter under **Other** and make it an **Instance** parameter. In the *Categories* area, filter the list based on **Structure** and select **Structural Columns,** as shown in Figure 6–133.

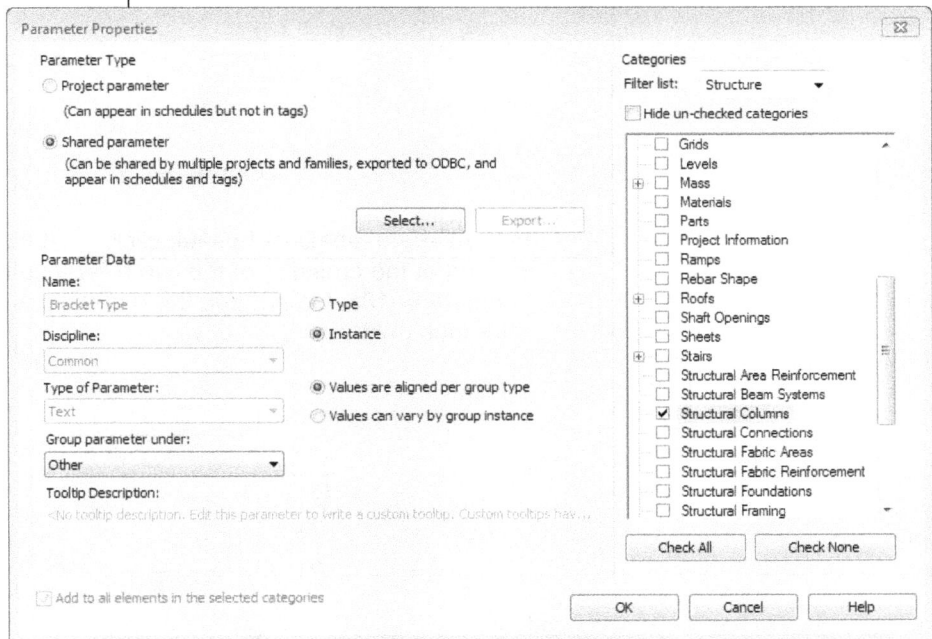

Figure 6–133

13. Click **OK**. **Bracket Type** is added to the shared parameters in the project.

14. Repeat the process to add **Bracket Offset from Base** and **Bracket Finish** to the Project Parameters list.

15. Click **OK** to finish creating the project parameters.

16. Save the project.

Task 2 - Create a Tag with Shared parameters.

1. Start a new family based on the **Generic Tag.rft** template found in the default library's *Annotations* folder.

2. Zoom in, read the information in red, and delete the note.

3. In the Properties panel, click 🔲 (Family Category and Parameters).

4. In the Family Category and Parameters dialog box, set the *Family Category* to **Structural Column Tags**, as shown in Figure 6–134. Click **OK**.

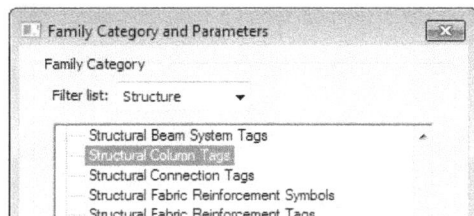

Figure 6–134

5. In the *Create* tab>Detail panel, click ✐ (Line). Draw a box, starting at the crossing of the two reference lines, as shown in Figure 6–135. Do not add the dimensions. They are for reference only.

Figure 6–135

6. In the *Create* tab>Text panel, click 🔤 (Label).

7. Use the default type, **Label: 3/32"**.

8. In the *Modify | Place Label* tab>Format panel, set Justification to ≡ (Align Center) and ≡ (Align Top).

9. Click inside the box you just created.

10. In the Edit Label dialog box, which includes a list of the multi-category parameters supplied with the Autodesk Revit software, click (Add Parameter).

In this dialog box, you can only create shared parameters.

11. In the Parameter Properties dialog box, click **Select...**.

12. In the Shared Parameters dialog box, the shared parameters you created earlier should be available by default. Select **Bracket Type**, as shown in Figure 6–136. Then, click **OK**.

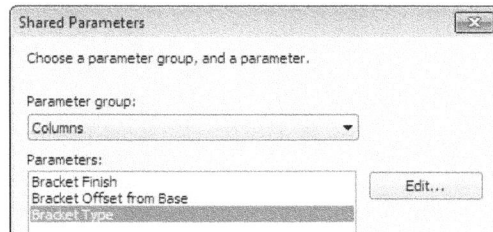

Figure 6–136

13. Click **OK** until you reach the Edit Label dialog box.

14. Select **Bracket Type** and click (Add parameter(s) to label).

15. Repeat with the **Bracket Offset from Base** and **Bracket Finish** parameters. In the *Break* column, select the option for the first two parameters, as shown in Figure 6–137. This forces each parameter to be on a separate line.

Label Parameters

	Parameter Name	Spaces	Prefix	Sample Value	Suffix	Break
1	Bracket Type	1		Bracket Type		✓
2	Bracket Offset from Base	1		Bracket Offset fro		✓
3	Bracket Finish	1		Bracket Finish		

Figure 6–137

16. Click **OK** to insert the label into the family.

17. Click (Modify) and select the new label. Resize the outline of the text box so that it fits inside the box, and move the label so that it is top-centered in the box, as shown in Figure 6–138.

Bracket Type
Bracket Offset
from Base
Bracket Finish

Figure 6–138

18. Save the new family with the name **Column-Bracket-Tag.rfa**.

19. Load the family into the project **Events-Plaza.rvt**.

20. The **Tag** command is automatically started. Tag one of the columns.

21. The tag is empty as shown in Figure 6–139, because no values have been added to the parameters.

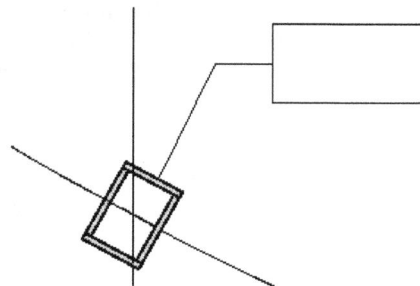

Figure 6–139

22. Save the project.

Task 3 - Add Tags and modify information.

1. In the *Annotate* tab>Tag panel, click (Tag All).

2. In the Tag All Not Tagged dialog box, select the *Category* **Structural Column Tags** with the *Loaded Tags* set to **Column-Bracket-Tag**. Select **Leader** and click **OK**.

   - All of the columns are tagged. The tags are blank but display question marks when selected, as shown in Figure 6–140. This is because the corresponding information has not been entered into the properties.

Figure 6–140

3. Select a column.

4. In Properties, scroll down to the *Other* area. The **Bracket Finish**, **Bracket Type**, and **Bracket Offset from base** parameters are available but have no information stored in them yet, as shown in Figure 6–141.

Figure 6–141

5. Right-click on the column and select **Select All Instances> Visible in View**.

   - In this case, you will set the default values for all columns once. Individual columns can be changed later.

6. In Properties, set the *Bracket Offset from Base* to **12'-0"**, set the *Bracket Type* to **Banner**, and set the *Bracket Finish* to **Metal**.

7. Select two or three individual columns, and in Properties change the *Bracket Type* to **Sculptural** and the *Bracket Offset from Base* to **15'-0"**. The tags update only for those columns, as shown in Figure 6–142.

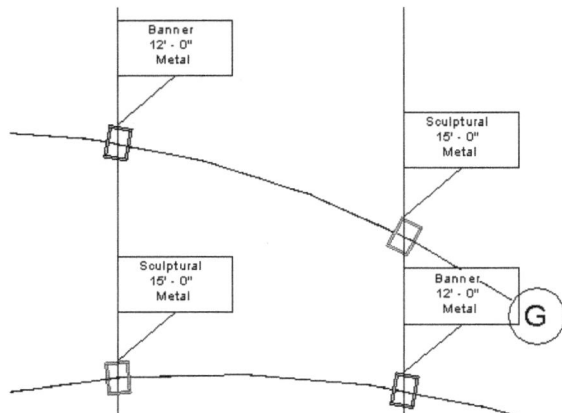

Figure 6–142

8. Save the project.

Task 4 - Create a Structural Column schedule.

---

1. Create a new building component schedule for structural columns.

2. In the Schedule Properties dialog box, in the *Fields* tab, add the **Column Location Mark** parameter and then add **Mark**, **Bracket Type**, **Bracket Offset from Base**, and **Bracket Finish**, as shown in Figure 6–143.

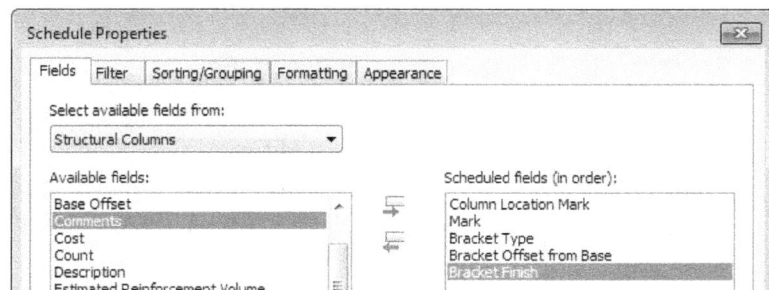

Figure 6–143

3. Sort by the Column Location Mark and modify the other schedule properties as required. Click **OK** when finished. The schedule should display the information you entered in the column's properties, as shown in Figure 6–144.

<Structural Column Schedule>				
A	B	C	D	E
Column Location M	Mark	Bracket Type	Bracket Offset fro	Bracket Finish
A-1	1	Banner	12' - 0"	Metal
A-2	2	Sculptural	15' - 0"	Metal
A-3	3	Banner	12' - 0"	Metal
A-4	4	Sculptural	15' - 0"	Metal
A-5	5	Banner	12' - 0"	Metal
A-6	6	Sculptural	15' - 0"	Metal
A-7	7	Banner	12' - 0"	Metal

Figure 6–144

4. Save the project.

Chapter Review Questions

1. An in-place family is created whenever you need a custom family that is:

   a. Not available in your library.

   b. Built using profiles.

   c. Directly connected to elements in the project.

   d. Requires shared parameters.

2. Which of the following are examples of elements for which you can create profiles? (Select all that apply.)

   a. Wall reveals

   b. The top rail of railings

   c. In-place Sweeps

   d. Curtain Wall mullions

3. At what size should you create the tag family elements, as shown in Figure 6–145?

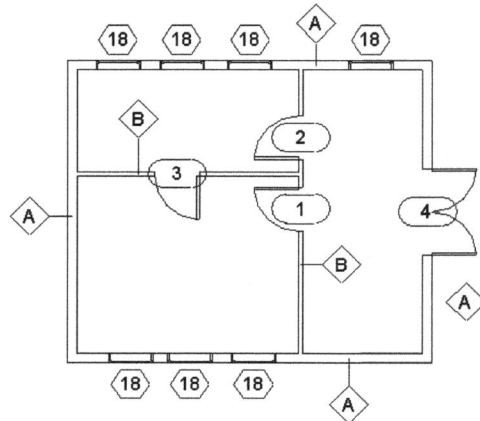

Figure 6–145

   a. Full scale to match the size of the tagged element in the project.

   b. Full scale to match the size of the annotation on the sheet.

   c. One size for each scale.

   d. It varies according to the type of annotation.

4. Where are shared parameters (access shown in Figure 6–146) stored?

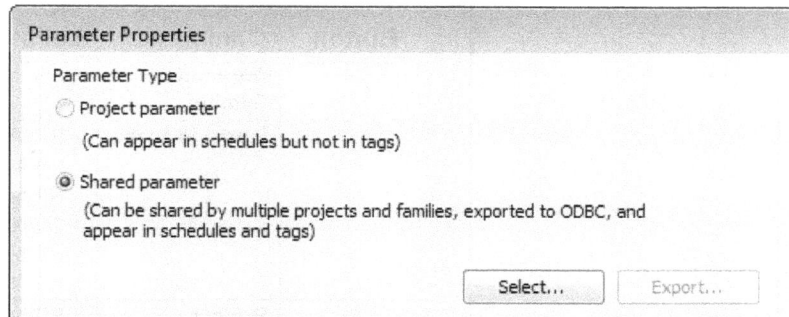

Parameter Properties

Parameter Type

○ Project parameter

(Can appear in schedules but not in tags)

◉ Shared parameter

(Can be shared by multiple projects and families, exported to ODBC, and appear in schedules and tags)

Select...   Export...

Figure 6–146

a. In a text file.

b. In the current project.

c. In a shared project.

d. In the family file.

Command Summary

Button	Command	Location
	Annotation Symbol	• **File** tab>expand New
	Model In-Place	• **Ribbon:** *Architecture* tab>Build panel> expand Component • **Ribbon:** *Structure* tab>Model panel> expand Component • **Ribbon:** *Systems* tab>Model panel> expand Component
	Project Parameters	• **Ribbon:** *Manage* tab>Project Settings panel
	Shared Parameters	• **Ribbon:** *Manage* tab>Project Settings panel

Creating Architectural Specific Families

Architectural families include elements that are created using standard component family methods (such as doors and windows). There are also ways to create other elements that use profiles and are best created directly in the project as in-place families (such as angled cornices and coping). Another important family is railings. These families are put together using other families, including rails, balusters, posts and panels.

Learning Objectives in this Chapter

- Create custom door and window families from existing families and templates.
- Use in-place families to create angled cornices, fascias, and copings.
- Create railing types, including the rails, balusters, posts, and panels.

7.1 Creating Custom Doors and Windows

You can create custom doors and windows by copying and modifying an existing family, enabling you to use all of the existing detailed elements and parameters. For example, in Figure 7–1 the full panel door family on the left can be transformed into the square panel on the right.

Figure 7–1

When you use a template, only the most basic elements are included. For example, in the Window with Trim template (shown in Figure 7–2), only the opening for the window, basic trim, and parameters are included. Everything else must be added.

Figure 7–2

Practice 7a | Create Custom Doors

Practice Objectives

- Create custom families based on an existing family.
- Add and modify parameters.
- Modify reference planes and dimensions.
- Set formulas for parameters.

In this practice, you will create new door family based on an existing door family, shown on the left in Figure 7–3. For the first family, you will add a material parameter and modify an existing extrusion to use the new glass material, as shown in the middle in Figure 7–3. You will then create a copy of the family and modify the dimension and parameters and add a formula to create square panels, as shown in the right in Figure 7–3.

Original Door   *Glass Panel Door*   *Square Glass Panel Door*

Figure 7–3

Task 1 - Create door types and specify new material.

1. In the Autodesk Revit Library's *Doors>Residential* folder, open **Door-Interior-Single-5_Panel_Vert-Wood.rfa**.
   - The family is also available in the practice files *Architectural* folder.

2. Save the file in the practice files folder with the name **Door-Interior-Single-5_ Panel_Vert-Wood and Glass.rfa**.

3. In the Family Types dialog box create a new type parameter named **Interior Panel Material** with *Type of parameter* set to **Material** and *Group parameter under* set to **Materials and Finishes**.

4. Assign the *Value* to **Glass**, as shown in Figure 7–4. Click **OK**.

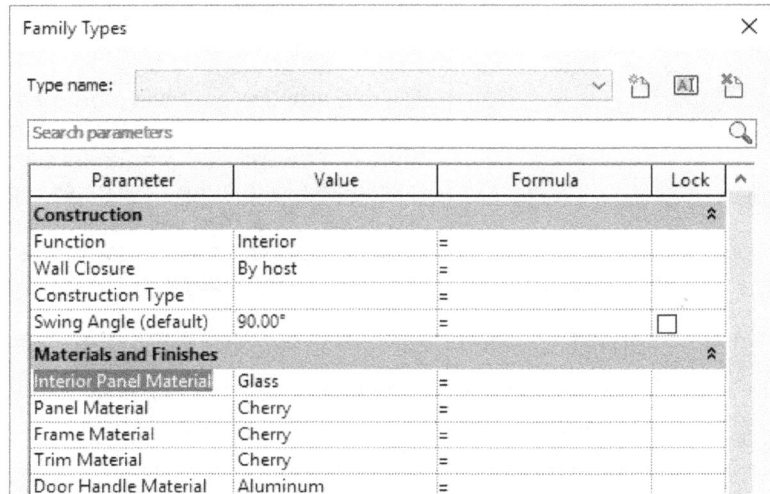

Family Types				×

Type name: [   ] ▽ ⬚ AI ⬚

Search parameters [   ] 🔍

Parameter	Value	Formula	Lock	^
Construction				≫
Function	Interior	=		
Wall Closure	By host	=		
Construction Type		=		
Swing Angle (default)	90.00°	=	☐	
Materials and Finishes				≫
Interior Panel Material	Glass	=		
Panel Material	Cherry	=		
Frame Material	Cherry	=		
Trim Material	Cherry	=		
Door Handle Material	Aluminum	=		

Figure 7–4

5. Select the Panel Extrusion as shown in Figure 7–5. (Press <Tab> to select the interior extrusion.)

6. In Properties, in the *Material and Finishes* area beside Material click ▣ (Associate Family Parameter).

7. In the Associate Family Parameter dialog box, select **Interior Panel Material** and click **OK**. The interior panels update to glass, as shown in Figure 7–6.

Figure 7–5   Figure 7–6

8. Create three Family Types. Modify the *Width* and *Height* values to match the name. You will use the new types to flex the parameters as you continue working.
   - **32" x 80"**
   - **36" x 80"**
   - **36" x 84"**

9. Save the family.

Task 2 - Modify the glass panel in a separate door family.

---

1. Save the family as **Door-Interior-Single-5_ Panel_Vert-Wood and Glass-Square.rfa**. (This enables you to have two different door styles based on one original.)

2. Open the **Elevations: Exterior** view.

3. Change the *Scale* to **1 1/2" = 1'-0"** to make the dimensions easier to modify.

4. Delete the right Stiles dimension shown in Figure 7–7.

5. Add a new dimension labeled **Interior Panel Width** (Type Parameter), as shown in Figure 7–8.

Figure 7–7

Figure 7–8

6. Open the Family Types dialog box.

7. Set the *Type name* to **32" x 80"** and click **Apply**.

8. Add the *Formula* to the **Interior Panel Width** parameter, as shown in Figure 7–9.

(Height - (Bottom Rail + Top Rail + (Intermediate Rail * 4))) / 5

Parameter	Value	Formula	L ^
Dimensions			
Interior Panel Width	9 163/256"	= (Height - (Bottom Rail + Top Rail + (Intermediate Rail * 4))) / 5	☑
Width	32"	=	☑
Height	80"	=	☑
Rough Width	34"	= Width + 2"	☑
Rough Height	81"	= Height + 1"	☑
Thickness	1 3/8"	=	☑
Stiles	4 3/4"	=	☑
Top Rail	4 11/16"	=	☑
Intermediate Rail	4 1/2"	=	☑
Bottom Rail	9 1/8"	=	☑

Figure 7–9

-   Ensure that you type in all the parameter names exactly and watch the parentheses. The *Value* should solve as **9 163/256"**.

-   This formula was developed because a reporting parameter based on the height of the interior panel cannot be used in this case.

9. Click **Apply**. The entire panel set changes to a square shape, as shown in Figure 7–10. Click **OK**.

Figure 7–10

10. Open the 3D Views>**Preview** view.

11. Use the Family Types you created earlier to flex the family.

12. Save the family.

13. Create a new project and add a wall into the project.

14. Load the two doors you created into the project and test them in the wall.

15. Save and close the families. You do not need to save the project.

Practice 7b | Create Custom Windows

Practice Objectives

- Create a custom family based on a template.
- Add trim and glass to the window.

In this practice, you will create a new window family based on a family template. You will modify the existing opening, trim it, and add materials and glass to the window, as shown in Figure 7–11.

Figure 7–11

Task 1 - Create a custom window family.

1. Create a new family based on the **Window with Trim.rft** template found in the Autodesk Revit Library.
   - The family is also available in the practice files *Architectural* folder.

2. Save the family to the practice files folder as **Arched Window with Trim.rfa**.

3. Open the **Elevations: Exterior** view.

4. Edit the sketch of the **Opening Cut** element and lock the tangency locks, as shown in Figure 7–12. Delete the extra horizontal sketch line.

Figure 7–12

5. Click ✎ (Finish Edit Mode).

6. Add a dimension to the arc and label it **Arch Radius** (a **Type** parameter in the *Dimensions* category), as shown in Figure 7–13.

7. Edit the **Trim: Extrusion** element and modify the sketch so that it matches the new arc opening, as shown in Figure 7–14.

Figure 7–13

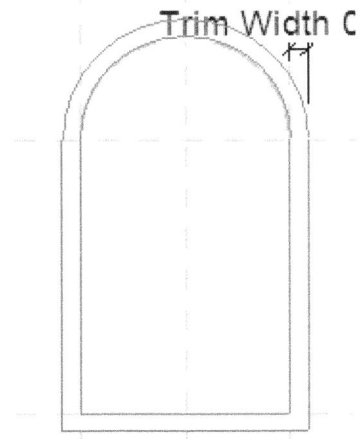

Figure 7–14

8. Click ✔ (Finish Edit Mode).

9. Open the Family Types dialog box and modify the **Radius** parameter to use the formula **Width/2**. Flex the model by trying different widths.

10. Set the final *Width* to **3'-0"** and click **OK**.

11. Save the family.

12. Start a new project and add a wall to the project.

13. Switch back to the window family and load it into the project to test it.

14. Open a 3D view and set the *Visual Style* to ▤ (Shaded). The window does not have glass or materials, as shown in Figure 7–15.

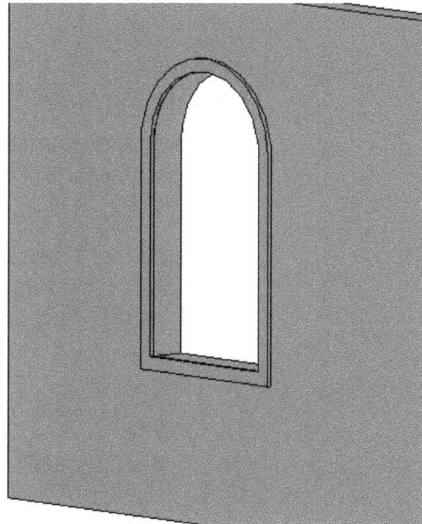

Figure 7–15

15. Save the project as **Window Test.rvt**.

Task 2 - Add a material to the window trim.

1. Switch back to the family file **Exterior** view.

2. Set the *Visual Style* to ▤ (Shaded).

3. Select the **Trim Projection : Extrusion**.

4. In Properties, next to the **Materials** parameter, select **<By Category>**. Click ⌷ (Browse) at the end of the row.

5. In the Materials Browser, under *AEC Materials>Wood*, select **Cherry** and click ⬆ (Add material to document), as shown in Figure 7–16.

Figure 7–16

6. Select the new material. In the *Graphics* tab, in the *Shading* area, select **Use Render Appearance**, as shown in Figure 7–17.

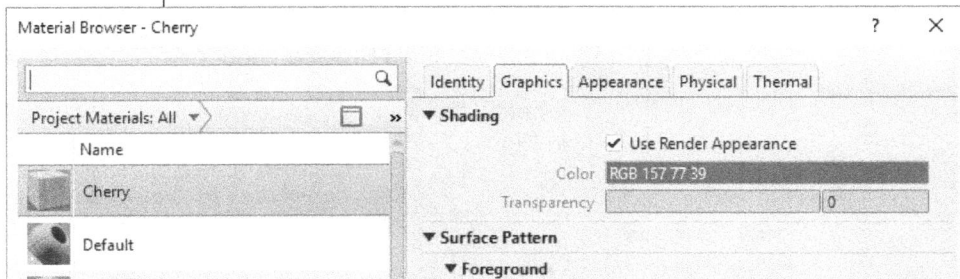

Figure 7–17

- By default, this material only displays when the *Visual Style* is set to **Realistic**. By using the **Render Appearance**, the color displays when the *Visual Style* is set to **Shaded** or **Consistent Colors**.

7. Click **OK** to close the Material Browser and apply the material.

8. Save the family file.

Task 3 - Add glass to the window.

1. In the family file, open the **Floor Plans: Ref. Level** view.

2. Draw a reference plane **1"** from the exterior face of the window and lock it in place, as shown in Figure 7–18. Name the reference plane **Glass**.

Figure 7–18

3. Open the **Elevations: Exterior** view.

4. In the *Create* tab>Work Plane panel, click ⊞ (Set).

5. In the Work Plane dialog box, select the new reference plane **Glass** and click **OK**.

6. In the *Create* tab>Form panel, click ▯ (Extrusion).

7. Sketch the outline of the glass inside the window.

8. In Properties, in the *Constraints* area, set the *Extrusion End* to **1/2"**.

9. In the *Materials and Finishes* area, click the **(...)** Browse button beside *Material*.

10. In the Material Browser, open the *AEC Materials* library and select the *Glass* category. Select **Glass, Clear Glazing** and click ⬆ (Add material to document), as shown in Figure 7–19.

Figure 7–19

11. In the *Project Materials* list, select the **Glass, Clear Glazing** material and in the *Graphics* tab, select **Use Render Appearance**.

12. Click **OK**.

13. Click ✔ (Finish Edit Mode). The glass material displays.

14. Save the family file.

15. Click ⬆ (Load into Project) and select **Overwrite the existing version and its parameter values**. The new glass and trim material display in the project.

7.2 Creating Angled Cornices and Copings

You might have tried to add a wall sweep to a wall at an angle, and found that it does not work. The **Wall Sweep** command only works horizontally or vertically. For example, to add a cornice to the top of a wall following the angled profile, as shown in Figure 7–20, you need to use a workaround, such as an in-place family using a solid sweep. A solid sweep can also be used to create a coping on the top of a short wall running beside steps.

Attempting to place a wall sweep   *In-place solid sweep family*

Figure 7–20

Creating Fascias

Another way to create profiles along an angle is to use a workaround to create a roof fascia on a model line, as shown in Figure 7–21. Typically, a fascia is applied to a roof edge but it can also be applied to a model line placed anywhere in a project.

Figure 7–21

How To: Create a Fascia Type

The process is similar for creating new Gutter types.

1. Load the profile for the fascia.
   - Many options are available in the Autodesk Revit library *Profiles*>Roofs folder.

2. In the *Architecture* tab>Build panel, expand 🔲 (Roof) and click 🔽 (Roof: Fascia).

3. In Properties, click 🔲 (Edit Type).
4. In the Type Properties dialog box, click **Duplicate**.
5. In the Name dialog box, type a name and click **OK**.
6. In the Type Properties dialog box, select the appropriate profile, as shown in Figure 7–22.

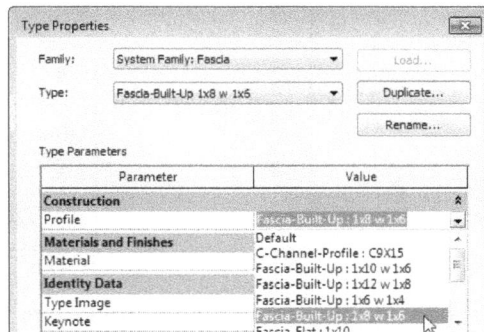

Figure 7–22

7. Click **OK** and the new fascia type is ready to be used.

How To: Add a Fascia Using Model Lines

1. In the *Architecture* tab>Work Plane panel, click 🔲 (Set) and select the appropriate work plane.

2. In the *Architecture* tab>Model panel, click 🔏 (Model Line). Draw the model lines on the face of the wall where you want to add a fascia.
   - Check the height of the fascia profile first so that you know where to put the model lines.

3. In the *Architecture* tab>Build panel, expand 🔲 (Roof) and click 🔽 (Roof: Fascia).
4. Select the model lines.

Hint: Object Style Subcategories

When creating an in-place family, you might want the family member to be modified in Visibility/Graphic Overrides separately from the main component. For example, if you are creating a cornice or coping for a wall and want to be able to toggle it off separately from the wall, you can create an Object Style subcategory.

1. In the *Manage* tab>Settings panel, click ⬚ (Object Styles).
2. In the *Modify Subcategories* area, click **New**.
3. In the New Subcategory dialog box, type a *Name* and select the category it is going to be a *Subcategory of*, as shown in Figure 7–23.

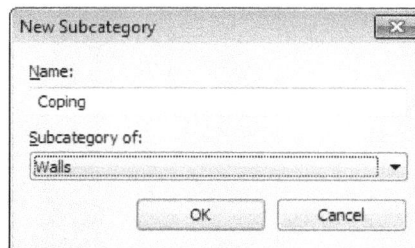

Figure 7–23

4. Click **OK** twice to finish the command.
5. The object style is now available in Visibility/Graphic Overrides, as shown in Figure 7–24.

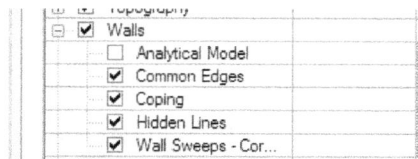

Figure 7–24

6. In the in-place family, select the object you want to add to the new subcategory. In Properties, under the *Identity Data* heading, select a *Subcategory* from the list (as shown in Figure 7–25), and then click **OK**.

Figure 7–25

Practice 7c

Create Angled Cornices and Copings

Practice Objectives

- Create a coping using an in-place family.
- Use Model Lines and Roof Fascia to add a Profile to a Sloped Wall.

In this practice, you will create a coping using an in-place family with a solid sweep. You will then add a profile to a sloped wall using the **Roof: Fascia** command and a model line, as shown in Figure 7–26.

Profile on sloped wall

Coping

Figure 7–26

Task 1 - Create a coping using an in-place family.

1. In the practice files *Architectural* folder, open **Plaza.rvt**. This is the beginning of a site design consisting of two slabs with retaining walls connected by a stair.

2. Open the **Floor Plans: Site** view. This project has three sections to help you draw additional elements.

3. Open the **Sections: East-West Site Section** view and zoom in on the lower wall, where you are going to add a stone coping to the top of the wall.

4. In the *Architecture* tab>Build panel, expand 🗗 (Component) and click 🗗 (Model In-Place).

5. In the Family Category and Parameters dialog box, select **Walls** and click **OK**.

You are placed in the Family Editor with the corresponding tabs in the ribbon

6. Name the family **Coping**.

7. In the *Create* tab>Forms panel, click ⬡ (Sweep).

8. In the *Modify | Sweep* tab>Sweep panel, click ✏ (Sketch Path).

9. In the Work Plane dialog box, select **Pick a plane** and click **OK**. Select the face of the concrete retaining wall.

10. Draw the path, as shown in Figure 7–27.

Figure 7–27

11. Click ✓ (Finish Edit Mode).

12. In the Sweep panel, click ✎ (Edit Profile).

13. In the Go To View dialog box, select **Section: Wall Section** and click **Open View**.

14. Zoom in and draw the profile, as shown in Figure 7–28.

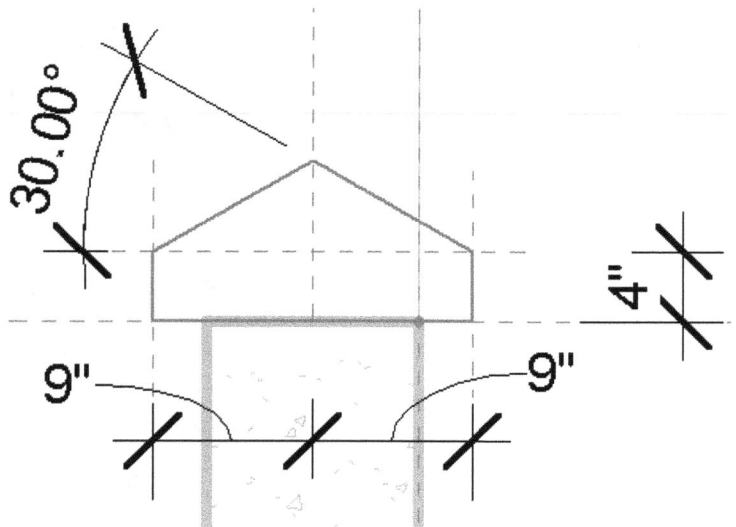

Figure 7–28

15. Finish the profile, sweep, and model.

16. Switch to a 3D view to see the coping in place.

Task 2 - Use Model Lines and Roof Fascia to add a profile to a Sloped Wall.

---

1. Open the **Sections: East-West Site Section** view and zoom in on the upper plaza.

2. In the *Insert* tab>Load from Library panel, click 🔽 (Load Family). Navigate to the practice files *Architectural* folder and load the **Wall-Profile.rfa.**

3. In the *Architecture* tab>Model panel, click ⌐ (Model Line).

4. In the Work Plane dialog box, select **Pick a Plane** and click **OK** and select the face of the concrete retaining wall.

If you use Pick Lines or draw from the right to the left, the fascia faces the wrong direction when it is applied.

5. Draw a model line from the left to the right, **7"** down from the top of the retaining wall.

6. In the *Architecture* tab>Model panel, expand ▱ (Roof) and click ⩔ (Roof: Fascia).

7. In Properties, click **Edit Type**.

8. In the Type Properties dialog box, create a new fascia type named **Wall Sweep** using the profile you loaded earlier, and set the *Material* to **Masonry-Stone**, as shown in Figure 7–29.

Type Parameters	
Parameter	Value
Construction	⌃
Profile	Wall-Design-Profile : Wall-Design
Materials and Finishes	⌃
Material	Masonry - Stone

Figure 7–29

---

9. Once you have finished creating the **Roof Fascia** type, select the model line to place it in the project, as shown in Figure 7–30.

If you do not see the fascia, switch to a plan view, select it and click the Flip control.

Fascias : Fascia : Wall Sweep

Figure 7–30

10. Save the project.

7.3 Creating Custom Railings

Creating a railing is more complex than creating a standard component family, as railings consist of several preset families for the rails, balusters, posts, and panels, as shown in Figure 7–31. Once you have the collection of families ready, you can create a Railing type.

Figure 7–31

- It helps to create all of the components for a Railing type (e.g., rails, handrails, top rails, posts, balusters, and panels) before creating the type.

- There are also Railing Supports (for handrails) and Railing Termination families that can be added to railings types.

Creating Rail Profiles

Top Rails, Handrails, and rails within a railing structure are all based on a rail profile. The rail profile is made of 2D elements that are swept along the railing lines, as shown in Figure 7–32.

Figure 7–32

- Existing profiles for rails are found in the Autodesk Revit library in the *Profiles>Railings* folders.

- The **Profile-Rail.rft** template is specifically created for railings. The template indicates where to start drawing the outline, as shown in Figure 7–33.

Rail Centerline

Rail Top

Figure 7–33

- Rail profiles must be closed shapes.

- Once you have created a rail profile, you can apply it to a Top Rail or Handrail system family type.

Creating Baluster, Post, and Panel Families

Balusters and posts are created from solid elements made with extrusions and revolves. Having the correct reference planes is important for flexibility. Standard balusters also require void elements to cut the angle on stair railings.

There are three baluster templates for standard balusters, posts, and panels. The example in Figure 7–34 shows a custom baluster modified from an existing baluster family supplied with the Autodesk Revit software.

When you are creating a family, see if you can modify an existing one to suit your needs. This is much faster than creating a new family from scratch and helps you learn how to construct the specific family.

Original Baluster   *Modified Baluster*

Figure 7–34

The templates for these families include reference planes for the slope angles, as shown for a baluster panel in Figure 7–35. For stair railings, you can lock the solid elements to these angles so that they respond to the slope of the stair.

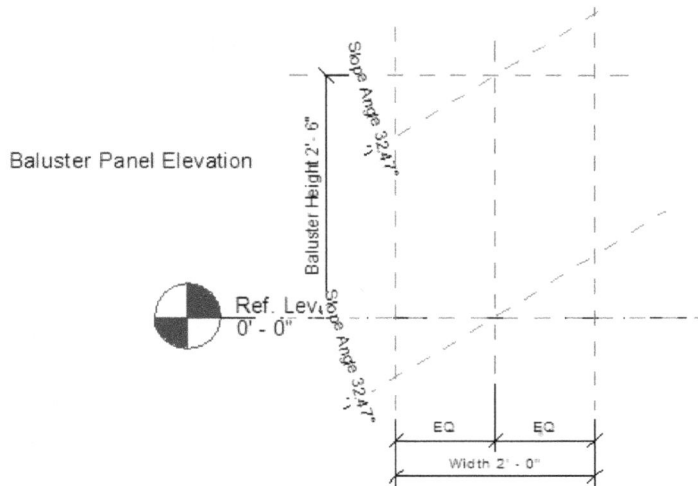

Figure 7–35

- Component families are found in the *Railings* folder, with subfolders for *Balusters*, *Supports*, and *Terminations*.

- To create elements from scratch, use the following family templates:
    - **Baluster.rft**
    - **Baluster-Panel.rft**
    - **Baluster-Post.rft**
    - **Railing Support.rft**
    - **Railing Termination.rft**

Hint: Adding Custom Posts

Posts are the point at which railings join. In many cases, this is the area in which railings need to change pitch and extend into adjacent railings, creating an integral, non-interrupted system. When designing a post, it is important to have a good grasp of creating custom families and to want to experiment. An example is shown in Figure 7–36.

Figure 7–36

*   If you create a post as a post family, you cannot insert it as an independent component in the model. However, if you create a post as a generic model, you cannot use it in the Baluster dialog box and add it to a rail system. For this reason, it is recommended that you create the post family as an actual post, and then save a copy as a generic model. This gives you the option of using the post in any situation.

Creating Railing Types

To create a railing type, select an existing railing, duplicate it, and modify the Type properties, as shown in Figure 7–37. Click **Preview** to display a thumbnail of the railing.

Figure 7–37

- When editing a type, any changes that you make to one type impacts all instances of the railing type, as shown in Figure 7–38. Make duplicate copies of the top rail and railing type before making changes so that you can have one without extensions, as shown in Figure 7–39.

Figure 7–38

Figure 7–39

How To: Set the Rail Structure (Non-Continuous)

1. In the Type Properties dialog box, next to the **Rail Structure (Non-Continuous)** parameter, click **Edit...**.
2. In the Edit Rails (Non-Continuous) dialog box, click **Insert** to add a new rail to the list. You can have a single rail or multiple rails in a Railing type, as shown in Figure 7–40.
   - If there are no other horizontal members, this dialog box remains empty.

Figure 7–40

3. Fill out the information about the rails as required:

Name	The name of the individual railing component. Select the name to modify it.
Height	The height for each rail from the base height.
Offset	The distance from the rail sketch line.
Profile	Select a profile in the drop-down list. You need to have the profile loaded before you can use it. (This is just a profile family, not a rail type as is required when you specify the top rails and handrails.)
Material	Specify a material for the rail. This is the only place where you can apply the material for rails.

4. Click **Up** and **Down** to move the rail to the correct location in the group.
5. Click **OK** to finish the command.

How To: Edit the Baluster Placement

1. In the Type Properties dialog box, next to the **Baluster Placement** parameter, click **Edit....** The Edit Baluster Placement dialog box has two main areas: *Main pattern* and *Posts*, as shown in Figure 7–41.

Figure 7–41

2. In the *Main pattern* area, add the baluster family and its sizes, such as the distance from the previous baluster. You can also add panels in this area.
3. If you are using a baluster on stairs and want a specific number per tread, select **Use Baluster Per Tread On Stairs** and specify the number per tread.
4. In the *Posts* area, specify the profiles for the *Start*, *Corner*, and *End* posts, and then specify their dimensions and locations.

How To: Set the Top Rail and Handrail

1. In the Type Properties dialog box, set up the information for *Top Rail, Handrail 1*, and *Handrail 2*, as shown in Figure 7–42.

The Top Rail is either the top of a guardrail (specify the handrail separately) or the top of the handrail (no separate handrail type needed).

Figure 7–42

2. To select a *Type*, click on the Browse (**...**) button, as shown in Figure 7–43. The Type Properties dialog box displays (as shown in Figure 7–43), where you can duplicate and modify type properties (including Extensions and Terminations).

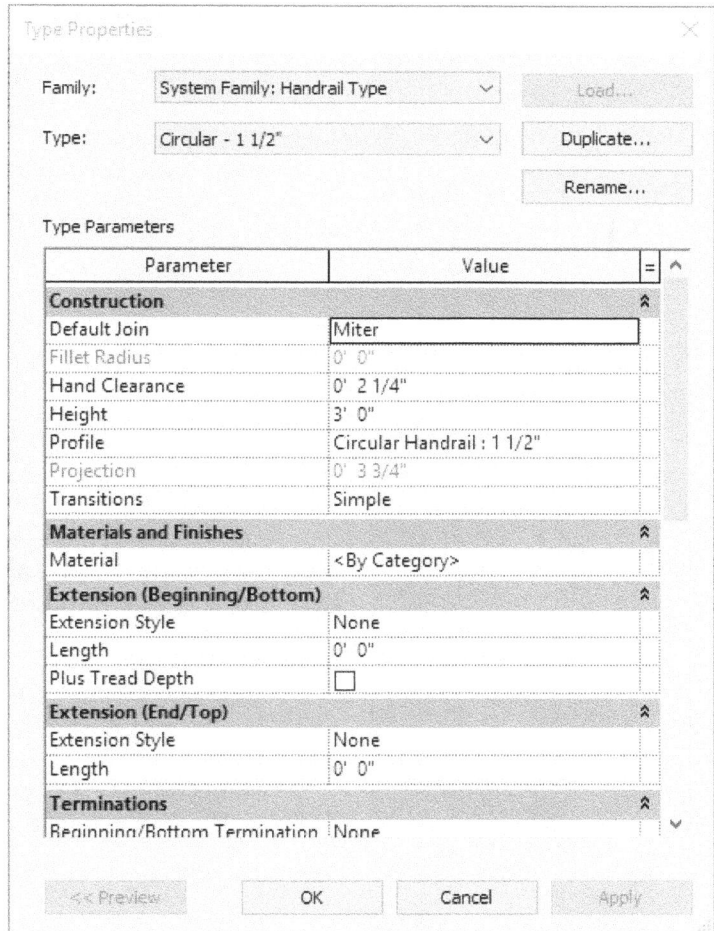

Figure 7–43

- In the *Extension (Beginning/Bottom)* area, set the *Extension Style*. The properties are **None**, **Wall**, **Floor**, and **Post**, as shown in Figure 7–44.

Wall

Floor

Post

Figure 7–44

- A Termination can be added if required. The default rectangular termination works best with the Floor Extension Style, but you can also create custom ones.
- For Handrail types, you can also specify *Supports*, as shown in Figure 7–45. These are typically used if you are creating a wall-based railing type.

Supports		☆
Family	Support - Metal - Circular	
Layout	Align With Posts	⬚
Spacing	None	
Justification	Fixed Distance	
Number	Align With Posts	
	Fixed Number	
Identity Data	Maximum Spacing	
Keynote	Minimum Spacing	

Figure 7–45

3. If you are creating a guardrail, you also need to specify the *Type* and *Position* of the handrail. The handrail can be set to **Left**, **Right**, or **Left and Right** of the main railing as shown in Figure 7–46. The **Lateral Offset** and **Height** are read-only parameters.

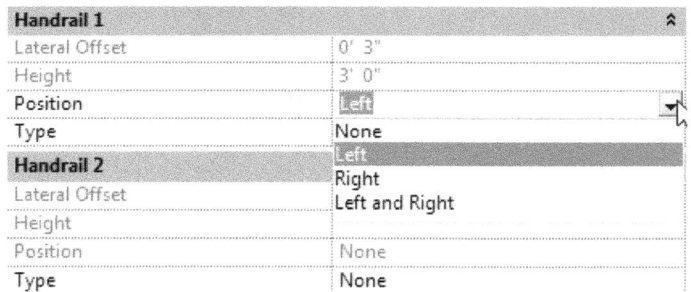

Handrail 1		☆
Lateral Offset	0' 3"	
Height	3' 0"	
Position	Left	⬚
Type	None	
Handrail 2	Left	
Lateral Offset	Right	
Height	Left and Right	
Position	None	
Type	None	

Figure 7–46

- If you do not want to include a separate handrail in the railing type, set the *Type* to **None**.

Hint: Additional Clean up Options

When railings are not cleaning up as expected, ensure that the Stair Properties are correct. For example, *Rail Connections* can be set to **Trim** (as shown in Figure 7–47) or **Weld**. The **Weld** option forces a miter joint, rather than a butt joint.

Type Parameters

Parameter	Value	
Construction		⟰
Railing Height	0' 0"	
Rail Structure (Non-Continuous)	Edit...	
Baluster Placement	Edit...	
Baluster Offset	0' 0"	
Use Landing Height Adjustment	No	
Landing Height Adjustment	0' 0"	
Angled Joins	Add Vertical/Horizontal Segments	
Tangent Joins	Extend Rails to Meet	
Rail Connections	Trim	

Figure 7–47

When a straight rail joins an arc rail, the Autodesk Revit software tends to distort the geometry. To fix this, select the segment of a rail in the railing's Sketch mode and modify the *Height Correction* in the Options Bar, as shown in Figure 7–48.

Slope: By Host	▼	Height Correction: By Type	▼	0.0

Figure 7–48

Practice 7d	# Create Custom Railings

Practice Objectives

- Duplicate and modify existing baluster and baluster panel families.
- Create a custom railing type using the baluster and baluster panel families.

In this practice, you will make copies of existing baluster and baluster panel families and modify them slightly. You will also create new Top Rail and Handrail types. You will then use the various families and types to create a new Railing type, as shown in Figure 7–49.

Figure 7–49

Task 1 - Set the material of a baluster family.

1. In the practice files *Architectural* folder, open **Modern-Hotel-Railings-BIM.rvt**.

2. Open the **3D Views: Hall Balcony** view. This is the railing style you are going to use to create a new railing style.

3. Switch to the **Floor Plans: Floor 2** view. Families cannot be opened when you are in a 3D camera view.

4. In the *File* tab, expand 📂 (Open) and click 🖳 (Family).

5. In the Library, expand the *Railings>Balusters* folder and open **Baluster-Round.rfa**.

- The family is also available in the practice files practice files *Architectural* folder.

6. Save the file as **Baluster-Round-Wood.rfa** in your practice files folder.

7. In the Baluster family file, in the *Manage* tab>Settings panel, click (Materials). A short list of materials is available in the family and no wood materials are available.

8. In the Material Browser, expand *AEC Materials* and select **Wood**. In the selection set next to **Birch**, select **Adds material to document**, as shown in Figure 7–50.

Figure 7–50

9. In the *Project Materials* area, select the **Birch** material and in the *Graphics* tab, select **Use Render Appearance**, as shown in Figure 7–51.

Figure 7–51

10. Click **OK**.

The material for balusters cannot be set in the railing style, only in the family.

11. In the *Create* tab>Properties panel, click ⊞ (Family Types).

12. In the Family Types dialog box, change the current type to **2"**.

13. Beside the *Type name*, click 📄 (New Type) and name the new type **2" - Birch**.

14. Set the *Baluster Material* to **Birch**, as shown in Figure 7–52.

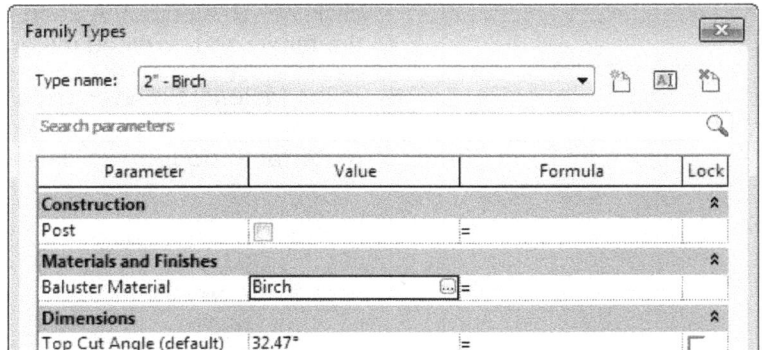

Figure 7–52

15. Click **OK**.

16. In the View Control Bar, set the *Visual Style* to ▱ (Consistent Colors) and then to ▱ (Realistic) to display the new wood shade.

17. Save the baluster family.

18. In the *Create* tab>Family Editor panel, click ⊟ (Load into Project and Close).

19. If the Modern Hotel project is the only one you have open, the family automatically loads and switches to the project file. If you have others open, select the Modern Hotel project from the list and click **OK**.

Task 2 - Modify a baluster panel family.

1. In the Revit Library's *Railings>Balusters* subfolder, open the family file **Baluster Panel - Glass w Brackets.rfa.**

   • The family is also available in the practice files practice files *Architectural* folder.

2. Save it as **Baluster Panel - Glass with Open Brackets.rfa** in your practice files folder.

3. Open the **Elevations: Left** view.

4. Zoom in on one of the brackets and select it.

5. In the *Modify | Extrusion* tab>Mode panel, click ⬚ (Edit Extrusion).

6. Sketch a **3/4"** radius circle inside the bracket, as shown in Figure 7–53. This creates a hole in the extrusion.

*To snap to the center of the arc, type the shortcut **SC** for Snap to Center.*

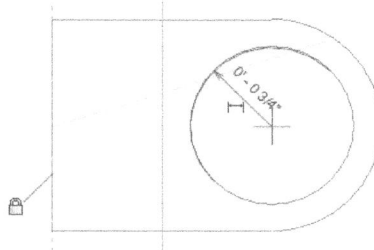

Figure 7–53

7. Click ✓ (Finish Edit Mode).

8. Repeat the process with the other three brackets.

9. Open the **3D Views: View 1** view and set the *Visual Style* to ▱ (Consistent Colors). The panel displays with the opening in the brackets, as shown in Figure 7–54.

Figure 7–54

10. In the *Modify* tab>Properties panel, click ⊞ (Family Types).

11. Create a new family type named **36" w 1" Gap**.

12. In the Family Types dialog box, change the *Width* to **3'-0"**.

13. Click **Apply**. The panel updates, as shown in Figure 7–55. Click **OK**.

Figure 7–55

14. Save the baluster panel and load it into the Modern Hotel project.

Task 3 - Create Top Rail and Handrail types.

1. In the Modern Hotel project, in the Project Browser, expand **Families>Railings>Top Rail Type** node.

2. Right-click on **Circular - 1 1/2"** and select **Type Properties**.

3. In the Type Properties dialog box, duplicate the type, and name it **Circular - 1 1/2" - Birch**.

4. Change the *Material* to **Birch** and set the *Extension (Beginning/Bottom)* and *Extension (End/Top)* to **Wall**, as shown in Figure 7–56.

Figure 7–56

5. Click **OK**.

6. Repeat the process to create a new Birch Handrail type.

7. Save the project.

Task 4 - Create custom Railing types.

---

1. In the Modern Hotel project, open the **3D Views: Hall Balcony** view.

2. Select the railing.

3. In Properties, click ⊞ (Edit Type).

4. In the Type properties dialog box, click **Duplicate** and name the new railing type **Hotel Balcony Guardrail - Glass Panel**.

5. Next to the **Rail Structure (Non-Continuous)** parameter, click **Edit...**.

6. In the Edit Rails dialog box, delete all of the Rails and click **OK**.

7. Click **OK**. The new railing displays with wooden guardrail and handrail and existing posts, as shown in Figure 7–57.

Figure 7–57

8. Select the railing and edit the Railing type again.

9. Next to the **Baluster Placement** parameter, click **Edit...**.

10. In the *Main pattern* area, next to *Regular Baluster* (in the *Baluster Family* column), change the type to **Baluster-Round-Wood: 2"-Birch**, as shown in Figure 7–58.

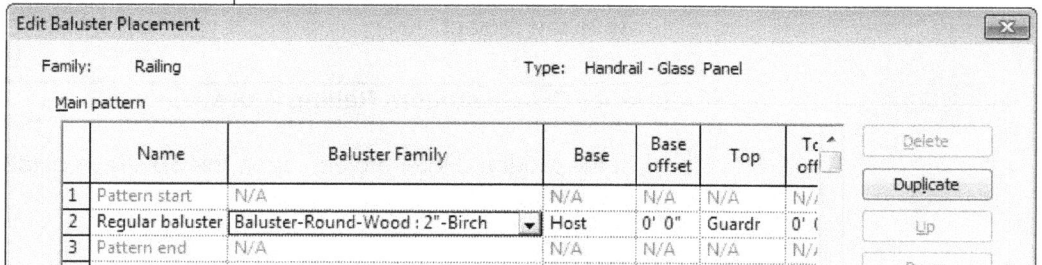

Figure 7–58

11. Click **Duplicate**.

12. In row 2, change the *Name* to **Panel** and the *Baluster Family* to **Baluster Panel-Glass w Open Brackets: 36" w 1" Gap**.

13. Click **OK** twice and view the railings. The panel displays, but it is not in the correct location in relation to the posts, as shown in Figure 7–59.

Figure 7–59

Distances between balusters is measured from center to center.

14. Edit the type again and open the Edit Baluster Placement dialog box. In the *Dist. from Previous* column, you can see that the settings are now **4'-0"** for both the baluster and the panel. Therefore, the baluster and panel placement is spread out.

15. Set the *Dist. from Previous* to **1'-7 1/8"** for both the baluster and panel.

16. Set *Justify* to **Beginning** and *Excess Length Fill* to **None**, as shown in Figure 7–60.

Main pattern

	Name	Baluster Family	Base	Base offset	Top	Top offset	Dist. from previous	Offset
1	Pattern sta	N/A	N/A	N/A	N/A	N/A	N/A	N/A
2	Panel	Baluster Panel - Gla	Host	0' 0"	Top Rai	0' 0"	1' 7 1/8"	0' 0"
3	Regular ba	Baluster - Round -	Host	0' 0"	Top Rai	0' 0"	1' 7 1/8"	0' 0"
4	Pattern en	N/A	N/A	N/A	N/A	N/A	0' 0"	N/A

Break Pattern at: Each Segment End   Angle: 0.000°   Pattern Length: 3' 2 1/4"

Justify: Beginning   Excess Length Fill : None   Spacing: 0' 0"

Figure 7–60

17. While still in the Edit Baluster Placement dialog box, in the *Posts* area, change the *Baluster Family* for all of the posts to **Baluster - Round - Wood: 2" - Birch** and click **OK**.

18. In the Type Properties dialog box, change the *Top Rail Type* to the new **Circular - 1 1/2" - Birch** top rail type and *Handrail 1* to the new **Circular - 1 1/2" - Birch** handrail type.

19. Close the dialog boxes and view the new Railing type. This time, the baluster to panel fit is better, as shown in Figure 7–61.

Figure 7–61

20. Save the project.

Chapter Review Questions

1. The door family shown in Figure 7–62 does not exist in the default library. Which one of the following methods should you use to create the door family?

Figure 7–62

   a. Start a new door family based on the default door template and build it from there.

   b. Copy the existing **Single-Flush.rfa** family as the base and draw the panel outlines using detail lines.

   c. Copy an existing panel-style family and modify the panel extrusions.

   d. Start a new door family based on the **Single-Panel.rfa** template and modify the panel extrusions.

2. Based on the information in the Family Types dialog box (shown in Figure 7–63), if you changed the *Trim Projection Ext* value, would the *Trim Projection Int* also update?

Family Types

Type name:	36" x 48"			

Search parameters

Parameter	Value	Formula	Lock	▲
Dimensions			☆	
Height	4' 0"	=	☑	
Default Sill Height	3' 0"	=	☑	
Trim Projection - Ext.	0' 0 1/2"	=	☑	
Trim Projection - Int.	0' 0 3/4"	=	☑	
Trim Width - Exterior	0' 3 1/2"	=	☑	
Trim Width - Interior	0' 3 1/2"	=	☑	
Width	3' 0"	=	☑	
Window Inset	0' 0 3/4"	=	☑	
Rough Width		=	☑	≡
Rough Height		=	☑	

Figure 7–63

   a. Yes

   b. No

3. Which of the following must be in place before you can add a fascia to an angled wall? (Select all that apply.)

   a. A profile

   b. A fascia type

   c. A wall sweep

   d. A model line

4. Which of the following parts of a railing type (shown in Figure 7–64) is created by a profile?

Figure 7–64

   a. Rail

   b. Post

   c. Baluster

   d. Baluster panel

5. What is the main difference between a Baluster family and a Post Family?

   a. A Baluster is created using a profile and a Post is created using solid forms.

   b. A Baluster has top and bottom angles programmed into the family, while a Post does not have any angles.

   c. Balusters can be placed on stair treads, but posts can only be placed on landings.

   d. Balusters are typically placed 4" apart, and Posts are placed 3'-0" apart.

Command Summary

Button	Command	Location
	Roof: Fascia	• **Ribbon:** *Architecture* tab>Build panel
	Object Styles	• **Ribbon:** *Manage* tab>Settings panel
	Model Line	• **Ribbon:** *Architecture* tab>Model panel

Creating MEP Specific Families

MEP families include elements such as plumbing fixtures, light fixtures, data devices, and pipe fittings. By working through practices, you can learn how to upgrade an architectural plumbing fixture to use connectors, create a custom light fixture, and create a data device with annotation options. For an advanced challenge you can also create a pipe fitting flange. Select the practices that you find most helpful and relevant to your work.

Learning Objectives in this Chapter

- Upgrade an architectural plumbing fixture with MEP connectors.
- Create a custom lighting fixture.
- Create a data device family that includes a tag in the family.
- Create a pipe fitting flange.

Practice 8a

Upgrade an Architectural Plumbing Fixture to MEP

Practice Objective

- Upgrade an existing architectural toilet fixture with pipe sizes and connectors for use in a MEP project.

In this practice, you will upgrade an existing architectural toilet fixture to be used in an MEP project. You will create parameters for pipe sizes. You will also add connectors for cold water and Sanitary systems, as shown in Figure 8–1.

Figure 8–1

Task 1 - Create parameters for pipe sizes.

1. In the practice files *MEP* folder, open **Toilet-Commercial-Wall-3D.rfa**.

2. Save the family as **Toilet-Commercial-Wall-3D-MEP.rfa**.

3. In the Family Types dialog box, add the following Type parameters:

Name	Discipline	Type of Parameter	Group
Sanitary Radius	Piping	Pipe Size	Dimensions
Cold Water Radius	Piping	Pipe Size	Dimensions

The related diameter parameters need to be Shared because they are often used in plumbing fixture schedules.

4. Set *Sanitary Radius* to **2"** and *Cold Water Radius* to **1/2"**. Lock the parameters.

5. Add shared type parameters selected from the **MEP.txt** parameter file:
   - Sanitary Diameter
   - Cold Water Diameter

6. Create formulas for *Sanitary Diameter* and *Cold Water Diameter* based on the corresponding radius parameters, as shown in Figure 8–2.

Dimensions			☆
Sanitary Radius	2"	=	☑
Sanitary Diameter	4"	= Sanitary Radius * 2	☑
Cold Water Radius	1/2"	=	☑
Cold Water Diameter	1"	= Cold Water Radius * 2	☑
Mounting Height	1' 3"	=	☑

Figure 8–2

7. Click **OK**.

8. Save the family.

Task 2 - Add connectors.

---

1. Rotate the view so that the back of the toilet displays. (If the wall displays, hide it temporarily or set the *Visual Style* to **Wireframe** while you are adding connectors.)

2. In the *Create* tab>Connectors panel, click (Pipe Connector).

3. In the Options Bar, select **Domestic Cold Water**.

4. Hover the cursor over the face of the pipe opening, as shown in Figure 8–3, and click to place the connector.

Figure 8–3

5. Click ⌖ (Modify) and select the Connector.

6. In Properties, set the following values for parameters:
   - *Flow Configuration*: **Fixture Units**
   - *Flow Direction:* **In**
   - Clear the **Allow Slope Adjustments** option.
   - *Fixture Units:* **2.5**

7. In the *Dimensions* area, and next to *Diameter*, click
   ▯ (Associate Parameter).

8. In the Associate Family Parameter dialog box, select **Cold Water Diameter**, as shown in Figure 8–4. Then, click **OK**.

Figure 8–4

9. The connector resizes to fit the correct pipe size.

10. Add a Pipe Connector for a Sanitary system to the back of the fixture, as shown in Figure 8–5.

Figure 8–5

11. Select the connector and set the following properties.
    - *Diameter:* Associate with **Sanitary Diameter** parameter
    - *Flow Configuration:* **Fixture Units**
    - *Flow Direction:* **Out**
    - Select **Allow Slope Adjustments**.
    - *System Classification:* **Sanitary**
    - *Fixture Units:* **4**

12. Add any other parameters or values required to make this a more useful MEP fixture.

13. Test the fixture in a project.

14. Save and the family and project files.

Practice 8b

Upgrade an Architectural Lighting Fixture to MEP

Practice Objectives

- Modify the light source.
- Apply a power connector.
- Create family types with different materials for the pendant and glass shade.

In this practice, you will modify a lighting fixture family with a specific light source and connector, as shown in Figure 8–6. You will also create family types using different materials.

Figure 8–6

Task 1 - Set up a new light fixture family.

1. In the practice files *MEP* folder, open the family **Pendant-Light-Fixture.rfa**.

2. Open the **Elevations: Front** view. It includes reference planes for the Ceiling and Light Source, a ceiling element, the fixture elements, and the Ref. Level, as shown in Figure 8–7.

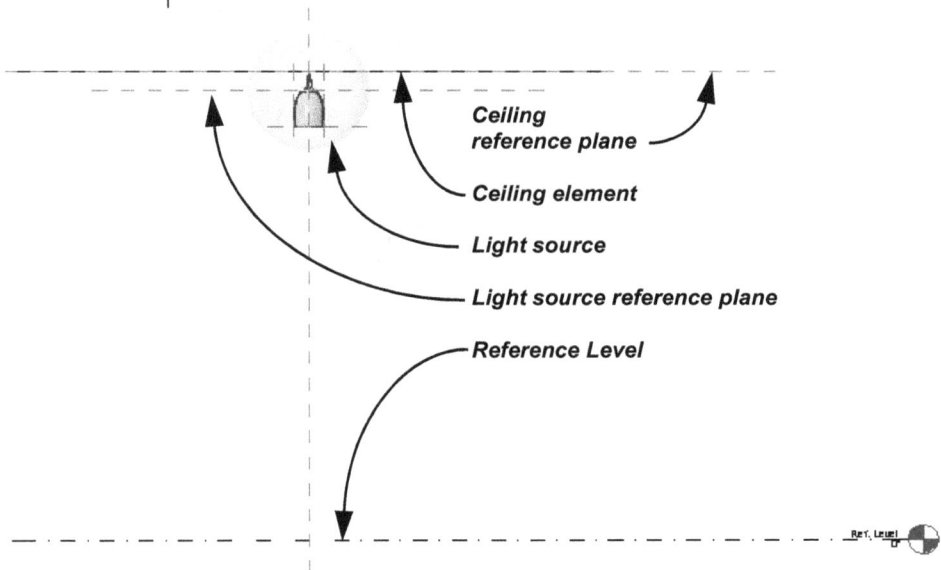

Figure 8–7

3. Select the light source. In the *Modify | Light Source* tab> Lighting panel, click (Light Source Definition).

4. In the Light Source Definition dialog box, change the Light distribution to (Photometric Web), as shown in Figure 8–8. Then, click **OK**.

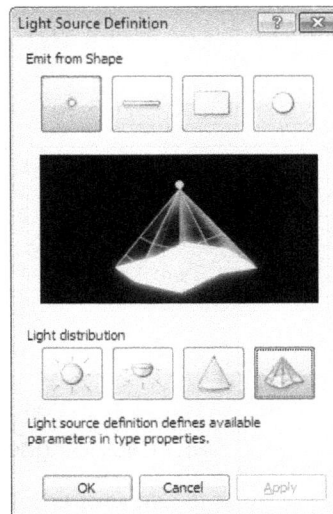

Figure 8–8

5. Open the Family Types dialog box and set the following values for the parameters:
   - *Lamp:* **CF42TRT**
   - *Apparent Load:* **44.21 VA**
   - *Tilt Angle:* **90**
   - *Photometric Web File:* Click [...] and select **spot_ideal.ies**.
   - *Light Loss Factor:* **0.85**
   - *Initial Intensity:* **Luminous Flux, 3200**

6. Save the family.

Task 2 - Add a connector.

1. Open a 3D view and set the *Visual Style* to **Wireframe**.

2. In the *Create* tab>Connectors panel, click ⤴ (Electrical Connector).

3. In the Options Bar, select **Power - Balanced**.

4. Attach the connector to the face of the pendant at the point where the pendant touches the ceiling, as shown in Figure 8–9.

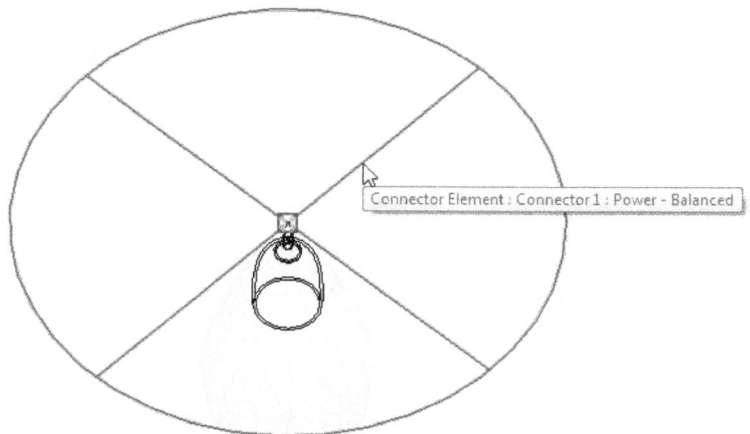

Connector Element : Connector 1 : Power - Balanced

Figure 8–9

5. Click ⟶ (Modify) and select the connector.

6. In Properties specify the values for the following parameters:
   - *System Type:* **Power - Balanced (verify)**

- *Load Classification:* **Lighting**
- *Voltage:* **277**
- *Power Factor:* **0.95**

7. While still in Properties, beside the *Apparent Load* parameter, click ⬜ (Associate Family Parameter).

8. In the Associate Family Parameter dialog box, select **Apparent Load**. Click **OK**.

9. Save the family.

Task 3 - Create Family types.

1. In the *Create* tab>Properties panel, click ⬛ (Family Types).

2. In the Family Types dialog box, click ⬜ (New Type).

3. In the Name dialog box, enter **Brass and Green Glass** as the name.

4. In the *Materials and Finishes* area, verify or set the following values for the parameters, as shown in Figure 8–10:

- **Pendent Material:** Metal - Brass
- **Glass Material:** Glass - Green

Parameter	Value	Formula	Lock
Materials and Finishes			☆
Pendent Material	Metal - Brass	=	
Glass Material	Glass - Green	=	

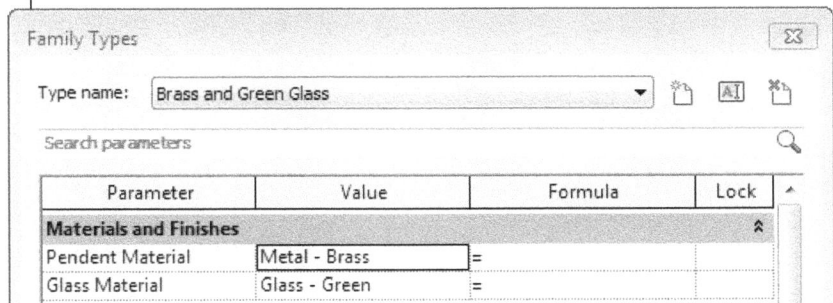

Type name: Brass and Green Glass

Search parameters

Figure 8–10

5. Click **Apply**.

6. Create several other Family Types that use different colors of glass and different pendant materials.

7. Test the family in a project that has a ceiling in it.

8. Save and close the family and the project.

Practice 8c

Create a Data Device with Annotation Parameters

Practice Objective

- Create a data device with both solid elements and annotation elements.

In this practice, you will create a data device using reference planes, extrusions, and connectors. You will then add an annotation symbol to the family with its related parameters, as shown in Figure 8–11. You will also test the family in a project.

Figure 8–11

Task 1 - Set up reference planes.

1. Create a new family based on the **Data Device Hosted.rft** template found in the Autodesk Revit Library.

2. Save the family to your practice folder as **Data Receptacle Type C.rfa.**

3. In the *Manage* tab>Settings panel, click [icon] (Project Units) or type **UN**.

4. In the Project Units dialog box, set the *Length* units to **Fractional Inches**. Click **OK** to close the dialog boxes.

5. In the **Floor Plans: Ref. Level** view, set the *View Scale* to **3"=1'-0"**.

6. Zoom in closer to the intersection of the reference planes.

7. Create and dimension the reference planes, as shown in Figure 8–12. You do not need to label these dimensions as all of the data receptacles are the same size.

Figure 8–12

8. Save the family.

Task 2 - Create the model extrusions.

1. Create the two extrusions shown in Figure 8–13. Set the *Depth* of the extrusions as follows:
   - Extrusion 1 = (negative) -**2 1/8"**
   - Extrusion 2 = **3/16"**

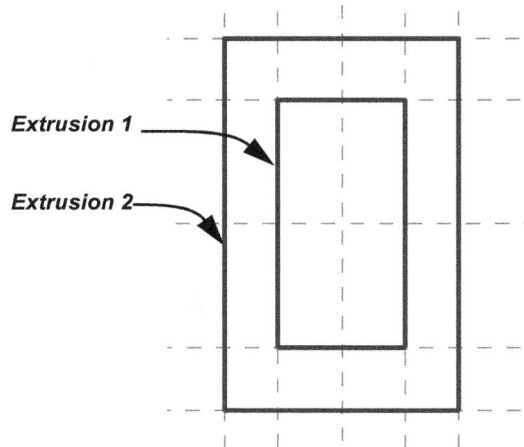

Extrusion 1

Extrusion 2

Figure 8–13

2. Open a 3D view and set the *Visual Style* to **Wireframe**. The finished view displays as shown in Figure 8–14.

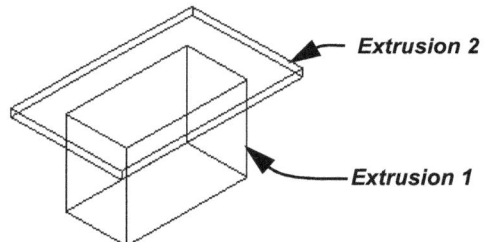

Extrusion 2

Extrusion 1

Figure 8–14

3. In the *Create* tab>Connectors panel, click ⚡ (Electrical Connector).

4. In the Options Bar, select **Data**.

5. Select the face of the top extrusion.

6. Click ⌖ (Modify) and select both extrusions.

7. In the *Modify | Extrusion* tab>Mode panel, click ⬜ (Visibility Settings).

8. In the Family Element Visibility Settings dialog box, clear **Front/Back**, **Coarse**, and **Medium**. Click **OK**.

   • This causes the 3D elements to display only at the Fine detail level where it is often used to coordinate the placement of items by their real dimensions. At the Coarse and Medium detail levels the tag is more useful.

9. Return to the **Ref. Level** view.

10. Save the family.

Task 3 - Create an Annotation symbol.

---

1. Create a new family based on the **Generic Annotation.rft** template found in the *Annotations* folder of the Autodesk Revit Library.

2. Save the family to your practice folder as **Data Device Annotation.rfa.**

3. Read and delete the red note. You will not modify the Family Category in this case because you need it to remain a generic annotation.

4. In the *Annotate* tab>Detail panel, click ⬜ (Symbolic Line) and using the Draw tools, sketch the shape shown in Figure 8–15.

Do not add the dimensions, they are for information only.

Figure 8–15

5. In the *Create* tab>Text panel, click ⊞A (Label).

6. Click inside the new symbol sketch.

7. In the Edit Label dialog box there are no parameters listed. Click ⬚ (Add Parameter).

Ensure that this is an instance parameter.

8. Create an Instance parameter named **Tag**, set *Type of Parameter* as **Text**, and set *Group parameter under* as **Identity Data**. Click **OK**.

9. Back in the Edit Label dialog box, add the parameter to the label and set the *Sample Value* to **A1**, as shown in Figure 8–16. Then, click **OK**.

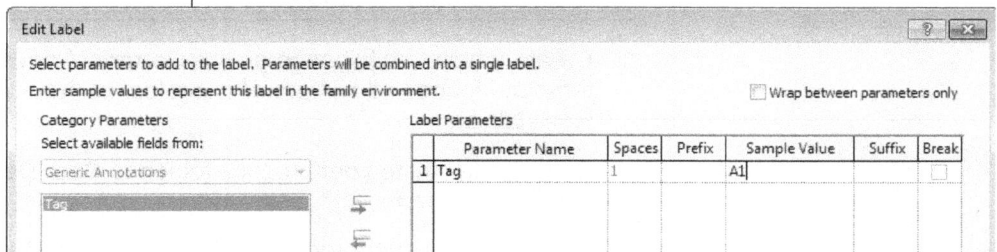

Figure 8–16

10. Select the new label and, in Properties, click ⊞ (Edit Type). In the Type Properties dialog box, set the *Background* to **Transparent** and click **OK**.

11. Relocate the label to fit inside the symbol sketch.

12. With nothing selected, in Properties, select **Rotate with component** and **Keep text readable.**

13. Save the annotation family and load it into the data receptacle family.

Task 4 - Add the Label Family to the Data Receptacle.

1. In the data receptacle family, place a copy of the Data Device Annotation family at the center of the elements, as shown in Figure 8–17.

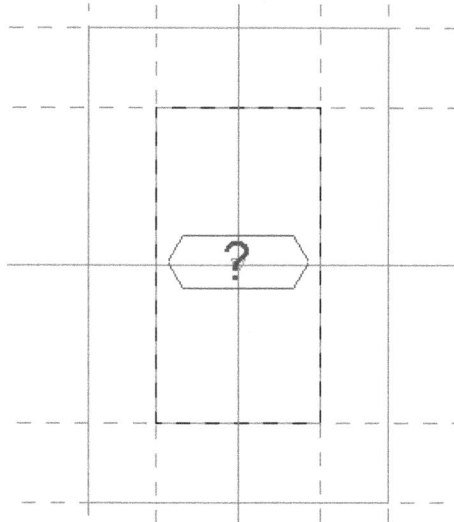

Figure 8–17

2. Open the Family Types dialog box and create an Instance parameter named **Tag**. Set *Type of Parameter* as **Text** and *Group parameter under* as **Identity Data**. Click **OK**.

3. Expand the *Identity Data* heading (if required) and set the *Tag* to **C7**, as shown in Figure 8–18.

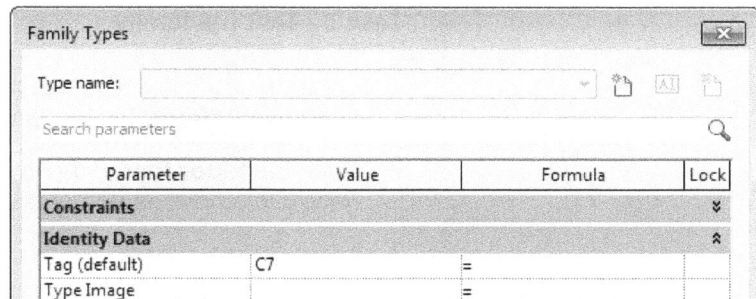

Parameter	Value	Formula	Lock
Constraints			⮟
Identity Data			⮝
Tag (default)	C7	=	
Type Image		=	

Figure 8–18

4. Click **OK**.

5. Select the Data Device Annotation element.

6. In Properties, under the *Identity Data* heading, beside the

   Tag parameter, click ⬚ (Associate Family Parameter).

7. In the Associate Family Parameter dialog box, select **Tag** and click **OK**.

8. When you finish, the parameters are associated together and the tag displays as **C7**, as shown in Figure 8–19.

Figure 8–19

9. If time permits, you can create Family Types for C1, C2, C3, C4, C5, C6, and C7. Change the value of the **Tag** parameter for each of these, as required.

10. Save the family.

Task 5 - Test the family.

---

1. Create a new project using the **Electrical-Default.rte** or **Systems-Default.rte** template.

2. Open the **Floor Plans: 1- Power** view and close the **1-Mech** view. (Data devices do not display in Mechanical views.)

3. Add a couple of walls.

4. Switch to the data receptacle family and load it into the project.

5. Add it several times using different types if you have created them.

6. Save and close the project and family files.

Practice 8d

Create a Pipe Fitting Flange (Advanced)

Practice Objectives

- Create reference planes, dimensions, and labels.
- Draw single-line representations for Coarse and Medium detail levels.
- Create solids for the Fine detail level.
- Create and apply Family Types.

In this practice, you will create a family file based on a template and add parameters, some of which include formulas. You will then add reference planes, dimensions, and labels and create family types to help you flex the framework. You will then create the flange components: a single-line representation for **Coarse** and **Medium** detail levels, and an extrusion and blend solid elements for **Fine** detail level, as shown in Figure 8–20. Finally, you will test the flanges in a project and draw pipe between them.

Figure 8–20

Task 1 - Open a family template.

1. Create a new family based on the **Plumbing Fixture.rft** template found in the Autodesk Revit Library.

2. Save the family to your practice folder as **Pipe Fitting Flange.rfa**.

3. In the *Create* tab>Properties panel, click (Family Category and Parameters).

4. In the Family Category and parameters dialog box, set the *Filter list* to **Piping** and in the *Family Category* area, select **Pipe Fittings**.

5. In the *Family Parameters* area, set the following options:
   - Clear the **Work Plane-Based** option.
   - Select **Always Vertical**.
   - For the *Part Type*, select **Transition**.
   - Clear the **Shared** option.

6. Click **OK**.

7. Type **UN** to open the Project Units dialog box.

8. Change the format of *Length* to **Fractional inches**, and set it to the nearest **1/16"**.

9. Set the *Discipline* to **Piping** and change the format of *Pipe Size* to the nearest **1/16"**.

10. Click **OK**.

11. Set the view *Scale* to **1" = 1'-0"**.

12. Save the family.

Task 2 - Create parameters.

---

1. In the *Create* tab>Properties panel, click ⊞ (Family Types).

2. At the bottom of the Family Types dialog box, click ⬜ (New Parameter).

3. In the Parameter Properties dialog box, in the *Parameter Type* area, select **Family Parameter** (if it is not already selected) and specify the following:
   - *Name:* **NomRad**
   - *Discipline:* **Piping**
   - *Type of Parameter:* **Pipe Size**
   - *Group Parameter Under:* **Dimensions**
   - Select **Type**.

4. Click **OK**.

5. Repeat the steps, creating instance parameters named **NomDia**, **FlgRad**, **FlgDia**, **PipeOD**, **PipeOR**, **RFD**, **RFR**, **RFT**, **FT**, **LTH**, **HT**, and **HubRad**. Define the parameters as follows:
   - *Parameter Type:* **Family Parameter**
   - *Discipline:* **Piping**
   - *Type:* **Pipe Size**
   - *Group Parameter Under:* **Dimensions**
   - Select **Instance**.

6. In the Family Types dialog box, specify the following values:
   - *FT:* **3/4"**
   - *FlgDia:* **9"**
   - *LTH:* **5"**
   - *NomRad:* **2"**
   - *PipeOD:* **4 1/2"**
   - *RFD:* **7"**
   - *RFT:* **1/16"**

7. In the Family Types dialog box, enter the following formulas for the parameters:
   - *FlgRad:* **FlgDia / 2**
   - *HT:* **LTH - (FT + RFT)**
   - *HubRad:* **PipeOR * 1.5**
   - *NomDia:* **NomRad * 2**
   - *PipeOR:* **PipeOD / 2**
   - *RFD:* **FlgDia - 2"**
   - *RFR:* **RFD / 2**

The final information displays as shown in Figure 8–21.

By default, the parameters are listed in alphabetical order.

Parameter	Value	Formula	Lock
Dimensions			⌃
FT (default)	3/4"	=	▢
FlgDia (default)	9"	=	▢
FlgRad (default)	4 1/2"	= FlgDia / 2	▢
HT (default)	4 3/16"	= LTH - (FT + RFT)	▢
HubRad (default)	3 3/8"	= PipeOR * 1.5	▢
LTH (default)	5"	=	▢
NomDia (default)	4"	= NomRad * 2	▢
NomRad	2"	=	▢
OffsetHeight (default)		=	
OffsetWidth (default)		=	
PipeOD (default)	4 1/2"	=	▢
PipeOR (default)	2 1/4"	= PipeOD / 2	▢
RFD (default)	7"	= FlgDia - 2"	▢
RFR (default)	3 1/2"	= RFD / 2	▢
RFT (default)	1/16"	=	▢

Figure 8–21

8. Click **OK**.

9. Save the family.

Task 3 - Create plan view reference planes.

1. Place three vertical reference planes 2" apart, with one to the left of the **Center (Left/Right)** reference plane, and two on the right, as shown in Figure 8–22.

2. Name the new reference planes, as shown in Figure 8–22, with the *Is Reference* parameter set to **Not a Reference**.

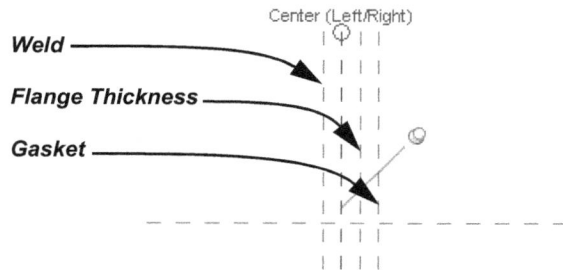

Figure 8–22

3. Dimension the reference planes, as shown in Figure 8–23. Apply the labels shown in Figure 8–24 to the dimensions.

Figure 8–23

Figure 8–24

4. Add horizontal reference planes, dimensions, and labels on either side of the **Center (Front/Back)** reference plane, as shown in Figure 8–25.

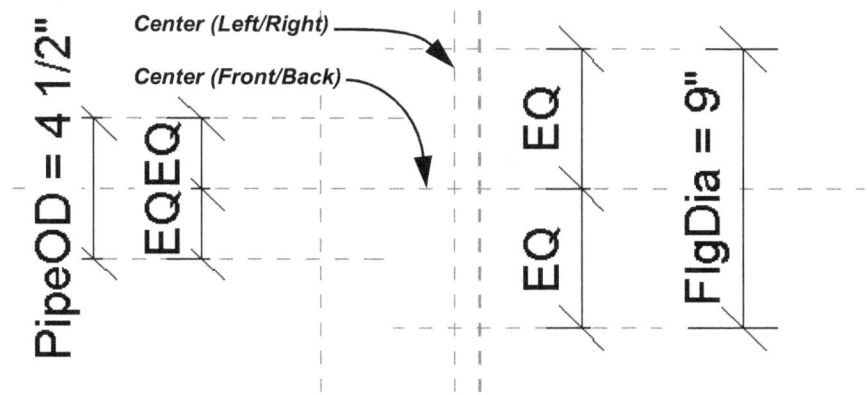

Figure 8–25

5. Save the family.

Task 4 - Create family types so that you can test the framework.

---

1. In the Properties panel, click ▦ (Family Types).

2. In the Family Types dialog box, beside the *Type name*, click 📄 (New Type).

3. In the Name dialog box, type **4"** and click **OK**. Note that the existing values are applied to this type by default.

4. Click 📄 (New Type) again. In the Name dialog box, type **6"**.

5. In the *Dimensions* area, change the parameter values as follows:
   - *FT:* **15/16"**
   - *FlgDia:* **11"**
   - *LTH:* **3 1/2"**
   - *NomRad:* **3"**
   - *PipeOD:* **6 5/8"**

6. Move the Family Types dialog box so that the reference planes display.

7. Click **Apply**. The reference plane locations change according to the new parameter values, as shown in Figure 8–26.

Family Types

Type name: 6"

Search parameters

Parameter	Value
Graphics	
Use Annotation Scale (d	☐
Dimensions	
FT (default)	15/16"
FlgDia (default)	11"
FlgRad (default)	5 1/2"
HT (default)	2 1/2"
HubRad (default)	4 31/32"
LTH (default)	3 1/2"
NomDia (default)	6"
NomRad	3"
OffsetHeight (default)	
OffsetWidth (default)	
PipeOD (default)	6 5/8"
PipeOR (default)	3 5/16"
RFD (default)	9"
RFR (default)	4 1/2"
RFT (default)	1/16"

Figure 8–26

8. In the Type Name drop-down list, select **4"**.

9. Click **Apply**. Note that the flange returns to its original size.

10. Click **OK** to close the dialog box.

11. Save the family.

Task 5 - Create plan view graphics.

1. Continue working in the **Floor Plans: Rev. Level** view.

2. Type **VV** to open the Visibility Graphics dialog box. In the *Model Categories* tab, click **Object Styles**.

3. In the Object Styles dialog box, click **Select All**. Change the *Projection Line Weight* to **5** for all objects, as shown in Figure 8–27.

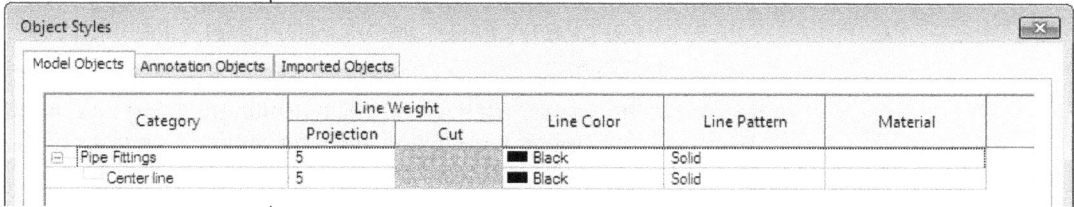

Figure 8–27

4. Click **OK** twice to close the dialog boxes.

5. In the *Create* tab>Model panel, click (Model Line).

6. Draw the lines shown in Figure 8–28. If you do not see the thickness, toggle (Thin Lines). Ensure that you draw from the intersections of the reference planes so that the lines will flex with the reference planes.

RFT = 1/16"

Draw this line on the vertical reference plane to the right

Figure 8–28

7. Open the Family Types dialog box. Use the new Types to verify that the lines work with the changes.

8. Reset the *Type Name* to **4"** and click **OK** to close the dialog box.

9. Select the three lines.

10. In the *Modify | Lines* tab>Visibility panel, click ⬚ (Visibility Settings).

11. In the Family Element Visibility Settings dialog box, in the *Detail Levels* area, clear the **Fine** option. Leave all of the others selected, as shown in Figure 8–29.

   • This enables the selected elements to be visible only at the Coarse and Medium detail levels.

Figure 8–29

12. Click **OK**.

13. In the View Control Bar, select ⬚ (Preview Visibility On). Test the *Detail Levels.* When you select **Fine**, the line elements should disappear. End on **Medium.**

14. Toggle off the preview visibility.

15. Save the family.

Task 6 - Create the Raised Face and Flange extrusions.

1. In the Project Browser, open the **Elevations: Left** view.

2. Select the model lines and temporarily hide the elements.

3. In the *Create* tab>Forms panel, click ⬚ (Extrusion).

4. In the *Modify | Create Extrusion* tab>Work Plane panel, click ⬚ (Set).

5. In the Work Plane dialog box, in the Name drop-down list, select **Reference Plane: Gasket** and click **OK**.

6. Draw a circle at the intersection of the **Ref Level** and **Center (Front/Back)** reference planes. Dimension and label it using the **RFR** parameter, as shown in Figure 8–30.

Figure 8–30

7. Click ⬉ (Modify).

8. In Properties, in the *Extrusion End* row, click the **Associate Family Parameter** button.

9. In the Associate Family Parameter dialog box, select **RFT**, as shown in Figure 8–31. Then, click **OK**.

Figure 8–31

10. Click ✓ (Finish Edit Mode).

11. Click ▯ (Extrusion).

12. Set the Work Plane to **Reference Plane: Center (Left/Right)**.

13. Draw a larger circle at the same intersection.

14. Make the temporary dimension permanent and label it as **FlgRad**.

15. In Properties, in the *Extrusion End* row, click the **Associate Family Parameter** button. In the Associate Family Parameter dialog box, select **FT** and click **OK**. The new radius displays as shown in Figure 8–32.

Figure 8–32

16. Click ✓ (Finish Edit Mode).

17. Open the **3D views: View 1** view. The two circular extrusions and the model lines should display. Shade and rotate the element as required, as shown in Figure 8–33. Flex it using the family types.

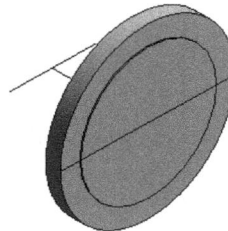

Figure 8–33

18. Save the family.

Task 7 - Create the pipe connection blend.

1. Return to the **Elevations: Left** view.

2. In the *Create* tab>Forms panel, click ⬭ (Blend).

3. Draw a circle at the same intersection. Dimension and label it **HubRad**.

4. In the *Modify | Create Blend Base Boundary* tab>Mode panel, click ⬭ (Edit Top).

5. Draw a smaller circle at the same intersection as the other element. Dimension and label it **PipeOR**.

6. In Properties, set the *Second End* to (negative) **-4"**.

7. Click ✔ (Finish Edit Mode).

8. Open the **Elevations: Front** view. Align and lock the small end of the blend to the Weld reference plane, as shown in Figure 8–34.

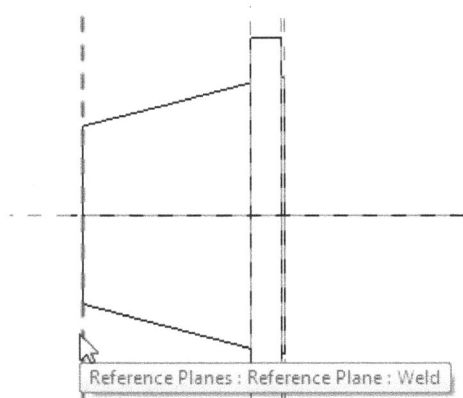

Reference Planes : Reference Plane : Weld

Figure 8–34

9. Open the **3D Views: View 1** view and flex the types to ensure that everything is working, as shown for two possible flexes in Figure 8–35 and Figure 8–36.

 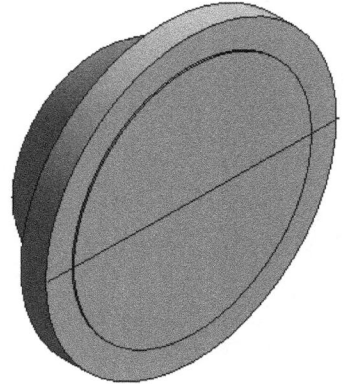

Figure 8–35 **Figure 8–36**

10. Temporarily hide the model lines.

11. Save the family.

Task 8 - Add connectors.

---

1. Continue working in the **3D Views: View 1** view.

2. In the *Create* tab>Connectors panel, click (Pipe Connector).

3. In the *Modify | Place Pipe Connector* tab>Placement panel, verify that (Face) is selected.

4. In the Options Bar, in the System type drop-down list, select **Hydronic Supply**.

5. In Properties, set the *Round Connector Dimension* parameter to **Use Radius**.

6. Rotate the view and press <Tab> as required to highlight the small face of the blend and click to add the connector.

7. The arrow of the connector should be pointing outward from the flange object, as shown in Figure 8–37. If the arrow is pointing inward, click the **Flip** control.

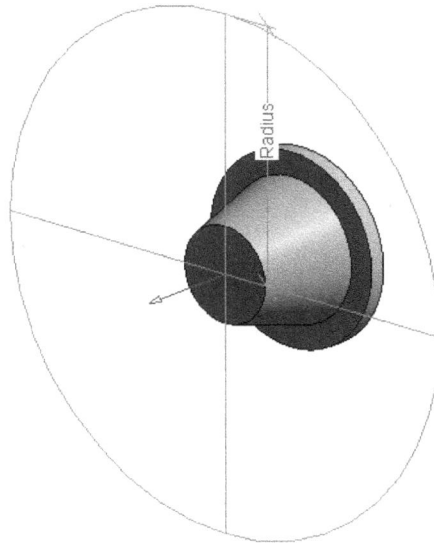

Figure 8–37

- The connector arrow does not indicate flow direction. Instead, it points in the direction from which the pipe is going to connect into it.

8. Spin the view so that the raised face is visible and apply another connector to that face, as shown in Figure 8–38.

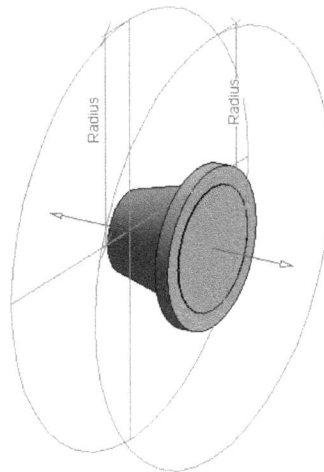

Figure 8–38

9. Select the first connector. In the *Modify | Connector Element* tab>Connector Links panel, click 🔗 (Link Connectors).

10. Click the second connector to link it to the first.

11. Select both connectors.

12. In Properties, for *Radius,* associate it with the **NomRad** parameter and click **OK**.

13. The connectors are resized as shown in Figure 8–39.

Figure 8–39

14. Save the family.

Task 9 - Test the flange in a project.

---

1. Start a new project using the default **Mechanical Template**, the **Plumbing-Default.rte**, or **Systems-Default.rte** templates.

2. Save the project as **Flange Test.rvt**

3. Open the Plumbing>Plumbing>Floor Plans: **1 - Plumbing** view.

4. Switch back to the family.

5. In the Family Editor panel, click 📤 (Load into Project).

   • If you have one project open, the new family loads directly into it. If you have more than one project open, select the right one(s) in the dialog box.

6. You are returned to the project.

7. Place an instance of each type into the drawing area of the project.

- If a command is not automatically started, in the *Systems* tab>Model panel, click (Component).

8. Zoom in to display the plan view of the flanges at a **Coarse** detail level. Ensure that **Thin Lines** is toggled off so that the line weight displays as shown in Figure 8–40.

9. With **Thin Lines** on, change the *Detail Level* to **Fine**. The flanges display in detail at full size, as shown in Figure 8–41.

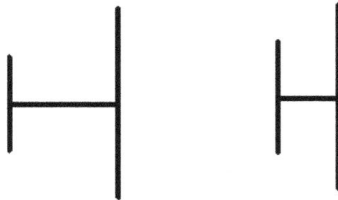

Figure 8–40   **Figure 8–41**

10. Ensure that the flanges are aligned with each other, and then draw pipe between them.

11. Open a 3D view.

12. Zoom in on the flanges and toggle on (Thin Lines) as required.

13. Change the *Detail Level* to **Fine** and type to **SD** to shade the view.

14. Spin the view to examine the flanges from all sides.

15. Save the project file.

16. Close the project and family files. Save any changes you want to keep.

Chapter Review Questions

1. An architect has requested that you use an architectural vanity family such as the one shown in Figure 8–42, but it does not work with MEP tools. What must you do to upgrade it so that it includes MEP parameters?

Figure 8–42

   a. Add pipes to the family where you want the project pipes to tie in.

   b. Add connectors to the family where you want the project pipes to tie in.

   c. Import an existing sink designed to work with MEP systems into the family.

   d. Use one of your own families even if it does not match the architect's request.

2. Which of the following Light Source Definition distribution options enables you to specify an IES file?

a. (Spherical)

b. (Hemispherical)

c. (Spot)

d. (Photometric Web)

3. If you want to include an annotation element, such as a label that references a parameter in a family, you can only do so by creating a separate annotation tag.

a. True

b. False

4. How do you have a family display different elements when you change the *Detail Level* from *Coarse* to **Fine**?

a. In the project file, select the family and in Properties change the detail level.

b. In the family file, select the elements and modify the *Visibility Settings*.

c. In the family file, in the View Properties, set the detail level.

d. In the project file, set the *Visibility Settings* for the view.

5. In the Family Types dialog box shown in Figure 8–43, if the *Pump Length* changed to **2'-0"**, what would the value of *Radius 2* be?

Family Types

Name: 5 Tons

Parameter	Value	Formula	Lock
Pump Length	3' 1 1/4"	=	☑
Pump Height	3' 5 1/8"	=	☑
Panel Height	1' 8"	=	☑
Outlet Radius	3/16"	=	☑
Outlet Diameter	3/8"	= Outlet Radius * 2	☑
Inlet Radius	9/16"	=	☑
Inlet Diameter	1 1/8"	= Inlet Radius * 2	☑
Fan Radius	1' 1 205/256"	= Fan Diameter / 2	☑
Fan Diameter	2' 3 77/128"	=	☑
C2 Offset 2	0' 8 5/8"	=	☑
C2 Offset 1	0' 3 3/8"	=	☑
C1 Offset 2	0' 6"	=	☑
C1 Offset 1	0' 3 7/8"	=	☑
Other			⌃
Radius 1	7' 9 1/8"	= 2.5 * Pump Length	☑
Radius 2	7' 8 1/8"	= Radius 1 - 0' 1"	☑

Family Types: New... Rename... Delete
Parameters: Add... Modify... Remove
Lookup Tables: Manage...

OK | Cancel | Apply | Help

Figure 8–43

a. 5'-0"

b. 4'-0"

c. 4'-11"

d. 5'-1"

Creating Structural Specific Families

Structural specific families include everything from column and beam design, to detail items such as gusset plates. By working through a series of practices, you learn about creating a parametric gusset plate, an in-place stiffener plate, an in-place slab depression, a built-up column, a tapered concrete column, a truss family, a precast hollow core slab and a tapered moment frame. Select the ones that are most helpful in your work.

Learning Objectives in this Chapter

- Create a gusset plate with parametric properties.
- Create an in-place column stiffener family.
- Create a floor-based family with a void that cuts out a depression in a floor when inserted in a project.
- Create a built-up column family made of steel plates.
- Create a tapered concrete column family.
- Create a truss family.
- Create a precast hollow core slab family that uses an imported CAD file for the profile.
- Create a tapered moment frame family that includes two columns with a connecting beam.

Practice 9a

Parametric Gusset Plate

Practice Objectives

- Create reference planes, dimensions, and parameters.
- Create solid geometry for the plates.
- Modify Visibility Settings and create Family Types.

In this practice, you will create a family file based on a template and create reference planes. You will then create gussets as a mass, create material parameters, and apply Family Types. Finally, you will toggle off the visibility of the gusset plate from the coarse detail to all views, as shown in Figure 9–1.

Figure 9–1

Task 1 - Start a new family using a template and add reference planes.

1. Create a new family based on the **Structural Stiffener.rft**. template found in the Autodesk® Revit® Library**.**

2. Save the family to your practice folder as **Parametric Gusset Plate.rfa**.

3. Open the Project Units dialog box. Change the *Length Format* to **Fractional inches**. This makes the dimensions easier to read.

4. Open the **Elevations: Left** view.

5. Create and dimension the new reference planes, as shown in Figure 9–2.

   • Ensure that the diagonal reference plane being added crosses the intersection of the **Center (Front/Back)** and **Ref. Level** reference planes.

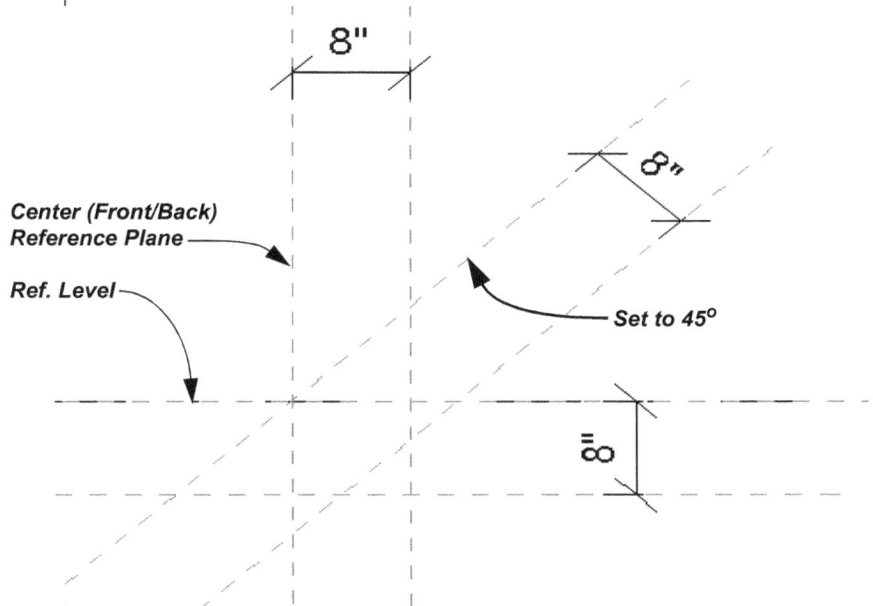

Figure 9–2

6. Label one of the dimensions with a new type parameter named **Width**.

7. Select the other two dimensions and apply the same parameter to them.

8. Flex the parameter to test the stability of the framework.

9. Set the *Width* to **8"**.

10. Save the family.

Task 2 - Create Front View reference planes.

1. Switch to the **Elevations: Front** view and create two reference planes, **1/4"** on either side of the **Center (Left/Right)** reference plane and add dimensions. Label the overall dimension as **Thickness**, as shown in Figure 9–3.

Figure 9–3

2. Flex the parameter to test the stability of the framework.

3. Set the *Thickness* to **1/2"**.

4. Save the family.

Task 3 - Creating family geometry.

1. Switch to **Elevations: Left** view.

2. In the *Create* tab>Forms panel, click (Extrusion). In the Options Bar, set the *Depth* to **1/2"**.

3. Draw individual lines across the outside intersections of the reference planes, and lock all five lines to the reference planes, as shown in Figure 9–4.

Modify the scale so that the dimensions are clearly displayed.

*Use the **Align** command to help lock the lines to the reference plane.*

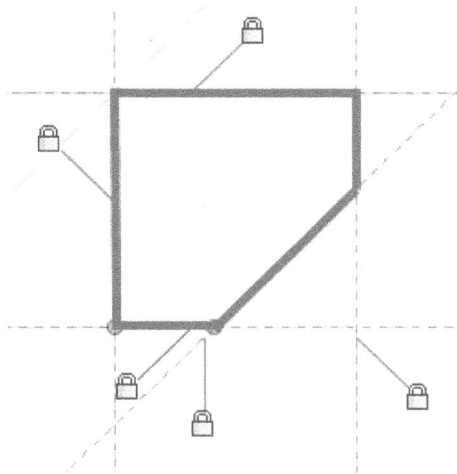

Figure 9–4

4. Click ✔ (Finish Edit Mode).

5. Switch to the **Elevations: Front** view. Align the left and right sides of the extrusion with the reference planes you created earlier and lock them.

6. Switch to a 3D view and shade the model.

7. In the *Create* tab>Properties panel, click ▦ (Family Types) to flex the model to ensure that everything is working together. The model displays as shown in Figure 9–5.

Figure 9–5

8. Save the family.

Task 4 - Add material parameters.

1. Open the Family Types dialog box.

2. At the bottom of the dialog box, click ⬜ (New Parameter).

3. Create an Instance parameter named **Material** and set the *Type of Parameter* to **Material**. The Group automatically updates to Materials and Finishes, as shown in Figure 9–6. Click **OK**.

*Setting the parameter as an **Instance** makes it easier to modify it in the project file.*

Parameter Data
Name:
Material   ○ Type
Discipline:
Common   ▼   ◉ Instance
Type of Parameter: ☐ Reporting Parameter
Material   ▼   (Can be used to extract value
Group parameter under: from a geometric condition and
Materials and Finishes   ▼   report it in a formula or as a
                                            schedulable parameter)
Tooltip Description:
<No tooltip description. Edit this parameter to write a custom tooltip. Custom t...
Edit Tooltip...

OK   Cancel   Help

Figure 9–6

4. In the 3D view, select the plate.

5. In Properties, in the *Materials and Finishes* area, in *Material* row, click ⬜ (Associate Family Parameter).

6. In the Associate Family Parameter dialog box, select **Material**, as shown in Figure 9–7. Then, click **OK**.

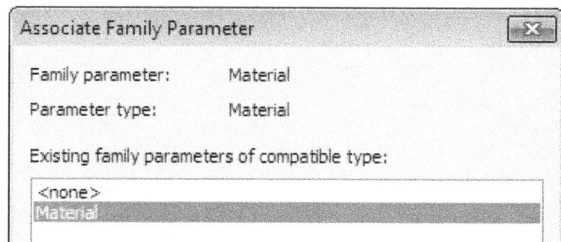

Associate Family Parameter   ✕

Family parameter: Material

Parameter type: Material

Existing family parameters of compatible type:

<none>
Material

Figure 9–7

7. In Properties, the **Material** parameter is now marked with the = sign, as shown in Figure 9–8. Therefore, when the family is loaded into a project, you can control its material using Properties.

Materials and Finishes		☆
Material	<By Category>	🗐
Identity Data		☆

Figure 9–8

Task 5 - Change the visibility settings in a family.

---

1. Select the extrusion.

2. In the *Modify | Extrusion* tab>Mode panel, click 🗗 (Visibility Settings).

3. In the Family Element Visibility Settings dialog box, clear the **Coarse** option, as shown in Figure 9–9, so that the gusset plate does not display at a **Coarse** detail level.

Figure 9–9

4. Click **OK**.

5. In the View Control panel, select 🖾 (Preview Visibility On).

6. Change the *Detail Level* to **Coarse**, **Medium**, and **Fine**. The outline of the Gusset Plate remains in the **Medium** and **Fine** detail levels but disappears in the **Coarse** detail level.

7. Toggle off the preview visibility.

8. Save the family.

Task 6 - Create family types.

1. Open the Family Types dialog box.

2. Create three Family Types. Set the *Name* and the *Width* parameter of each as follows:
   - **8"**
   - **10"**
   - **12"**

3. Use the new types to flex the gusset plate family.

4. Save the family.

5. Ensure that you have a structural project open and then load the family into the project.

6. In the project, open a 3D View and set the *Detail Level* to **Medium**.

7. Insert one of each Plate type into the project.

8. Switch to a 3D view to see the differences.

9. Shade the view, using the shortcut **SD** as required.

10. Select one of the Plates. In Properties, apply a material to it. Repeat with the others using different materials.

11. Save and close the family and project files.

Practice 9b

In-Place Column Stiffeners

Practice Objective

- Create an in-place family in a detail view

In this practice, you will create a stiffener plate to strengthen a column's flange, as shown in Figure 9–10.

Figure 9–10

Task 1 - Create an in-place family in a detail view.

1. In the practice files *Structural* folder, open **Column-Stiffeners.rvt**. The file opens in the **Structural Plans: Level 2** view.

2. In the Project Browser, open **Detail Views: Detail 0**. It displays a column supporting a beam and concrete on metal deck slab, as shown in Figure 9–11.

Figure 9–11

3. The column requires stiffeners to strengthen its flanges. In the *Structure* tab>Model panel, expand ⬜ (Component) and click ⬜ (Model In-Place).

4. In the Family Category and Parameters dialog box, set the *Filter list* to **Structure** and select **Structural Stiffeners**, as shown in Figure 9–12. Click **OK**.

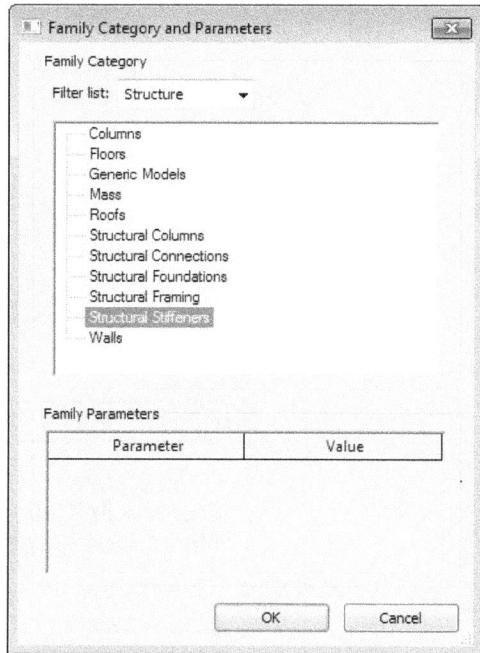

Figure 9–12

5. Enter a name for the stiffener plate, as shown in Figure 9–13.

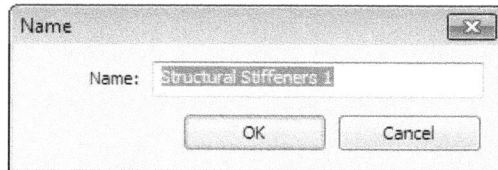

Figure 9–13

6. You are now in the In-Place Editor. In the **Detail 0** view, draw two horizontal reference planes and name them, as shown in Figure 9–14. These reference planes assist in locating the stiffener plates.

Top of Beam

Bottom of Beam

Figure 9–14

7. In the *Create* tab>Forms panel, click ▯ (Extrusion).

8. In the Work Plane dialog box, in the drop-down list, select **Reference Plane: Top of Beam**, and then click **OK**.

9. In the Go To View dialog box, select **Structural Plan: Level 2**. This view is used to draw the stiffener plate.

10. Click **Open View**.

11. In the **Structural Plans: Level 2** view, zoom into the grid intersection **1/A**.

12. In the *Modify | Create Extrusion* tab>Draw panel, click

⬚ (Pick Lines). In the Options Bar, select **Lock**. This ensures that the stiffener edges adjust to any changes to the column size.

13. Select and trim the perimeter of the inside face of the column, as shown in Figure 9–15.

You might need to zoom in very close to display the faint background image.

Figure 9–15

14. In Properties, set the *Extrusion End* value to (negative) **-1"**, as shown in Figure 9–16.

Figure 9–16

15. Click ✓ (Finish Edit Mode).

16. Switch to the **Detail 0** view. Note that the stiffener plate is located under the **Top of Beam** reference planes.

17. Select the stiffener plate and click (Copy). In the Options Bar, clear the **Constrain** option. Select the starting point as the bottom of the stiffener plate and copy it halfway down between the two reference planes.

18. Select the copied stiffener plate.

19. In the *Modify | Extrusion* tab>Work Plane panel, click **Edit Work Plane**.

20. In the Work Plane dialog box, select **Reference Plane: Bottom of Beam** and click **OK**. The plate moves into a new position.

21. The stiffener plate thickness must be adjusted upward. Select the new stiffener plate and change the *Extrusion End* to **1"**.

22. The new plates are now in place, as shown in Figure 9–17.

Figure 9–17

23. In the In-Place Editor panel, click ✓ (Finish Model).

24. In the project file, navigate through the different views to see the stiffener plates.

25. Save and close the project.

Practice 9c | In-Place Slab Depression

Practice Objectives

- Create a floor-based family by setting up the parametric framework.
- Create a void form for a depression in the floor.
- Apply the family in a project.

Slab depression family is an important host-based family that you need to modify for your projects. In this practice, you will create a slab depression using a template file and apply it in a project, as shown in Figure 9–18.

Figure 9–18

Task 1 - Create a family and add reference planes, insertion points, and dimensions.

1. Create a new family based on the **Generic Model floor based.rft** template found in the Autodesk Revit Library**.**

2. Save the family to your practice folder as **Slab Depression Component.rfa**.

3. In the Create Tab>Properties panel, click ⬚ (Family Categories and Parameters).

4. In the Family Category and Parameters dialog box, select **Structural Foundations** and click **OK**.

5. In the *Create* tab>Datum panel, click ◿ (Reference Plane).

6. Add the horizontal and vertical reference planes and dimensions, as shown in Figure 9–19.

Figure 9–19

7. Label the horizontal dimension as **Slab Depression Length** and the Vertical dimension as **Slab Depression Width**. In both cases set the parameter to **Instance**. The parameters display as shown in Figure 9–20.

*Ensure that you set these parameters and the one below to **Instance** parameters. This ensures that they can be set in the project.*

Figure 9–20

8. Flex the parameters to test them.

9. Open the **Elevations: Front** view where you create the depth of the depressed slab.

10. Add another reference plane **3"** down from the reference level. Add a dimension between the reference level and the new reference plane. Label the dimension as **Slab Depression Depth**, as shown in Figure 9–21.

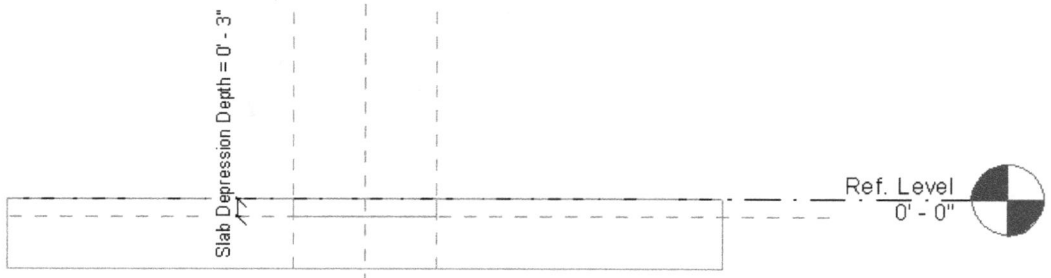

Figure 9–21

11. Flex the parameters to test them.

12. Save the family.

Task 2 - Create the depressed area for the slab.

1. Now you will create the depressed area for the slab by creating a void form and locking it to the reference planes. Switch to the **Floor Plans: Ref. Level** view.

2. In the *Create* tab>Forms panel, expand ⬜ (Void Forms) and click ⬚ (Void Extrusion).

3. In the Draw panel, click ⬚ (Rectangle).

4. Add the rectangle by clicking at the top left corner of the intersecting reference planes and then the bottom right corner. Click the lock controls to constrain the void form to the reference planes, as shown in Figure 9–22.

Figure 9–22

5. Click (Finish Edit Mode).

6. Open the **Elevations: Front** view.

7. In the *Modify* tab>Modify panel, click (Align).

8. Select the lower reference plane first and then pick the bottom of the void form, as shown in Figure 9–23. Select the lock control to constrain the bottom of the void form to the reference plane.

Figure 9–23

9. Still in the **Align** command, select the reference level and pick the top of the void form. Select the lock control to constrain the top of the void form to the reference level.

10. In the *Modify* tab>Geometry panel, click (Cut Geometry) and pick the void form and the slab object. (The order of the selection does not matter.)

11. Open a 3D view to see the depression in the slab object. Type **SD** to shade the view, as shown in Figure 9–24.

Figure 9–24

12. Use the Family Types dialog box to flex the depression.

13. Close the dialog box.

14. Save the Depressed Slab component family file. Do not close the family file.

Task 3 - Test the component family file.

---

1. Create a new project and save the file as **Depressed Slab Example.rvt**.

2. In the *Structure* tab>Foundation panel, click ⬭ (Structural Foundation: Slab). Create an **8" Foundation Slab** in the new project.

3. When the slab has been created in the project file, return to the **Slab Depression Component.rfa** family file.

4. In the Family Editor panel, click 📤 (Load into Project).

5. If it is not automatically started, start the **Component** command.

6. Pick a location for the slab depression. The insertion is based on the origin in the family file. In the family file you based the insertion point at the center of the recessed slab.

7. Select different views to display the depression. Cut some sections through it.

8. To change the size of slab depression, return to the **Floor Plans: Level 2** view, and select the component.

9. In Properties, change the values to any required size, as shown in Figure 9–25.

Properties	✕

Slab Depression Component ▾

Structural Foundations (1) ▾ Edit Type

Constraints	⁂
Structural	⁂
Dimensions	⁂
Slab Depression Depth	0' 6"
Slab Depression Length	4' 0"
Slab Depression Width	2' 0"

Figure 9–25

10. Return to the 3D view and Section view to see the new shape of the depressed slab.

11. Save and close the project and family files.

Practice 9d | Built-Up Column

Practice Objectives

- Set up the parametric framework for a column.
- Use extrusions to create the sides of the column.

The Autodesk Revit Structure software has an extensive structural columns library to meet many standard types and sizes in the industry. However, there is still a need for built-up (custom) made columns. In this practice, you will create a built-up column from steel plates, as shown in Figure 9–26.

Figure 9–26

- The analytical line is already incorporated into the family in the structural system family template. Therefore, it is not required to be created in the new family.

Task 4 - Set up reference planes and dimensions.

1. Create a new family based on the **Structural Column.rft** template found in the Autodesk Revit Library.

2. Save the family to your practice folder as **Built-Up Column.rfa**.

3. In the **Structural Plans: Lower Ref. Level** view, add reference planes to the inside of the four exterior reference planes using ⚲ (Pick Lines) with an *Offset* of **2"**, as shown in Figure 9–27.

Figure 9–27

4. Delete the vertical **EQ** dimensions to prevent over-constraining and re-insert new vertical EQ dimensions at the inner reference planes, as shown in Figure 9–28.

Figure 9–28

5. Place single dimensions horizontally and vertically above the EQ dimensions, as shown in Figure 9–29.

Figure 9–29

6. Select the horizontal dimension and label it. Set the *Name* to **Primary Plate Length** and select **Instance**, as shown in Figure 9–30.

*The **Instance** option enables the value to be modified per element.*

Figure 9–30

7. Follow the same procedures for the vertical dimension, naming it **Secondary Plate Length**.

8. Add four more dimensions, as shown in Figure 9–31. Set the parameters for these new dimensions to determine the thickness of the primary and secondary plates.

Primary Plate Length 2' - 0"

EQ   EQ

Secondary Plate Thickness 0' - 2"

Primary Plate Thickness 0' - 2"

Secondary Plate Length 1' - 8"

EQ

EQ

Primary Plate Thickness 0' - 2"

Secondary Plate Thickness 0' - 2"

Figure 9–31

9. Flex the sizes to ensure that they are moving together.

10. Save the family.

Task 5 - Create the plates.

---

1. In the *Create* tab>Forms panel, click ⬜ (Extrusion) to create the plates. Only one plate can be created at a time because each extrusion must be a closed loop.

2. Sketch the rectangle, based on the start and end points shown in Figure 9–32.

   - Lock the lines to the reference planes.
   - Leave the **Extrusion Start** and **Extrusion End** parameters as default. The column height is adjusted later by aligning with other reference planes.

Figure 9–32

3. Click (Finish Edit Mode).

4. Select the primary plate created and mirror it using the center line as the axis of reflection.

5. Create the secondary plate (sketch shown in Figure 9–33) and mirror it to the other side.

Figure 9–33

6. Flex the sizes to ensure that the extrusions move as expected.

7. Open the **Elevations: Front** view to establish the height of the column.

8. Use ⬚ (Align) to align the four plates to the **Upper Ref. Level.** Select the **Upper Ref. Level** and then the top of a plate and lock it in place. Repeat this procedure until all four plates are locked to the **Upper Ref. Level** and **Lower Ref. Level**, as shown in Figure 9–34.

Ensure that the view is in Wireframe mode to see all of the plates.

Figure 9–34

9. Set the *Visual Style* of the view to **Hidden Line**. Note that the secondary plates behind the primary plates disappear.

10. Use Symbolic Lines to display the secondary plates with hidden lines. In the *Annotate* tab>Detail panel, click ⬚ (Symbolic Line).

11. In the *Modify | Place Symbolic Lines* tab>Subcategory panel Type Selector, select **Hidden Lines (projection)**.

12. In the Options Bar, verify that the **Chain** option is cleared. Draw a line from the intersection of the **Upper Ref. Level** and the inside reference planes on both sides of the column, as shown in Figure 9–35. Lock these lines to both the **Upper** and **Lower Ref. Levels**.

Figure 9–35

13. Temporarily hide the reference plane category so you can see the new lines.

14. Flex the sizes and **Upper Ref. Level** height.

15. Reset Temporary Hide/Isolate.

16. Save the family.

17. To test the Built-Up Column, open a new project and load the **Built-Up Column** family into the new project. Insert a column, as shown in Figure 9–36, and navigate from one view to another to see the new column. Add other columns and change the size and offset from the level.

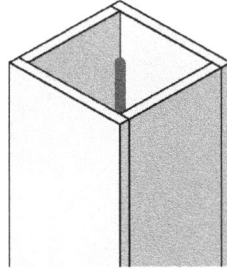

Figure 9–36

18. Save and close the family and project files.

Practice 9e | Tapered Concrete Column

Practice Objectives

- Create Reference Planes and Parameters as the framework of the column family.
- Create geometry using a solid blend.

In this practice, you will create a tapered concrete column using a column family template. You will create its geometry using a solid blend and add a taper parameter that can be modified as shown in Figure 9–37.

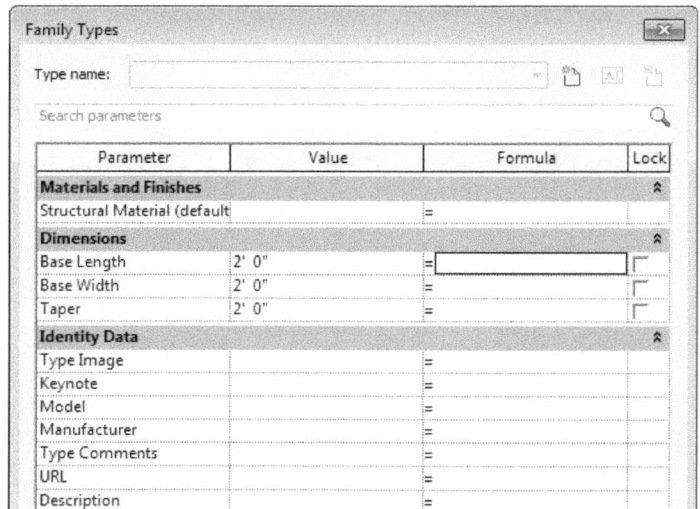

Figure 9–37

Task 1 - Create Reference Planes and Parameters.

1. Create a new family based on the **Structural Column.rft** template found in the Autodesk Revit Library.

2. Save the family to your practice folder as **Tapered-Concrete-Column.rfa**.

3. Add dimensions and labels for the **Base Width** and **Base Length**, as well as a reference plane named **Taper**. Dimension and label it, as shown in Figure 9–38.

Figure 9–38

4. Flex the sizes to test the framework.

5. Save the family.

Task 2 - Create geometry.

1. In the *Create* tab>Forms panel, click ⬠ (Blend).

2. Sketch the base of the blend, as shown in Figure 9–39.

3. Click ⬠ (Edit Top) and sketch the top of the blend (the overhanging taper - it is larger than the base), as shown in Figure 9–40.

Figure 9–39

Figure 9–40

4. In the Mode panel, click ✎ (Finish Edit Mode).

5. Open the **Elevations: Front** view.

6. Align and lock the blend to the **Upper Ref. Level**, as shown in Figure 9–41.

7. Open the **3D Views: View 1** view and shade it. Rotate to display the taper side of the column, as shown in Figure 9–42.

Figure 9–41   **Figure 9–42**

8. Use the Family Type dialog box to flex the column.

9. Reset the default values and close the Family Types dialog box.

10. Save the family.

11. If time permits, you can create Family Types using various dimensions and test them in a project.

12. Save and close the project and family files.

Practice 9f | Truss Family

Practice Objectives

- Start a truss family and add reference planes and labels.
- Add Top Chord, Bottom Chord, and Web layout lines.

In this practice, you will create a truss using a truss family template. You will add reference planes, create parameters, and add chords and webs to form the structure of the trusses, as shown in Figure 9–43. You will then test it in a project.

Figure 9–43

Task 1 - Add reference planes and labels.

1. Create a new family based on the **Structural Trusses.rft** template found in the Autodesk Revit Library.

2. Save the family to your practice folder as **Custom Truss.rfa**.

3. Add the reference planes, dimensions, and labels (Instance parameters) shown in Figure 9–44.

Figure 9–44

4. Open the Family Types dialog box and scroll down to the *Dimensions* area. Add the formula *Top Chord Length* = **Truss Length / 3**, as shown in Figure 9–45.

If you forgot to set any of the labels as Instance parameters, you can edit it in the Family Types dialog box.

Dimensions			
End Height (Left) (default)	4' 0"	=	☐
End Height (Right) (default)	4' 0"	=	☐
Top Chord Length (default)	26' 8"	= Truss Length / 3	☑
Truss Length (default)	80' 0"	=	☑
Truss Height (default)	10' 0"	=	☑

Figure 9–45

5. Click **OK**.

Task 2 - Add the Top Chord, Bottom Chord, and Web layout lines.

---

1. In the *Create* tab>Detail panel, click ⋙ (Top Chord).

2. In the Options Bar, verify that the **Chain** option is cleared so that you can lock each line as it is created.

3. Starting from the left vertical reference plane, draw the top chord, locking each sketch before you draw the next, as shown in Figure 9–46.

Figure 9–46

Alternatively, in the Create tab>Detail panel,

click 𝖭𝖭 *(Bottom Chord).*

4. In the *Modify | Top Chord* tab>Draw panel, click 𝖭𝖭 (Bottom Chord).

5. Draw the bottom chord, across the bottom of the truss, as shown in Figure 9–47. Lock the bottom chord sketch line in place.

Figure 9–47

6. In the *Create* tab>Detail panel, click 𝖭𝖭 (Web). In the Options Bar, verify that the **Chain** option is not selected.

7. Draw vertical web lines, as shown in Figure 9–48. Dimension and set them EQ in three different sets.

Figure 9–48

*   Start at the far left reference plane and work over to the right.
*   Ensure that you dimension to the vertical reference planes where available or the truss will not flex correctly.

• DO NOT mirror the Web lines as this might cause undesirable results or errors in the truss family.

8. Add diagonal web members to the left of the truss, from the top chord to the bottom chord. Start from the far left side working toward the center of the truss. Repeat the process from the other direction. The final outcome is shown in Figure 9–49.

Figure 9–49

• Snap to the intersections of elements. Type **SI** to force the snap points.
• DO NOT mirror the web lines, as this might cause errors when the truss is loaded into a project.

9. Flex the geometry.

10. Reset the values to the dimensions shown in Figure 9–49.

11. Save the family.

12. Load the truss into a project and test it.
    • Note that the default framing sizes might be too large. In the truss family (or in the truss type in the project), set appropriate framing members for the chords and webs.

13. Save and close the project and family files.

Practice 9g | Precast Hollow Core Slab

Practice Objectives

- Create a family using the Structural Framing - Beams and Braces template.
- Use a CAD file to modify the sketch of an extrusion.
- Assign a material to the extrusion.
- Set visibility settings for Medium and Fine detail levels along with simple geometry for the Coarse detail level.

In this practice, you will use the **Structural Framing - Beams and Braces.rft** file as the base of the hollow core slab. You will modify an existing extrusion and import a CAD drawing to assist in setting up the new profile. You will assign a material to the extrusion and establish the visibility settings for **Medium** and **Fine** detail levels. You will then draw a second extrusion with a simple rectangular profile, assign the material and set the visibility settings so that it only displays at a **Coarse** detail level as shown in Figure 9–50.

Detail Level: Coarse   *Detail Level: Medium and Fine*

Figure 9–50

Task 1 - Import a CAD file into a family template to create the hollow core geometry.

1. Create a new family based on the **Structural Framing - Beams and Braces.rft** template found in the Autodesk Revit Library.

2. Save the family to your practice folder as **Precast-Hollow-Core-Slab.rfa**.

3. Close any other projects or family files that you might have open.

4. Open and tile the following views:
   - **Floor Plans: Ref Level**
   - **Elevations: Front**
   - **Elevations: Left**
   - **3D Views: View 1**

5. In the **Elevations: Left** view, zoom in on the geometry.

6. Select the extrusion. In the *Modify | Extrusion* tab>Mode panel, click ⬚ (Edit Extrusion).

7. Select the outline geometry (as shown in Figure 9–51) and the reference planes that are part of the extrusion and delete them from the view.

Figure 9–51

In this example, a CAD drawing is used to create the geometry of the hollow core slab.

8. In the *Insert* tab>Import panel, click 🗎 (Import CAD).

9. In the Import CAD Formats dialog box, navigate to the practice files *Structural* folder. Select **Precast-Hollow-Core-Slab.dwg** and then and set the following options, as shown in Figure 9–52:
   - Select **Current View Only**.
   - *Colors:* **Black and White**
   - *Layers:* **All**
   - *Import units:* **Auto-Detect**
   - *Positioning:* **Auto - Center to Center**

Figure 9–52

10. Click **Open**.

11. A message box opens prompting you about exploding import instances. Click **Yes** to continue. The family now includes the sketch lines from the AutoCAD drawing, as shown in Figure 9–53.

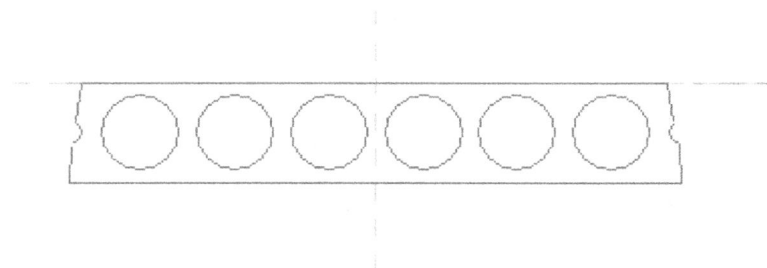

Figure 9–53

12. To select the material for the hollow core slab, in Properties, in the *Materials and Finishes* area, select **<By Category>**, and then click ⎯ (Browse).

13. In the Material Browser, select **Concrete-Precast Concrete**, as shown in Figure 9–54.

Figure 9–54

14. Click **OK** to close the dialog boxes. The Material is assigned.

15. Click (Finish Edit Mode).

16. Click in empty space to release the selection.

17. In the 3D view, zoom out as required to display the slab. Set the *Visual Style* to ☐ (Shaded) to display the new slab with the concrete material applied, as shown in Figure 9–55.

Figure 9–55

18. Save the file.

Task 2 - Establish visibility settings.

1. Select the new extrusion.

2. In the *Modify | Extrusion* tab>Mode panel, click ☐ (Visibility Settings).

3. In the Family Element Visibility Settings dialog box, in the *Detail Levels* area, verify that **Coarse** is cleared, as shown in Figure 9–56.

Figure 9–56

4. Click **OK**.

5. In the View Control Bar, click ☐ (Preview Visibility On).

6. Test the *Detail Levels.* In the **Coarse** detail level, the extrusion should not display.

7. Activate the **Elevations: Left** view.

8. In the *Create* tab>Forms panel, click ⬭ (Extrusion). In the Work Plane dialog box, select **Pick a plane** and click **OK**. Select the face of the existing extrusion.

9. Draw a rectangle around the perimeter of the hollow core slab and lock it in place.

    • Start the rectangle at the lower left corner.
    • To select the appropriate upper right corner, press <Tab> once to force the horizontal temporary dimension, as shown in Figure 9–57.

Figure 9–57

10. In Properties, set the *Extrusion End* to (negative) **-8'-0"** and the *Material* to **Concrete - Precast Concrete**.

11. Click ✔ (Finish Edit Mode).

12. Activate the **Floor Plans: Ref. Level** view.

13. Align and lock the new extrusion to the **Member Left** reference plane, as shown in Figure 9–58.

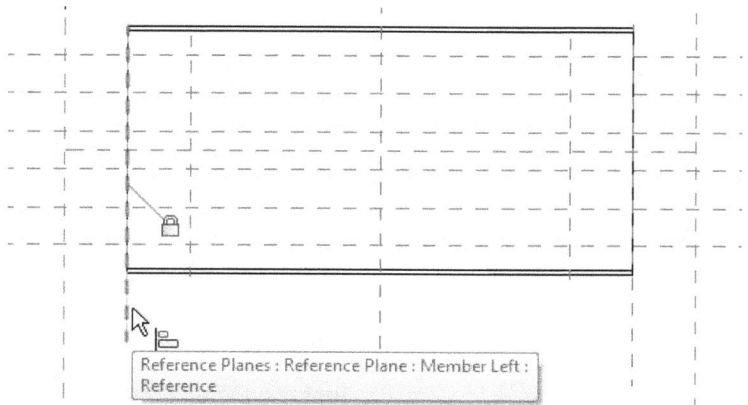

Reference Planes : Reference Plane : Member Left :
Reference

Figure 9–58

14. Align the other end to the **Member Right** reference plane.

15. Select the new simple rectangular extrusion.

16. In the *Modify | Extrusion* tab>Mode panel, click ⬚ (Visibility Settings).

17. In the Family Element Visibility Settings dialog box, in the *Detail Levels* area, clear **Medium** and **Fine**, as shown in Figure 9–59.

Detail Levels

☑ Coarse   ☐ Medium   ☐ Fine

| OK | Cancel | Default | Help |

Figure 9–59

18. Click **OK**.

19. Release the selection and preview the different *Detail Levels*.

20. Save the file.

Task 3 - Add hidden lines.

---

1. Activate the **Floor Plans: Ref. Level** view.

2. In the View Control Bar, set the *Visual Style* to ⬚ (Wireframe).

3. In the *Annotate* tab>Detail panel, click ⬚ (Symbolic Line).

4. In the *Modify | Place Symbolic Lines* tab>Subcategory panel, set *Subcategory* to **Hidden Lines [projection]**.

5. In the *Modify | Place Symbolic Lines* tab>Draw panel, click ⬚ (Line). In the Options Bar, clear the **Chain** option.

6. Draw hidden lines horizontally along the edges, as shown in Figure 9–60. You cannot see them as you draw because they are in the same location as the elements displayed through the wireframe view.

Figure 9–60

7. In the View Control Bar, set the *Visual Style* to ▱ (Hidden Line). The hidden lines should be displayed. ↘

8. Select the 12 hidden lines that you just created.

9. In the *Modify | Lines* tab>Visibility panel, click 🗗 (Visibility Settings).

10. Set the visibility of only the lines to the **Medium** and **Fine** detail levels.

11. Save the family.

12. Load the family into a project.

13. Using 🗇 (Beam) draw a beam using the new **Precast-Hollow-Core-Slab** family.

14. Test the visibility settings in the plan and elevation views.

15. Close but do not save the project.

16. Save and close the family.

Practice 9h | Tapered Moment Frame

Practice Objectives

- Set up reference planes, reference lines, and parameters as the framework of the family.
- Create geometry for the columns and beams of the family.

In this practice, you will use the family template file **Structural Column.rft** as the basis of the Tapered Moment Frame. You will create reference planes, reference lines, and parameters and then create the geometry for the columns and tapered beam using both solid sweeps and extrusions, as shown in Figure 9–61.

Figure 9–61

Task 1 - Set up the reference planes and parameters.

1. Create a new family based on the **Structural Column.rft** template found in the Autodesk Revit Library.

2. Save the family to your practice folder as **Tapered-Moment-Frame.rfa**.

3. Add dimensions and labels for **Overall Length** and **Column Width** to the existing reference planes, as shown in Figure 9–62. Create them as **Type** parameters.

Figure 9–62

4. Open the Family Types dialog box

5. In the Family Types dialog box, change the values of *Overall Length* to **26'-0"** and *Column Width* to **1'-0"**, as shown in Figure 9–63. Click **OK**.

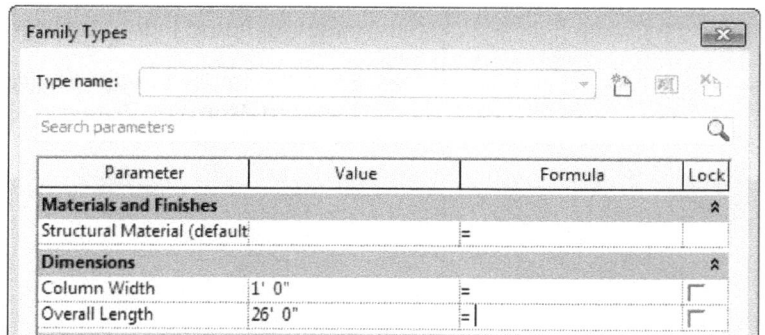

Figure 9–63

6. Zoom out and extend the horizontal reference planes beyond the new vertical reference planes, as shown in Figure 9–64.

   • Unpin the **Front/Back** reference plane to lengthen it. Click on the **Pin** icon to pin the reference plane back in place so that it will not move when you add dimensions and labels.

Figure 9–64

7. Add two new horizontal reference planes with associated dimensions and label (type parameter) to represent the **Beam Width**, as shown in Figure 9–65.

   • **Hint:** Use **Pick Lines** with an *Offset* of **2"** and place them inside the existing outer reference planes.

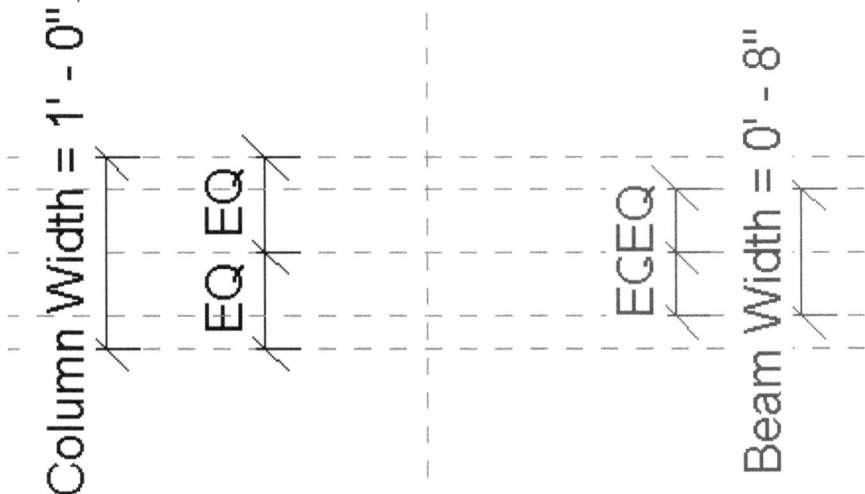

Figure 9–65

8. Open the **Elevations: Front** view.

9. Change the *elevation* of the **Upper Ref. Level** to **13'-0"**.

10. Extend the reference planes and levels so that they all overlap.

11. Add a reference plane on top of the **Upper Ref. Level**, as shown in Figure 9–66, and lock it into the level.

12. Add reference planes and labels (type parameters), as shown in Figure 9–66.

Column Top = 2' - 0"

Reference plane on top of Upper Ref. Level.

Beam Middle Height = 12' - 0"

Knee Height = 10' - 0"

Column Base = 1' - 0"

Figure 9–66

13. Add **Column Base** and **Column Top** reference planes and labels on the other end of the frame. (Do not use Mirror.)

14. Temporarily hide the **Upper Ref. Level**, but not the associated reference plane.

15. Draw two reference lines from the intersection of the top and outside reference planes to the center vertical reference plane, as shown in Figure 9–67. Lock the reference lines to the related reference planes.

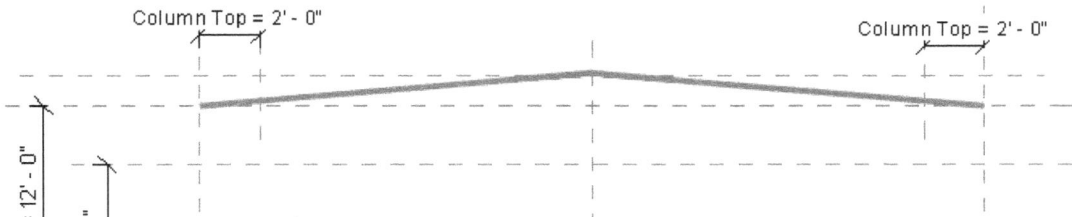

Figure 9–67

16. Reset **Temporary Hide/Isolate**.

17. Flex the framework. End with the **Upper Ref. Level** height of **13'-0"** and **Beam Middle** height of **12'-0"**.

18. Save the family file.

Task 2 - Create the geometry for the Tapered Columns.

---

1. In the *Create* tab>Forms panel, click ⬡ (Sweep).

2. In the *Create* tab>Work Plane panel, click ⊞ (Set).

3. In the Work Plane dialog box, select **Reference Plane: Center (Front/Back)**, as shown in Figure 9–68. Click **OK**.

Figure 9–68

4. In the *Modify | Sweep* tab>Sweep panel, click ✐ (Sketch Path).

5. In the Draw panel, ✐ (Line) is selected by default. In the Options Bar, verify that the **Chain** option is selected.

6. Sketch the path for the column of the moment frame. Align the two vertical sketch lines to their parallel reference planes.

7. Align and lock the angular sketch line to the reference line, as shown in Figure 9–69.

Draw the left vertical sketch first. The profile is drawn in this plane.

Column Top = 2' - 0"

Beam Middle Height = 12' - 0"

Knee Height = 10' - 0"

Column Base = 1' - 0"

Figure 9–69

8. In the Mode panel, click ✔ (Finish Edit Mode).

9. In the *Modify | Sweep* tab>Sweep panel, click ✎ (Edit Profile).

10. When the Go To View dialog box opens, select **Floor Plan: Lower Ref. Level**. Click **Open View**.

11. If you have not already done so, zoom out to see the full framework and expand the Reference lines to the ends.

12. Zoom in on the Profile target and draw a rectangle **3/4" x 1'-0"**. Lock it to the reference planes, as shown in Figure 9–70.

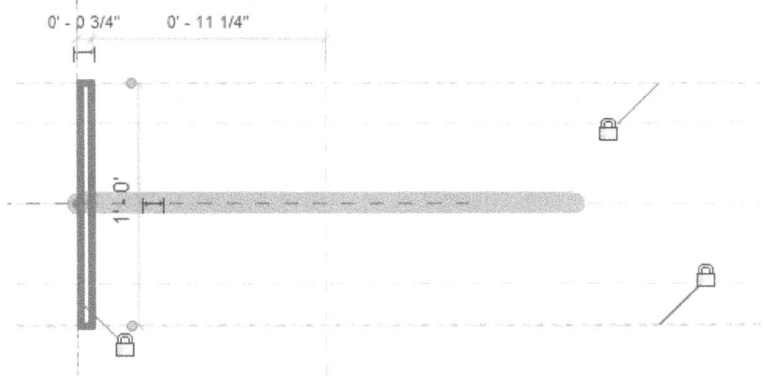

Figure 9–70

13. Click ✔ (Finish Edit Mode) twice to finish the Profile and the Sweep.

14. Open the **3D Views: View 1** view. Rotate and shade it to display the column up to this point, as shown in Figure 9–71.

Figure 9–71

15. Return to the **Elevations: Front** view.

16. Click ⬚ (Extrusion) and set the *Work Plane* to **Reference Plane: Center (Front/Back)**.

17. In the *Modify | Create Extrusion* tab>Draw panel, click ⬚ (Pick Lines). In the Options Bar, select **Lock**.

18. Zoom into the sweep that was created earlier and select all of the interior lines, as shown in Figure 9–72.

*The lines are automatically locked to the selected lines because you selected the **Lock** option.*

Figure 9–72

19. In Properties, set the values of the *Extrusion End* to **3/8"** and *Extrusion Start* to (negative) **-3/8"**, as shown in Figure 9–73.

Figure 9–73

20. Click ✓ (Finish Edit Mode)

21. Display the column profile in a shaded 3D View and return to the **Elevations: Front** view. (**Hint:** Press <Ctrl>+<Tab>.)

22. Mirror the new tapered column (both extrusion and sweep) along the center vertical reference plane, as shown in Figure 9–74.

Edit this sketch and align it to the angled reference line

Column Top = 2' - 0"

Column Top = 2' - 0"

Beam Middle Height = 12' - 0"

Knee Height = 10' - 0"

Column Base = 1' - 0"

Column Base = 1' - 0"

Figure 9–74

23. Edit the path sketch of the mirrored sweep and align and lock the sketch to the reference line.

24. Flex the framework to ensure that everything is working as expected.

25. Save the family file.

Task 3 - Create the geometry for the Tapered Beam.

1. Start the **Sweep** command and add a path, as shown in Figure 9–75. Use **Pick Lines** with the **Lock** option on and select the angled reference lines.

Figure 9–75

2. Click ✓ (Finish Edit Mode).

3. In the *Modify | Sweep* tab>Sweep panel, click 📓 (Load Profile).

4. In the Load Family dialog box, navigate to the practice files *Structural* folder. Select **Tapered-Frame-Profile.rfa** and click **Open**.

5. In the *Profile:* drop-down list, select **Tapered-Frame-Profile**, as shown in Figure 9–76.

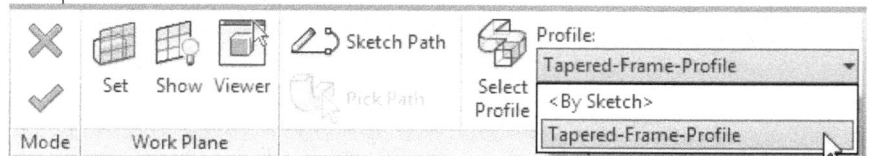

Figure 9–76

6. Click ✓ (Finish Edit Mode).

7. Display the top plate of the beam profile in a 3D View, as shown in Figure 9–77.

Figure 9–77

8. Return to the **Elevations: Front** view and create another sweep for the beam's bottom flange using the sketch for the path shown in Figure 9–78 and the same profile family.

Hint: You can temporarily hide existing solid elements so that you can attach the sketch to the reference planes.

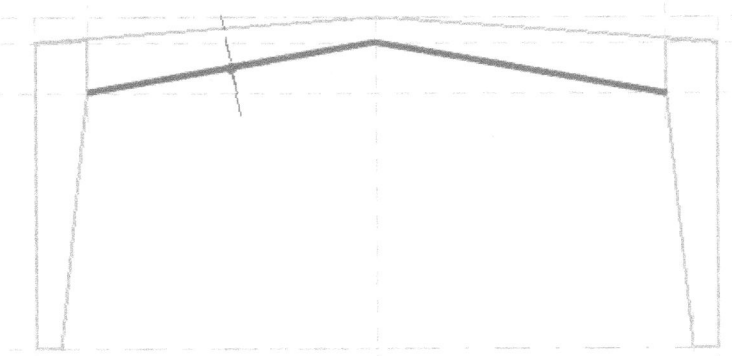

Figure 9–78

9. The final 3D view should display, as shown in Figure 9–79.

Figure 9–79

10. Return to the **Elevations: Front** view and add an extrusion using the interior of the previously created sweeps, as shown in Figure 9–80. Set the *Extrusion End* to **3/8"** and *Extrusion Start* to (negative) **-3/8"**.

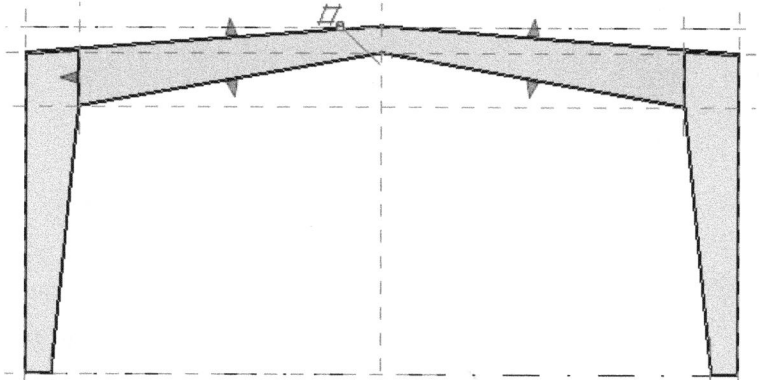

Figure 9–80

11. Open the 3D view and move it to one side. Open the Family Types dialog box and flex the geometry of the **Tapered Moment Frame** parameters, as shown in Figure 9–81.

Figure 9–81

12. Save the family file.

13. Create a new structural project, load the family, and test it.

14. Save and close the project and family files.

Chapter Review Questions

1. How do you change a standard dimension to a parameter-based dimension, as shown in Figure 9–82?

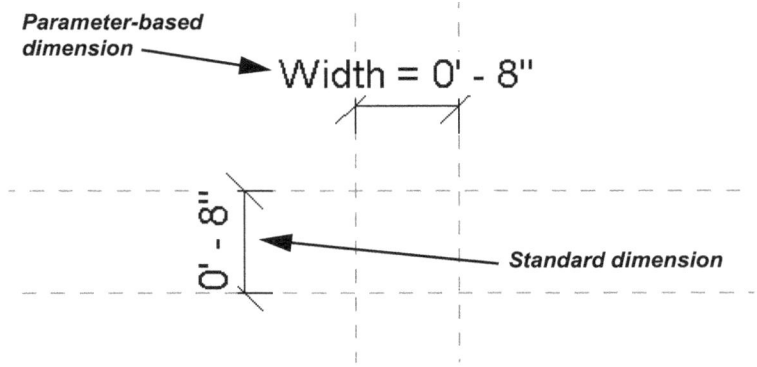

Figure 9–82

    a. In the Type Selector, select a parameter-based type.

    b. In Properties, change the *Value*.

    c. In the ribbon, click **Create Parameter**.

    d. In the Family Types dialog box, in the *Parameters* area, click **Add**.

2. Why would you create an in-place family rather than a component family?

    a. An in-place family can be used several times in the current project only.

    b. An in-place family is used once in the current project for a specific location and size.

    c. A component family cannot be modified to fit the specific location.

    d. A component family cannot be joined to other elements in the project.

3. Which of the following Generic Model family templates would you use to create a slab depression?

    a. **Generic Model wall based.rft**

    b. **Generic Model face based.rft**

    c. **Generic Model line based.rft**

    d. **Generic Model floor based.rft**

4. In a truss family, is the highlighted element shown in Figure 9–83 a Chord or a Web?

Figure 9–83

   a. Chord

   b. Web

5. When assigning material to a solid form you can select the **Associate Family Parameter** option. The option to select the material is grayed out, as shown in Figure 9–84. Where do you assign the material?

Figure 9–84

   a. In the Family Types dialog box, select the associated parameter and select the material.

   b. In the *Manage* tab>Settings panel, click ⊗ (Materials) and select the material.

   c. In the *Modify* tab>Geometry panel, click ⊗ (Paint).

   d. In the Family Category and Parameters dialog box, specify the material in the *Family Parameters* area.

Additional Management Tools

There are many tools available in the Autodesk® Revit® software that you can use when creating and using templates and projects. This appendix provides details about several additional tools and commands that are related to those covered in this learning guide.

Learning Objectives in this Appendix

- Set up units, snaps, temporary dimensions, and arrowheads.
- Create object styles for components that include line weight, color, pattern, and material.
- Create patterns used in the Filled Region command and for cut and surface patterns in materials.
- Create materials and material libraries that can be used in multiple projects.
- Review mechanical settings (for ducts and pipes)
- Review electrical settings (for wiring, cable trays, and conduits).
- Review structural specific settings.
- Create sheet list schedules.
- Modify the keyboard shortcuts and double-click function of the mouse.
- Create new Project Browser organization layouts for views, schedules, and sheets.

A.1 General Settings

A variety of settings are available to help you customize the projects you create and keep everything consistent with your office's standards. Other settings can make the process of working in Autodesk Revit more productive.

Specifying Units

Although you select Imperial or Metric units when you create the project template, you can set up the Project Units with specific formats and options. For example, if you are working on a Civil project where everything is set up in feet, you specify **Decimal Feet** as the Length Format. For an international metric project, you can specify the length units as Meters, Centimeters, or Millimeters.

How To: Set Up Project Units

1. In the *Manage* tab>Settings panel, click (Project Units) or type **UN**.
2. In the Project Units dialog box, in the *Format* column, click the button next to the unit type that you want to modify, as shown in Figure A–1. The related Format dialog box opens, as shown in Figure A–2.

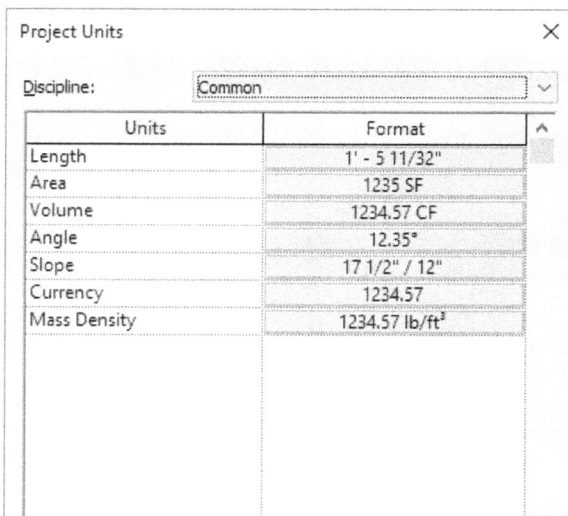

Figure A–1

Figure A–2

3. Set the *Units*, *Rounding*, and other options as required.

4. In the Project Units dialog box, you can also select the *Discipline* (**Common** by default) and change the Unit format for each discipline. The other options are **Structural**, **HVAC**, **Electrical**, **Piping**, and **Energy**. The options vary according to the discipline-specific software in use.
5. Click **OK** to close each dialog box.

Format Options

Each unit has specific formatting options. The option is grayed out if it is not applicable to that unit type.

Units	Select the type of units in the Units drop-down list.
	Units: Feet and fractional inches ▼
	Decimal feet
	Rounding: Feet and fractional inches
	Decimal inches
	To the nearest 1/32" Fractional inches
	Meters
	Unit symbol: Centimeters
	Millimeters
	Meters and centimeters
Rounding	Specify how precisely you want the dimensions to be rounded. The options depend on the *Units* you selected.
Unit Symbol	If you are using metric units, you can select a unit symbol, such as **cm** for centimeters or **None**.
Suppress trailing 0's	(For decimal-based units) If selected, this option removes any trailing 0s. For example, it displays 1.5 instead of 1.50 if you are using two decimal places.
Suppress 0 feet	(Imperial Units only) If selected, this option removes the 0 in front of a dimension in inches only. For example, the dimension displays as 0'-4", rather than 4".
Use digit grouping	If selected, the unit uses the Decimal symbol/digit grouping specified in the Project Units dialog box.
	123,456,789.00
	123,456,789.00
	123.456.789,00
	123 456 789,00
	123'456'789.00
	12,34,56,789.00
	12.34.56.789,00
	12 34 56 789.00
Suppress spaces	(Imperial Units only) If selected, this option removes the spaces between the feet and inches, so that a dimension reads 1'-2", rather than 1' - 2".

- The **Use project settings** and **Show + for positive values** options are grayed out when setting units for the project. This dialog box is used when creating dimension styles or specifying label formats when the options are available.

Snap Settings

The Snaps dialog box controls *Dimension Snaps,* which are the increments you see in temporary dimensions, and *Object Snaps,* which are the points on elements that you can select. In the

Manage tab>Settings panel, click 🧲 (Snaps) to open the dialog box, as shown in Figure A–3.

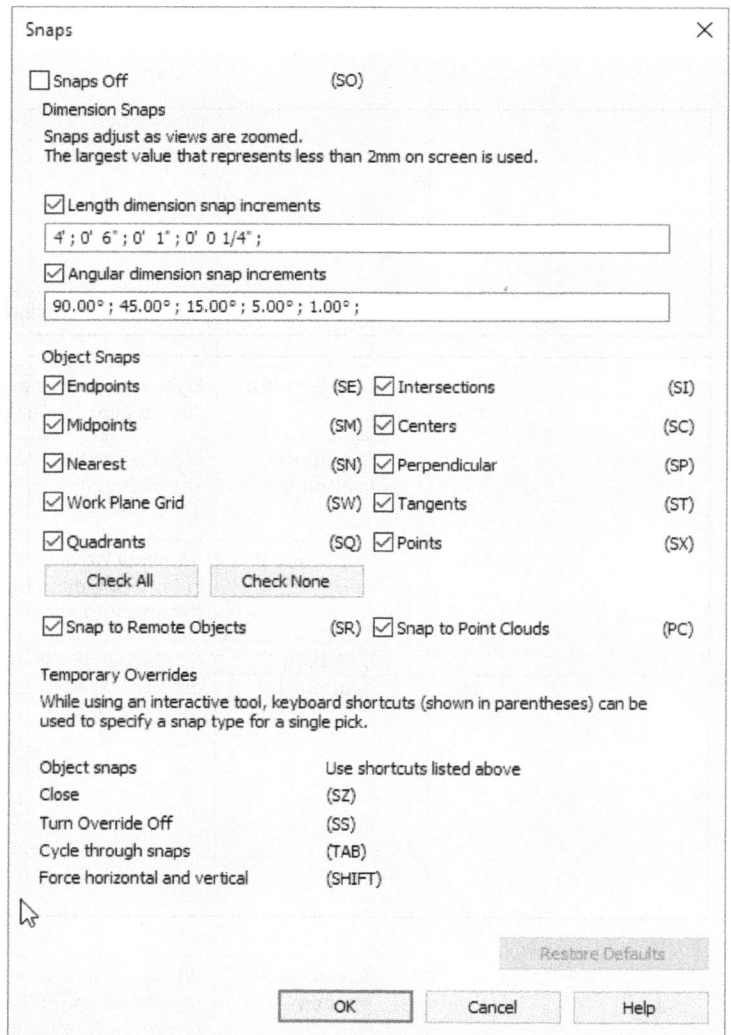

Figure A–3

Keyboard shortcuts, such as the ones listed here, are part of the User Interface and apply to all projects.

- Snap overrides are listed as keyboard shortcuts in parentheses, next to the corresponding snap. When a snap override is used, the cursor finds that specified snap type in your view until something is selected.

- Snap overrides can be used while inside a command by right-clicking and selecting **Snap Overrides** and then selecting the one that you want to use from the list.

Temporary Dimension Settings

Temporary dimensions display when you draw or edit building elements in the software. By default, they measure from the center lines of walls to the center lines of openings, as shown in Figure A–4.

Figure A–4

- When you move a witness line to another element or part of an element, the location is remembered in the current session of program.

You can control where temporary dimensions are placed by default. In the *Manage* tab>Settings panel, expand

(Additional Settings) and click (Temporary Dimensions) to open the Temporary Dimension Properties dialog box, as shown in Figure A–5.

Figure A–5

- You can set up these properties in the project template file or modify them at any time. They do not affect existing elements in your project.

- You can control the size of the temporary dimension text in the Options dialog box in the *Graphics* area.

Setting Up Arrowheads

A variety of arrowhead types are supplied with the Autodesk Revit software, including open and filled arrow styles, tick marks, and dots. You can also create custom styles by duplicating an existing style and defining the parameters, such as the *Arrow Style* shown in Figure A–6. In the *Manage* tab>Settings panel, expand 🔧 (Additional Settings) and click ⇄ (Arrowheads) to open the dialog box.

Type Parameters

Parameter	Value
Graphics	⌄
Arrow Style	Arrow
Fill Tick	☐
Arrow Width Angle	30.000°
Tick Size	1/8"
Heavy End Pen Weight	7

Figure A–6

- Arrowheads are used by both text (with a leader) and dimensions.

- The templates include loop leaders, typically used in MEP projects, that can be set as *Tick Mark* for dimensions and *Leader Arrowhead* for text, as shown in Figure A–7. You can also create an Arrow Style using Loop in the Arrowhead settings.

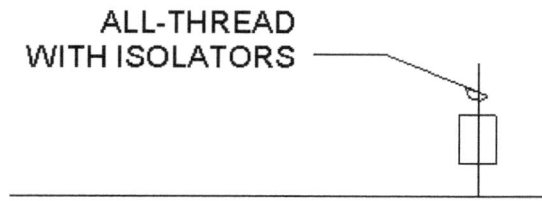

Figure A–7

A.2 Creating Object Styles

Every element in the Autodesk Revit software contains object styles that control how its components display in various views. For example, the *Doors* element includes the *Elevation Swing*, *Frame/Mullion*, *Glass*, *Hidden Lines*, *Opening*, *Panel*, and *Plan Swing* as components, as shown in Figure A–8. The *Elevation Swing* is set to a light line weight, displayed in black with a dashed line pattern. It does not have any material attached to it, but the *Glass* component does.

Object Styles					✕

Model Objects   Annotation Objects   Analytical Model Objects   Imported Objects

Filter list: Architecture ˅

Category	Line Weight		Line Color	Line Pattern	Material
	Projection	Cut			
⊞ Casework	1	3	■ Black	Solid	
⊞ Ceilings	2	5	■ Black	Solid	
⊞ Columns	1	4	■ Black	Solid	
⊞ Curtain Panels	1	2	■ Black	Solid	
⊞ Curtain Systems	2	2	▨ RGB 000-127-000	Solid	
⊞ Curtain Wall Mullions	1	3	■ Black	Solid	
⊞ Detail Items	1		■ Black	Solid	
⊟ Doors	2	2	■ Black	Solid	
Elevation Swing	1	1	■ Black	Dash 1/16"	
Frame/Mullion	1	3	■ Black	Solid	
Glass	1	4	■ Black	Solid	Glass
Hidden Lines	2	2	▨ Blue	Dash	
Opening	1	3	■ Black	Solid	
Panel	1	3	■ Black	Solid	
Plan Swing	1	1	■ Black	Solid	
⊞ Electrical Equipment	1		■ Black	Solid	
⊞ Electrical Fixtures	1		■ Black	Solid	

Modify Subcategories

[Select All] [Select None] [Invert]   [New] [Delete] [Rename]

[OK] [Cancel] [Apply] [Help]

Figure A–8

- In the *Manage* tab>Settings panel, click ▥ (Object Styles) to open the Object Styles dialog box.

- To modify an object style, select the element to change and then select an option in the appropriate column in the drop-down list or dialog box.

- Most categories enable you to create subcategories. For example, you can create subcategories for reference planes that can be toggled off while leaving other reference planes visible in a view.

Line Weights

Line weights for model elements can be set for a **Projection** (in elevations) or **Cut** (in section and plan). For example, a wall displays a heavy line weight while the door and window cuts are lighter, as shown in Figure A–9.

Figure A–9

- Annotation elements are only set for projection.

Hint: Setting Line Weights

In the *Manage* tab>Settings panel, expand (Additional Settings) and click (Line Weights) to open the Line Weights dialog box, as shown in Figure A–10. It contains three tabs: *Model Line Weights* (vary by scale), *Perspective Line Weights* (control elements like walls and windows in perspective views), and *Annotation Line Weights* (not dependent on the scale).

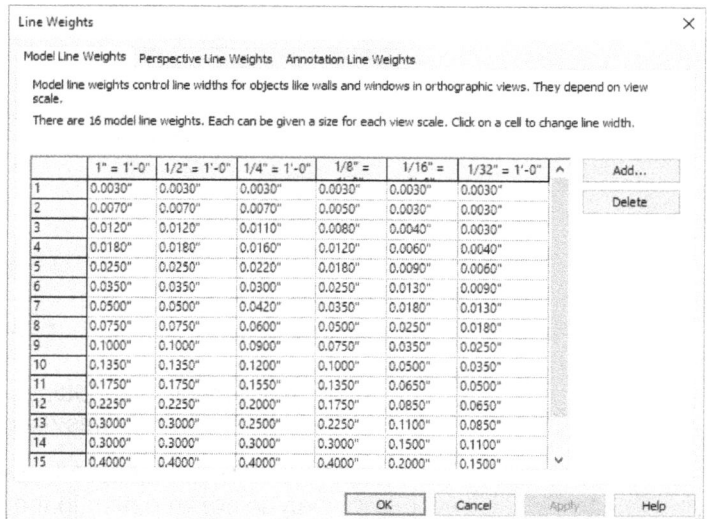

Line Weights						
Model Line Weights	Perspective Line Weights	Annotation Line Weights				

Model line weights control line widths for objects like walls and windows in orthographic views. They depend on view scale.

There are 16 model line weights. Each can be given a size for each view scale. Click on a cell to change line width.

	1" = 1'-0"	1/2" = 1'-0"	1/4" = 1'-0"	1/8" =	1/16" =	1/32" = 1'-0"
1	0.0030"	0.0030"	0.0030"	0.0030"	0.0030"	0.0030"
2	0.0070"	0.0070"	0.0070"	0.0050"	0.0030"	0.0030"
3	0.0120"	0.0120"	0.0110"	0.0080"	0.0040"	0.0030"
4	0.0180"	0.0180"	0.0160"	0.0120"	0.0060"	0.0040"
5	0.0250"	0.0250"	0.0220"	0.0180"	0.0090"	0.0060"
6	0.0350"	0.0350"	0.0300"	0.0250"	0.0130"	0.0090"
7	0.0500"	0.0500"	0.0420"	0.0350"	0.0180"	0.0130"
8	0.0750"	0.0750"	0.0600"	0.0500"	0.0250"	0.0180"
9	0.1000"	0.1000"	0.0900"	0.0750"	0.0350"	0.0250"
10	0.1350"	0.1350"	0.1200"	0.1000"	0.0500"	0.0350"
11	0.1750"	0.1750"	0.1550"	0.1350"	0.0650"	0.0500"
12	0.2250"	0.2250"	0.2000"	0.1750"	0.0850"	0.0650"
13	0.3000"	0.3000"	0.2500"	0.2250"	0.1100"	0.0850"
14	0.3000"	0.3000"	0.3000"	0.3000"	0.1500"	0.1100"
15	0.4000"	0.4000"	0.4000"	0.4000"	0.2000"	0.1500"

Add...

Delete

OK   Cancel   Apply   Help

Figure A–10

You can customize the line weights in each tab and add scales as required for the model line weights.

Line Color

When you select **Line Color** in Object Styles or elsewhere, the Color dialog box opens, as shown in Figure A–11.

Figure A–11

You can select from thousands of colors, including options from the Pantone color system, as shown in Figure A–12. Typically, most elements in the Autodesk Revit software are black for printing purposes. When you shade and render, the elements take on the color of the assigned material. Therefore, these dialog boxes are opened when you create materials.

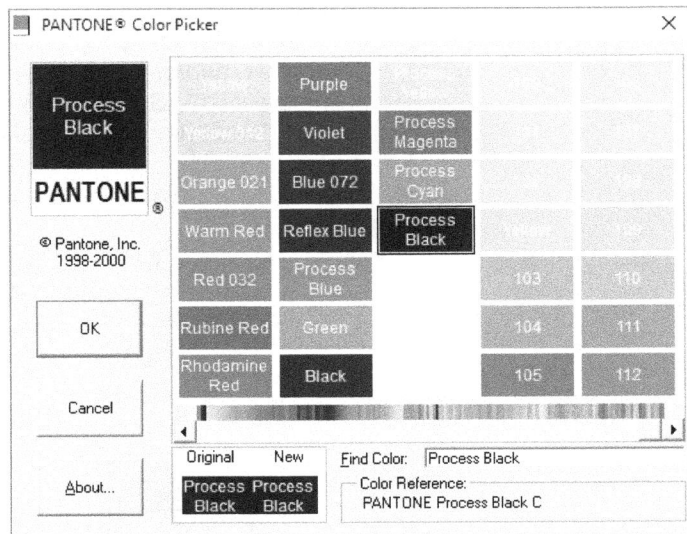

Figure A–12

Line Patterns

Line Patterns can be specified for various components in the Object Styles dialog box. In the example shown in Figure A–13, the line pattern **Dash** is used for the elevation door swing and the line pattern **Dash dot** is used for the callout bubble.

Figure A–13

How To: Create Line Patterns

A wide variety of patterns are supplied with the Autodesk Revit software and you can create your own with a series of dashes, spaces, and dots.

1. In the *Manage* tab>Settings panel, expand (Additional Settings) and click (Line Patterns) to open the Line Patterns dialog box.
2. In the Line Patterns dialog box, click **New**.
3. In the Name dialog box, type a name for the pattern and click **OK**.
4. In the Line Pattern Properties dialog box, add a list of dashes, spaces, and/or dots and specify their values, as shown in Figure A–14. *Space* is always the option after a dash or dot. You do not have to enter a value for dots.

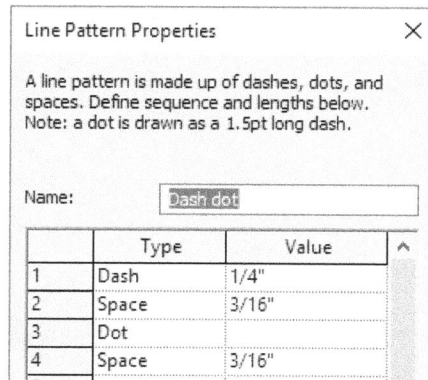

Figure A–14

Line Styles

Line styles are a specific type of object style used with the sketching tools. They are not part of the Object Styles dialog box, but are created in a similar way.

In the *Manage* tab>Settings panel, expand ✐ (Additional Settings) and click 🗦 (Line Styles). In the Line Styles dialog box (shown in Figure A–15), specify the *Line Weight*, *Line Color*, and *Line Pattern* for each line style.

Category	Line Weight Projection	Line Color	Line Pattern
Lines	1	RGB 000-166-000	Solid
<Area Boundary>	6	RGB 128-000-255	Solid
<Beyond>	1	Black	Solid
<Centerline>	1	Black	Center 1/4"
<Demolished>	1	Black	Demolished 3/16"
<Fabric Envelope>	1	RGB 127-127-127	Dash
<Fabric Sheets>	1	RGB 064-064-064	Solid
<Hidden>	1	Black	Hidden 1/8"
<Overhead>	1	Black	Overhead 1/16"
<Room Separation>	1	Black	Solid
<Sketch>	3	RGB 225-000-255	Solid
<Space Separation>	1	Black	
Axis of Rotation	6	Blue	Center 1/4"
Hidden Lines	1	RGB 000-166-000	Dash
Insulation Batting Lines	1	Black	Solid
Lines	1	RGB 000-166-000	Solid
Medium Lines	3	Black	Solid

Select All Select None Invert

Modify Subcategories

New Delete Rename

OK Cancel Apply Help

Figure A–15

A.3 Creating Fill Patterns

Fill patterns are used by the various **Filled Region** commands and material specifications. In the *Manage* tab>Settings panel, expand ✎ (Additional Settings) and click ▦ (Fill Patterns). Select from two types: **Drafting** and **Model**.

- Fill Patterns can also be created while you are working in the Visibility/Graphics dialog box. When you select a Fill Pattern override, the dialog box displays ⌐...⌐ (Browse), which opens the Fill Patterns dialog box.

Drafting patterns are symbolic. The view scale controls the size of the pattern, as shown in Figure A–16. These are used in details and in plan or section cuts.

Model patterns are full scale to the actual elements they represent. They do not change if the view scale changes, as shown in Figure A–17. These patterns are primarily used in elevation and plan views.

Figure A–16

Figure A–17

- In the Type Properties of filled regions, you can set the background to **Opaque** or **Transparent**.

How To: Create New Fill Patterns

1. In the *Manage* tab>Settings panel, expand ✎ (Additional Settings) and click ▨ (Fill Patterns).
2. In the New Pattern dialog box, select the type of pattern you want to create: **Drafting** or **Model**.
3. Click ⬚ (New Fill Pattern).
4. In the New Pattern dialog box, type a name for the pattern.
5. For a simple pattern (as shown in Figure A–18), specify the *Type* as **Basic** and select **Parallel lines** or **Crosshatch** and type values for the *Line angle* and *Line spacing*.
6. For a complex patter (as shown in Figure A–19), specify the *Type* as **Custom**. Then, click **Import...** and select a PAT file and a pattern. Set the *Import Scale* as required.
7. Specify the *Orientation in Host Layers* as **Orient to View**, **Keep readable**, or **Align with element**.

The PAT file can be created specifically for the Autodesk Revit software or it can be based on an AutoCAD® PAT file.

Figure A–18

Figure A–19

8. Click **OK** to finish. The pattern can now be used to create a filled region type or used in a material.

Importing Patterns from AutoCAD

Pattern files (PAT) can be imported from the AutoCAD software, such as the Escher pattern shown in Figure A–20.

Figure A–20

One change must be made in the pattern file for it to be usable in the Autodesk Revit software. Open the PAT file and add the following line after the title of a custom hatch, as shown in Figure A–21.

```
*AR-HBONE, Standard brick herringbone pattern @ 45 degrees
;%TYPE=MODEL
45,        0,0,         4,4,                          12,-4
135,       2.828427125,2.828427125,   4,-4,           12,-4
```

Figure A–21

- A line with a semicolon in front it is ignored by the AutoCAD software, while the type is specified for the Autodesk Revit software.

- Any pattern in the **Acad.pat** file can be automatically brought in as a drafting pattern. However, you must add the string above to specify model patterns.

A.4 Creating Materials

When you shade or render Autodesk Revit models, their appearance depends on the materials that have been associated with the elements, as shown in a shaded view in Figure A–22. Materials also include information that can be used in material takeoff schedules and in energy and structural analysis. You can use materials supplied with the Autodesk Revit software or create custom materials.

Figure A–22

- Materials can be assigned in several ways: using ⊘⊡ (Paint) on faces, setting it in the layers of system families (such as walls and floors), and in object styles. You also assign materials when you create other component families, such as doors and furniture.

- Materials consist of 2D graphic settings for shading, surface, and cut patterns and the 3D rendering appearance, as well as physical and thermal properties. You can also include identity data, such as manufacturer, model, and keynotes.

Material Libraries

Materials are stored in libraries, which can be shared between Autodesk Revit projects and the AutoCAD, Autodesk® Inventor®, Showcase and Autodesk® 3ds Max® software. Before creating custom materials it is recommended that you create a custom library. Materials can be copied between the current project and the library.

- You can also use Transfer Project Standards to bring in all the materials from another project into the current project.

- Older versions of materials may need to be updated with appearance assets, as shown in Figure A–23. All legacy materials still work but they may not be as complex and nuanced when rendering.

Figure A–23

How To: Create a Material Library

1. In the *Manage* tab>Settings panel, click ⬡ (Materials).

2. At the bottom of the Material Browser, expand 📖 (Creates, opens and edits user-defined libraries) and select **Create New Library** as shown in Figure A–24.

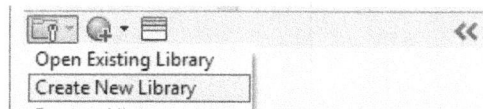

Figure A–24

3. In the Select File dialog box, navigate to the appropriate folder, type a *File name* and save the library. The Material Library displays in the Library list without any materials displayed.

4. Create new materials as required in the current project. Then drag and drop both new and existing materials from the project materials into the new library as shown in Figure A–25.

Libraries that come with the Autodesk Revit software are locked. You can copy materials from them but cannot add or change materials in them.

Figure A–25

How To: Create a Material

1. In the *Manage* tab>Settings panel, click (Materials).

2. In the Material Editor, expand (Creates or duplicates a material), and select either **Create New Material** or **Duplicate Material** as shown in Figure A–26. If you are duplicating a material, select an existing material similar to what you want to use first.

*You can also right-click on an existing material in the Material Browser and select **Duplicate**.*

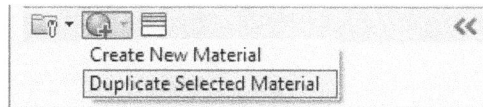

Create New Material
Duplicate Selected Material

Figure A–26

3. A new material is added to the current project. Modify the name of the material or right-click on the Material name in the Material Browser and select **Rename**.

   • Duplicated materials include all of the properties of the existing material as shown for a new Aluminum material in Figure A–27.

Figure A–27

4. Fill out the information on each of the tabs.
5. Click **Apply** and add additional materials as required.
6. Click **OK** when you are finished.

Identity Tab

In the *Identity* tab, you set up the *Descriptive Information*, *Product Information*, and *Revit Annotation Information* for the material, as shown in Figure A–28. This information can be used in material takeoff schedules.

Figure A–28

Graphics Tab

In the *Graphics* tab (shown in Figure A–29), you set how a material displays in shaded or hidden line mode.

Figure A–29

- The *Shading* area controls how the material displays when an element is shaded. If you want the shaded view to resemble the rendered view, select **Use Render Appearance**. The color and other options are modified to match the Render Appearance selection. Alternatively, you can set up a color and transparency ratio. Only use this if the render appearance would be too dark or otherwise not suit the use.

- The *Surface Pattern* and *Cut Pattern* areas enable you to select a fill pattern and color to display on a surface or in a section cut. Surface patterns stay true to size. Cut patterns are drafting patterns, which change size according to the view scale.

Appearance Tab

In the *Appearance* tab, you can set different aspects of a rendered material, including **Information**, the type of material (in this example Masonry is selected as shown in Figure A–30) and other parameters depending on the type of material you are working with. Note that changing the asset changes all of the information, so check if that is an option first.

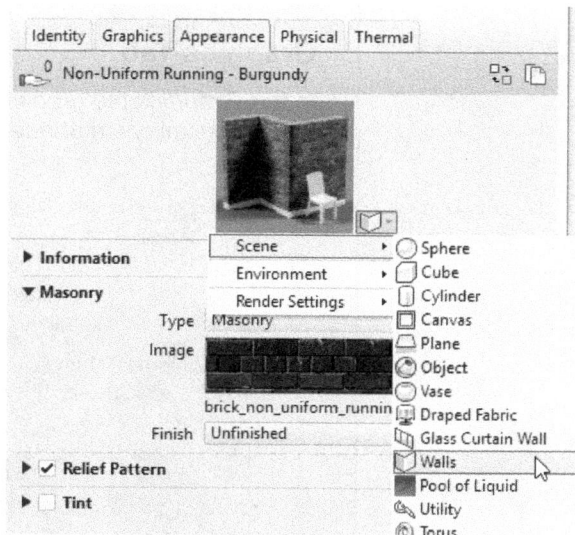

Figure A–30

- You can select how to display the preview of the material by expanding the Scene list next to the graphic, as shown in Figure A–30, above.

- You can modify the *Render Settings* of the preview to either **Draft Quality** or **Production Quality**.

- If you duplicate a material and then change asset-related information (such as the Image or Color) the original material also updates. To prevent this from happening, duplicate or change the asset before making changes.

Physical Tab

In the *Physical* tab, you can specify information about the physical properties of the material. The options vary by material type, as shown in Figure A–31.

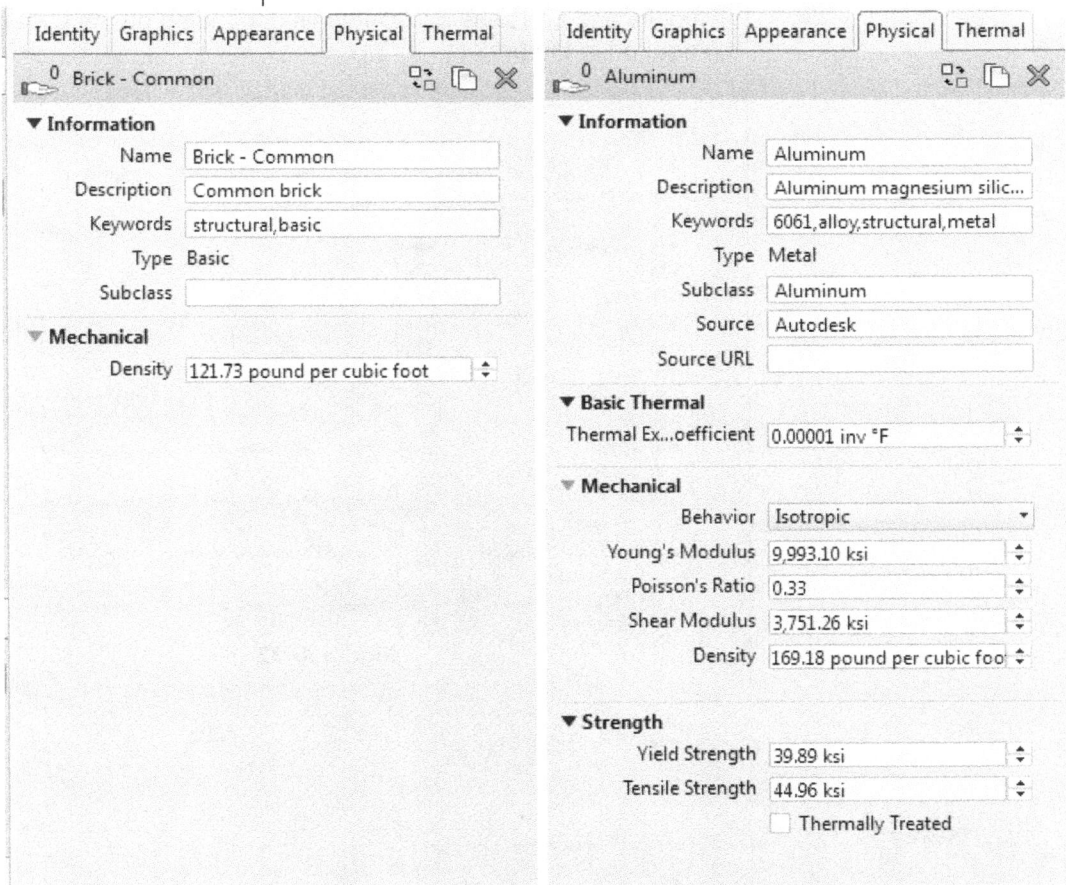

Figure A–31

- Some materials, such as **EPDM Membrane** or **Vapor Retarder**, do not have physical properties, but do have thermal properties.

- Analytical surface and Default materials do not have physical or thermal properties.

- As changing the asset changes all of the information, you should check to see if that is an option first.

Working with Assets

Physical Assets contain preset parameters for materials. These assets are available in the *Appearance*, *Physical* and *Thermal* tabs. Autodesk provides an extensive library of assets that are divided by material type as shown in Figure A–32. You can modify and add assets to materials depending on the variables required in the project.

Figure A–32

Assets updated with higher rendering capabilities do not have a triangle in the lower left corner, as shown in Figure A–33.

Original Cherry Asset   *Updated Cherry Asset*

Figure A–33

How To: Replace an Asset for a Material

1. In the Material Browser, select the material that you want to modify.
2. In the *Appearance*, *Physical*, or *Thermal* tab, click

   (Replaces this asset).
3. In the Asset Browser, hover the cursor over the required

   asset and click (Replaces the current asset in the editor with this asset), as shown in Figure A–32.
4. Close the Asset Browser.

- The assets are filtered by type. Therefore, you need to modify the Appearance asset by clicking through the *Appearance* tab, etc.

- You can create new assets by duplicating an existing one and then modifying the parameters.

A.5 Settings for Mechanical Projects

In addition to the standard settings common to all Autodesk Revit projects, the Autodesk Revit MEP software also has specific Mechanical settings that can be used in a template or a project.

In the *Manage* tab>Settings panel, expand 📇 (MEP Settings) and click 📄 (Mechanical Settings), or in the *Systems* tab> HVAC, (or Mechanical, or Plumbing & Piping) panel title, click ⌄ (Mechanical Settings), as shown in Figure A–34. Alternatively, you can type **MS**.

Figure A–34

Mechanical Settings

Mechanical settings enable you to preset many items relating to duct and pipe sizes, conversion settings, and other key defaults, as shown in Figure A–35.

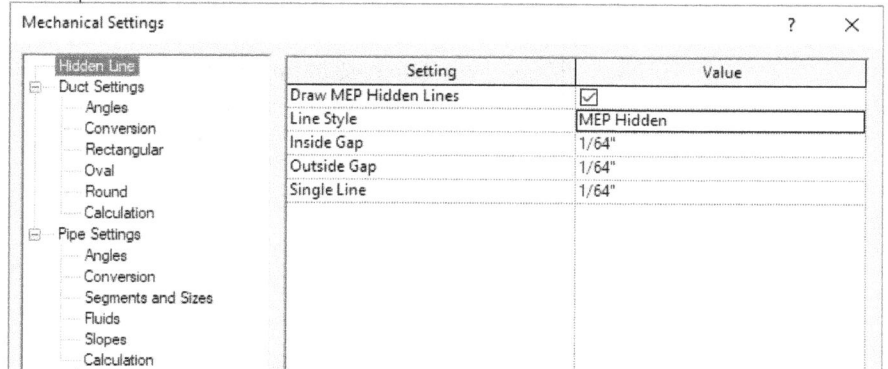

Figure A–35

Hidden Line

If the **Draw MEP Hidden Lines** option is selected, hidden lines display to indicate pipes and ducts that are below other pipes and ducts, as shown in Figure A–36.

Figure A–36

The **Line Style**, **Inside Gap**, and **Outside Gap** options enable you to specify how the hidden lines display.

Angles

In the *Angles* category you can specify the limits on the angles that can be used as ducts or pipes are being drawn, as shown in Figure A–37. This is most often used with piping.

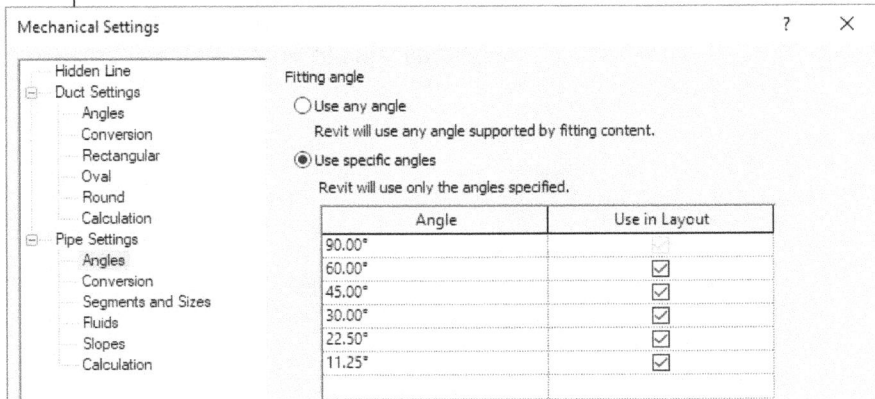

Figure A–37

- The **Duct Settings>Angles** options also include **Set an angle increment** for determining the angle values.

Duct Settings

For the **Single Line Fittings** option, the first two settings relate to how fittings display in a single line view, as shown in Figure A–38. If the **Use Annot. Scale for Single Line Fittings** option is selected, the single line fittings display at the same size on every sheet, regardless of the view scale. The **Duct Fitting Annotation Size** option enables you to specify the size at which the fittings should be displayed.

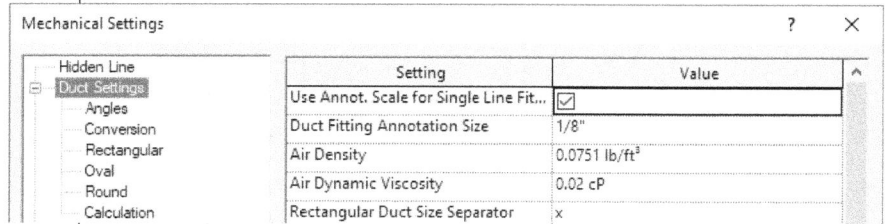

Figure A–38

The **Air Density** and **Air Viscosity** options (not shown) are used when sizing the ducts. The remaining options set the separators and suffixes that are used for duct objects.

Conversion

The *Conversion* area is used to set the routing solutions for ductwork. The settings for the **Main** and **Branch** options can be set separately for each system type. You can specify the **Duct Type**, **Offset** from level, and **Flex Duct Type** settings (this is only applicable to branches), as shown in Figure A–39.

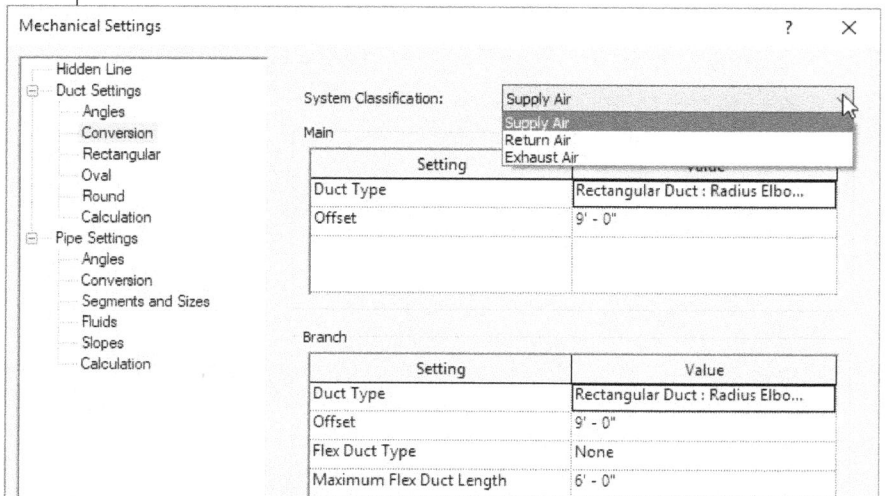

Figure A–39

Rectangular, Oval, and Round

The **Rectangular, Oval,** and **Round** options enable you to adjust the sizing tables. The *Size* column lists all of the sizes. You can click **New Size...** to add a size to the list and **Delete Size** to remove sizes from the list.

In addition, you can specify whether a size displays in the size lists (to be available when you place a new duct or select existing ducts) or if the size is used by the sizing routine (automatic sizing of duct branches and systems), as shown in Figure A–40.

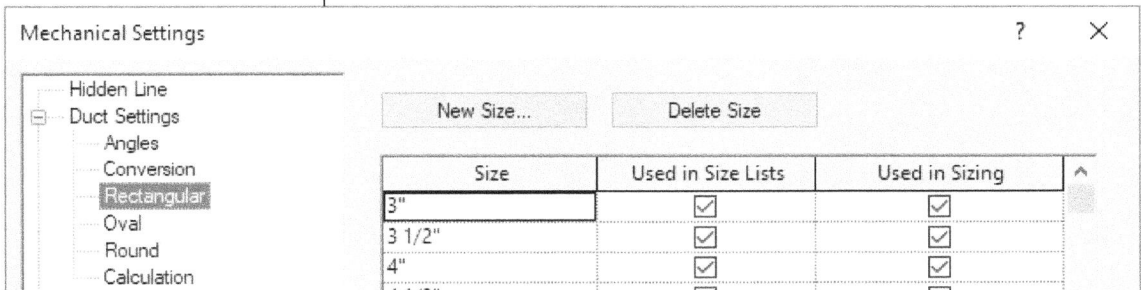

Mechanical Settings			? ✕

Hidden Line
⊟ Duct Settings
    Angles
    Conversion
    Rectangular
    Oval
    Round
    Calculation

New Size...	Delete Size

Size	Used in Size Lists	Used in Sizing	^
3"	☑	☑	
3 1/2"	☑	☑	
4"	☑	☑	
4 1/2"	☐	☐	

Figure A–40

- For example, if you do not want the sizing routine to use any odd numbered sizes, clear the **Used in Sizing** option for all odd-numbered sizes.

Pipe Settings

Most of the options in the *Pipe Settings* area are identical to or similar to those in the *Duct Settings* area.

Pipe Segments and Sizes

Pipe segment and size settings are more complex due to the many different materials and connections available. Each material has its own roughness, connection types, schedule/types, and sizes that correspond to each combination, as shown in Figure A–41.

Mechanical Settings ? ✕

- Hidden Line
- ⊞ Duct Settings
- ⊟ Pipe Settings
  - Angles
  - Conversion
  - **Segments and Sizes**
  - Fluids
  - Slopes
  - Calculation

Segment: Copper - K

Properties

Roughness: 0.00010"

Segment Description:

Size Catalog

New Size...   Delete Size

Nominal	ID	OD	Used in Size Lists	Used in Sizing	^
1/4"	5/16"	3/8"	☑	☑	
3/8"	13/32"	1/2"	☑	☑	
1/2"	17/32"	5/8"	☑	☑	
3/4"	3/4"	7/8"	☑	☑	
1"	1"	1 1/8"	☑	☑	

Figure A–41

The actual size lists are identical in function to those for ducts, except for the inclusion of the **ID** (inside diameter) and **OD** (outside diameter) parameters.

- Click ⬚ (Create New Pipe Segment) to open the New Segment dialog box (as shown in Figure A–42), where you specify new Material, and/or Schedule/Type for the segment.

Figure A–42

- To delete a segment, click ⬚ (Delete Pipe Segment).

Fluids

The *Fluids* area enables you to specify the viscosity and density of fluids at different temperatures, as shown in Figure A–43. You can add or delete fluid types, and for each type, add or delete temperatures.

Figure A–43

Slopes

In the *Slopes* area, you can add or delete typical slopes used in a project, as shown in Figure A–44.

Figure A–44

Calculation

Both Duct and Pipe settings include methods for Pressure Drop that are specific to their needs, as shown for Pipe Settings in Figure A–45. For pipes, the calculation method for converting fixture units to flow for plumbing fixtures is also included.

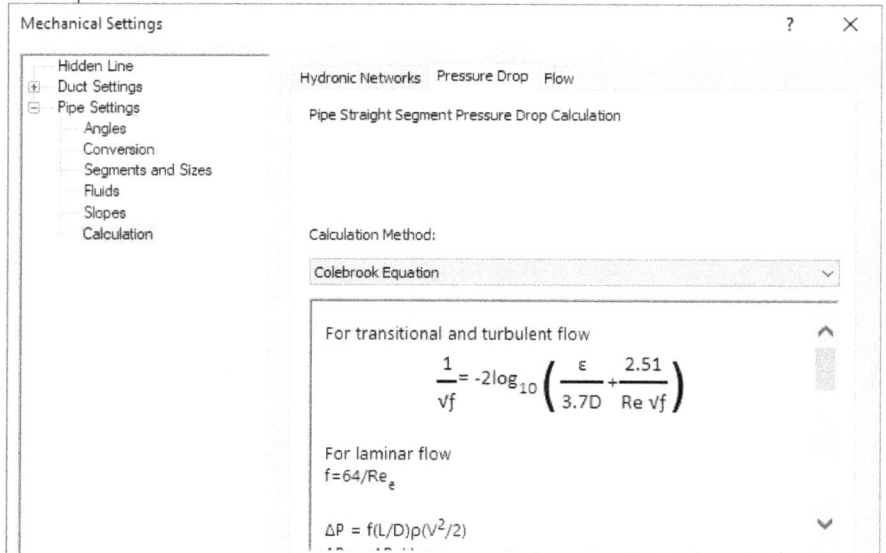

Figure A–45

A.6 Settings for Electrical Projects

In addition to the standard settings common to all Autodesk Revit projects, the Autodesk Revit MEP software also has specific Electrical settings that can be used in a template or a project.

- In the *Manage* tab>Settings panel, expand 🖳 (MEP Settings) and click 🖳 (Electrical Settings), or in the *Systems* tab>Electrical panel title, click ⩔ (Electrical Settings), as shown in Figure A–46. Alternatively, you can type **ES**.

Figure A–46

In the Electrical Settings dialog box, you can preset many options relating to wiring, voltage, cable trays and conduits as well as Load Calculations and Panel Schedules, as shown in Figure A–47. Setting these up in the template for all of the commonly used electrical settings, saves time for individual projects and increases consistency.

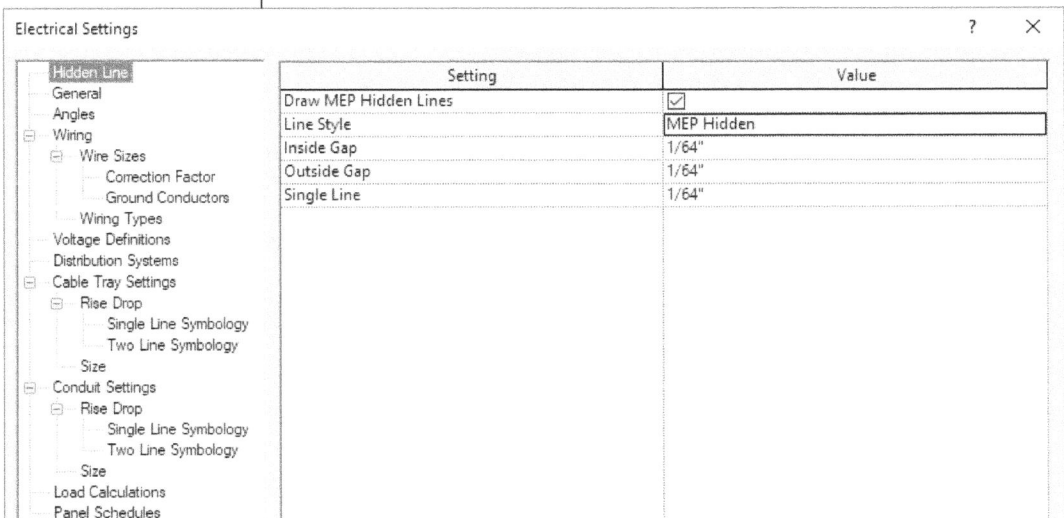

Setting	Value
Draw MEP Hidden Lines	☑
Line Style	MEP Hidden
Inside Gap	1/64"
Outside Gap	1/64"
Single Line	1/64"

Figure A–47

General

The parameters in the *General* area affect the display of electrical information. The **Electrical Data Style** option sets how the power information displays in the **Electrical Data** parameter in the Instance Properties of the electrical component. The **Circuit Description** option sets the formatting of the circuit description.

Wiring

The *Wiring* area enables you to specify the ambient temperature for wiring and some annotation settings related to wiring. The **Tick Mark** families need to be preloaded into the template so that they can be selected in this area, as shown in Figure A–48.

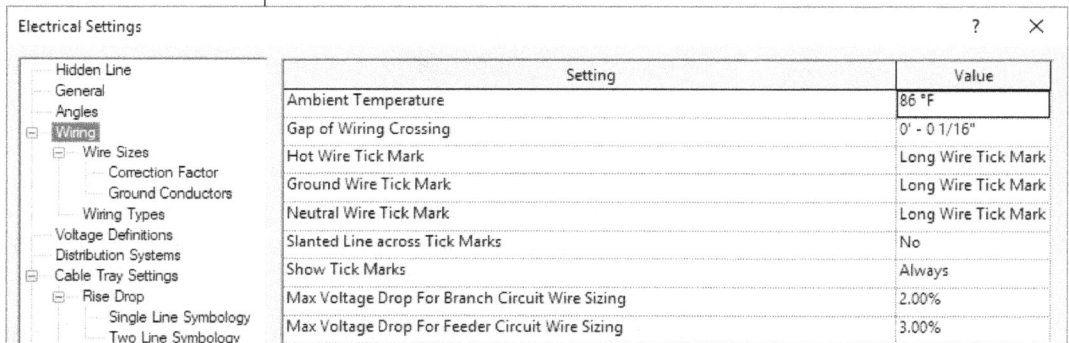

Electrical Settings ? ✕

| Hidden Line | | |
| General | | |
Angles	Setting	Value
Wiring	Ambient Temperature	86 °F
Wire Sizes	Gap of Wiring Crossing	0' - 0 1/16"
Correction Factor	Hot Wire Tick Mark	Long Wire Tick Mark
Ground Conductors	Ground Wire Tick Mark	Long Wire Tick Mark
Wiring Types	Neutral Wire Tick Mark	Long Wire Tick Mark
Voltage Definitions	Slanted Line across Tick Marks	No
Distribution Systems	Show Tick Marks	Always
Cable Tray Settings	Max Voltage Drop For Branch Circuit Wire Sizing	2.00%
Rise Drop	Max Voltage Drop For Feeder Circuit Wire Sizing	3.00%
Single Line Symbology		
Two Line Symbology		

Figure A–48

Wire Sizes

The Wire Size settings enable you to create new wire materials, temperature ratings, and insulation types. You can then specify the ampacity, size, diameter, and if the size is used by the wire sizing tools.

- The functionality in the *Wire Sizes* area is similar to that in the *Pipe Sizes* and *Fluids* areas.

Correction Factor

The *Correction Factor* area enables you to specify the correction factors for different temperatures and for each wire type, as shown in Figure A–49.

Figure A–49

Ground Conductors

The Autodesk Revit software sizes ground conductors according to their circuit rating. The *Ground Conductors* area enables you to customize the sizes it uses for each wire material and ampacity, as shown in Figure A–50.

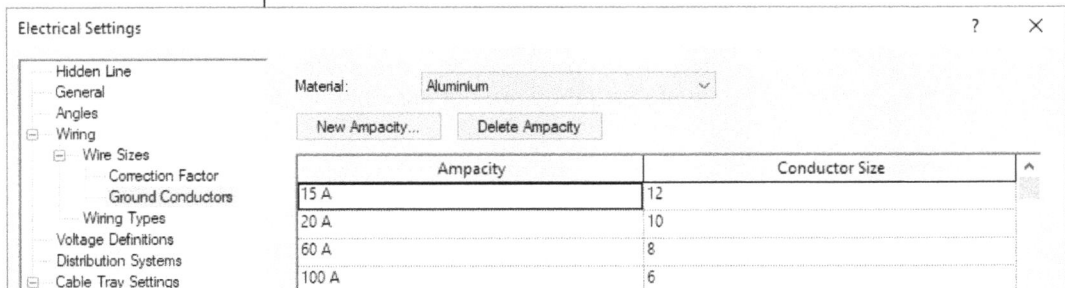

Figure A–50

Wiring Types

The *Wiring Types* area enables you to create wiring types by clicking **Add** and to delete them by clicking **Delete**. You can also specify their properties.

Voltage Definitions

In the *Voltage Definitions* area, you can specify the minimum and maximum voltages of devices that can be added to the distribution systems of a specified voltage. For example, the Autodesk Revit software permits devices ranging from 110V to 130V on a 120V distribution system, as shown in Figure A–51. You can also add or delete definitions.

Electrical Settings

	Name	Value	Minimum	Maximum
1	120	120.00 V	110.00 V	130.00 V
2	208	208.00 V	200.00 V	220.00 V
3	240	240.00 V	220.00 V	250.00 V
4	277	277.00 V	260.00 V	280.00 V
5	480	480.00 V	460.00 V	490.00 V

Figure A–51

Distribution Systems

The *Distribution Systems* area sets the distribution systems that are available in your project, as shown in Figure A–52. You can edit the names by selecting them. The options for *Phase* are preset and affect the options that are available in the *Configuration* and *Wires* columns and whether L-L Voltage is available. You can add more systems and delete existing systems if they are not assigned to devices in the current project.

Electrical Settings

	Name	Phase	Configuration	Wires	L-L Voltage	L-G Voltage
1	120/208 Wye	Three	Wye	4	208	120
2	120/240 Single	Single	None	3	240	120
3	480/277 Wye	Three	Wye	4	480	277

Figure A–52

Cable Tray and Conduit Settings

Cable Trays and Conduits settings include annotation, Rise Drop Symbology, and sizing, as shown in Figure A–53.

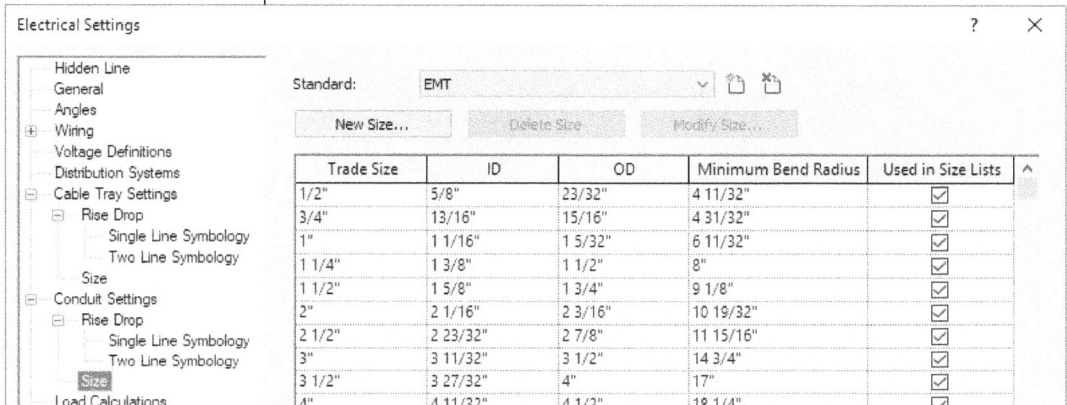

Figure A–53

Load Calculations and Panel Schedules

The *Load Calculations* area gives you access to additional dialog boxes where you can set Load Classifications (as shown in Figure A–54) and Demand Factors.

Figure A–54

The *Panel Schedules* area (shown in Figure A–55) enables you set up labels and other options for the default panel schedule.

Electrical Settings   ?   ✕

- Hidden Line
- General
- Angles
- Wiring
- Voltage Definitions
- Distribution Systems
- Cable Tray Settings
- Conduit Settings
- Load Calculations
- Panel Schedules

Setting	Value
Spare Label:	Spare
Space Label:	Space
Include Spares in Panel Totals	☑
Merge multi-poled circuits into a single cell	☐

Figure A–55

A.7 Settings for Structural Projects

In addition to the standard settings common to all aspects of the Autodesk Revit software, there are structural settings that need to be customized.

- In the *Manage* tab>Settings panel, expand Structural Settings and click (Structural Settings), or click the arrow in the *Structure* tab>Structure panel title.

Symbolic Representation

There are several tabs at the top of the Structural Settings dialog box, as shown in Figure A–56. The first tab, *Symbolic Representation Settings*, contains options that are mainly used for the graphical model and the common defaults.

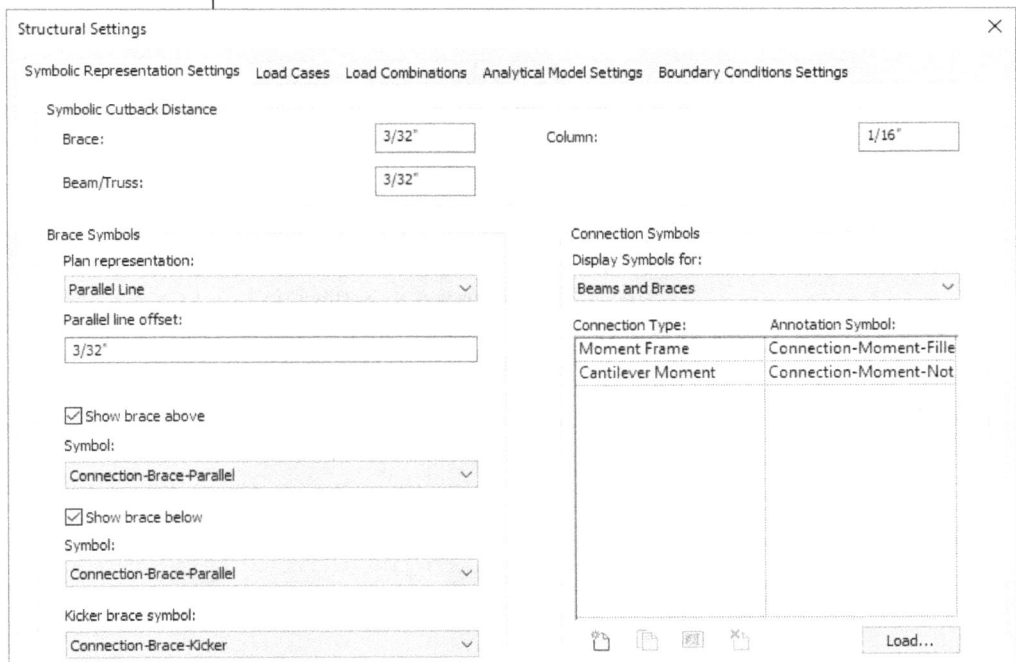

Figure A–56

The **Symbolic Cutback Distance** setting represents the distance that cuts a framing member back from a column or into another framing member. This cutback distance is symbolic and does not affect the 3D view. For example, in plan, beams do not extend into the column and there is a gap between them, as shown in Figure A–57. The same connection in 3D displays the beams back from the column, which is more consistent with a real-world situation.

Figure A–57

The *Brace Symbols* and *Connection Symbols* areas enable you to specify the kinds of symbols that are shown for the braces in plan, and for frame and shear connections. For many of these items, only one symbol is loaded into the default template.

Load Cases and Load Combinations

Two tabs are related to setting up Load Cases and Load Combinations. These vary by project and by region and typically requires the input of a company's engineer.

See the Autodesk Revit Structure Fundamentals learning guide for additional information about creating Load Cases and Load Combinations.

Analytical Model Settings

The process of modeling a building simultaneously creates a digital model and its corresponding analytical model. As this is done, the software can check for consistency between these two models. The *Analytical Model Settings* tab contains settings for automatic checks, tolerances, and checks, as shown in Figure A–58.

Structural Settings   ✕

Symbolic Representation Settings   Load Cases   Load Combinations   Analytical Model Settings   Boundary Conditions Settings

Automatic Checks

☐ Member Supports   ☐ Analytical / Physical Model Consistency

Tolerances

Support distance: `1' 0"`   Analytical auto detect - Horizontal: `1' 0"`

Analytical-to-physical model distance: `0' 6"`   Analytical auto detect - Vertical: `1' 0"`

Analytical Link auto detect: `1' 0"`

Member Supports Check

☑ Circular references

Analytical / Physical Model Consistency Check

☑ Analytical model connectivity

☑ Analytical model adjusted away from default location

☑ Analytical Beam and Floor overlap check

☑ Possible instability based on release conditions

☑ Analytical model outside physical model

☐ Valid Physical Material Asset

Analytical Model Visibility

☑ Differentiate ends of linear analytical models

Figure A–58

It is a best practice not to enable **Automatic Checks** in the template, as in the early stages of design there might be many elements that are not supported, causing many warning boxes to open. Automatic Checks are very useful when most of the structure has been modeled and should be enabled at that time.

The values in the *Tolerances* area informs the kind of tolerance that is permitted for supports, differences between the analytical and physical distance, adjusting, and auto-detects. For example, when the **Analytical Model** parameters for a wall are set to auto-detect, the software adjusts the analytical lines, provided it can do so within the specified tolerances.

The *Analytical/Physical Model Consistency Check* area enables you to specify the kinds of consistencies to be checked for.

Boundary Condition Settings

In the last tab, you can select the family symbols used for boundary conditions, as shown in Figure A–59 (from left to right: **Fixed**, **Pinned**, **Roller**, and **User**).

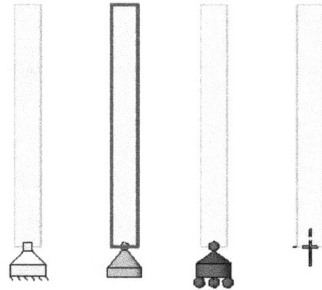

Figure A–59

The structural templates typically include four boundary condition families: **Fixed**, **Pinned**, **Roller**, and **Variable**. They are assigned to the corresponding boundary conditions, as shown in Figure A–60.

Figure A–60

- You can create new boundary condition families, load them into the template, and select them from the drop-down lists as required.

A.8 Additional Schedule Types

In addition to the standard Schedule/Quantities and Material Takeoff Schedules, several other schedule types can be created in Autodesk Revit, as shown in Figure A–61. Sheet List schedules keep track of all the sheets and View List schedules keep track of all of the views used in a project. Note Block Schedules can be used to create a custom style of keynotes.

For more information on Graphical Column Schedules, see the Autodesk Revit Fundamentals for Structure learning guide.

Figure A–61

Sheet List Schedules

Sheet List schedules (as shown in Figure A–62) are used to keep track of all of the sheets in a project and any list sheets that could be added. Sheet lists are often used by architects to display all of the sheets in a building project. This includes any consultant sheets that are not in the architectural project file, as they would only be in the Sheet List schedule and not created as actual sheets.

Figure A–62

How To: Create a Sheet List Schedule

1. Open a project template file (or a project).

2. In the *View* tab>Create panel, expand ⊞ (Schedules) and click ⌗ (Sheet List).

3. In the Sheet List Properties dialog box, in the *Fields* tab, select the **Sheet Number** and **Sheet Name** and add them to the *Scheduled fields* list, as shown in Figure A–63.

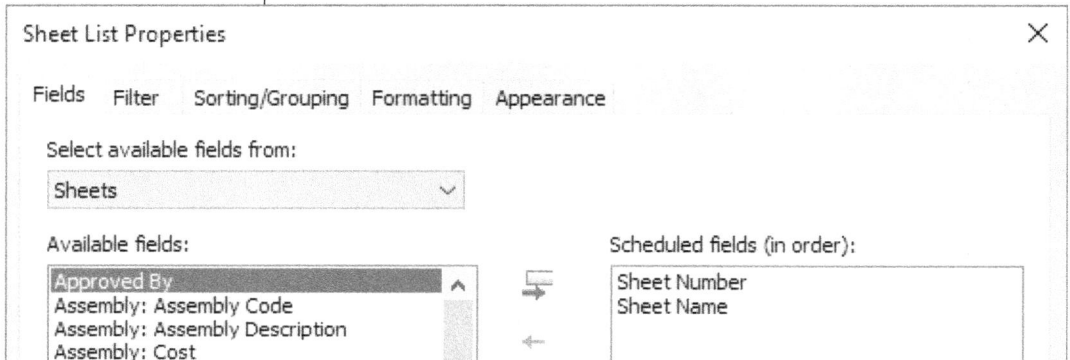

Sheet List Properties   ✕

Fields   Filter   Sorting/Grouping   Formatting   Appearance

Select available fields from:

| Sheets | ⌄ |

Available fields: Scheduled fields (in order):

Approved By	Sheet Number
Assembly: Assembly Code	Sheet Name
Assembly: Assembly Description	
Assembly: Cost	

Figure A–63

4. Depending on the complexity of your sheet naming scheme, you can also modify items on the *Filter* and *Sorting/Grouping* tabs.

5. Click **OK** when you are finished.

6. You are placed in the schedule view with the two parameters displayed. Stretch out the columns as shown in Figure A–64.

Sheet List	
Sheet Number	Sheet Name

Figure A–64

If sheets are already in the project, they display here.

7. In the *Modify Schedule/Quantities* tab>Rows panel, click

   🔲 (Insert Data Row).

8. A new row is added below the schedule names. If no sheets are in the project, it comes in automatically as **A101** and **Unnamed**.

9. Add as many rows as you have sheets. If you are using a numbering scheme such as A1xx for site plans, A2xx for Floor Plans, A3xx for Detail plans, etc., then you should rename the sheet number for the first row of a set before creating more rows so that they increment automatically.

10. Enter the name of each sheet. Once you have added a new name, it is available in the drop-down list, as shown in Figure A–65.

<Sheet List>	
A	**B**
Sheet Number	Sheet Name
CS000	Cover Sheet
A201	First Floor Plan
A202	Second Floor Plan
A203	Fifth Floor Plan
A204	First Floor Plan
A205	Fouth Floor Plan
A206	Second Floor Plan
A101	Site Plan
	Sixth Floor Plan
	Third Floor Plan

Figure A–65

How To: Use Sheet List Tables

1. Create a new sheet. In the Sheet List Schedule view, in the *Modify Schedule/Quantities* tab>Create panel, click ⬚ (New Sheet), You can also access the command on the *View* tab or right-click on *Sheets* in the Project Browser.

2. In the New Sheet dialog box, select the placeholder sheets you want to use, as shown in Figure A–66. To select more than one, hold <Ctrl> or <Shift> as you select.

Figure A–66

3. Click **OK**. The new sheets are created in the project.

- This sheet list is available in all projects based on the project template where it was created.

- You can import the sheet list schedule into another project, but it does not import the associated sheets. That is because they are part of the project, not the schedule view.

View List Schedules

View List schedules are similar to other schedules in their construction. The difference is that the available fields are gathered from the view, as shown in Figure A–67 . This type of schedule can be very helpful when you are creating copies of view and want to modify the phase, discipline, or other information about the view.

In the *View* tab>Create panel, expand ⊞ (Schedules) and click ▣ (View List).

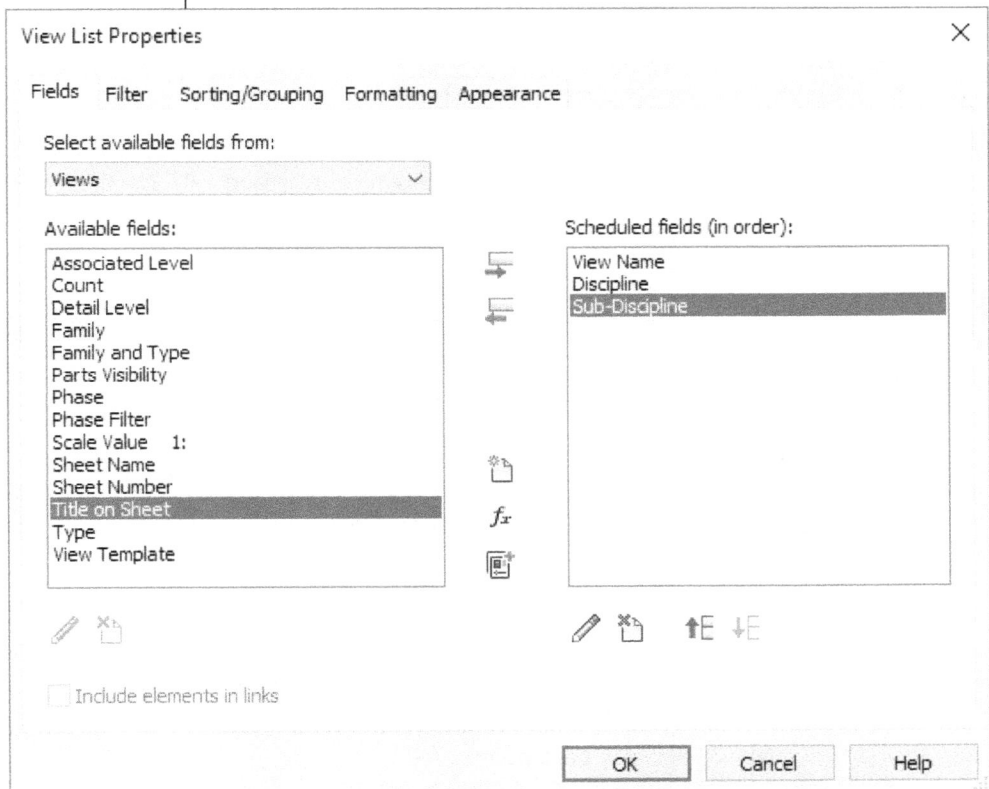

Figure A–67

- You can also add fields from Project Information.

Note Blocks

Note Blocks are a way of creating a custom keynoting system if the internal system in Autodesk Revit does not work for you. It requires you to create an annotation symbol with at least two parameter labels for a number and text (shown in Figure A–68) and a note block schedule that uses the same options.

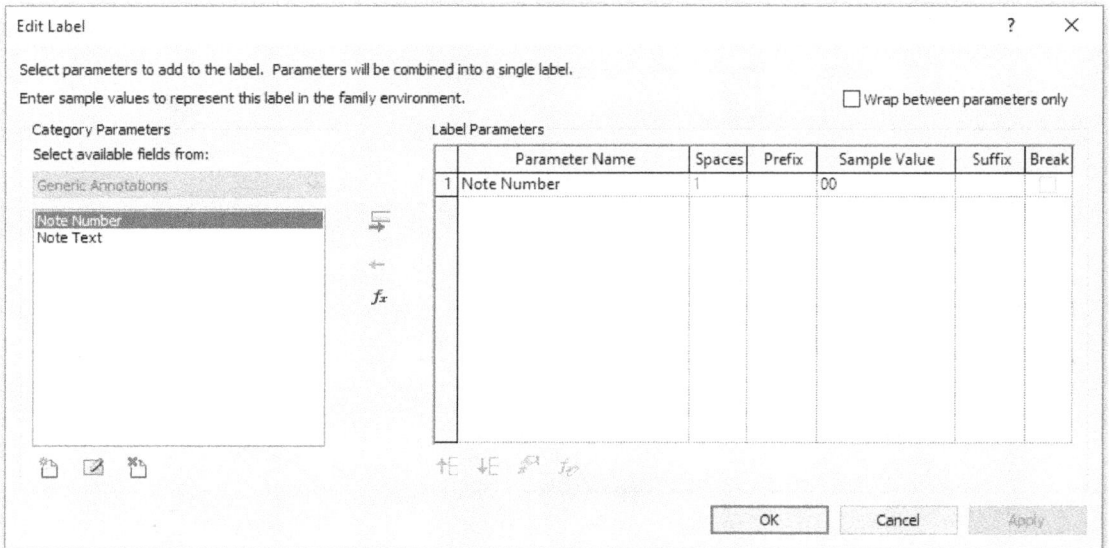

Edit Label

Select parameters to add to the label. Parameters will be combined into a single label.

Enter sample values to represent this label in the family environment.

☐ Wrap between parameters only

Category Parameters

Select available fields from:

Generic Annotations

Note Number
Note Text

Label Parameters

	Parameter Name	Spaces	Prefix	Sample Value	Suffix	Break
1	Note Number	1		00		

OK   Cancel   Apply

Figure A–68

How To: Create and use Note Blocks

1. Create a generic annotation symbol with the required parameters.
2. Load it into the project.
3. Using the **Symbol** command, place the note block symbol in the project. You can add a leader after you have placed it, as shown in Figure A–69.

4. Select the symbol and in Properties, assign the number and text, as shown in Figure A–69.

Generic Annotations (1)	⌄ 🔲 Edit Type
Text	⟩
Note Number	1
Note Text	Gypsum Drywall with

Figure A–69

5. In the *View* tab>Create panel, expand 🔲 (Schedules) and click 🔲 (Note Block).
6. In the New Note Block dialog box, select the Family, as shown in Figure A–70. Then, click **OK**.

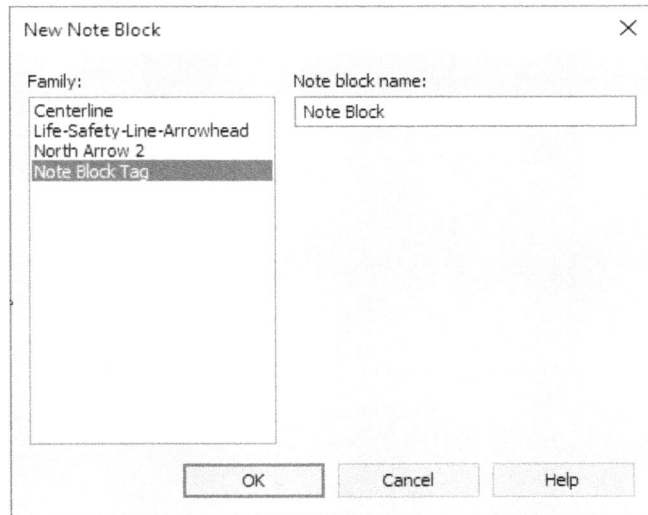

Figure A–70

7. In the Note Block Properties dialog box, select the required fields (as shown in Figure A–71), make any other modifications as required, and click **OK** to created the schedule.

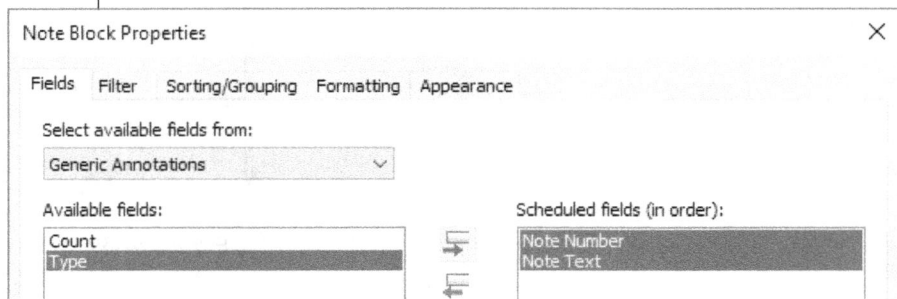

Figure A–71

8. Modify the schedule as required and place it on the sheet with the corresponding view, as shown in Figure A–72.

Figure A–72

A.9 Basic User Interface Customization

The Revit User Interface has a variety of features that can be customized. From moving ribbon panels around by dragging and dropping them to a new location, to the activation and location of palettes, and items that display on the status bar. For example, if you do not use Design Options you can clean up the Status Bar by clearing **Status Bar - Design Options**, as shown in Figure A–73.

Figure A–73

You can also customize other parts of the Autodesk Revit software, including which tabs display in the ribbon, customizing keyboard shortcuts, specifying how the double-click functions work and setting up the Project Browser organization.

Configuring the Ribbon

The Autodesk® Revit® software is used by many different disciplines including Architecture, Structure, Mechanical, Electrical, and Plumbing. All of these tools are setup to display in the ribbon by default. Most users only need access to a specific set of tools and the interface can be customized to suit those needs.

How To: Configure the Ribbon to Suit Your Needs

1. In the *File* tab, click **Options**.
2. In the Options dialog box, in the left pane, select **User Interface**.
3. In the *Configure* area, under *Tools and analyses* (as shown in Figure A–74), clear all of options that you do not want to use.

You are not deleting these tools, just removing them from the current user interface.

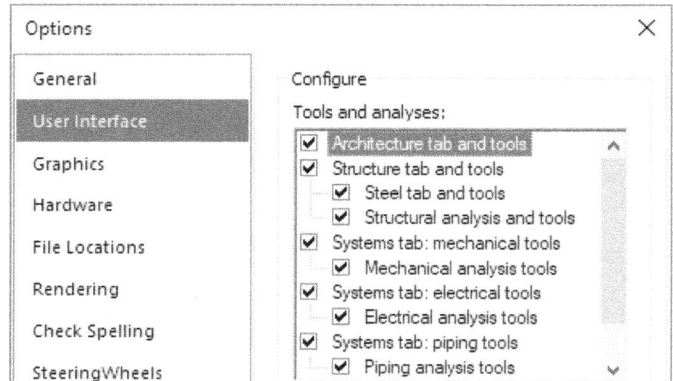

Figure A–74

Customizing Shortcuts

A helpful customization is to set up the keyboard shortcuts for frequently used commands. These are not saved by project, but on each computer. To display the shortcuts that are already available, hover the cursor over a tool, such as **Text**, to display the tooltip that displays the associated shortcut, as shown in Figure A–75.

When you type keyboard shortcuts, you do not need to press <Enter> or the <Spacebar>.

Figure A–75

How To: Customize the Keyboard Shortcuts

1. In the *View* tab>Windows panel, expand (User Interface) and click (Keyboard Shortcuts) or, in the *File* tab, click **Options**. In the Options dialog box, in the *User Interface* pane, in the *Configure* area, next to *Keyboard shortcuts:* click **Customize...**.

2. In the Keyboard Shortcuts dialog box, use **Search** or **Filter** to narrow the search, as shown in Figure A–76.

Figure A–76

3. Select the command that you want to add or modify.
4. In the Press new keys edit box, type the shortcut that you want to use, as shown in Figure A–77. Then, click **Assign**.

Figure A–77

5. Click **OK** when you have finished.

- To remove shortcuts, select the shortcut, and click **Remove**.

- You can import or export the shortcut file to be used in other stations of the Autodesk Revit software than the one on which they were created. When you export to XML, all of the commands are exported. You can then add the required shortcuts to the XML file and import them into your program

If a shortcut has already been assigned, you can still use it. Press the <Spacebar> to cycle through the options.

Customizing Double-click Settings

When you double-click on elements, you can specify what you want this to do. For example, by default, double-clicking on a family, such as a chair, column, or plumbing fixture, opens the element in the Family Editor. In most cases that is not something you want to do, editing the type would be better. You can change this in the Customize Double-click Settings dialog box, as shown in Figure A–78.

Element Type:	Double-click action:
Family	Edit Family
Sketched Element	Edit Element
Inside Views / Schedules on Sheets	Activate View
Outside Views on Sheets	Deactivate View
Assemblies	Edit Element
Groups	Edit Element
Stairs	Edit Element

Figure A–78

How To: Customize Double-Click Settings

1. In the *File* tab, click **Options**.
2. In the Options dialog box, in the *User Interface* pane, in the *Configure* area, next to *Double-click Options:* click **Customize...**.
3. Select the method that you want to use for each of the element types.

Customizing the Browser Organization

The Project Browser is the heart of the Autodesk Revit software. It is where you access all of the different views, sheets, family types, etc. When working with complex projects, it can help to organize the views, schedules, and sheets so that it is most useful to the methods used in your firm. It is easy to switch between different organizations and you can create custom ones to suit your work.

- To switch between existing organization types, in the Project Browser, select the **Views** node at the top of the palette, and in the Type Selector, select the type that you want to use, as shown in Figure A–79.

The name of the current organization type is in parentheses.

Figure A–79

- You can also switch schedule and sheet organizations by selecting the *Schedules/Quantities* or *Sheets* node and changing the type in the Type Selector.

How To: Customize the Browser Organization

1. In the *View* tab>Windows panel, expand ⬚ (User Interface) and click ⬚ (Browser Organization) or, in the Project Browser, right-click on the *Views, Schedules*, or *Sheets* node and select **Browser Organization**.
2. In the Browser Organization dialog box, select the *Views, Schedules* or *Sheets* tab, and click **New**.
3. Name the new browser organization and click **OK**.
4. In the Browser Organization Properties dialog box, in the *Filtering* tab, specify the filtering rules, as required.

5. In the *Grouping and Sorting* tab, assign the various groups as required. The example shown in Figure A–80 is by discipline, an organization that is used most often in the MEP templates.

Figure A–80

6. Click **OK** to finish the property changes.
7. In the Browser Organization dialog box, you can continue to create the new organization and then select the current organization. Click **Apply** between sets if you are creating multiple organizations. Click **OK** when you have finished.

- In the Options dialog box, in the *General* tab, in the *View Options* area, you can set the *Default view discipline* that is used when you create new views, such as sections, callouts, and elevations, as shown in Figure A–81.

Figure A–81

- When you duplicate a view, it automatically assumes the discipline and other view properties of the original view.

Command Summary

Button	Command	Location
	Arrowheads	• **Ribbon**: *Manage* tab>Settings panel> expand Additional Settings
	Browser Organization	• **Ribbon**: *View* tab>Windows panel> expand User Interface • *File* tab: Options>*User Interface* tab
	Electrical Settings	• **Ribbon**: *Manage* tab>Settings panel> expand MEP Settings
	Fill Patterns	• **Ribbon**: *Manage* tab>Settings panel> expand Additional Settings
	Keyboard Shortcuts	• **Ribbon**: *View* tab>Windows panel> expand User Interface • *File* tab: Options>*User Interface* tab
	Line Patterns	• ***Ribbon**: Manage* tab>Settings panel> expand Additional Settings
	Line Styles	• **Ribbon**: *Manage* tab>Settings panel> expand Additional Settings
	Line Weights	• **Ribbon**: *Manage* tab>Settings panel> expand Additional Settings
	Materials	• **Ribbon**: *Manage* tab>Settings panel
	Mechanical Settings	• **Ribbon**: *Manage* tab>Settings panel> expand MEP Settings
	Note Block	• **Ribbon**: *View* tab>Create panel, expand Schedules
	Object Styles	• **Ribbon**: *Manage* tab>Settings panel
Options	**Options**	• **Ribbon**: *File* tab
	Project Units	• **Ribbon**: *Manage* tab>Settings panel • **Shortcut**: UN
	Sheet List	• **Ribbon**: *View* tab>Create panel, expand Schedules
	Snaps	• **Ribbon**: *Manage* tab>Settings panel, expand Schedules
	Structural Settings	• **Autodesk Revit Structure** • **Ribbon**: *Manage* tab>Settings panel
	Temporary Dimensions	• **Ribbon**: *Manage* tab>Settings panel> expand Additional Settings
	User Interface	• **Ribbon**: *View* tab>Windows panel
	View List	• **Ribbon**: *View* tab>Create panel

Autodesk Revit 2019 BIM Management: Template and Family Creation

Autodesk Revit Certification Exam Objectives

Autodesk Revit Architecture

The following table will help you to locate the exam objectives in the chapters of the Autodesk® Revit® learning guides to help you prepare for the Autodesk Revit Architecture Certified Professional exam.

Exam Topic	Exam Objective	Learning Guide	Chapter & Section(s)
Collaboration			
	Copy and monitor elements in a linked file	• Revit Collaboration Tools	• 2.3
	Use worksharing	• Revit Collaboration Tools	• 4.1, 4.2, 4.3
	Import DWG and image files	• Revit Fundamentals for Architecture	• 3.4
		• Revit Collaboration Tools	• 3.1, 3.2, 3.3
	Use Worksharing Visualization	• Revit Collaboration Tools	• 4.4
	Assess review warnings in Revit	• Revit Fundamentals for Architecture	• 12.1

Exam Topic	Exam Objective	Learning Guide	Chapter & Section(s)
Documentation	Create and modify filled regions	• Revit Fundamentals for Architecture	• 16.3
	Place detail components and repeating details	• Revit Fundamentals for Architecture	• 16.2
	Tag elements (doors, windows, etc.) by category	• Revit Fundamentals for Architecture	• 15.1
	Use dimension strings	• Revit Fundamentals for Architecture	• 14.1
	Set the colors used in a color scheme legend	• Revit Architecture: Conceptual Design and Visualization	• 2.3
	Work with phases	• Revit Collaboration Tools	• 1.1
Elements and Families	Change elements within a curtain wall (grids, panels, mullions	• Revit Fundamentals for Architecture	• 6.2, 6.3, 6.4
	Create compound walls	• Revit BIM Management	• 3.1
	Create a stacked wall	• Revit BIM Management	• 3.3
	Differentiate system and component families	• Revit BIM Management	• 3.1 • 4.1
	Work with family parameters	• Revit BIM Management	• 4.2
	Create a new family type	• Revit Fundamentals for Architecture	• 5.3
		• Revit BIM Management	• 4.4
	Use family creation procedures	• Revit BIM Management	• 4.1 to 4.4
Modeling	Create a building pad	• Revit Architecture: Site and Site Designer	• 1.2
	Define floor for a mass	• Revit Architecture: Conceptual Design and Visualization	• 1.7
	Create a stair with a landing	• Revit Fundamentals for Architecture	• 12.1
	Create elements such as floors, ceilings, or roofs	• Revit Fundamentals for Architecture	• 9.1 • 10.1 • 11.2, 11.4
	Generate a toposurface	• Revit Architecture: Site and Site Designer	• 1.1
	Model railings	• Revit Fundamentals for Architecture	• 12.3
	Edit a model element's material (door, window, furniture)	• Revit Fundamentals for Architecture	• 5.3 • B.4

Exam Topic	Exam Objective	Learning Guide	Chapter & Section(s)
Modeling *(continued)*	Change a generic floor / ceiling / roof to a specific type	• Revit Fundamentals for Architecture	• 9.1 • 10.1 • 11.2
	Attach walls to a roof or ceiling	• Revit Fundamentals for Architecture	• 11.2
	Edit room-aware families	• Revit BIM Management	• 5.1
Views	Define element properties in a schedule	• Revit Fundamentals for Architecture	• 15.3
	Control visibility	• Revit Fundamentals for Architecture	• 7.1
	Use levels	• Revit Fundamentals for Architecture	• 3.1
	Create a duplicate view for a plan, section, elevation, drafting view, etc.	• Revit Fundamentals for Architecture	• 7.2
	Create and manage legends	• Revit Fundamentals for Architecture	• 14.4
	Manage view position on sheets	• Revit Fundamentals for Architecture	• 13.2
	Organize and sort items in a schedule	• Revit Fundamentals for Architecture	• B.10
		• Revit BIM Management	• 2.2

Autodesk Revit Electrical Building Systems

The following table will help you to locate the exam objectives in the chapters of the Autodesk® Revit® learning guides to help you prepare for the Autodesk Revit Certified Professional Exam for Electrical Building Systems.

Exam Topic	Exam Objective	Learning Guide	Chapter & Section(s)
Collaboration	Import AutoCAD files into Revit	• Revit Fundamentals for MEP	• 3.1
	Link Revit models	• Revit Fundamentals for MEP	• 3.2
	Copy levels and setup monitoring	• Revit Fundamentals for MEP	• 3.3 & 3.4
	Create floor plans	• Revit Fundamentals for MEP	• 3.3
	Use Worksets	• Revit Collaboration Tools	• 4.1 to 4.3
	Resolve Coordination Review Errors	• Revit Fundamentals for MEP	• 3.5

Exam Topic	Exam Objective	Learning Guide	Chapter & Section(s)
Documentation	Electrical: Tag components	• Revit Fundamentals for MEP	• 14.1
	Create sheets	• Revit Fundamentals for MEP	• 12.1
	Electrical: Create panel schedules	• Revit Fundamentals for MEP	• 11.4
	Add and modify text	• Revit Fundamentals for MEP	• 13.2
	Add and modify dimensions	• Revit Fundamentals for MEP	• 13.1
Elements	Differentiate system and component families	• Revit BIM Management	• 3.1 • 4.1
	Edit Family Connectors	• Revit BIM Management	• 5.1
	Create a new family type	• Revit BIM Management	• 4.4
Modeling	Electrical: Add and modify receptacles	• Revit Fundamentals for MEP	• 11.2
	Electrical: Add and modify panels	• Revit Fundamentals for MEP	• 11.2
	Electrical: Add and modify lighting fixtures	• Revit Fundamentals for MEP	• 11.2
	Electrical: Add and modify switches	• Revit Fundamentals for MEP	• 11.2
	Electrical: Create and modify switching circuits	• Revit Fundamentals for MEP	• 11.3
	Electrical: Create and modify lighting circuits	• Revit Fundamentals for MEP	• 11.3
	Electrical: Add and modify conduit	• Revit Fundamentals for MEP	• 11.5
	Electrical: Use cable trays	• Revit Fundamentals for MEP	• 11.5
	Electrical: Add and modify switch systems	• Revit Fundamentals for MEP	• 11.3
	Electrical: Create Distribution System	• Revit Fundamentals for MEP	• 11.1
	Electrical: Add and modify security devices	• Revit Fundamentals for MEP	• 11.2
	Electrical: Add and modify wiring	• Revit Fundamentals for MEP	• 11.3
	Electrical: Generate automatic wire layouts	• Revit Fundamentals for MEP	• 11.3
	Electrical: Check circuits and disconnects	• Revit Fundamentals for MEP	• 11.6
	Perform interference check	• Revit Collaboration Tools	• 2.4
	Electrical: Work with Spaces	• Revit Fundamentals for MEP	• 5.1 to 5.3

Exam Topic	Exam Objective	Learning Guide	Chapter & Section(s)
Modeling *(continued)*	Electrical: Perform a Lighting Analysis	• Revit Fundamentals for MEP	• 11.6
	Electrical: Work with Fire Alarm Devices	• Revit Fundamentals for MEP	• 11.2
	Electrical: Work with Site Lighting	• Revit Fundamentals for MEP	• 11.2
Views	View models	• Revit Fundamentals for MEP	• 1.4
	Apply view templates	• Revit Fundamentals for MEP	• 4.1
	Create detail views	• Revit Fundamentals for MEP	• 15.1
	Electrical: Create and label wiring plans	• Revit Fundamentals for MEP	• 3.3 • 11.3 • 13.1 to 13.3 • 14.1

Autodesk Revit Mechanical Building Systems

The following table will help you to locate the exam objectives in the chapters of the Autodesk® Revit® learning guides to help you prepare for the Autodesk Revit Certified Professional Exam for Mechanical Building Systems.

Exam Topic	Exam Objective	Learning Guide	Chapter & Section(s)
Collaboration	Import AutoCAD files into Revit	• Revit Fundamentals for MEP	• 3.1
	Link Revit models	• Revit Fundamentals for MEP	• 3.2
	Copy levels and setup monitoring	• Revit Fundamentals for MEP	• 3.3 & 3.4
	Create floor plans	• Revit Fundamentals for MEP	• 3.3
	Use Worksets	• Revit Collaboration Tools	• 4.1 to 4.3
	Resolve Coordination Review Errors	• Revit Fundamentals for MEP	• 3.5

Exam Topic	Exam Objective	Learning Guide	Chapter & Section(s)
Documentation	Mechanical: Tag ducts and piping	• Revit Fundamentals for MEP	• 14.1
	Create sheets	• Revit Fundamentals for MEP	• 12.1
	Add and modify text	• Revit Fundamentals for MEP	• 13.2
	Add and modify dimensions	• Revit Fundamentals for MEP	• 13.1
	Mechanical: Create duct/pipe legends	• Revit Fundamentals for MEP	• B.2
Elements	Differentiate system and component families	• Revit BIM Management	• 3.1 • 4.1
	Edit Family Connectors	• Revit BIM Management	• 5.1
	Create a new family type	• Revit BIM Management	• 4.4
Modeling	Mechanical: Add and use mechanical equipment	• Revit Fundamentals for MEP	• 8.1
	Mechanical: Add and modify air terminals	• Revit Fundamentals for MEP	• 8.1
	Mechanical: Add and modify ducts	• Revit Fundamentals for MEP	• 8.2 & 8.3
	Mechanical: Add and modify return ducts	• Revit Fundamentals for MEP	• 8.2 & 8.3
	Mechanical: Add and modify duct accessories and fittings	• Revit Fundamentals for MEP	• 8.3
	Mechanical: Work with heating and cooling zones	• Revit Fundamentals for MEP	• 6.1
	Plumbing: Add and modify fixtures	• Revit Fundamentals for MEP	• 9.1
	Plumbing: Add and modify piping	• Revit Fundamentals for MEP	• 9.2
	Plumbing: Add and use plumbing equipment	• Revit Fundamentals for MEP	• 9.1
	Plumbing: Create a plumbing system	• Revit Fundamentals for MEP	• 10.1
	Plumbing: Add and modify pipe accessories	• Revit Fundamentals for MEP	• 9.3
	Mechanical: Add and modify placeholder duct	• Revit Fundamentals for MEP	• 8.2 & 8.3
	Mechanical: Define a duct system	• Revit Fundamentals for MEP	• 10.1
	Mechanical: Work with spaces	• Revit Fundamentals for MEP	• 5.1 to 5.3
	Plumbing: Add and modify placeholder pipe	• Revit Fundamentals for MEP	• 9.2

Exam Topic	Exam Objective	Learning Guide	Chapter & Section(s)
Modeling *(continued)*	Size duct and pipe systems	• Revit Fundamentals for MEP	• 8.3
	Perform interference check	• Revit Collaboration Tools	• 2.4
	Check duct and pipe systems and disconnects	• Revit Fundamentals for MEP	• 10.3
Views	View models	• Revit Fundamentals for MEP	• 1.4
	Apply view templates	• Revit Fundamentals for MEP	• 4.1
	Create detail views	• Revit Fundamentals for MEP	• 15.1
	Mechanical: Create and label HVAC plans	• Revit Fundamentals for MEP	• 3.3 • 13.1 to 13.3 • 14.1
	Plumbing: Create a plumbing view	• Revit Fundamentals for MEP	• 4.1
	Plumbing: Create and label plumbing plans	• Revit Fundamentals for MEP	• 3.3 • 13.1 to 13.3 • 14.1

Autodesk Revit Structure

The following table will help you to locate the exam objectives within the chapters of the Autodesk® Revit® learning guides to help you prepare for the Autodesk Revit for Structures Certified Professional exam.

Exam Topic	Exam Objective	Learning Guide	Chapter & Section(s)
Collaboration	Create and modify levels	• Revit Fundamentals for Structure	• 3.3
	Create and modify structural grids	• Revit Fundamentals for Structure	• 5.1
	Import AutoCAD files into Revit	• Revit Fundamentals for Structure	• 3.1
		• Revit Collaboration Tools	• 3.1
	Link Revit models	• Revit Fundamentals for Structure	• 3.2
		• Revit Collaboration Tools	• 2.1
	Control the visibility for linked objects	• Revit Collaboration Tools	• 2.2

Exam Topic	Exam Objective	Learning Guide	Chapter & Section(s)
Documentation	Using temporary dimensions	• Revit Fundamentals for Structure	• 2.1
	Annotate beams	• Revit Fundamentals for Structure	• 13.3
	Add and modify text annotations	• Revit Fundamentals for Structure	• 13.2
	Add and use dimensions and dimension labels	• Revit Fundamentals for Structure	• 13.1
	Use detail components	• Revit Fundamentals for Structure	• 14.2
	Create and modify column schedules	• Revit Fundamentals for Structure	• 15.2
	Create and modify footing schedules	• Revit Fundamentals for Structure	• 15.3 • B.8
		• Revit BIM Management	• 2.2
	Create and modify standard sheets	• Revit Fundamentals for Structure	• 12.1, 12.2
Modeling	Place and modify structural columns	• Revit Fundamentals for Structure	• 5.2
	Place and modify walls	• Revit Fundamentals for Structure	• 6.1
	Create custom wall types	• Revit BIM Management	• 3.1
	Place footings	• Revit Fundamentals for Structure	• 6.2, 6.4
	Create concrete slabs and/or floors	• Revit Fundamentals for Structure	• 8.1
	Create and modify stepped walls in foundations	• Revit Fundamentals for Structure	• 6.2
	Place rebar	• Revit Fundamentals for Structure	• 9.2
	Add beams	• Revit Fundamentals for Structure	• 7.1
	Add beam systems	• Revit Fundamentals for Structure	• 7.1
	Add joists	• Revit Fundamentals for Structure	• 7.1
	Add cross bracing to joists	• Revit Fundamentals for Structure	• 7.1
	Create and use trusses	• Revit Fundamentals for Structure	• 7.3
	Create and modify floors	• Revit Fundamentals for Structure	• 8.1

Exam Topic	Exam Objective	Learning Guide	Chapter & Section(s)
Modeling *(continued)*	Create and modify custom floors	• Revit BIM Management	• 3.1
	Create and modify sloped floors	• Revit Fundamentals for Architecture	• 9.3
	Add floor openings for stairs	• Revit Fundamentals for Structure	• 8.2
	Create and modify stairs	• Revit Fundamentals for Architecture	• 12.1
	Create and modify ramps	• Revit Fundamentals for Architecture	• 12.5
	Model and use roofs	• Revit Fundamentals for Structure	• 8.1
		• Revit Fundamentals for Architecture	• 11.2, 11.4
Views	Create section views	• Revit Fundamentals for Structure	• 4.4
	Create framing elevations	• Revit Fundamentals for Structure	• 4.4
	Use callout views	• Revit Fundamentals for Structure	• 4.3

Index

www.ingramcontent.com/pod-product-compliance
Lightning Source LLC
Chambersburg PA
CBHW082101220326
41598CB00066BA/4601